Toward a Pragmatist Philosophy of the Humanities

Toward a Pragmatist Philosophy
of the Humanities

SAMI PIHLSTRÖM

Published by State University of New York Press, Albany

© 2022 State University of New York

All rights reserved

Printed in the United States of America

No part of this book may be used or reproduced in any manner whatsoever without written permission. No part of this book may be stored in a retrieval system or transmitted in any form or by any means including electronic, electrostatic, magnetic tape, mechanical, photocopying, recording, or otherwise without the prior permission in writing of the publisher.

For information, contact State University of New York Press, Albany, NY
www.sunypress.edu

Library of Congress Cataloging-in-Publication Data

Name: Pihlström, Sami, author.
Title: Toward a pragmatist philosophy of the humanities / Sami Pihlström.
Description: Albany : State University of New York Press, [2022] | Includes bibliographical references and index.
Identifiers: LCCN 2022013232 | ISBN 9781438491059 (hardcover : alk paper) | ISBN 9781438491073 (ebook) | ISBN 9781438491066 (pbk. : alk. paper)
Subjects: LCSH: Humanities—Philosophy. | Pragmatism. | History—Philosophy. | Literature—Philosophy. | Religion—Philosophy.
Classification: LCC AZ101 .P54 2022 | DDC 001.301—dc23/eng/20220525
LC record available at https://lccn.loc.gov/2022013232

10 9 8 7 6 5 4 3 2 1

Contents

Preface   vii

1. Introduction: Why This Book?   1

2. Realism, Practices, and Inquiry: What Is Pragmatist Philosophy of the Humanities?   31

3. Developing Pragmatist Philosophy of Literary Theory, Historiography, and Religious Studies   79

4. Pragmatic Naturalism and Transcendental Arguments in the Philosophy of the Humanities   127

5. Conclusion: The Values and Limits of the Humanities   171

Notes   183

References   241

Index   265

Preface

We are living through challenging times in our Western liberal democracies. In addition to the planetary threat of the climate crisis and more acute crises such as the COVID-19 pandemic in 2020–2022 and Russia's criminal invasion of Ukraine in 2022, we are witnessing an alarming discontent with democracy itself. Not only are increasingly authoritarian and aggressive powers like China and Russia a serious global concern, but antidemocratic trends have unfortunately gained strength in the Western world as well. We are all familiar with what happened during Donald Trump's disgraceful presidency in the United States, and even within the European Union there are nations—and a considerable number of citizens—who are tempted to follow the global leadership of antidemocratic countries such as China and Russia instead of the liberal tradition of the West. Liberal democratic processes protecting universal human rights and the rule of law are challenged and disturbed all over the world, and we clearly cannot take for granted any smooth progress toward increasing freedom and respect for humanity.

In this situation, we need not only new advancements in the natural sciences, as vital as they are in combating urgent problems like the COVID-19 pandemic and the climate crisis, but also increased and deeper understanding of human actions, meanings, and values, as well as their complex histories. In short, we need the kind of knowledge that the humanities—such as history, literary studies, arts studies, and law, as well as theology and religious studies—can provide to us.

Unfortunately the crisis of liberal democracy also affects the state of the humanities. Humanist scholars have for a long time been worried about what is going to happen to their disciplines, but in contemporary academia these worries are perhaps more clearly justified than previously.

Politicians often expect scientific research to deliver immediately applicable results, and this is precisely what the humanities do not seem to be able to do. Moreover, political pressures may affect the ways in which humanistic research itself is conducted. Authoritarian rulers have never honored historical truth, but the frankness with which the current leaders of (again) China and Russia deny plain historical or scientific facts—such as the war crimes of the Red Army during World War II, the extreme violations of human rights during the post–World War II Soviet occupation of Eastern Europe, the murderous events on the Tiananmen Square in 1989, the persecution of the Uighur minority in contemporary China, the false claims used by Russian President Putin to justify his war against Ukraine, and the indisputable biological basis of the diversity of human sexual orientations—is as astounding as the clearly untrue claim by a (democratically elected) President of the United States that he had won the 2020 election. If the writing of history were subordinated to political power, the humanities as a serious scholarly enterprise would indeed be a lost cause. We see a hint of this even in my relatively happy and peaceful home country Finland, where in 2020 a historian was heavily attacked in social media by a group of nationalist right-wing activists and politicians who maintained that the prestigious grant he had received for a project on the role of Finland in the Holocaust was a "communist" sham.

Nor is the situation helped by the claims by those humanistic scholars who maintain that the humanities only "tell us stories" or offer interesting novel perspectives on human experience rather than aspiring to tell the truth. What is needed is a rigorous philosophical defense of humanistic scholarship as a serious cognitive project in its own right. However, this defense must not pretend that the humanities are exactly like the sciences. Rather, it must respect the distinct ways in which humanistic scholarship seeks knowledge and objectivity while at the same time perceiving the important similarities shared by all rational pursuits of truth. My discussion will start from the conviction that even though we may say, for instance, that literature and the arts pursue something like the truth about the human condition—about the right and the wrong, or about love or suffering or human mortality, among many other things—there is nevertheless a vital distinction to be made between the pursuit of truth via fictional writing and the rational pursuit of truth that at a general level is shared by the humanities and the sciences. The world we live in is a complex one, inviting multiple human perspectives and interpretations, but there is a real world around us that we need to understand better.

This book will not solve the crisis of liberal democracy nor what some scholars view as the "crisis of the humanities" today. What it does aim at is a philosophical examination of what the humanities are and in particular, the nature of their ontology and epistemology—that is, their understanding of the "reality" they seek to interpret and theoretically represent, as well as their distinctive ways of pursuing the truth. The philosophical approach that I have found particularly relevant for this purpose is pragmatism. As I will explain in the following chapters, this is because pragmatism acknowledges the ("humanly speaking") realistic and objective character of humanistic scholarship while appreciating the fact that humanistic inquiries are value-laden processes serving human needs and interests within the practices of research that we, as scholars, engage in.

I like to think of this book as a synthesis of two seemingly different and rather independent dimensions of my academic career.

First, I have, since my doctoral dissertation (1996), published extensively on pragmatism and related topics in philosophy, including metaphysics, ethics, philosophy of religion, philosophical anthropology, and philosophy of science.[1] I have also tried to contribute to the development of pragmatism scholarship in Europe and globally by being actively involved in pragmatism-related associations and networks—such as the European Pragmatism Association, the Central European Pragmatist Forum, and the Nordic Pragmatism Network, as well as, more recently, the William James Society—since the early 2000s. Having followed the outstanding work on pragmatism by many of my colleagues, near and remote, I have occasionally wondered why pragmatist philosophers, while defending pluralistic and antireductionist views in general, have only rarely systematically discussed the nature of the humanities from a pragmatist perspective. Pragmatist philosophy of science has a long tradition with many twists and turns (as will be seen in chapter 2 below), and pragmatism can be regarded as a general theory of critical inquiry (as this book as a whole also emphasizes), but more specific yet sufficiently broad pragmatist analyses of the status of humanistic scholarship have up to now been relatively rare.

Secondly, quite independently of my scholarly work on pragmatism and other topics in philosophy, I have had a unique opportunity to develop and facilitate humanistic scholarship more administratively in my home country Finland, with active international and interdisciplinary networks and connections. In addition to my own research and my regular professorial duties, I have had the privilege of serving in positions related more broadly to *all* the humanities and social sciences: I was, from 2009 to 2015, the director of the Helsinki Collegium for Advanced Studies, an institute for advanced study within the University of Helsinki specializing in the humanities and the social sciences, with a strongly interdisciplinary and international profile; later, I served as the vice-chair (2016–2018) and the chair (2019–2021) of the Research Council for Culture and Society at the Academy of Finland, the main national research funding organization in Finland. As the Research Council chair, I also participated in basically all the activities of the board of the Academy of Finland, as well as its subcommittees responsible for a number of rather important research funding allocation decisions at the national level across all academic disciplines (i.e., not merely the humanities). Due to this position of trust, I was also engaged in the international activities of our Research Council, among other things, as the Finnish board member of the HERA (Humanities in the European Research Area) network (2016–2021). On a smaller scale, one of my interesting interdisciplinary duties over the recent years was the directorship of the doctoral program in Theology and Religious Studies at the University of Helsinki (2018–2021). In all these and many related responsibilities, I have seen and been involved in decision-making processes about literally thousands of research proposals representing all the human sciences.

My experiences in both scholarly and administrative work have convinced me that a sustained philosophical discussion of the nature of the humanities is necessary. The humanities constantly need to define and redefine themselves in relation to other academic fields and to the society in which they exist. Moreover, in order to contribute to the development and renewal of, for example, research funding instruments serving the researcher community consisting of scholars representing a variety of career stages as well as scholarly orientations, a broad and ultimately philosophical understanding of the nature of humanistic research as a human activity is essential. A pragmatist philosophy of the humanities—to which this book can offer only a prolegomenon, though—will, I believe, provide a solid, philosophically sound basis for such ongoing discussions of the nature of the humanities and their relation to other areas of inquiry. It will be vital for evaluating the appropriateness of the various academic, political, cultural, and other expectations that humanities scholars face in their work. Indirectly, therefore, this book is also a defense of the very project of liberal democracy as a foundation for universal human rights, about which contemporary events provide good reasons to be concerned. There can be no humanistic scholarship without fundamental ethical respect for the irreducible significance of the individual human being at the center of all research—both as its subject and as its object. Therefore, I suppose this book is implicitly (unfortunately) rather timely, given how dramatically humanity itself has become under attack by Putin's troops invading Ukraine.

❧

A few portions of this book are drawn from previously published articles. Some fragments of chapters 1 and 2 include ideas that originally appeared in my short paper "Developing a Pragmatist Philosophy of the Humanities," published in a special issue of the open access journal *Pragmatism Today* 12:2 (2021) titled *Pragmatic Naturalism Today: Essays in Honor of John Ryder* (https://www.pragmatismtoday.eu/winter2021/Pragmatism_Today_Volume12_Issue2_Winter2021.pdf); warm thanks to the issue guest editor Lyubov Bugaeva for the invitation. Chapter 2 incorporates my essay, "How (Not) to Write the History of Pragmatist Philosophy of Science?" (*Perspectives on Science* 16:1, 2008), while some sections of chapter 4 loosely build on my brief entry "Transcendental Arguments," published in Byron Kaldis, ed., *Encyclopedia of Philosophy and the Social Sciences* (SAGE Publishing, 2013). Thanks are due to The MIT Press and SAGE Publishing for the permissions to use this copyrighted material. Otherwise the chapters have either been specifically written for this volume or employ material that has appeared only in unpublished conference presentations and guest talks. Sections of chapters 1 and 2 were presented as an online guest lecture at the École Normale Supérieure (Paris) in November 2020 (warm thanks to Mathias Girel), while some portions of chapter 4 were initially presented as a paper on transcendental arguments in a workshop on the philosophy of social science at the Forum Scientiarum, University of Tübingen, in November 2013 (thanks are due to Niels Weidtmann). Some of this material was also used at my lecture course on pragmatism and realism in theology and religious studies at the University of Helsinki in September 2021.

In addition to the individuals already mentioned, I am grateful to a large number of friends and colleagues who may not have provided explicit feedback on this particular project but whose views and ideas have, over the years, crucially shaped my thinking about the topics of this book. All or even most of such colleagues would be impossible to list here, but the ones whose influence is, explicitly or implicitly, most relevant to what I am trying to do in this book include Hanne Appelqvist, Dirk-Martin Grube, Logi Gunnarsson, Leila Haaparanta, Sara Heinämaa, Ana Honnacker, Matthias Jung, Heikki Kannisto, the late Erkki Kilpinen, Simo Knuuttila, Timo Koistinen, Heikki J. Koskinen, the late Joseph Margolis, Ilkka Niiniluoto, Wayne Proudfoot, Henrik Rydenfelt, Risto Saarinen, Naoko Saito, Magnus Schlette, Friedrich Stadler, Emil Višňovský, and Ulf Zackariasson. I would also like to thank the innumerable people encountered in the context of developing the humanities and social sciences within the international networks of institutes for advanced study and the administrative bodies of the Academy of Finland, as well as my colleagues at the Faculty of Theology, University of Helsinki (where I am academically based since 2015) and the Philosophical Society of Finland (which I have had the pleasure of chairing since 2016). Furthermore, I am deeply grateful to the three anonymous reviewers whose comments on the manuscript were valuable in many ways and to Michael Rinella and Susan Geraghty at SUNY Press for crucial help and guidance.

Most importantly, Sari Kivistö's support and her influence on the development of my ideas on the humanities—and academic life generally—are at least implicitly manifested throughout the book. Finally, I have been pleased to perceive that my two daughters, Meeri and Katri, seem to be developing (broadly) humanistic study and career pursuits of their own, and I hope they will have a chance to advance humanist ideals in their unique ways, probably different from mine.

Sami Pihlström
Wolfenbüttel, Germany, May 2022

Chapter 1

Introduction
Why This Book?

This volume develops a program for articulating and defending a novel pragmatist philosophy of the humanities, aiming at a philosophical theory of the basic character, objects of study, and general epistemology and ontology of humanistic inquiry from the perspective of pragmatism. The topic is, on the one hand, extremely comprehensive and wide-ranging, as I will deal with *the humanities in general* (albeit focusing on three main areas selected for closer case studies), but it is, on the other hand, very specific, because my articulation of the nature of the humanities will be based on a philosophical framework provided by *pragmatism*—a tradition initiated in the United States in the late nineteenth century by Charles S. Peirce, William James, and John Dewey, and later developed by many of their interpreters, critics, and followers. More precisely, my pragmatist philosophy of the humanities will build upon a distinctive Kantian version of pragmatism that I have defended in my own work since the late 1990s.

As a concept naming a field of study, *philosophy of the humanities* is only relatively rarely encountered—at least in comparison to analogous expressions denoting various other special fields in the philosophy of science, such as *philosophy of physics*, *philosophy of biology*, or *philosophy of economics*. *Philosophy of social science* is, of course, a well-established discipline, while *philosophy of the humanities* can hardly be regarded as such—even though the history of the humanities is an increasingly recognized area of scholarship.[1] As a first approximation, we may understand the philosophy of the humanities to mean the application of the problems, ideas, and arguments originally developed in general philosophy of science to humanistic inquiry in particular. The philosophy of the humanities is, then, something like a general theory of scientific or rational inquiry as applied to the humanities (with the word *scientific* corresponding roughly here to the meaning of the German word *Wissenschaft* rather than to its usually more restricted meaning in English, referring only to the natural sciences), while the humanities themselves, broadly conceived, can be taken to include historically established and normatively constrained disciplines as diverse as aesthetics and arts studies, art history, anthropology, cultural studies, history, law and legal studies, linguistics, literary studies (or comparative literature), philosophy, religious studies, and theology—and no such list can aim at any exhaustiveness.[2] There are, then, both analogies and differences between what I am calling the philosophy of the humanities and other special areas of the philosophy of science and inquiry.

It might be objected right away that the philosophy of the humanities has been developed at least since the emergence of hermeneutics in the eighteenth and nineteenth centuries by thinkers such as Friedrich Schleiermacher, Wilhelm Dilthey, Wilhelm Windelband, and others. However, the present book does not build upon this tradition but seeks a new opening for the philosophy of the humanities in the form of a pragmatist investigation of the ontology and epistemology of humanistic inquiry, especially focusing on the issue of realism. Moreover, pragmatism, while appreciating the insights of hermeneutical philosophers, adopts a critical distance from that tradition, which usually presupposes a sharp dualism between the natural and the human sciences. Nothing like that will be assumed in my pragmatist philosophy of the humanities; on the contrary, as will become clear shortly, my approach will be based on a general pragmatist theory of inquiry. On the other hand, the refusal to view the different branches of science and inquiry in dualistic terms does not at all mean that we would not have to appreciate the enormous differences between different practices of inquiry: theology and physics, for example, are certainly *very* different from each other. Pragmatism, with its pluralistic emphases, is ideally suited for defending this kind of diversity. It will also become clear in due course that the pragmatist tradition contains excellent philosophical resources for dealing with the humanities in their diversity in a manner that does not claim them to be essentially different from the other sciences.

Moreover, insofar as the humanities need to be "defended" in global academia today (perhaps more than previously), as many scholars seem to think,³ it may be advisable to understand academic politics as something like applied philosophy of science; thus, we arguably need the philosophy of the humanities in order to ground and systematize our attempts to articulate and defend the nature and value of the humanities also in more practical contexts of academic life. Therefore, explorations in the philosophy of the humanities may serve "political" goals, too, even though that is *not* a main purpose of this book. The chief intention of this volume is to understand more deeply what the humanities are about. Yet, while my focus will be more philosophical (and, indeed, epistemic and metaphysical) than political, it ought to be recognized that the humanities may certainly seem to be in the need of a defense protecting them from both external and internal threats or challenges, including a *technocratic instrumentalism* that views all research in terms of its explicit practical utility, a *reductionist scientism* that considers only the fundamental physical sciences to be capable of "limning the true and ultimate structure of reality" (to quote a well-known phrase by W. V. Quine), and a *radical postmodern relativism* that may in a sense collapse the humanities "from within" by suggesting that there is no room for any rational and critical scholarly discussion at all, as everything—including the most basic criteria of rational thought—is just relative to interpretation, discourse, or historical circumstances (cf., e.g., Pihlström 2011b).⁴ Pragmatism, in the way I will characterize it here, is, I argue, able to offer such a defense based on a thoroughgoing philosophical account of what the humanities are in the business of doing, without succumbing to the temptations of instrumentalism, reductionism, or radical relativism. Therefore, it may be politically relevant in academia, too.

It should be noted right in the beginning that even though the humanities study cultural phenomena such as art and literature, historical events, and religious practices, I will not be directly engaging in any scholarly discussions in, say, the philosophy of art, of literature, of history, or of religion. In relation to these subdisciplines of philosophy, the philosophy of the humanities, in the sense I mean it, adopts a metalevel standpoint that is at the same time more abstract and more concrete. It is *more abstract* in the sense that it does not directly ask what, for example, literature, history, or religion *are* but more indirectly what literary critics, historians, and scholars of religion (along with other humanistic scholars) are doing, or what they ought to be doing, when investigating what they consider the "realities" studied in their disciplines. Thus, I will be concerned with the nature of literature, history, and religion *only* to the extent that these are understood as objects of humanistic inquiry. I will not examine how, for instance, literature or religion may themselves be ways of pursuing "truth" (in some sense) but only how humanistic scholars investigating these human practices (ought to) pursue the truth about them. My discussion is also *more concrete* (insofar as a philosophical discussion can be concrete at all) in the sense that it examines the purpose-driven *practices* of humanistic disciplines rather than some presupposed abstract philosophical conceptions of what such disciplines are "about." Humanistic inquiry is something in which real human beings engage, and this—in itself humanistic—point of departure should never be overlooked. Indeed, one of the virtues of my pragmatist reflection will, I hope, be its ability to maintain a "human perspective" even when the philosophical issues themselves are examined at a rather abstract (more specifically, transcendental) level. What I am aiming at is an increased philosophical understanding of the activities of the humanistic inquiries that in turn focus on art and literature, history, and religion (as elements of human culture more generally), an understanding that may also contribute to the critical appreciation of what may be permanently and irreducibly valuable for human culture in humanistic scholarship.

Thus, while the philosopher of art and literature may ask highly relevant questions about the nature of literary works of art, for instance, I will here ask questions about the nature of the scholarship in literary theory and criticism that studies literary works of art. I will not be mainly interested in the ontological criteria of identity of a literary work, the ontology and semantics of fictional discourse (e.g., the sense, if any, in which a work of fiction can teach us truths about the human condition), or the ways in which fictional literature may convey philosophical (or other) cognitive information (cf. Haapala 1989; Mikkonen 2013; Geisenhanslüke 2015; Selleri and Gaydon 2016). Rather, I will be interested in what the literary critic and/or theorist is (or should be) aiming at when making theoretical and interpretive claims about such works and discourses. Analogously, while the philosophy of history, traditionally conceived, may inquire into, say, historical progress and teleology (or the lack thereof) in the development of civilizations,[5] my pragmatist philosophy of the humanities contributes to the philosophy of historiography by asking questions about the nature and epistemic status of historical inquiry, including the objects and methods of historiography. Thus, my goal is not the interpretation of history itself but a philosophical interpretation of what is (or should be) going on in scholarly interpretations of history, especially at the ontological level (rather than, say, the level of historical explanation and understanding). This distinction roughly corresponds to the one traditionally drawn between "speculative" and "critical" philosophy of history or what is, rather, usually described today as the distinction between the philosophy of history and the philosophy of historiography, where the former explores, for example, historical "laws" or teleology while the latter focuses on the epistemology and methodology of historiography[6]—even though my focus will be primarily ontological. Furthermore, instead of contributing to the philosophy of religion characterized by questions concerning, for example, the nature of religious language or the relation between faith and reason (or the history of such questions), I hope to make a contribution to our understanding of theology and religious studies as fields of inquiry into religion; thus, again, this book does not deal with the philosophy of religion but aims at a philosophical investigation of the kinds of inquiries into religion that scholars in theology and religious studies (or comparative religion) may engage in.[7]

An obvious question is why I am proposing a *pragmatist* approach to the philosophy of the humanities instead of some of the other presumably better known and more widely discussed philosophical orientations that might be relevant to the topic I have chosen. What added value does pragmatism bring to our picture of the humanities, over and above the well-established accounts of the nature of the humanistic disciplines based on, say, hermeneutics as a general theory of interpretation and understanding, on deconstruction as a poststructuralist method of reading historical texts, or on many analytic philosophers' careful theorization of the concept of interpretation and the structure of historical explanations? Clearly, I cannot possibly deal with these and many related approaches in the philosophical study of the nature of the humanities in a single book. In particular, the "postmodern" developments in poststructuralism and deconstruction, though clearly relevant to my concerns, will be more or less left aside here. Rather than engaging with the rivals of pragmatism in any detail, I will only be able to sketch a pragmatist approach to the kinds of issues—particularly realism—that I believe philosophers interested in the humanities ought to take seriously, no matter which theoretical (or antitheoretical) background they come from.[8]

Answering the question "why pragmatism?" is one of the overarching purposes of this volume, but I will in this introductory chapter outline the project by preliminarily providing some key reasons for adopting the pragmatist point of view in this context. It will also become clear in due course that one of the metalevel questions to be addressed is how exactly pragmatism itself—in its historical and contemporary manifestations—ought to be interpreted and developed in order to best sustain a comprehensive philosophy of the humanities. I cannot claim expertise on the various methodological debates within the slightly more detailed case study areas I propose to explore; what I primarily intend to do in this book is to sketch a pragmatist *approach*—indeed, merely a *program* or a *prolegomenon* opening up certain key questions without being able to provide any full-fledged theory—to the philosophy of the humanities, suggesting a certain way of looking at the ways reality gets represented in these fields.

Few previous contributions address the philosophy of the humanities at the general level this inquire operates at, let alone within a pragmatist framework. One exception is Jan Faye's (2012) naturalistic program for a "reconstruction" of the humanities, to be occasionally cited in relevant contexts below. Another important recent book is the comprehensive introduction to the history and philosophy of the humanities by Michiel Leezenberg and Gerard de Vries (2019). Many of its themes are relevant to my project as well: Leezenberg and de Vries emphasize the Kantian background of the rise of the modern humanities (see ibid., 61–69, 141–143), focusing on the *possibility* of both scientific and humanistic knowledge as well as of the objects of knowledge, and observing that major twentieth-century thinkers like Thomas Kuhn and Michel Foucault (whose historicist ideas have to a considerable extent shaped our understanding of the development of both science and the humanities) in a sense worked within this broadly Kantian framework (cf. ibid., 121–126, 133–139). Leezenberg and de Vries fail to consider pragmatism in any detail, though (apart from a few remarks on, e.g., Richard Rorty's neopragmatism: see ibid., chapter 4 and 304–309). This provides, for my undertaking, a natural way of both relying on work that has already been done on the emergence and development of the humanities—there is certainly no need to repeat the historical discussions that other, much more competent scholars have provided before me—and advancing from it by proposing what is lacking in earlier research, namely, a (broadly) Kantian yet pragmatist articulation of the humanities.[9]

However, for my pragmatist taste, Leezenberg and de Vries's discussion, though in many ways excellent and informative, operates too much with the dualism between science as seeking the truth and the humanities as pursuing new interpretations (see, e.g., ibid., 24, 35).[10] This is one of the dichotomies that a pragmatist philosophy of the humanities should, in my view, avoid by taking seriously the idea that the humanities are also cognitive projects in search of knowledge and truth. Before explicating my own pragmatist standpoint, let me, however, add some further thoughts on why we should examine the philosophy of the humanities in the first place.

Why Study the Philosophy of the Humanities?

Scholars across the humanities seem frequently to suggest that the humanistic disciplines constantly need to define and redefine themselves in contemporary academia. Some fear that the humanities may face the danger of being reduced to other (more obviously "relevant") fields or narrowed down in the interest of practical applications and "useful knowledge," a fear exacerbated by the reduction in recent decades of the resources of humanities departments in many countries—though certainly not everywhere. (In some cases there seems to be a collectively held belief among humanities scholars that their resources have been or are at permanent risk of being steeply reduced, even if nothing like that has happened or is planned.) A major worry, in brief, is that the humanities may be losing their own distinctive "voice" in academia, at least in comparison to their central position in traditional "Humboldtian" research universities. Reacting to this situation, international and national scholarly networks and other actors have powerfully defended the humanities and their special value both within academia and more generally in society. The academic as well as societal *impact* of the humanities—in its many different meanings and across different time periods—is thus constantly discussed, and for good reasons, also taking into consideration the kind of larger political contexts with the various threats to universal human rights we are painfully familiar with. We certainly vitally *need* whatever it is that the humanities are able to deliver.

My philosophical examination of the nature of the humanities takes its departure from the conviction that a pragmatist analysis of the status, objects, aims, and value of the humanities will be able to crucially enlighten these discussions and to offer a novel way of accounting for the distinctive impact potential of the humanities. Moreover, it is very important to study the humanities *in general*, because—even for the pragmatist antiessentialist—many of the problems concerning the status and value of the humanistic disciplines are common to most or all of these fields of scholarship. On the other hand, in order to keep this book within a reasonable size, I have chosen specifically to comment on three case studies concerning traditional—and also interestingly different—areas of humanistic scholarship: literary theory and criticism, historiography, and theology and religious studies. As a fourth such area, we might, at the metalevel, view this entire undertaking as, implicitly, a pragmatist investigation of the nature of philosophy (of the humanities) itself as a humanistic discipline. The reasons for my choices of exemplary cases are mostly practical; however, the arguments to be formulated will, I hope, be relevant to the other fields within the humanities and, mutatis mutandis, outside them, too.[11]

I will deliberately focus on *traditional* fields of humanistic scholarship such as literary theory, history, and theology. It is, I believe, a more difficult and therefore also more interesting philosophical challenge to develop a pragmatist philosophy of those fields than of more "dynamic" (and for that reason currently more "trendy") interdisciplinary areas. As is well known, various relatively recent transformations have shaped the general understanding of the humanities among both their practitioners and university administrators. These include the increasing *interdisciplinarity* (not only within the humanities but also between the humanities and the natural and social sciences) and the strengthening *research group structure* of humanistic scholarship, as well as the growing emphasis on *digital research materials and methods* that have led to novel research questions utilizing "big data"—at least in comparison to the traditional image of the humanistic scholar sitting in the learned solitude of their "study chamber" immersed in reading and writing about obscure old texts.

The present book suggests that these developments, despite their obvious importance for the practice and self-understanding of the humanities, are relatively minor trends in comparison to the fundamental need to increase our deeper philosophical comprehension of the nature of the knowledge-acquisition characteristic of the humanities in general (both in contemporary digital and interdisciplinary contexts and in more traditional scholarly contexts), and especially the relation of that characteristic to the "reality" about which knowledge is to be acquired. We cannot afford to lose our philosophical sense of how the autonomous role of the humanities can be maintained in an academic culture and environing society that may increasingly expect direct applicability and concrete results. More specifically, we cannot, I argue, lose the idea of the individual human being at the center of humanistic inquiry—and this is one reason that we need a pragmatist philosophy of the humanities. I am, of course, not at all opposed to the ways in which the humanities are being developed today (e.g., within "digital humanities" or "environmental humanities"), but I also wish to defend the permanent value of traditional humanities. The fact that something is "new" does not by itself make it better than something "old."[12]

One possible source for the worry—perhaps primarily among humanistic scholars themselves—that the (especially traditional) humanities may not be taken sufficiently seriously as "sciences" among natural scientists might be the idea that the *ontological* status of the objects of research in the humanities is somewhat less clear than the ontological status of natural-scientific research objects. The meanings of texts are ontologically more obscure entities than, for instance, electrons, molecules, or genes. Therefore, a philosophical question concerning the very existence of humanly created cultural entities as objects of humanistic inquiry needs to be asked—and it is, clearly, a question prior to the more practical questions concerning more practical issues of methodology, such as interdisciplinarity and digital methods. I will, accordingly, focus on fundamental ontological and epistemic questions concerning the humanities rather than methodological ones.[13] But I will do so in a pragmatist context defined by the understanding of ontology itself as ineliminably pragmatic (cf. Pihlström 2009, 2013, 2020).

My ontological orientation also indicates the kind of issues concerning the humanities' objects of study that will be considered and those that will remain beyond the scope of this discussion. A simple example may enlighten this. In his famous work, *The Great Chain of Being* (1936), Arthur O. Lovejoy suggested that the history of ideas should study what he called "unit ideas," such as the "principle of plenitude" whose long and complex history he sought to uncover. These unit ideas may, according to Lovejoy, take rather different shapes as implicit elements of more comprehensive philosophical systems and ways of thinking ("compounds") characteristic of their authors and their times. A few decades later, another major twentieth-century thinker, Jaakko Hintikka (1976), vigorously challenged this view, arguing not only that the principle of plenitude is *not* a unit idea in Lovejoy's sense but more generally that there are no general unit ideas in that sense *at all* and that a historian of ideas should rather focus on more detailed ideas that more accurately reflect historical philosophers' ways of thinking, as well as on their logical connections. Now, my aim is of course not to settle this dispute, even though both Lovejoy and Hintikka wrote immense *oeuvres* that could be relevant to my own project in various ways.[14] (Even less is my aim to settle specific methodological controversies in the methodology of historiography, for example.) My main interest lies in *what kind of entities* Lovejoyian unit ideas would be, if any such ideas existed, and in what kind of *ontological assumptions or presuppositions* the philosopher of historiography (or the philosopher seeking to understand the conceptual, ontological, and methodological structures of the history of ideas as a humanistic discipline) makes in claiming that such ideas ought to be studied—or that there is nothing of that kind to be studied, as the case might be. My philosophy of the humanities lies at a metalevel with regard to the kind of philosophical controversies exemplified by the Lovejoy v. Hintikka case.[15]

The pragmatic frameworks of humanistic inquiries also manifest remarkable differences in the ontological status of the objects of study within different fields of the humanities. Literary critics are concerned with works of literature and their meaningful structures, as well as, for example, the representational relations they may bear on historical and/or contemporary social and political events and processes, while historians examine what really happened in the past, why it happened, and why something else did not happen.[16] Theologians and religious studies scholars may investigate the meanings involved in religious documents, practices, and institutions from a wide range of historical, textual, and systematic (including philosophical) points of view. It is not at all clear that the ontological questions concerning the existence of these different types of entities—that is, works of art, past (chains of) events, and religious meanings—are the same. It also needs to be understood that religious studies and theology[17] need *not* be concerned with questions about the existence of supernatural or transcendent beings (which are, rather, a concern of religion itself); these academic fields, in contrast to religious activities, need to operate within an ontology that may resemble both literary studies (meaningful textual structures) and history (past events and actions)—a cultural ontology, in short. Pragmatism will, I suggest, prove useful in its ability to acknowledge not only the methodological but also the ontological *pluralism* of such research fields.[18] It goes without saying that pragmatism is generally opposed to ontological reductionisms that find only some privileged class(es) of entities fully real; such monistic ontologies cannot serve as a ground for the philosophy of the humanities. Rather, pragmatism recognizes that "humanistic entities" such as meanings, values, and historical events are as fully real as, say, electrons or atoms, or other theoretical entities postulated by fundamental physics.[19]

It might be suggested, however, that at least some elements of both theology and philosophy—such as philosophy of religion or "analytic theology," which utilizes analytic philosophical concepts and arguments for theological purposes (cf., e.g., Vainio 2020)—do seek to engage with the transcendent. One might thus claim that in some sense philosophy is *not* a humanistic discipline, as it cannot be defined in terms of its subject matter—and here it differs from basically all other academic disciplines. Philosophy can investigate reality in general—not just humanly made cultural reality but also fundamental metaphysical questions, including the theologically relevant one concerning the existence or nonexistence of God (or other "religious entities," as we might call them, such as souls, the afterlife, and so on). To the extent that (analytic, systematic) theology relies on such philosophical investigations, it could also be taken to reach beyond the merely human. However, such a metaphysical characterization of the tasks of philosophy and theology already presupposes an essentially non-Kantian and (thus) nonpragmatist account of the nature of these disciplines based on what may be called metaphysical realism (cf. also chapter 2). From a Kantian critical and/or pragmatist perspective, even theology and philosophy, including philosophy of religion, primarily investigate human reality, *our attempts* to refer to God, the world in general, transcendence, and other metaphysical realities beyond the "merely human."[20] The metaphysical realist could maintain that the Kantian conception of theology and philosophy as humanistic disciplines that investigate only human language, culture, and world-categorization (rather than the "world in itself") begs the question against stronger realism that claims the fundamental metaphysical nature of reality itself to be among the legitimate objects of study in these fields. However, the very fact that this metalevel dispute remains an open issue in my view counts in favor of the basically Kantian (and pragmatist) position. This issue indeed needs to be settled first, and *it* is an inescapably humanistic question concerning the very possibility of referring, by means of human language-use, to a transcendent reality; it is an inquiry into human inquiry.[21] Accordingly, I do believe it is justified to maintain that theology, religious studies, and even the philosophy of religion are primarily humanistic practices of inquiry into human meanings that shape, for us, the world—even if we did believe that the world thus shaped exists independently of those meanings (see, however, also chapter 4 below).

As we indeed shape the world we live in through our meaning-making activities and interpretations, the broader *societal context* of our discussion of the philosophy of the humanities is also, I believe, remarkable. Academic life and universities may change significantly and perhaps even permanently due to the COVID-19 pandemic of 2020–2022 and the ensuing, possibly long-lasting social, educational, and economic crises. At the time of this writing, we do not know how these developments will unfold, but the crisis could fundamentally affect the long-term future of the humanities in ways that are still hard to predict. Further potential contextual significance—as well as potential societal impact—characteristic of this inquiry can be expected because the humanities may yield results that are culturally and politically controversial. An obvious example is the politics of history (and what has come to be called interdisciplinary "memory studies") in post-communist countries, sometimes resulting in deliberate, politically opportunistic misinterpretations of historical events such as World War II (as, notoriously, in Vladimir Putin's increasingly authoritarian and nationalistic Russia today, a "post-truth" society by any decent judgment).[22] Another example is the constant tension between secular and religious worldviews, which has political consequences in, say, the struggle between liberal and conservative social and cultural forces. Such an interplay of political power struggles and academic research needs *holistic*—and, I argue, pragmatic—evaluation. Indeed, one reason for approaching the humanities from a pragmatist viewpoint is that we need to understand academic research and politics as *human practices* with their distinctive aims and goals that nevertheless overlap and entangle with each other, for better and for worse. We also need to realize that the very ontologies of humanistic research may reflect our various practice-embedded needs, interests, and value commitments. One book can only make a very small contribution to the kind of critical discussion that is needed in order to tackle these vast themes, but a philosophical articulation of the nature of the humanities will, I hope, be helpful for those hoping to examine more directly, for instance, the political significance of historical interpretations.

Investigating the ontology and epistemology of the humanities may also have what might be called a very significant *weltanschaulich* (worldview-related) impact; that is, it may profoundly affect our understanding of the reality we live in. For example, in the philosophy of science, it has been debated for decades whether electrons and other unobservable theoretical entities postulated in scientific theories to explain observable data "really exist."[23] Indeed, questions like this played a vital role in the emergence of twentieth-century philosophy of science in the context originally provided by logical empiricism, which sought to reduce the language of scientific theories via explicit translations to language only referring to the observable world. Accordingly, the extent to which we are justified in believing in the existence of unobservable theoretical entities on the basis of observational evidence has been debated (see, e.g., van Fraassen 1980; Hacking 1983; Niiniluoto 1999; Psillos 1999)—in a sense continuing the age-old discussion of David Hume's problem of induction. Not only have most philosophers rejected the empiricist restriction to the observable, but there are even strong scientific realists who go as far as to claim that *only* the scientific entities in the last analysis exist: the theoretical entities postulated by best-explaining scientific theories are what is ultimately real, as the "scientific image" ontologically replaces the "manifest image" (cf. Sellars 1963; Tuomela 1985). However, even when such radical formulations of scientific realism and materialism are rejected, serious ontological attention is usually not directed in the same way to the ontological postulations (or ontologically relevant background assumptions) of humanistic scholarship—even apart from the question of the ontological status of historical facts and events, which is a big discussion in its own right. If we have good philosophical reasons to believe in the reality of, say, literary meanings or interpretive possibilities (as Peircean-like "real generals," for instance, as explained in chapter 3), our world is, ontologically speaking, considerably *richer* than the world as seen merely from the point of view of the natural (physical) sciences. Understanding the humanities philosophically thus contributes to understanding the human world. Therefore, we can also say that the philosophy of the humanities may contribute to the classical philosophical project of human *self-understanding*. Enhancing our philosophical understanding and appreciation of humanistic scholarship contributes to our understanding and appreciation of some of the central dimensions of the human world we live in and the activities we engage in.

On the other hand, this of course does not mean that the humanities scholar should or could simply accept whatever ontological postulations are made in or by their objects of study (e.g., the texts whose meanings they are analyzing). Historical documents may postulate any number of truly weird ontologies, and humanistic scholarship may and often does focus on products of human thinking containing manifestly false statements about what there is. It scarcely needs to be argued in any great detail that our humanistic inquiry ought to be compatible with a reasonably comprehensive natural-scientific (and social-scientific) picture of the world.[24] In particular, as already remarked, the scholar of theology and religious studies can by no means presuppose the existence of God or other religious "realities" that their objects of study—for example, religious documents, doctrines, or groups of people—may have postulated but must critically study those postulations themselves. Indeed, ontological postulations of various kinds—ways of thinking about the existence (or nonexistence, as the case might be) of various types of entities—and the more or less problematic reasonings behind such postulations may themselves be among the very objects of inquiry in the humanities.[25]

The Philosophy of the Humanities Today

Even though there is no agreement among scholars engaged in the philosophy of the humanities about the precise scope or even definition of this field, there are, of course, plenty of scholarly contributions on specific areas such as the philosophy of literary criticism, the philosophy of historiography, and the philosophy of religious studies.[26] When canvassing the conceptual and scholarly background of this project, it is important to realize that a wealth of previous work has already been done and that only a very small fragment of it can really be taken into consideration here. For example, both philosophers and historians have actively discussed the methodology of historiography (see again Tucker 2009 for a comprehensive collection of relatively recent essays), and controversies on the epistemology and methodology of literary interpretation and religious studies, raising issues of interpretive objectivity and relativism are also well known.

On the other hand, the philosophy of history and the philosophy of historiography, have not always been clearly distinguished from each other conceptually even by central figures in the field—not until relatively recently, that is (cf. ibid., "Introduction"; Kuukkanen 2015). It may be difficult to draw such a distinction in any principled and ahistorical (!) way; this division, as all conceptual distinctions, is itself subject to historical change (and must be pragmatically evaluated on the basis of the purposes it serves in different contexts).[27] What has been called critical philosophy of history examines, among other things, the objectivity of historical knowledge and the nature of historical explanation (see, e.g.,

Mandelbaum 1977), topics clearly relevant to the question of realism about historiography and its objects (to be considered in more detail below). Some major scholars in the philosophy of history and historiography, such as William Dray (1980), have investigated *both* philosophical issues of (the methods of) historiography—including, say, R. G. Collingwood's classical views on historical understanding as reenacting past experiences or rethinking past thoughts (see Collingwood 1946), as well as the traditional idea of objectively reconstructing the past "as it actually was"—*and* more speculative or "metaphysical" issues in the philosophical interpretation of history itself, such as historical progress, human freedom in its historical contexts, and Spenglerian cultural pessimism.[28]

The present undertaking will focus—from its distinctive pragmatist angle—on the former kind of topics instead of the latter, while recognizing that a sharp division between them will be quite impossible. The pragmatist philosopher of history and historiography should therefore, in my view, be strongly opposed to, for example, Hegelian historical teleology, but arguing for that general view is only tangentially relevant to my investigations in this book. On the other hand, the way in which Karl Popper (1972 [1957], 1977) both criticizes historicist accounts of historical inevitability or "laws of history" and offers a philosophical articulation of realism about history would certainly be significant for a (more comprehensive) pragmatist study of history and historiography, too, even though Popper himself never sympathized with pragmatism at all. Furthermore, when exploring, say, historical or interpretive objectivity, the philosophy of the humanities is primarily concerned with fundamental philosophical questions concerning the very possibility of such objectivity—in its social and historical contingencies (cf. also Hacking 2002, 181).

Moreover, a monumental scholarly work like Paul Ricoeur's *Memory, History, Forgetting* (2004) may successfully combine deep insights into the historicity of human existence and the ethical and political issues of memory[29] with careful philosophical examination of the methodology of historiography, including explanation, understanding, and historical representation. It is a clear indication of the entanglement of philosophy of history and philosophy of historiography. Furthermore, if we read G. H. von Wright's classic *Explanation and Understanding* (1971), dealing with the methodology of historical explanation in particular and developing the theory of intentional explanation understood in terms of the famous "practical syllogism,"[30] in the context of his overall philosophical oeuvre, which also includes essays on the historical development of the

Western civilization and critical analyses of the state of humanity and the environmental crisis (e.g., von Wright 1993), we can appreciate the profound connections between the epistemology of historical scholarship and the broader philosophical attempts to understand human beings as historical beings ethically concerned with their past, present, and future.[31] Even though specific methodological issues in historiography will not be centrally present in this book, the well-known contributions by major thinkers including Dray, Ricoeur, von Wright, and Hayden White (among others) would potentially be among the kind of materials that would have to be critically studied in more comprehensive investigations of the philosophy of the humanities. Whatever I will have to say (primarily in chapter 3) about the kinds of issues these scholars have worked on will only be in relation to the pragmatist views I will develop.

Analogous examples characterizing the contemporary state of the philosophy of the humanities can be found in the other case study areas. For example, when Paisley Livingston (1988) examines the knowledge that literary theory may offer us, he also comments on the epistemic status of literature itself; in comparison, again, my discussion focuses on the former kind of issues rather than the latter.[32] Moreover, while debates over the methodology of theology and religious studies are primarily confined to the epistemic credentials of scholarly contributions to those fields, it is almost inevitable that the possibility of "religious knowledge" is thereby also discussed. Even what is sometimes labeled "methodological naturalism" (see chapter 4 below) is not entirely neutral. For a thoroughgoing naturalist, the commitment to naturalism (or atheism) as a background assumption of religious studies can hardly remain "merely methodological"; it is at the same time a commitment to a conception of the world according to which religious experience (due to its aspiration to the transcendent), for example, should not be regarded as being cognitively in touch with reality in the same way in which scientific experimentation and theorization may be, and should not therefore play an evidential role in the methodology of the study of religion. A naturalist account of religion—based on, for example, Dewey's nonreductive pragmatic naturalism (cf. Pihlström 2005, 2013)—will thus have to determine exactly how scholarly perspectives on religious practices and their practitioners' experiences are related to religious worldviews themselves (see several essays in Bagger 2018, esp. Proudfoot 2018 and Davis 2018).

In a comprehensive philosophy of the humanities, the relations between humanistic scholarship and the "world" such scholarship aims at representing, understanding, and explaining are therefore complex.

This "world" also contains human beings' (e.g., literary or religious) ideas about and attempts to "know" something about the reality they (we) live in, and those cognitive pursuits themselves also need to be critically explored, in connection with the very attempt to study the philosophical foundations of humanistic scholarship generally. This reflexive structure is nicely manifested in historiography, in particular: the writing of history is itself an element of the historicity of human beings.

What we need, then, is an enriched philosophy of the humanities exploring the status of our scholarly endeavors seeking to understand the literary, historical, and (possibly) religious aspects of human beings' "being-in-the-world" (to adopt a Heideggerian expression out of context) in their reflexive complexity. Humanities scholars typically analyze human practices that are themselves (purportedly) *about* the world, and the philosophical assessments of those practices will, to a certain degree, inevitably include an assessment of their successes and failures in this "aboutness."[33] Hence, philosophical discussions of literary theory or religious studies will also to some extent have to engage with literary and religious attempts to cope with the world we live in, even though that is not my primary aim in this study.

It should be observed that, in comparison to the plethora of scholarship available within, for example, the philosophy of historiography in general, specifically pragmatist contributions to this field have been few and far between. Yet, two pragmatist giants—both recently deceased—stand out. In the philosophy of historiography and more generally in the philosophy of culture, Morton White (e.g., 2002) defended what he called holistic pragmatism (to be further discussed below), while Joseph Margolis (e.g., 1993) wrote extensively over the years on what he labeled the "flux" of history, developing a complex form of historicist pragmatism. Interestingly, special issues of relatively new but well-established journals such as *European Journal of Pragmatism and American Philosophy* and *Journal of the Philosophy of History* have been devoted to pragmatism in historiography, offering a rich set of perspectives on both pragmatist classics' views on history and the ways in which the methods of historiography might be developed along pragmatist lines (see Gronda and Viola 2016; Kuukkanen et al. 2019; and esp. Grigoriev and Piercey 2019, an informative introduction to the aforementioned *Journal of the Philosophy of History*'s special issue).[34]

Giles Gunn (2014, 2017) has proposed a pragmatist approach to the study of literature and examined the history of American literature that emphasizes its connections with pragmatism.[35] But probably by far the best-known pragmatist philosopher of literary theory, and of the humanities generally, is Richard Rorty,[36] whose work emphasizes the radical contingency of our historically developing practices, including the ways we speak about and conceptualize reality. In a sense, Rorty extends a broadly "Kuhnian" understanding of the historicity of the development of the sciences (cf. Kuhn 1970 [1962]) to philosophy and human culture generally, proposing an "ironist" attitude to the contingency of even our most fundamental "final vocabularies," while creatively engaging with some of the most profound literary works of modern times, including Vladimir Nabokov's and George Orwell's great novels (see esp. Rorty 1989; on Orwell, cf. also chapter 3 below). However, while Rorty's radical neopragmatism certainly needs to be taken seriously by the pragmatist philosopher of the humanities,[37] it is not easy to find any systematically developed philosophical account of the humanities in his work. I am also on a rather different track from Ulf Schulenberg's (2015) defense of a pragmatist "humanism" as a Rortyan antifoundationalist and postmetaphysical "poeticized culture," as my own version of pragmatist humanism (as developed, e.g., in Pihlström 2021) is Kant-inspired and thus "transcendental"; yet, the Rortyan "uses of literature" in moral and political emancipation, as analyzed by Schulenberg (and many others), could be among the research objects of humanistic inquiry (arguably characterizable as Peircean-like "real generals"; cf. chapter 3).

In comparison to pragmatist philosophy of literary theory, there is a lot of discussion available on pragmatism as applied to religion. However, in most cases this is, at least primarily, pragmatist philosophy of religion rather than pragmatist philosophy of theology and religious studies (cf., e.g., Pihlström 2013, 2020; see, however, also Bagger 2018). In some of my own previous work, I have tried to develop a pragmatically realist and nonreductively naturalist approach to religion and its academic study, and clearly whatever I will have to say about the study of religion in this book is intended to be compatible with such a broadly pragmatist philosophy of religion.

In any event, I am not claiming that I can always clearly maintain the distinction between the philosophy of the humanities, on the one hand, and the philosophy of the "objects" of the fields of humanistic scholarship to be studied (viz., the philosophy of literature, the philosophy of history, and the philosophy of religion), on the other hand; to a certain degree this can only be a matter of emphasis rather than any strict division. But trying to maintain a distinction like this will determine my focus.

Why Study the Philosophy of the Humanities from a Pragmatist Perspective?

Very few among the major theorists cited above have approached the philosophy of the humanities in an explicitly pragmatist manner. However, pragmatism, I will argue, is considerably better suited to the task of philosophically understanding the nature and value of the humanities than, for example, "pure" analytic philosophy, hermeneutics, or phenomenology. This is so especially because the pragmatist tradition has developed a *general theory of inquiry* (cf., e.g., Capps 2015) not restricted to either the natural sciences or the humanities, or to any other specific field of inquiry, for that matter; nor does it presuppose any principled dichotomy or dualism between the natural and the human sciences.[38] The very concept of inquiry, as articulated by pragmatist philosophers, is extremely broad yet specific in its own way. Pragmatism provides philosophical tools for developing a general conception of rational inquiry that can be fruitfully applied to humanistic inquiry in particular and to investigating what is distinctive in such inquiry in comparison to other forms of inquiry. We need, moreover, a philosophical theory of the humanities that can also be appreciated from the perspective of the natural sciences, as well as from the standpoint of general philosophy of science (often focusing on scientific rather than humanistic inquiry as a model of all rational science). Few philosophers of natural science care much for hermeneutics, but many of them could without difficulties embrace pragmatism. This is a further practical (external) reason for developing a pragmatist philosophy of the humanities, in addition to the intrinsic philosophical value such a development may embody.

Thus, while I have nothing against the kind of philosophy of the humanities that has been articulated in the tradition of hermeneutics since Schleiermacher and Dilthey, up to and including contemporary hermeneutic scholars such as Charles Taylor, my pragmatist approach offers, I think, unique advantages, especially in its understanding of the problem of realism as fundamentally similar across all the disciplines of inquiry.[39] This adds a kind of *commensurability* to the philosophy of science and the philosophy of the humanities: the pragmatists' insights concerning realism, truth, and objectivity in the philosophy of science are arguably directly relevant to the problem of realism in the philosophy of the humanities, though the latter cannot be reduced to the former. The pragmatist tradition also equips us with a number of specific philosophical ideas that can be usefully applied to the philosophy of the humanities, even though they were originally developed in more general contexts of metaphysics, epistemology, and theory of inquiry; these include the value-embeddedness of all ontology (as thematized by both classical figures like James and Dewey and modern pragmatists like Hilary Putnam) as well as, for example, Peircean realism concerning "real generals" (see chapter 3).

I believe it is indeed fair to say that pragmatist thinkers, early and late, have successfully formulated sophisticated approaches to general epistemology and philosophy of science, integrating the most plausible insights from both *realism*—affirming the mind- and theory-independence of reality as an object of inquiry—and *constructivism*—emphasizing the constitutive significance of human practices of inquiry for the emergence of the objects of scientific and humanistic investigations.[40] This book will ask to what extent a *pragmatic realism* offering a middle path between strong realism and radical constructivism is available in the philosophy of the humanities (again, see chapter 3 for more elaborated questions along these lines, as well as some attempts to answer them). This basic issue entangling pragmatism and realism will be tackled in a number of specific dimensions, potentially also leading to a careful critical reevaluation of the ways we think about concepts such as rationality, progress, and impact in the context of humanistic inquiries.[41]

Precisely in its project of integrating realism with constructivism, pragmatism is an inherently *pluralistic* philosophy, both in general philosophy of science and inquiry and more broadly in other areas of philosophy, including metaphysics, ethics, social and political philosophy, and philosophy of religion (see, e.g., Pihlström 2013, 2020, 2021). Pragmatism is therefore well equipped to take up the task of philosophically systematizing the structure of humanistic scholarship in a thoroughly *nonreductive* and *antifoundationalist* framework that recognizes the radical historicity of human culture, including our inquiries into human culture and its history. It is, I will argue, only within an overall pragmatist context that we can plausibly hope to avoid the opposite challenges of *reductive naturalism*, which ultimately yields a form of *scientism*, culminating in the view that cultural phenomena are in the end "nothing over and above" natural or even physical phenomena, based on biological or eventually just physical contingencies and laws of nature,[42] and *radical relativism*, which can take the form of *historicism* claiming that the humanities can reach no objectivity, or no realistic truth about their objects of study, because they are always open to multiple historically contextualized interpretive points of view.[43] A pragmatist philosophy of the humanities should be able to secure *a critical middle path* between these—and many other—implausible extremes. In this respect, my pragmatism, or pragmatic realism, shares, for example, Livingston's (1988) project of defending (moderate) realism about literary theory—analogous to nonreductive scientific realism—but unfortunately Livingston is (again) one of those scholars who make no reference whatsoever to pragmatism.

This book will, in any event, seek to render plausible the view that pragmatism is actually a vital sine qua non of a successful account of realism in the philosophy of the humanities; a plausible form of realism avoiding the pitfalls of both reductionism and radical relativism (among others) can in the end be developed only on pragmatist grounds. Properly arguing for this strong claim would only be possible as a result of a much more comprehensive investigation, though. As noted earlier, here I can only provide a prolegomenon to a properly pragmatist philosophy of the humanities in general, and this also applies to the contribution this book will be able to make to the realism discussion.

Due to its relatively general philosophical approach, this volume will, as already remarked, focus on pragmatist ontology and epistemology of the humanities—with the realism issue largely defining that focus—instead of any detailed questions of specific methodologies. Thus, for example, the methodological opposition between explanation and understanding in the humanities is, despite its enormous philosophical significance, of secondary importance for the purposes of my discussion and will be referred to here only to the extent that it is relevant to a deeper understanding of the problem of realism in the humanities. I will, moreover, suggest throughout the book—in striking contrast to many neopragmatists' (e.g., Rorty's) antimetaphysical characterizations of pragmatism—that pragmatism ought to be developed in the philosophy of the humanities in an *ontologically serious* manner (cf. Pihlström 1996, 2009, 2020). Ontology will be relevant not despite pragmatism but because of it—and this insight will also be crucial for developing an understanding of pragmatism itself that avoids the naïve conception of pragmatism as a merely instrumental philosophy of "useful consequences" (as it is occasionally understood in popularized contexts).

One of the main reasons that we need a unified philosophy of the humanities is precisely that the ontological status of the objects of inquiry in the humanities remains unclear. A key pragmatist suggestion I hope to develop emphasizes the role played by the *valuational* activities of humanistic inquirers in the constitution of the objects of study in these fields.[44] Pragmatist metaphysics generally takes very seriously the value-laden perspectives from which ontologies are constituted within human practices of engaging with the world. We human beings—in particular, in our role as inquirers, both in the humanities and more generally—"select" the objects we focus our attention on, as James already insisted in his "teleological" theory of the human mind in the early days of the pragmatist movement and as many other pragmatists have continued to insist in their analyses of inquiry as a practice-embedded process. No object of study comes "ready-made" to us; the inquirer needs to be active in constituting the very object of inquiry in order for that inquiry to be so much as possible. This is particularly clear in the philosophy of historiography, where it can be argued that historians "select" past events that are worthy of examining on the basis of their scholarly (and perhaps other) interests and values.[45] But the same holds for any inquiry, even to the extent that all fields of inquiry are "human sciences" in the sense of being based on human values (cf., e.g., Putnam 1981, 2002; Margolis 1995, 2012).

However, it is a fundamental insight of pragmatic *realism* that this value-embeddedness of our inquiries does not entail that, say, historiography would just be more or less like writing imaginative literary narratives (cf. Hayden White 1973, 1978; Ankersmit 2001, 2009).[46] Even as pragmatists, we cannot deny the dimension of realistic objectivity (cf. also Pihlström 2017a) to our inquiries that are themselves value-laden and interest-driven processes but nevertheless aim at (humanly speaking) objective knowledge about elements of the real world that we may (within our value-guided practices themselves) regard as existing mind-independently. Pragmatism, in short, is the only philosophy of inquiry that is able to maintain sufficiently robust realism and objectivity while acknowledging the irreducibly valuational nature of inquiry and its objects.[47] This is particularly important in any serious attempt to develop a philosophy of the humanities. Moreover, pragmatists have from early on insisted on the need to investigate values themselves rationally, critically, and objectively; values are not to be reduced to mere subjective preferences but can and should themselves be subordinated to pragmatically conducted rational inquiry, which, in turn, is itself always guided by values (see, e.g., Putnam 2002, 2016). Values can be among the objects to be investigated in the humanities themselves while driving those very investigations, and this reflexive process also needs to be appreciated in a pragmatist philosophy of the humanities.

Pragmatism, as already noted, offers us a plausible *general* philosophy of inquiry—not only of scientific inquiry but inquiry as an element of human life and societies more broadly—with smooth transitions between the philosophy of science, ethics, metaphysics, the philosophy of religion, and other fields. Pragmatism is *not* like phenomenology or hermeneutics, insofar as the latter can be seen as restricted to analyzing human experience and humanistic understanding. Pragmatism, rather, synthesizes, unites, and integrates realism with relativism and constructivism, explanation with understanding, and natural causes with normative reasons and values—thus overcoming dichotomies that have historically been taken to be fundamental to the distinction between the sciences and the humanities (as will be explained in more detail below). Furthermore, pragmatism is able to appreciate both the relative *autonomy* of philosophy itself (i.e., its irreducibility to any special humanistic—or other—empirical disciplines) and the *continuity* between philosophy and the special scholarly disciplines, both natural and human sciences.

It is, furthermore, more natural for pragmatism than for many other philosophical orientations to defend and further articulate a genuinely *emergentist*, and hence antireductionist, ontology of cultural phenomena,[48] which are typical objects of study in the humanities. Cultural entities such as artworks, religious practices, and social institutions (together with their complex histories) are, from a pragmatist perspective, fully and irreducibly real; moreover, they exist relatively autonomously in comparison to the material world yet without therefore being any Platonic abstract entities that could exist without their material emergence base. One does not have to be a pragmatist in order to embrace an antireductionist and emergentist metaphysics of culture of this kind, but it is certainly easier to make sense of such a metaphysics within pragmatism. This is because the pragmatist, as explained above, typically understands ontology in relation to human practices structured by their interests and goals, guiding the relevance criteria according to which anything whatsoever can be regarded as real. Something's being real depends on its being considered real for definite pragmatic purposes within normatively guided practices (of inquiry). The relation between natural (material) reality and humanly created cultural reality can, then, be plausibly examined within the pragmatist framework recognizing the plurality of human interests, values, and practices—much more naturally than within monistic philosophies privileging some particular viewpoint (e.g., narrowly conceived analytic philosophy, phenomenology, or hermeneutics).[49]

Pragmatism, moreover, is able to account for what is truly distinctive in the "human perspective" that scholarship in the humanities brings to its subject matter. This is inherently related to the value-laden and value-driven character of our practices of inquiry. We also need to appreciate *both* the individual pursuit of truth *and* the intersubjective social and/or cultural normative contexts of truth-seeking inquiries (cf. Pihlström 2021). Therefore, specific fields such as pragmatist philosophy of religion are also highly relevant to the pragmatist philosophy of the humanities (and of science), as they may draw attention to the irreducible value of *the individual scholarly perspective* (traditionally epitomized in the often-ridiculed idea of a scholar's "study chamber") and its existential and worldview-related ("*weltanschaulichen*") dimensions. I will thus argue that a pragmatist account of the humanities also involves, in the end, a form of *humanism* affirming the irreducible value of the human being at the center of *any* (not only humanistic) scholarship—a human being always concerned not merely with advancing inquiry but also with living a life.[50]

Pragmatism, then, provides us with what I take to be a uniquely plausible account of why and how we need to be (ethically, normatively) committed to the pursuit of truth also in the humanities,[51] in which pursuing the truth may be much more controversial—deeply controversial—than, for example, the truth-seeking methods of the natural sciences are. This controversiality is not a sign of the "immaturity" of the humanities as "sciences" but follows from their character as the kind of value-laden practices they are. Pragmatism can make sense of this value-ladenness in the pursuit of truth because it starts from a general understanding of any human pursuit of truth as a value-driven practice. Moreover, what we need here is, as I will argue, a holistic form of pragmatism, viewing values and facts—as well as our normative and factual beliefs and statements—as encompassing a comprehensive totality with no essential or principled dualisms or metaphysical (or epistemic) gaps (cf. White 2002).

This kind of holism also requires that we appreciate both the argumentative rigor of logico-analytic philosophy and the historical detail of careful scholarship in the history of philosophy. However, the ultimate philosophical purpose of inquiry may be somewhat different, irreducible to either logic or history; both technical and scholarly manifestations of philosophical skills may in the end be subordinate to the fundamental project of ever deeper understanding. This *existential* character of the pursuit of philosophy may distinguish this particular discipline from the other humanities, and this is also something that the pragmatist philosopher of the humanities appreciating the plurality of the values guiding different disciplinary practices should be able to take seriously. A pragmatist philosophy of the humanities will also duly recognize that all disciplines are historically changing, value-laden, and critically developing responses to human needs and interests in understanding reality; accordingly, our philosophy of the humanities must accommodate both disciplinary and interdisciplinary practices of inquiry as our value-driven ways of being-in-the-world-as-inquirers.

In so doing, it may also appreciate the sense in which philosophical inquiries (like, presumably, historical ones) both aim at truth and are comparable to literary writing. As aptly put by Arthur Danto (1984, 19): "Philosophy is literature in that among its truth conditions are those connected with being read and reading those texts is supposed to reveal us for what we are in virtue of our reading. Really to reveal us, however, not metaphorically, which is why, I think, I cannot finally acquiesce in the thought that philosophy is literature. It continues to aim at truth, but when false, seriously false, it is also so fascinatingly false as to retain a kind of perspectival vitality as a metaphor." I hope something like this could be true about my pragmatist philosophy of the humanities, too, even if what I am saying were entirely false. Philosophy is always written by real-life human beings with their needs, interests, and worries, living and acting in real-life political, cultural, institutional, environmental (etc.) contexts; a philosophical theory inevitably reflects those wider concerns that its author may have simply because philosophizing is a human activity.

In brief, the unique profile of this book lies, I suppose, in its attempt to outline a pragmatist philosophy of the humanities in general (that is, not just, say, a philosophy of historiography or a philosophy of literary theory) from the perspective of a pragmatist account of realism ("pragmatic realism") based on a transcendental rearticulation of pragmatism itself (to be carefully specified), taking seriously the ontological function and status of values as what enables objects of inquiry to be, and to become, real for us—in such a way that what is regarded as "real" here is (as will be explained in chapter 3) understood in a sense broad enough to include (in Peircean terms) "real generals," for example, specifically in humanistic ontologies, interpretive possibilities (across the spectrum of the different humanistic disciplines). My basic view is, then, that the humanities—no less than the sciences—are human epistemic practices pursuing truth and objectivity that need, indeed, to be understood as practice-embedded concepts. The practice- and value-ladenness of these pursuits does not render them any less serious in terms of realism; on the contrary, pragmatism offers a human form of realism that can save the humanities from being thoroughly mistakenly understood as merely ideological, fictional, or incommensurably culturally relative.

A Methodological Remark

This brings us to a point where a few words need to be added on the methodology of a scholarly undertaking such as this one. As has already become clear and will hopefully become clearer in what follows, one of the purposes of this discussion is to reflect on, and critically renew, the (antifoundationalist) philosophical foundations of the humanities in general.[52] While I will primarily focus on humanistic ontology and epistemology, my investigation definitely has methodological aspects, too, as it seeks to account for the practice-embeddedness of the distinctive ways in which humanistic inquiries deal with their objects of study. On the other hand, my discussion itself mostly employs relatively traditional methods of philosophical scholarship and humanistic inquiry, that is, conceptual and argumentation analysis, as well as what may be simply described as a critical close reading of philosophical and other relevant texts, including both classical pragmatist sources (and their historical predecessors in the Kantian tradition, in particular) and works by contemporary pragmatists and other philosophers and/or other scholars who have examined the nature of humanistic inquiry or whose work may be relevant to this task. To a certain extent, this could also involve close critical reading and appropriation of scholarly work in fields such as literary criticism, historiography, and theology and religious studies, though I will keep such extraphilosophical references to a minimum here.

The methodology I am employing is thus relatively strongly internal to what is generally regarded as philosophical methodology, without being restricted to any specific account of "the philosophical method," such as the method of logical and/or conceptual analysis, the hermeneutic method, the Wittgensteinian "grammatical method," or the phenomenological method. To the extent that something like the "pragmatic method" will be employed, this will take place in a manner explicitly relying on the classical pragmatists' writings (e.g., Peirce's and James's views on the pragmatic maxim).

So what exactly is *my* method in this book? In contrast to particular philosophical methods such as the phenomenological, hermeneutic, or pragmatist ones, it is, I suppose, the (above-mentioned) very simple humanistic method of reading piles of books and thinking about them. On the other hand, I also employ—and urge pragmatist philosophers of the humanities to employ—the both historically and systematically important method of *transcendental argumentation* seeking to identify and analyze the conditions for the possibility of things we take as "given" in our experience and practices. This method is so central for my examination that I will devote the entire chapter 4 to an investigation of the place of transcendental arguments in the philosophy of the humanities, especially in relation to the debates over naturalism and naturalization (concerning the problem of realism, in particular, but also more generally).[53] I will not, however, advance any specific metaphilosophical theory of philosophical methodology but will just employ the methods I find relevant. Moreover, I am not claiming that all philosophers of the humanities (let alone all scholars in the humanities) should use pragmatist and transcendental arguments. The fact that my pragmatist articulation of realism in the humanities can be taken to philosophically "work" (or so I claim) constitutes a metalevel argument for the significance of pragmatic methodology in philosophy generally—even though this line of thought will not be further pursued here.[54]

The Structure of the Book

I have chosen to organize the discussion in the following way. After having in this first, introductory chapter explained in broad strokes why I think it is important to investigate the philosophy of the humanities, why I think it is a good idea to do so from a pragmatist point of view, and what pragmatism in very general terms means in this context, I will in the second chapter move on to a historical account of pragmatism in general philosophy of inquiry. One of the main points of that discussion is that pragmatist explorations of the constitutive dependence of the objects of inquiry on the practices of inquiry can be (mutatis mutandis) carried over from general philosophy of science and theory of inquiry to the philosophy of the humanities. However, it is crucially important to understand this dependence and, in particular, its implications concerning the issue of realism in a correct way. Therefore, I strongly emphasize the Kantian nature of pragmatism (in the specific sense in which I am defending pragmatism here): the objects of inquiry are dependent on the practices of inquiry instead of existing "ready-made" prior to inquiry, not in the straightforward causal or factual sense that our human practices would directly produce them but in the transcendental sense that it is only in the context of a practice of inquiry that certain (kinds of) objects become *possible* as objects of knowledge for us (which also entails that the relevant inquiries themselves become possible as the kind of inquiries they are). This is as much the case in the humanities as it is the case generally in human inquiries into the ways the world is.[55]

The third chapter will take up some more specific themes, research questions, and hypotheses regarding pragmatist philosophy of the humanities, especially as they emerge in the contexts of my three case study areas, namely, pragmatist philosophies of literary theory and criticism, historiography, and theology and religious studies. In addition to recognizing the differences between these research fields and their pragmatist philosophies, I will emphasize their similarities, particularly regarding the transcendental yet practice-laden constitution of their objects of inquiry, also exploring more comprehensively some key pragmatist themes and ideas, including Peircean "real generals" in humanistic ontology.

Clearly, the relation between pragmatic naturalism—as a general pragmatist conception of the world—and the strategy of transcendental reflection and/or transcendental argumentation that (I am claiming) pragmatism inherits from the Kantian tradition needs a more substantial discussion, to which the fourth chapter will be devoted. This is necessary in this context, because the above-mentioned idea of transcendental constitution needs to be understood correctly in order for pragmatist philosophy of the humanities to be able to contain a plausible pragmatist response to the vexing question of realism with regard to the humanities. The fourth chapter thus first considers "naturalized" conceptions of inquiry that leave no room for specifically "philosophical knowledge" about the basic character of (humanistic) inquiry and/or its objects (including the question of realism), and then engages in a critique of such naturalism by investigating the legacy of transcendental argumentation in philosophy generally and the philosophy of the humanities in particular.

In addition to transcendental methodology, it might be suggested that we also need to explore the ways in which the humanities may aspire to examine transcendence.[56] There are *limits* to what the humanities can do. There are manifestations of *inhumanity* that must be investigated by the humanities with full acknowledgment that such an investigation can never entirely succeed. As examples of this (pragmatic and transcendental) engagement with the transcendent, one might mention literary scholars' attempts to understand literary works deliberately breaching the limits of language and meaning, theologians' (and perhaps philosophers' of religion) dealings with personal religious experiences that defy conceptual articulation, as well as historians' studies of extreme historical atrocities such as the Holocaust, whose shocking reality can presumably never be captured by any ordinary use of scientific, scholarly, everyday, or even artistic language. These cases cannot be examined in any great detail in this book, but the phenomenon of humanistic scholarship taking us to the limit of the humanities—while never literally transgressing that limit onto the side of the transcendent (as that could only be done by religion, which lies out of the scholarly endeavor as such)—must be duly recognized by any adequate philosophy of the humanities. Therefore, the fifth, concluding chapter will very briefly pay attention to the ethical limits of the humanities, particularly to how those limits are reached when it comes to humanistically representing something nonrepresentable, such as the Holocaust. Some final reflections will then close the volume with a brief concluding discussion and summarizing thoughts, emphasizing both academic freedom and our motivation for engaging in humanistic scholarship.

Chapter 2

Realism, Practices, and Inquiry
What Is Pragmatist Philosophy of the Humanities?

The historical canon of the pragmatist tradition runs from the late nineteenth- and early twentieth-century founding figures Peirce, James, Dewey, and George Herbert Mead, via mediating thinkers such as Jane Addams, C. I. Lewis, and Sidney Hook, to later pragmatists including, among others, Hilary Putnam, Richard Rorty, Morton White, Joseph Margolis, Richard Bernstein, Hans Joas, and Susan Haack—and all the way to contemporary pragmatism scholarship in its multidisciplinary and increasingly international variety.[1] I will explicate my commitment to pragmatism in this context by first briefly commenting on three major aspects of the pragmatist philosophy of the humanities I am seeking to develop: Kantian (transcendental) pragmatism, the pragmatic maxim and the related pragmatist theory of inquiry, as well as the relation between pragmatism and realism. I will then outline the history of pragmatist philosophy of science, suggesting that most of the insights of that historical development are readily applicable to the philosophy of the humanities, while recognizing that the open issues and tensions characterizing the tradition of pragmatism generally also apply to the pragmatist philosophy of the humanities. The bulk of this chapter will thus investigate the philosophy of scientific inquiry in a broader sense, with no specific reference to the humanities, while the next chapter will more explicitly turn to the humanities again, applying to humanistic inquiry the general insights of pragmatism and pragmatic realism achieved in this chapter.

It should be noted that I am not proposing my pragmatist philosophy of the humanities as a position or a program based on any close reading of any particular historical pragmatist. What I am doing in this book is grounded in my own synthesis of a number of ideas—most of them present in one way or another in the writings of either the classical or more recent pragmatists, or both—that I find relevant to a development of a philosophy of the humanities within the pragmatist tradition. More detailed scholarly studies on pragmatist philosophers' views on the humanities are, of course, strongly encouraged, and I hope other scholars of pragmatism will take up such challenges in the future.

Kantian Pragmatism

When proposing a pragmatist philosophy of the humanities, or of anything else, one cannot just take the pragmatist tradition as a totality and directly apply it to a given problem. Particularly in the interest of articulating the idea of the value-ladenness of the ontology of humanistic inquiry (as sketched in chapter 1), I will now continue to develop and defend a specific version of pragmatism, that is, a Kantian transcendental version, locating the roots of pragmatism—both historically and in a more systematic-argumentative sense—in Kantian critical (transcendental) philosophy. I have in a series of previous publications, spanning more than two decades,[2] defended such a transcendental form of pragmatism, according to which our purpose-driven human practices provide contextually necessary (in a Kantian vocabulary, transcendental) conditions for the possibility of the kinds of entities postulated within them.[3] Roughly, our social participation in shared practices—or in what Ludwig Wittgenstein called the human "form of life"—occupies the role of the traditional Kantian transcendental self in the ongoing process of world-constitution through conceptualization and inquiry. The objects of inquiry, including humanistic inquiry, are only *possible* within value-laden practices of inquiry, analogously to the way in which the objects of human cognition are, according to Kant, necessarily constituted by the transcendental features of the human cognitive faculty (i.e., space and time as forms of pure intuition, and the categories, or the pure concepts of the understanding). Just as there are no *possible* objects of cognition beyond such pervasive features of human experience according to Kant, no ontological postulation *can*, according to pragmatism, reach beyond our purposive practices.

In these terms, the main novelty of my pragmatist philosophy of the humanities in comparison to various other actual or potential philosophies of the humanities (e.g., those available in the traditions of hermeneutics and analytic philosophy) can perhaps be expressed as follows. The ontological postulations of the humanities—for example, historical facts and processes studied by the historiographer—are *ontologically dependent* on our value systems and commitments, that is, on values guiding our practices of inquiry, ethical and intellectual alike. Accordingly, our purposive practices of historiographical (and more generally humanistic) scholarship, driven by their ethical and epistemic interests and needs, guide the selection of whatever we may take to be historically factual and what, for us, *is* thereby factual. However, this value-dependence, though ontological, is *not* a dependence at the "first-order level," so to speak. It is, rather—and here my specific entanglement of Kantian and pragmatist standpoints comes to the picture—transcendental in the sense that only in the context of purpose-driven, practice-embedded selection is it possible for us to have (let alone know anything about) any historical facts or events whatsoever—and similarly, mutatis mutandis, for other kinds of topics and "objects" in humanistic inquiry. The transcendental ontological dependence is not at all a relation of causal or factual production or construction. This formulation reemphasizes the idea that it is only within a transcendental pragmatism (treating values and value commitments as the transcendental scheme enabling inquiry and objects of inquiry) that any empirical realism about such objects (e.g., historical facts and events) is so much as possible. In brief, historical facts depend on our values and practices not so much as to their first-order ontological status but with regard to their being possible as facts at all (and, again, similarly for facts and objects of other fields of inquiry in the humanities).[4] The analogy to Kant is clear: for him, empirical realism requires transcendental idealism.

This is not at all to suggest that a quasi-Kantian transcendental articulation of pragmatism could be uncritically assumed. On the contrary, within a pragmatist philosophy of the humanities it will be vitally important to critically examine how far this form of pragmatism is able to function as a comprehensive philosophy of the humanities (see also several essays in Skowronski and Pihlström 2019, some of them also highly critical of any Kantian accounts of pragmatism). The choice to integrate Kantian critical philosophy with pragmatism should itself be regarded as a relatively controversial philosophical hypothesis to be pragmatically tested by its success in formulating a plausible overall philosophy of the humanities. *If* a comprehensive philosophical account of the humanities can be based on transcendental pragmatism, this will yield an important metalevel (pragmatic) argument for the viability of such pragmatism. This chapter or this book will not, of course, finally resolve the matter either way, but I hope my proposal can be taken, precisely, as a hypothesis worthy of critical discussion.

I must also note that few pragmatists have explicitly investigated the philosophy of the humanities in the sense in which I will focus on this field. Two late twentieth- and early twenty-first-century pragmatists do stand out as key figures in any pragmatist philosophy of the humanities worth developing, though. These two major pragmatist thinkers are, as noted in chapter 1, Morton White and Joseph Margolis—though neither can be regarded as a Kantian pragmatist in my sense. While White (e.g., 2002, 2005) developed, as early as the 1950s or even the late 1940s, a novel understanding of pragmatism that he labeled "holistic pragmatism" (to be discussed below), he was also a historian of ideas himself, writing on the epistemology of historiography from the internal perspective of someone engaging in historical research. His understanding of the relationship between the factual and normative in historiography will be revisited in due course below.

Margolis, in turn, argued in a series of works for a thoroughly historicized understanding not only of historical interpretation itself but also of cultural practices generally. His reflections on the historicity of human existence and culture, including history as a practice of inquiry (e.g., 1993, 1995)—that is, his complex, pragmatism-inspired theory of the "flux" of history and the human world in general—are, for me, an important (though here largely only implicit) background for the development of a broader pragmatist philosophy of the humanities. This is especially because Margolis, despite his historicism and his rejection of Kantian transcendental philosophy along with any fixed "invariances,"[5] never downgrades the significance of "second-order" questions of normative legitimation even in a radical historicist context. Indeed, Margolis powerfully argues that history, in penetrating "our conception of the entire intelligible world and the structure of inquiry set to understand that world"—scientific as much as humanistic—not only penetrates the "facts" but also "*the legitimation of facts*" (Margolis 1993, 90; original emphasis).[6] Margolis's project of coming to terms with our inescapably historicized existence in a "postmetaphysical" era (in a way that may be moderately relativistic but need not end up with irresponsible relativism) is shared by many other scholars, not all of whom explicitly view the matter from a pragmatist standpoint (cf., e.g., Roberts 1995). At the same time, Margolis claims that classical pragmatism lacked a sustained theory of history (see, e.g., Margolis 2019, 306–307), as such a theory can only emerge on the basis of a nonreductively naturalist account of how human beings acquire language, discursive practices, and thereby selves (ibid., 309, 312–313).[7] Historicity, at any rate, is an ineliminable existential condition for human beings understood as culturally emerging selves.

Within my proposed construal of pragmatism as a (nonreductively, moderately) naturalized and historicized form of Kantian transcendental philosophy replacing the transcendental subject by our naturally evolving social practice of inquiry, it is entirely possible to endorse (with qualifications, of course) various insightful findings of, say, phenomenological and hermeneutic approaches to human historicity, insofar as these are subordinated to the overall pragmatist framework. For example, the pragmatist can very well appreciate Ricoeurian hermeneutics of memory (cf. Ricoeur 2004) as well as Soren Gosvig Olesen's (2013) more recent defense of a phenomenologically grounded understanding of the historicity of human beings as a transcendental condition of all knowledge.[8] Pragmatist philosophy of the humanities may also naturally enter into interesting dialogues with other approaches, say, Foucault-inspired conceptions of the radical historicity and (hence) contingency of the discourses, categories, and practices in terms of which we organize our experience and social institutions. For example, Ian Hacking's (2002) "historical ontology"—as well as, of course, Foucault's own (e.g., 1970 [1966]) seminal contributions analyzing the historicity of discursive practices and institutions—may and should be critically digested and appropriated by the pragmatist philosopher of historiography.

No matter how exactly the (transcendental) pragmatist develops the ontology of human history and culture in more detail,[9] the key idea in the kind of pragmatism defining the present undertaking is that the historical and/or interpretive existence (or reality)[10] of cultural entities and structures, including meanings and meaningful human actions, is only *possible* within the historicized and always already interpretively structured contexts established by our practices of inquiry. For example, past objects and events are not "there" in a "ready-made" form independently of us and *our* historically developing practices, but they are possible for us as objects of historical and interpretive study only in such contexts. A crucial pragmatist insight is that those contexts themselves, qua historical, also *point toward the future*, manifesting our purposive habits of action and their inevitably future-oriented interests, values, and goals. For the pragmatist, then, even historical truth is not merely "backward-looking" but "forward-looking" in the sense that we have to evaluate *all* our commitments to historical interpretation from the point of view of their potentially serving human interests and values (very broadly conceived) whose ultimate aim is always in our future actions and the amelioration of our practices. The objectivity of historical and cultural phenomena is therefore, for the pragmatist, not reducible to the paradigm of objectivity drawn from the natural sciences and the objects they deal with (e.g., natural laws and mind-independent theoretical entities); as a thoroughly pluralistic philosophical approach, pragmatism is well suited to investigating the distinctive kind of reality and objectivity that the objects of humanistic scholarship, including historical events, may enjoy.[11]

Examining history as "transcendental," we may also ask whether history—our historicized human condition—"makes us" or whether we "make" (or perhaps even "make up") history. Are we, as the kind of historical beings we are, ourselves possible only within a transcendental context of history, or is the pragmatist equivalent of the transcendental (human) subject not only an actor *in* history but the metaphysical "maker" *of* history? These questions demonstrate the significance of Kantian transcendental pragmatism for the philosophy of the humanities (in this case, the philosophy of historiography in particular). We pragmatically need to be able to develop a position that answers, "Both."[12] History, we may suggest, is indeed transcendental in the sense that historicity (or historicality) is a necessary condition for the possibility of any human relationship to the world—be it epistemic, ethical, political, educational, or whatever. For us humans, there can be no way of being outside history (cf., again, Olesen 2013—but also, e.g., Foucault's and Hacking's works cited above). Yet *we* are the agents of that history, not only in the straightforward "humanistic" sense that history is the history of human beings but also in the more robustly transcendental sense that there can be no historical truths or facts independently of our interest- and value-relative pragmatic choices directing the focus of our historical inquiries into such truths and facts.[13]

However, the kind of pragmatic pluralism and holism outlined here do not entail, say, Paul A. Roth's (2020) radical "irrealism" or constructivism about history, according to which historical facts are "made" by the historians' imaginative theorization and constructive activities, just as Putnam's (1981) pragmatic realism (or what he used to call "internal realism" in the 1980s) does not entail Nelson Goodman's (1978) irrealist, radically pluralistic theory of "worldmaking," according to which we make a plurality of (actual) worlds, or "world-versions," by using our symbol systems (see also Pihlström 1996).[14] Again, the golden middle ground between excessively strong metaphysical realism with a ready-made world of historical facts, on the one hand, and an antirealist constructivism denying even mild forms of objective independence of history, on the other hand, must be maintained, and a crucial task for Kantian pragmatism is to show ways of doing this.[15] Historiography, just like any serious inquiry into the ways the world is, is a critical interplay of our contribution and whatever there is independently of us.

The Pragmatic Maxim and the Theory of Inquiry

No matter how exactly the relation between pragmatism and Kantian critical or transcendental philosophy should be understood, the conception of pragmatism that shapes this book is fully committed to, and will seek to apply, the classical *pragmatist theory of inquiry* (cf. Capps 2015) as well as the *pragmatic maxim* originally proposed by the founders of the tradition. Regarding these constitutive pragmatist principles, we may apply to humanistic inquiry the seminal ideas we find in Peirce's early essays on the scientific method, "The Fixation of Belief" (1877) and "How to Make Our Ideas Clear" (1878), as well as James's and Dewey's elaborations of them in their central works, such as James's *Pragmatism* (1907) and *The Meaning of Truth* (1909) as well as Dewey's *The Quest for Certainty* (1929) and *Logic: The Theory of Inquiry* (1938).[16]

The pragmatist conception of inquiry, often labelled the "doubt-belief" model of inquiry, takes its departure from the fact that we cannot begin our inquiries—in any area of life—from any Cartesian-like universal doubt. We always have to start from within the beliefs about reality we already have—in media res, so to speak. In pragmatism, beliefs are literally understood as *habits of action*: to believe something to be the case is not merely to have a cognitive representation of something mind-independent that is taken to be the case outside one's cognitive mechanism but to be prepared to act in certain purposive ways in the world those beliefs are about. Believing anything, however ordinary and primitive, is always already to be committed to definite ways of acting. This is a fundamental pragmatist starting point for the present investigation as well: like any other beliefs and theories, the beliefs and theories we formulate within the humanities are also *constitutively* habits of action emerging in and through our humanistic practices of inquiry. As already suggested above, this even concerns our beliefs about the human past; even those beliefs are ultimately habits of acting in certain ways with an eye to our future, not merely to the past that those beliefs are directly "about."

A key point according to the pragmatist model of inquiry is reached when we in our habitual action (in which our beliefs are manifested) encounter something unexpected, a surprising fact or result. Then, and only then, is inquiry properly speaking launched. Stimulated by a surprise, we start doubting the original beliefs and thus inquiring into the matter, and thereby we may revise or give up our initial belief(s), that is, the habit(s) of action it was manifested in. And then the process will continue—arguably roughly analogously to the way the hermeneutic circle moves back and forth between an overall interpretation and textual evidence based on the details of the interpreted text. It is not difficult to see how naturally this model of the inquiry process can be applied to humanistic scholarship. We may analyze our beliefs and theories about literary works, historical events, or religious meanings and institutions as (broadly speaking) habits of action in terms of which, and by means of which, we are able to organize and orientate in the cultural world of literature, history, and religion or theology. From a pragmatist perspective, the value of humanistic scholarship lies to a significant extent in its ability to provide us with such orientation structuring our lives.

A related idea, the pragmatic maxim, is based on Peirce's (1992–98 [1878], vol. 1, 132) original principle: "Consider what effects, which might conceivably have practical bearings, we conceive the object of our conception to have. Then the whole of our conception of those effects is the whole of our conception of the object." Applied to the present topic, what this means is the following. Our conception of any object of humanistic study—be it a literary text, a historical event or a chain of events, a meaningful human action, or a religious set of beliefs and rituals, for instance—is *completely* expressed in terms of our conception of the potential (conceivable) practical effects that we consider that object might have in or for our habits of action. This, however, does *not* mean that those practical effects would necessarily have to be actualized in our current or future experience; it is essential that we draw attention to the *potential*, that is, conceivable, effects that the objects of our conception (or our study and interpretation) may have in order to determine the meaning of that conception.[17]

Just as Peirce himself applied the pragmatic maxim to clarify, for example, the concept of *reality*, ending up with his famous definition of truth as the "final opinion" of scientific inquiry at the ideal limit, an opinion to which the view of an idealized community of rational inquirers would converge if they were able to employ the scientific method for an indefinitely long time, we may systematically apply pragmatism and the pragmatic maxim to determine what exactly we should mean by "reality" in humanistic scholarship. A profound entanglement of pragmatism and realism emerges as the outcome of such an application of the pragmatic maxim, and it is this entanglement that I believe needs to be interpreted in terms of transcendental pragmatism. In this sense, the aspects of my preferred form of pragmatism—its Kantian character, the emphasis on the pragmatic maxim, and the need to entangle pragmatism and realism with each other—are all interrelated.

Pragmatism and Realism

As explained above, the problem of realism, particularly in its ontological dimension, is a key issue of this entire investigation. However, realism is such a multifaceted topic that it cannot be examined *exclusively* from the ontological point of view. A pragmatist philosophy of the humanities must explore the question of realism with regard to the humanities in a comprehensive manner, taking into consideration a number of different aspects of this fundamental philosophical problem.

One may begin this task by asking the questions that Ilkka Niiniluoto (1999, chapter 1) finds central for his articulation of *scientific realism* and by bringing them to address the special case of the humanities (see also Livingston 1988). *Ontologically*, the realism issue in the humanities concerns the mind-independent existence of the objects of humanistic inquiry (whatever those objects in the end are). The realist about the humanities affirms that at least some of these objects—particularly theoretical entities postulated for theoretical and interpretive reasons within humanistic research—exist and have the properties they do independently of our conceptualizations, inquiries, and theories, more or less analogously to the way in which the scientific realist (with regard to the natural sciences) claims that theoretical entities such as electrons, molecules, or genes exist mind- and theory-independently.[18] *Epistemologically*, the question concerns the knowability (cognizability) of such objects of humanistic research; here the realist claims that we may, at least to some extent, get to know the objects of humanistic inquiry and their properties—though of course it further needs to be asked what exactly it means to "know" such things.

Semantically, the realism issue focuses on the reference of our theoretical terms and the applicability of the concept of truth to theoretical statements; according to the realist, the theoretical vocabularies employed by humanistic scholars at least purportedly refer to objects existing in an ontologically realist sense, and the notion of truth can, at least in principle, be applied to theories in the humanities. That is, according to the realist, our use of theoretical terms in the humanities either refers or fails to refer to really existing things depending on whether such things exist or fail to exist (independently of our individual minds, though not independently of human minds in general), and our statements about those (or any) objects are true or false depending on whether they correspond to the way things are.

Methodologically, we may ask whether it is possible to develop research methods that (tend to) lead us to the truth or that yield an inquiry progressing toward the truth (in a quasi-Peircean sense) in the humanities;[19] again, the realist affirms this. Finally, there is the *axiological* question about the values, aims, and goals of research: Does humanistic inquiry aim at truth at all, as the realist claims, or does it pursue something else, such as practical problem-solving, individual or cultural welfare and self-understanding, or merely social or political empowerment?

A full-scale realism about the humanities would, when faced by these questions, state roughly the following. There is a real cultural world "out there" independently of individual humanistic scholars' (and research groups') use of concepts, language, and theories. It is, admittedly, a world created by human beings and their activities, containing objects such as meanings, norms, actions, and institutions, but its existence and properties are largely independent of any particular inquirers' or groups' of inquirers views, beliefs, opinions, and theories. By means of theoretical research and its rational methods of inference, explanation, and interpretation, we may at least to some extent get to know this humanly created cultural world more deeply. We may refer to its objects, events, and properties by using theoretical language, and our statements about it are typically true or false depending on the way the world—conceived as consisting of those objects, events, and properties—is. Humanistic inquiry pursues truth about this cultural reality and seeks to develop methods that may bring scholars closer to the truth.

Pragmatist answers to the list of questions concerning realism are not immediately obvious, and pragmatists may take various stands between realism and antirealism. Arguably, no sane pragmatist will deny realism altogether—either in the sciences or in the humanities. As indicated in chapter 1, a reasonable form of *pragmatic realism* needs to be distinguished *both* from strong realism committed to a "ready-made" world existing with its own precategorized ontological structure *and* from radical antirealisms, such as thoroughgoing relativism and/or constructivism that deny the theory-independent reality of any objects of study (in their most radical form even in the natural sciences). On the other hand, whether these questions characterizing the discourse on scientific realism are as appropriate in the humanistic context as they are in general philosophy of science also needs to be investigated; we will perceive that a pragmatist perspective can yield a balanced assessment of the relevance of these issues and thus of the relevance of whatever exactly is the analogy of scientific realism that can be developed to account for the humanities. As pointed out in the introductory chapter, pragmatists have been able to defend plausible and sophisticated accounts of pragmatic realism (or realism integrating key insights from constructivism) in general epistemology and philosophy of science; it is a major task for pragmatist philosophers of the humanities to investigate how far these conceptions may be applied to the philosophy of the humanities.[20]

Clearly, the issue of realism is also a key to the history of pragmatism in general philosophy of science. It is to that history that we will next turn in some more detail. Having now preliminarily explained what I mean by pragmatism—specifically invoking the Kantian transcendental interpretation of pragmatism, the pragmatic maxim and the theory of inquiry, and the question of realism—I will draft an outline of the history of pragmatist philosophy of science and inquiry, emphasizing what I find the central features of the tradition, especially focusing on the realism issue and hopefully making clearer how the pragmatist is able to integrate realism and constructivism in the philosophy of science and inquiry, including humanistic inquiry. After this historical survey, we will in the next chapter return to more specific issues concerning the philosophy of the humanities, equipped with a pragmatist understanding of the ontological and epistemological questions concerning the reality and knowability of the objects of inquiry.

How (Not) to Understand the History of Pragmatist Philosophy of Science and Inquiry

The task of identifying a coherent pragmatist tradition in general philosophy of science is challenging, because pragmatism, originating with Peirce's writings on the pragmatic maxim as a logical method of "making our ideas clear" in the 1870s, is a background *both* for Peircean forms of scientific realism and related dynamic theories of scientific progress (e.g., Isaac Levi, Ilkka Niiniluoto) *and*, via the pragmatist views of James and Dewey, for the more relativist and/or constructivist forms of neopragmatism (e.g., Rorty, Putnam) that have sometimes been seen as sacrificing the very ideas of scientific rationality and objectivity as responsive to the mind-independent reality around us. In contrast to realism, these constructivist neopragmatists claim that scientific objects, or even reality in general, are not "ready-made" or mind- and theory-independent but constructions based on our scientific or scholarly (and other) perspectives of inquiry and, more generally, our cultural and social practices and/or schemes and "vocabularies" employed within them. The continuing debate over realism and truth is, hence, crucial in not only the kind of pragmatism I am developing here but in this entire tradition in a historical sense—*if*, indeed, such a tradition is usefully identifiable—and it is only from the perspective of this debate, in some of its key dimensions, that I will now try to survey the history of pragmatist philosophy of science and inquiry. Moreover, the simplified picture of there being two basically different pragmatisms—realistic and relativistic, or objective and subjective (cf., e.g., Haack 1998, 2004; Rescher 2000, 2005)—ought to be enriched by a considerably more nuanced historical narrative (see also de Waal 2021).

In addition to the realism versus relativism and realism versus constructivism controversies, the history of pragmatism in the philosophy of science can also be approached from the perspective of another opposition, namely, the one between scientific realism and *instrumentalism*. (Indeed, as we have already preliminarily seen above, the problem of realism is so complex that realism takes a number of different antirealisms as its contrasts.) While James, as we will perceive, clearly maintained an instrumentalist interpretation of scientific theories and Dewey explicitly labeled his view "instrumentalism," though in a sense broader than the one in which the term is used today, it would also be extremely simplistic to identify pragmatism with instrumentalism, if the latter is understood as a denial of scientific realism (that is, as the claim that theories lack truth-values, being mere instruments for prediction and control of observable phenomena). Karl Popper, for example, characteristically ignored pragmatism, equating it with such antirealist instrumentalism, as well as with the somewhat vague idea that knowledge or truth per se is not valuable, but only practically "useful" knowledge is worth striving for—and many have followed him in adopting this negative attitude to pragmatism.[21] Given Popper's status as a towering figure among twentieth-century philosophers of science, and the simultaneous rise of scientific realism, such accusations cannot have failed to affect the credentials of virtually all forms of pragmatism in this field. However, pragmatism and instrumentalism, though distinguishable, do meet in Rudolf Carnap's (1950) logical empiricism, which was "pragmatist" in the sense of treating the "external questions" about the choice of a linguistic framework as only pragmatically decidable, avoiding "metaphysical" postulations of entities.[22]

A major event in the history of twentieth-century pragmatist philosophy of science was W. V. Quine's attack on the "dogmas of empiricism" in 1951, yielding (in Quine's own words) "a more thorough pragmatism" than Carnap's (and C. I. Lewis's), as well as a "shift toward pragmatism" within a more holistic, undogmatic empiricism (see Quine 1980 [1953], 20, 46). However, as several neopragmatists and scholars of classical pragmatism have argued, Quine's views, while grounding an influential synthesis of logical empiricism and American pragmatism, and thereby playing a crucial role in the emergence of the later "postpositivist" consensus in the philosophy of science, were actually quite far from classical pragmatism. Quine, perhaps unlike many of the actual logical empiricists, philosophized about science rather purely "from a logical point of view," drawing little attention to actual scientific practices and their historical development. More genuinely pragmatist perspectives on science, often without explicit commitments to pragmatism, have emerged in the work of, among others, Putnam, Thomas Kuhn, Larry Laudan, and (more recently) Joseph Rouse and Hasok Chang, as well as in the interdisciplinary discussions within science and technology studies, often examining concrete cases of scientific practice.[23]

This, roughly, is the story I will sketch in the rest of this chapter. It is obviously impossible to review all of the relevant material in a single chapter, though. I will try to show, through a selective discussion focusing on some of the key figures of pragmatist philosophy of science (old and new), how the issues of realism versus relativism (constructivism) and realism versus instrumentalism emerged in the pragmatist tradition, and I will briefly indicate how a synthesis or a via media that we may call "pragmatic realism" can be (and has been) defended. I will try to demonstrate that, and how, pragmatism can be viewed as a tradition (with a relatively loose identity and fuzzy boundaries) whose viability partly results from its openness. This openness is partly constituted by the frequently recurring of questions about whom to include in the tradition, and on the basis of which criteria.[24] This should have some impact on how we think about the prospects of pragmatist philosophy of the humanities, too.

One of the conclusions of my inquiry in the rest of this chapter is that pragmatist philosophy of science (and, hence, of the humanities) cannot be simply reduced to any particular position defined in terms of the straightforward oppositions between scientific realism and its alternatives. However, pragmatist theorists of science and inquiry cannot, I will argue, set the realism issue aside, either, but must live with it. A certain kind of *openness*—the recognition that the realism issue in its diversity will remain on our philosophical agenda—thus characterizes a genuinely pragmatist approach to the philosophy of the humanities, too. Before elaborating on this argument and its relevance to the philosophy of the humanities, we must begin with a historical sketch that illustrates why the pragmatist tradition has so easily been saddled with instrumentalist interpretations, especially among realist philosophers of science.

Instrumentalism and Operationalism in James and Dewey

Peirce's influence on later philosophy of science was, though slow in its emergence, eventually so enormous that I must largely set him aside here, in order to keep my discussion within a manageable size (but see chapter 3 below for my employment of the Peircean notion of "real generals"). In any case, Peirce's role in the pragmatist tradition is quite clear: without him, there would be no pragmatism at all. On the other hand, so many theorists of scientific inference, especially abduction (cf., e.g., Niiniluoto 2018), have drawn influence from Peirce that to include them all within pragmatism would be *too* open-minded. Peircean insights in logic, semiotics, and the theory of inference can be utilized quite independently of his pragmatism.[25] Yet the tension between scientific realism and constructivism or idealism (though, in Peirce's case, not relativism) is already present in Peirce's early writings on the pragmatic method (see the early sections of this chapter), particularly in his application of this method of "making our ideas clear" to the concept of reality, which is explained as the object of the "final opinion" of the scientific community of researchers employing the scientific method. Which comes first—the mind- and research-independent reality itself, or the process of fixing the final opinion—is left (perhaps deliberately) undecided. This is, essentially, the historical tension between realism and idealism.[26] The other key tension in the realism discussion, between scientific realism and instrumentalism, can also be traced back to Peirce, because his pragmatic conception of meaning influenced later verificationist and logically empiricist theories, although the proponents of those theories seldom realized that Peirce was not only a logician and a philosopher of science but also a highly original speculative metaphysician, contrary to the spirit of the Vienna Circle.[27]

Despite these interpretive issues, Peirce, the founder of pragmatism, was clearly a precursor of scientific realism—particularly of the idea that the advancement of science can be understood as a progression toward the truth, or as an increase in the truthlikeness of theories.[28] His concept of abduction has also been employed in the debate over whether realism itself can be defended as the best (or only) explanation of the empirical success of science.[29] Thus, in an important sense, Peirce is a classical figure of what is today known as scientific realism—and therefore cannot be overlooked in a discussion of realism in the humanities, either, as witnessed by the current interest in a Peircean approach to the philosophy of historiography, for instance.[30] The same cannot, however, be exactly said about his friend James. On the contrary, it is easy to see James as a precursor of instrumentalism, one of the major orientations opposed to realism in twentieth-century philosophy of science. Thus, when we move from Peirce to James and Dewey, the tensions centering around the issue of scientific realism become deeper and more essential. In James's main works, we find, for instance, the following somewhat overlapping remarks:

> As the sciences have developed farther, the notion has gained ground that most, perhaps all, of our laws are only approximations. The laws themselves, moreover, have grown so numerous that there is no counting them; and so many rival formulations are proposed in all the branches of science that investigators have become accustomed to the notion that no

theory is absolutely a transcript of reality, but that any one of them may from some point of view be useful. Their great use is to summarize old facts and to lead to new ones. They are only a man-made language, a conceptual shorthand [. . .] in which we write our reports of nature. (James 1975 [1907], 33)

We are witnessing a curious reversion of the common-sense way of looking at physical nature, in the philosophy of science favored by such men as Mach, Ostwald and Duhem. According to these teachers no hypothesis is truer than any other in the sense of being a more literal copy of reality. They are all but ways of talking on our part, to be compared solely from the point of view of their *use*. The only literally true thing is *reality*; and the only reality we know is, for these logicians, sensible reality, the flux of our sensations and emotions as they pass. (Ibid., 93)

There are so many geometries, so many logics, so many physical and chemical hypotheses, so many classifications, each one of them good for so much and yet not good for everything, that the notion that even the truest formula may be a human device and not a literal transcript has dawned upon us. We hear scientific laws now treated as so much 'conceptual shorthand,' true so far as they are useful but no farther. Our mind has become tolerant of symbol instead of reproduction, of approximation instead of exactness, of plasticity instead of rigor. (James 1978 [1909], 40)

Theories, then, are for James essentially "*instruments, not answers to enigmas*" (James 1975 [1907], 32; original emphasis). They enable us to cope with the world we live in; their purpose is not to "copy" the facts or the world. Their "truth" lies, pragmatically, in their usefulness.[31] Scientific ideas, in particular, "agree" with their real objects only in the more or less operationalist sense of a practical process of conduction leading from a present idea to a future one: "The term 'energy' doesn't even pretend to stand for anything 'objective.' It is only a way of measuring the surface of phenomena so as to string their changes on a simple formula" (ibid., 103). An obvious follow-up question in our context would be whether this also holds for theoretical terms and "ideas" employed in humanistic research. James does not develop this issue, but certainly the pragmatist philosopher of the humanities may agree with him that humanistic theories also enable us to "cope" with the world rather than seeking to "copy" a theory-independent reality.[32] Indeed, this may, at least prima facie, be more plausible in the humanities than in the sciences—though, as we will see, it does not follow that we could not develop a pragmatist analogy of scientific realism for the humanities, too.

James does talk about "approximation," but he does not seem to have in mind the scientific realists' (roughly Peircean) view on the approximation of truth by means of successive theories increasing in verisimilitude (cf. Niiniluoto 1984, 1999). Rather, contrasting approximation with truth as a "literal copy," he rejects the realist idea that our theories could ever represent the way things mind- and theory-independently are. James's empiricism, influenced by Mach, Ostwald, Duhem, Poincaré, and others,[33] thus brought him at least close to what later became known as instrumentalism. Another factor that led James to pursue these ideas was presumably his hope to acknowledge both science and religion as equally legitimate, and equally well experientially anchored, perspectives on reality, or practices of coping with human experience and the world.

However, immediately after the second of the above-quoted passages, James points out that the view he discusses "seems to be too economical to be all-sufficient," because "profusion, not economy, may after all be reality's key-note" (James 1975 [1907], 93). He also rejects Berkeleyan phenomenalism ("*esse est percipi*") on pragmatic grounds, emphasizing that "the category of trans-perceptual reality is now one of the foundations of our life" (James 1978 [1909], 43). Hence, in James we can observe, instead of any clear acceptance of instrumentalism, a *tension* between instrumentalist and realist ideas, pretty much as we find in his work a tension between idealist and realist viewpoints and between scientific and religious perspectives on reality.

Something similar seems to take place in Dewey's pragmatic naturalism, as articulated in major books such as *Experience and Nature* (1986 [1929]), *The Quest for Certainty* (1960 [1929]), *Logic: The Theory of Inquiry* (1938), and *Reconstruction in Philosophy* (1957 [1948]). In these and other works, Dewey often labeled his position "instrumentalism," "experimentalism," or "operational thinking." This is no place to describe even in general terms Dewey's complex views any more than James's; we should primarily observe that while his position has clearly instrumentalist and more generally empiricist elements, his talk about instrumentalism should *not* be simply equated with the narrower treatment by later philosophers of science of the empiricist doctrine carrying the same title. It is evident that Dewey is not innocent regarding the subsequent association, by Popper and others, of pragmatism and instrumentalism (in the narrower sense). When, for instance, Percy Bridgman (1960 [1927], 5, 31–32) speaks about "operational thinking" and suggests, notoriously, that the meaning of theoretical concepts is to be defined with reference to practical operations in the laboratory, one cannot help noticing a similarity to Dewey's insistence—roughly at the same time—on scientific practice, operationality, and the instrumental use of theories.[34] However, the similarities between operationalists' (like Bridgman's) and Dewey's views must not be exaggerated, as significant differences remain. For example, when acknowledging Peirce as a precursor of his operational thinking, Dewey (1936) endorsed, in a qualified manner, a Peircean view of universals (or "generals") yet avoiding hypostatizing them as real entities.[35]

Dewey (1960 [1929], 79) celebrates the "overtly executed operations of interaction" that are needed for obtaining scientific knowledge, thereby rejecting the gap traditionally thought to lie between knowledge and action. This seems to lead to antirealism:

> There is something both ridiculous and disconcerting in the way in which men have let themselves be imposed upon, so as to infer that scientific ways of thinking of objects give the inner reality of things, and that they put a mark of spuriousness upon all other ways of thinking of them, and of perceiving and enjoying them. It is ludicrous because these scientific conceptions, like other instruments, are hand-made by man in pursuit of realization of a certain interest—that of the maximum convertibility of every object of thought into any and every other. [. . .] When the physical sciences describe objects and the world as being such and such, it is thought that the description is of reality as it exists in itself. [. . . However, the] business of thought is not to conform to or reproduce the characters already possessed by objects but to judge them as potentialities of what they become through an indicated operation. [. . .] To think of the world in terms of mathematical formulae of space, time and motion is not to have a picture of the independent and fixed essence of the

universe. It is to describe experienceable objects as material upon which certain operations are performed. (Ibid., 135–137)

Science, then, has no more privileged relation to the real than (some) other human practices, arguably including the humanities (as well as practices such as art, education, and democratic engagement, all of which are, in a broad sense, forms of "inquiry" for Dewey). "There are as many conceptions of knowledge as there are distinctive operations by which problematic situations are resolved," Dewey tells us (ibid., 221). In brief, "scientific conceptions" are not "revelations of antecedent properties of real Being and existence" but "instrumentalities which direct operations of experimental observations" (ibid., 192). Natural laws, similarly, are "intellectual instrumentalities," *formulae for the prediction of the probability of an observable occurrence*,[36] instead of being statements about "ultimate and rigid uniformities of being" (ibid., 205–206; original emphasis). A law that was supposed to "govern phenomena" ought to be understood as "a way of transacting business effectively with concrete existences" (ibid., 207). The universality typically claimed to characterize laws and theories "is not that of inherent content fixed by God or Nature, but of range of applicability" (Dewey 1957 [1948], xv).[37] Scientific concept(ion)s and theories are tools, "open to development through use" (ibid., 145).

Similarly, in his naturalist magnum opus, *Experience and Nature*, Dewey (1986 [1929], 115) equates "the proper objects of science" with "nature in its instrumental characters." The key point is to stop treating the object of science as "complete and self-sufficient"; this will only result in an insoluble problem, namely, the question concerning the relation between the "perceptual order" and the order of "inferred and logically constructed real objects," with two incompatible kinds of knowledge and of the objects of knowledge (ibid., 116). In this context, Dewey also makes clear that his "instrumentalism" is not a theory about personal satisfaction in knowing, but about "the proper objects of science" (ibid., 126).[38] Precisely as such, it might, however, be regarded as straightforwardly antirealistic.

Dewey's commitment to instrumentalism is relatively obvious when he argues that the problem of the "two tables" (the so-called "Eddington tables") is illusory, because the table we perceive and use is "the only table[. . .] for it alone has both individuality of form [. . .] and also includes within itself a continuum of relations or interactions brought to a focus" (Dewey 1960 [1929], 240).[39] Is Dewey saying, then, that the scientific table, or the "scientific image" according to which the table is not a concrete, perceived, practically used object but a collection of microphysical particles, is unreal or illusory? If so, he is subscribing to a classical instrumentalist position, which several realist philosophers of science, especially following Wilfrid Sellars (1963), have powerfully called into question (cf. Tuomela 1985; Niiniluoto 1999). Or is he, rather, subscribing to some form of idealism, or to what would today more accurately be called constructivism, when maintaining that scientific objects are not independent of inquiry (cf. also Shook 2000)?

In an earlier work, Dewey (1916, 30) admits that he may sound like an idealist when he holds that thinking, which "is instrumental to a control of environment,"[40] in a way constructs its objects: "Processes of reflective inquiry play a part in shaping the objects—namely, terms and propositions—which constitute the bodies of scientific knowledge. [. . .] Insofar as it is idealistic to hold that objects of knowledge *in their capacity of distinctive objects of knowledge* are determined by intelligence, [this view] is idealistic. It believes that faith in the constructive, the creative, competency of intelligence was the redeeming element in historic idealisms" (ibid., 30–31; see also 60). Dewey's Hegelian background is visible here, though he immediately adds that his instrumentalism (or idealism) does not postulate an entity or substance which constitutes the world but "defines thought or intelligence by function, by work done, by consequences effected" (ibid., 31). Moreover, the ultimate justification of scientific theorization, for Dewey, seems to be humanistic, not narrowly instrumental, and therefore Dewey's philosophy of science must in the end be seen as indistinguishable from what we might mean by his philosophy of the humanities (though as far as I know he never uses that label): "Natural science loses its divorce from humanity; it becomes itself humanistic in quality. It is something to be pursued not in a technical and specialized way for what is called truth for its own sake, but with the sense of its social bearing, its intellectual indispensableness. It is technical only in the sense that it provides the technique of social and moral engineering" (Dewey 1957 [1948], 173).

The charges of instrumentalism and idealism have their obvious justification, but it would be overhasty to judge Dewey to be simply an antirealist[41] in his philosophy of science. For one thing, he—just like James—uses the terminology of *objects, concepts, conceptions, theories, hypotheses*, and so on, more loosely than is customary in (analytic) philosophy of science; I have, in fact, quoted extensively from his writings partly in order to bring this fact to the fore. This habit of usage makes confusions easy. For another thing, Dewey was, perhaps primarily, a *naturalist*, always arguing that experience and knowledge, including the production of scientific knowledge (and its objects), as well as (by extension) humanistic knowledge and its objects, are natural phenomena in a natural world in which we try to cope, to settle the problematic situations emerging within our world-engaging practices. Whatever is "natural" to our practices of inquiry, of resolving indeterminate situations and thus moving on in our experience and action, is to be accepted rather than treated with philosophical suspicion. A philosophical skepticism about, say, the existence of unobservable theoretical entities would have been, from Dewey's point of view, an utterly *unpragmatist* and *unnatural* attitude. Rather, we should take ontologically seriously the natural practices of inquiry we engage in. It was always the actual practice of inquiry itself that Dewey appealed to when, for instance, attacking the ancient ideal of certainty and the "spectator theory of knowledge" (Dewey 1960 [1929]).[42] It was science as it is actually conducted, rather than any abstract philosophical account of science, that he admired when we wrote: "In science the order of fixities has already passed irretrievably into an order of connections *in process*" (Dewey 1957 [1948], xl).

In the context of my attempt to develop a pragmatist philosophy of the humanities, it is particularly important to note that skeptical doubts concerning theoretical postulations may be as far from the actual practices of inquiry in the humanities as they are in the natural sciences. The "naturalist" pragmatist can, then, be a pragmatic realist—also regarding humanistic "entities." This thought, to be fully developed only in chapters 3 and 4 below, can arguably already be found in an initial form in Dewey's conception of inquiry.

We may conclude, with Steven French (1989, 293–294, 298–299), that antirealist forms of empiricism, such as the logical empiricists' instrumentalism or Bas van Fraassen's (1980) "constructive empiricism," are unpragmatic views because they are, above all, forms of *skepticism*, blocking the road of inquiry by doubting the existence of theoretical entities— which is something not actually doubted in the course of scientific (or, arguably, humanistic) inquiry itself.[43] This is close to saying, with Quine, that skeptical doubts, if real (and not the kind of "paper doubts" famously mocked by Peirce), are themselves scientific doubts; analogously, doubts about the reality of "humanistic entities" (e.g., historical events or chains of influence) can be seen as internal to humanistic scholarship itself. A critically realist view of the explanatory postulations of theories is thus a necessary condition for the possibility of scientific and humanistic practices of inquiry as we know them, and pragmatists, if anything, ought to take such humanly natural practices seriously. Therefore, pragmatism should acknowledge our habitual scientific practices in which unobservable theoretical entities are postulated without paying too much attention to the relatively uninteresting possibility of entertaining skeptical doubts about their existence on narrowly empiricist grounds. Insofar as the classical pragmatists (particularly James and Dewey) to some extent refused to do this, their instrumentalism ought to be significantly modified by the contemporary pragmatist.[44]

Our preliminary conclusion at this point is that the classical pragmatists—we are specifically speaking about James and Dewey here—were definitely *not* scientific realists, if scientific realism is defined as the thesis that scientific theories provide us with the only true (or truthlike) picture of reality, or that the "scientific image" is ontologically prior to the "manifest image" we are acquainted with in our ordinary human experience.[45] But they were scientific realists, or at least their views were compatible with scientific realism, in the sense of rejecting unnatural skeptical doubts about the existence of theoretical entities postulated in the actual course of scientific theorization (as long as such theorization is firmly rooted in its humanly natural practical contexts of inquiry). Of course, all pragmatists—and all rational inquirers—should admit that any specific postulations of unobservable entities in (current) scientific theories might turn out to be ill-founded. Yet, as fallibilists, we should adopt such a critical, open attitude to any human claims and ideas whatsoever. The key pragmatist move is to liberate not only science but also scientific realism—and all other philosophical interpretations of science—from foundationalist pursuits of certainty, essences, and other remnants of "first philosophy" also motivating skeptical doubts. Classical pragmatism offers, then, a middle path (or, rather, several such paths) between scientific realism and instrumentalism.

This is a key to the pragmatist philosophy of the humanities as well. While there is no simple equivalent of instrumentalism in that area, an analogy of instrumentalist views on science in the philosophy of the humanities could be the idea that humanistic theorization is not to be taken literally or at face value at all but only as an instrument to something like human welfare or the good life. That is, according to what could be called "humanistic instrumentalism," we would not, say, interpret literature in order to understand more deeply the meanings of a literary work of art (and what it may say about the human condition, for example), but only in order to, for example, "exercise" our minds and brains to imagine complex moral situations and to strengthen our capacities for empathy, and perhaps thus enhance our individual and social welfare. Similarly, we would not study history in order to understand better what "really" happened in the past and why, but only to live better today amidst the documents of the past we may have around us, for example, by developing political institutions that would avoid the "mistakes of history." And we would not study theology and religion in order to understand more profoundly why and how people believe in divinities and what kinds of religious meanings they have formulated in their religious documents and practices, but primarily, or even exclusively, in the interest of living forward amidst the confusing plurality of religious frameworks surrounding us in contemporary societies. In all these cases, humanistic theories and ideas would be mere instruments for something purely practical.

Now, the pragmatist philosopher of the humanities should, in my view, be a moderate realist in the sense of affirming that humanistic inquiry and theorization are indeed in the business of referring to real entities and processes in the world—in addition to perhaps (hopefully) also ameliorating our individual and social lives and experiences. The ontological status of the humanistic "entities" postulated in inquiry will, of course, have to be examined more closely, but something like the distinction between realism and instrumentalism (in an analogous form) is, we may conclude, as important in a pragmatist philosophy of the humanities as it is in general pragmatist philosophy of science and theory of inquiry. Clearly, the history of classical pragmatism offers us a tension—rather than any simple view to be just subscribed to—here.

Before moving on to later stages of the pragmatist tradition, I want to note that my brief survey of Peirce's, James's, and Dewey's ideas in this section by no means exhausts the relevance of so-called classical pragmatism to our topic. While there are important figures within classical pragmatism itself who were crucial for the development of the tradition but perhaps not so central in pragmatist philosophy of science and inquiry—such thinkers arguably include, among others, Josiah Royce and Jane Addams—some other early pragmatists were clearly highly significant regarding the pragmatist theory of inquiry. One such philosopher, often unfortunately neglected even by serious scholars of pragmatism, was George Herbert Mead, who should be considered equally a modern classic of pragmatist philosophy and social psychology.[46] The pragmatist philosopher of the humanities can appreciate both Mead's general views on realism and the objects of science and inquiry[47] and, more specifically, the sophisticated exploration of the (un)reality of the past included in Mead's posthumously published *The Philosophy of the Present*. The past, Mead (2002 [1932], chapter 1) there argues, is only available from the standpoint of the present, and as seen from the perspective of a different present, it is a different past, a "rewritten" one (see ibid., 43). Any "accepted past," according to Mead, "lies in a present," remaining subject to "possible reconstruction" (ibid., 58). This view postulating a constantly dynamically changing and rearticulated past could be regarded as a special case—clearly relevant to the philosophy of historiography, in particular—of the ontological dependence of all theoretical postulations, and any humanly cognizable reality, on the ongoing practices of inquiry through which (only) we encounter the world. Mead's exact position remains hard to interpret, but he seems to exemplify a tension analogous to the one already perceived in James's and Dewey's struggles with realism: on the one hand, there is a "real" reality—"reality exists in a present" (ibid., 35)—but this reality is unstable, renewed as experiential novelties emerge.

Quine's "More Thorough Pragmatism"?[48]

As important as Mead's views on realism, as well as his more famous account of intersubjectivity, are for any pragmatist conception of the human world, I will now move on to later twists in the pragmatist tradition. This is an obvious place for an excursus from the classical pragmatists' relaxed naturalism toward the more scientistic Quinean naturalism, according to which normative philosophical prescriptions, such as the strict principles of logical empiricism, should never be prior to scientific theorization itself. There is, famously, no "first philosophy" over and above science, according to Quine. In pragmatist terms, this radical *naturalization* of the philosophy of science can be expressed by saying that "first-philosophical" norms of justification, rationality, theory-choice, and so on, can never override the practices of inquiry that scientists themselves engage in. The reason we need to dwell on these issues here is not only because naturalism in one or another sense is a key dimension of pragmatism. Even more importantly, the relation between (pragmatic) naturalism and irreducible *normativity* must preoccupy pragmatist theorists of inquiry and pragmatist philosophers of the humanities (as further discussed in chapter 4 below).[49]

In "Two Dogmas of Empiricism," Quine (1980 [1953], chapter 2) advanced a "shift toward pragmatism" and claimed to represent a more thorough pragmatism than Carnap had done in his seminal "Empiricism, Semantics and Ontology" (1950).[50] However, Quine hardly ever commented—any more than Carnap[51]—in any historical detail on the actual pragmatist philosophers of the American tradition. It is not clear, then, what exactly Quine's place in the history of pragmatist philosophy of science and theory of inquiry is. Insofar as he occupies such a place at all, it is in the interesting intersection of pragmatism and logical empiricism.[52]

Still, among recent surveys of pragmatism, Susan Haack's (2004) contains a section on Quine (27–28), as does Nicholas Rescher's introduction to pragmatism (2000, 37–39). For a long time, Quine has been discussed, in general presentations of pragmatism, as a (neo)pragmatist of some kind (see, e.g., Murphy 1990). L. E. Hahn's preface to the *Library of Living Philosophers* volume dedicated to Quine described Quine's position as "pragmatic naturalism" (Hahn and Schilpp 1986, xv). The conviction that Quine represented pragmatism or that he was a major actor in the "pragmatic turn" in twentieth-century philosophy of science is, hence, widespread.

However, did the "endorsements of pragmatism" one finds in both "Two Dogmas" and "On What There Is" (Quine 1980 [1953], chapters 1–2) curiously vanish from Quine's later work, as Christopher Hookway (1988, 50) claims? This shift of emphasis is, perhaps, related to Quine's increasing tendency to describe himself as a naturalist and a "robust realist." However, even in the early works, the use of the term *pragmatic* and related expressions is subordinated to empiricism and thereby to a treatment not of individual pragmatic purposes or interests but of scientific objectivity: the talk about "pragmatic standards" refers "to an appeal to the pursuit of efficient predictive control over experience which serves as the 'duty' of science. Here Quine's empiricism intervenes to assign a meaning to the 'pragmatic' which puts into question the claim that the presence of pragmatic considerations in scientific growth is in tension with a realist construal of science" (ibid., 53). One might, therefore, view Quine's "pragmatism" as a descendant—philosophically, not historically—of Peirce's objective, realistic pragmatism (cf., e.g., Haack 1998, 2004; Rescher 2000, 2005; Pihlström 2004a, 2008), according to which the relevant kind of pragmatic results or conceivable practical consequences that our concepts and conceptions ought to have are, primarily or even exclusively, scientific, empirical ones—in contrast to James's more pluralistic, less science-oriented conception of the "practical consequences" of beliefs and their objects. This might lead us to view Quine's version of pragmatic naturalism as less relevant to the philosophy of the humanities than, say, the pragmatisms developed by James and Dewey—but it is precisely for this reason that we must investigate how the issue of normativity arises in Quine.

Several (neo)pragmatists and scholars of classical pragmatism have challenged the standard account of Quine as a pragmatist—with good reason, given Quine's own doubts about his place in the pragmatist tradition, and about what pragmatism even means (cf. also Quine 1981). As Haack (2004, 27) points out, "it is hard to take Quine's reference to pragmatism [in 'Two Dogmas'] as seriously historically intended, given that he includes Carnap, surely by any standards more positivist than pragmatist."

In order to enrich our picture, we may take a brief look at the ways in which Quine's philosophy of science can be claimed to differ, often significantly, from pragmatists'—old and new—ideas. This is important for the purposes of my pragmatist philosophy of the humanities not because Quine himself would have contributed to that field (famously, for him, philosophy of science was "philosophy enough") but because his project of naturalization sets limits to what a naturalistic pragmatism can do and achieve. In this chapter (or this book), there is no need to focus in any detail on the relations between pragmatism and logical empiricism (cf. Pihlström 2017c, 2018; Pihlström et al. 2017), but my brief discussion of Quine metonymically serves, I hope, the need to recognize the significance of this issue also for humanistically inclined pragmatists.

Putnam's criticism of Quine is particularly relevant here, because Putnam—in good pragmatist company (e.g., James)—rejects Quinean reductive scientism, a view that can be regarded as one of the threats that pragmatism may face due to excessive naturalization.[53] Putnam attacks Quine's views because they actually (albeit unexpectedly) lead, by his lights, to something very much like Rorty's (in Putnam's view irresponsibly relativist) neopragmatism.[54] From Putnam's perspective, then, Quine's version of pragmatic naturalism ought to be rejected pretty much for the same reasons that the responsible pragmatist ought to reject Rorty's radical neopragmatism. The key to this criticism—obviously highly relevant to the philosophy of the humanities—is the claim that both Quinean scientistic naturalism and Rortyan relativism tend to lose the humanly inescapable normativity of semantic and epistemic practices. Putnam has written on Quine for decades, and obviously we cannot pay attention to everything he has to say about Quine here (see, e.g., Putnam 1990, chapters 20 and 21; 1994, chapters 12 and 18). His main argument seems to be that Quine is led, through his radical naturalism, to a form of meaning skepticism and thus to global relativism and antirealism—in any case to a devastating loss of normativity, which no pragmatist should tolerate.[55] Such a fragmentation of normativity is, from a pragmatist point of view, at least as serious for our understanding of the humanities as it is for our understanding of the scientific method.

Putnam is not alone in his criticism. According to Michele Marsonet (1993), for example, Quine's views have encouraged "scientific anti-realism." David Weissman (2003), in turn, places Quine in the Cartesian tradition, with language replacing the self-sufficient mind, and argues that his "pragmatism" faces a tension between naturalism and idealism (see ibid., 71): Is the natural or physical world mind-independently real, or is it somehow made up by the mind—or, rather, language (in particular, scientific language-use)? A version of this tension can be perceived in the pragmatist tradition generally (as we have seen and will further emphasize here); accordingly, in *this* sense, Quine easily qualifies as a pragmatist. On the other hand, nonpragmatist philosophers may face similar difficulties in steering a plausible middle course between (scientific) realism and antirealism, for example, idealism, constructivism, or relativism. The openness of the issue of realism is certainly not unique to pragmatism.

Other, perhaps more clearly pragmatist, critics of Quine have formulated their complaints differently. For instance, John Shook (2002) argues that Quine's "global realism" postulates experience-transcendent unobservable entities, while Dewey's more properly pragmatic philosophy of science precludes such a realist postulation. This may or may not be accurate, depending on how realistically Quine's ontology is understood (cf. Koskinen 2004) and on how exactly we construe Dewey's (above-discussed) contribution to these issues. Independently of the realism debate, Shook's charge that Dewey's naturalism is far broader than Quine's scientism is, however, a traditional one among pragmatism scholars.[56] Shook (2002) is one of those viewing Quine's position as a pragmatist one "only in the most marginal of senses," that is, only in specific comparison to Carnap's. Most Deweyan pragmatists would probably agree with Shook that Quinean empiricism is simply too narrow to cover the practice-embedded richness of human experience, or with Leemon B. McHenry (1995) that the elements of (ontological) pragmatism in Quine are insufficient to significantly connect him with classical pragmatism. Accordingly, they would also agree with Matthew Brown's (2005) rejection of the myth—explicitly formulated, as Brown notes, by Ernest Gellner—of Quine as "the last pragmatist," because Quine was not merely an inaccurate interpreter of pragmatism but always more clearly an empiricist (or a positivist) than a pragmatist, admitting that it was never clear to him what it takes to be a pragmatist.[57]

We may conclude at this point that *if* Quine can be said to have been a pragmatist at all, he was a pragmatist of a reductively scientistic type, very far even from Peirce, whose pragmatism was far more strongly inclined toward the natural sciences than, say, James's. Quine's role in the history of pragmatist philosophy of science and inquiry might even be reduced to his having made, in "Two Dogmas," the term *pragmatism* (like the term *ontology* in "On What There Is") more widely used and legitimate among philosophers emerging from logical empiricism and developing analytic philosophy further. Moreover, Quine, like Carnap, does carry the instrumentalist heritage of logical positivism; hence, if we wish to draw a distinction between pragmatism proper and instrumentalism bearing only superficial resemblance to pragmatism (cf. the previous section), then we certainly should *not* include Quine among our paradigmatic pragmatists. Quine's place in the pragmatist tradition in the philosophy of science should, then, be approached only with utmost care (cf. Koskinen and Pihlström 2006). Even so, he remains an extremely important mediating figure, without whom later neopragmatist twists in the development of twentieth century philosophy of science and inquiry—especially in the work of philosophers such as Putnam and Rorty—could hardly have taken the form they did.[58] Clearly, Quine was instrumental in rehabilitating pragmatism as a philosophical tradition, whether or not he ever really even cared about the classical pragmatists' ideas, apart from his generally sympathetic remarks on Dewey's naturalism (e.g., Quine 1969) and his appreciation of Peirce as a logician.

This qualified result is important for the pragmatist philosophy of the humanities, even though for Quine the humanities were relatively uninteresting. There is no reason the pragmatist philosopher of the humanities could not be inspired by Quine's ideas, including not only the repudiation of the "dogma" of the analytic/synthetic dualism but even his naturalism (sufficiently nonreductively reinterpreted), despite Quine's own relative lack of interest in anything else but science and logic. We will see in chapter 4 the importance of finding a sustainable balance between pragmatic naturalization and full-blown normativity guiding all our inquiries in science and the humanities alike.

Paradigms and Reality: Kuhn, Putnam, and Pragmatic Realism

I will next try to further substantiate one of my main theses in this chapter, namely, that pragmatism need *not* amount *either* to an empiricist instrumentalism opposed to scientific realism about unobservable theoretical entities and processes *or* to a radical relativism (constructivism) sacrificing the objectivity of the scientific method and scientific knowledge—that is, that pragmatist philosophy of science and inquiry need not be "antirealist" in any standard sense. Of course, I am not the first pragmatism scholar to make such a suggestion. In discussions of Dewey, as already noted, it has been repeatedly emphasized that Dewey's instrumentalism is quite different from the one influential in and after logical empiricism and even that Dewey's version is compatible with scientific realism, because the Deweyan instrumentalist can accept unobservable theoretical entities while denying that theories simply mirror reality (see Morgenbesser's "Introduction" to his 1977, xvi-xvii, xxix; cf. Tiles 1988). In James's case, this would be slightly more difficult to document, but we have already said something in this regard above; also, James's pragmatism cannot be reduced to any straightforward instrumentalism or antirealism. More generally, the fact that the classical pragmatists rejected any simple "copy" theory of truth—or any version of the view Rorty (1979) later called the conception of the human mind or language as a "mirror of nature"—should not be taken to entail that they were committed to any simple antirealism, either.

In any case, while both of these classical pragmatists firmly denied that science—even our most advanced science—describes "reality as it exists in itself" (Dewey 1960 [1929], 136–137; cf. James 1975 [1907], Lectures V and VII), this is *not* necessarily to deny the ontological status of the theoretical postulations of science.[59] Nor is it to deny the (relative) objectivity, "humanly speaking"—to borrow a term from Putnam—of scientific as well as humanistic theories and methods. The pragmatist need not hold, with Paul Feyerabend (1993 [1975], chapter 1), that "anything goes" or that a pluralist proliferation of scientific practices and methods is *simply* or unproblematically a good thing as it stands, because scientific practices have their own inbuilt normativity, and normative distinctions between good and bad (or better and worse) science are internal to those practices themselves, hence something that the pragmatist always ought to take seriously. However, this does not mean that the norms of scientific methodology—or humanistic methodology, for that matter—would be handed down to us from above; to the contrary, inquiry (in any field) is a continuing critical process, in which not only theories but the methods used to justify them are constantly open for reevaluation. Instead of celebrating pluralism and anarchy as such, the pragmatist should follow Dewey in emphasizing the *critical* function of philosophy, its role as "the critical method of developing methods of criticism" (Dewey 1986 [1929], 354; cf. Pihlström 2020, chapter 3).

In general outline, the view these inevitably incomplete reflections yield (I hope) is the following. The pragmatist can and should try to develop a pragmatic realism about scientific knowledge and its objects, including unobservable ones—even when agreeing with James and Dewey that theories are, above all, practical instruments for coping with experience, that is, for living in the natural world surrounding us and settling the various problematic situations life brings with it. Nothing prevents us from viewing many of our problematic situations as highly "theoretical" ones. This understanding of the relation between theory, experience, and reality subordinates scientific realism to pragmatism. The realist makes an ontological commitment to the unobservable entities that a theory postulates on a pragmatic basis, from the point of view of scientific practice. The practice of science *is* a realistic practice, and the pragmatist should explore the normativity guiding it from within instead of instituting external norms foreign to it.[60] The same goes, analogously, for the normativity of humanistic research practices and thus for pragmatist philosophy of the humanities.

The instrumentalist view, according to which theories do not genuinely purport to describe reality at all but only structure and systematize the connections between observable phenomena, is extremely restrictive and, therefore, foreign to the habitual actions and deliberations standardly performed within our practices of inquiry and theory-choice. Instrumentalism and its later manifestations, such as constructive empiricism, according to which our theories should merely aim at "empirical adequacy" instead of truth (cf. van Fraassen 1980), can be regarded as essentially skeptical views blocking the road of inquiry, as noted above. Pragmatists and pragmatic naturalists, however, do not aim at "refuting the skeptic" in the first place; consequently, they need not worry about refuting the instrumentalist, either—not, at any rate, in any foundationalist manner. Skeptical issues should, as Quine correctly saw, be understood as issues arising *within* science (or more generally inquiry), if genuinely arising at all, and this is one reason that Quine's naturalism, though in some ways far from any core views of the pragmatist tradition, is important for pragmatist philosophy of the humanities, too. Such science-internal questions are not autonomous problems of an alleged first philosophy prior to science; conceived as such, they would amount to what Peirce called "paper doubts."[61] Yet, the truly pragmatic naturalist also rejects Quine's extremely restricted conception of scientific (empirical) experience as sheer physical stimulation of an organism's sensory receptors. Science qua practice is ineliminably normative,[62] and no adequate understanding of this normativity is achieved within a philosophy of science defined by Quinean restrictions. Quine's pragmatism is not more but less thorough than a desirable version of pragmatism in this situation.

Now, where should we look for a reconciliation of normatively rich pragmatism and scientific realism—and the corresponding detachment of pragmatism from both radical relativism and extreme empiricist instrumentalism?[63] Somewhat surprisingly, I propose, in the work of major late twentieth-century thinkers whose "pragmatist" thought is often associated with antirealism rather than realism: Hilary Putnam and Thomas Kuhn. We will, however, only discuss the latter in some detail here. Just like Putnam, whose "internal realist" or "pragmatic realist" views have often been characterized as yielding a combination of pragmatism and Kantian idealism (see, e.g., Pihlström 1996, 2009), Kuhn can be interpreted as a naturalistically relaxed, post-Darwinian and historically concerned Kantian transcendental idealist—with as firm a commitment to a form of empirical realism as in Kant himself. In this respect, Kuhn and Putnam stand close to each other, despite their disagreements over the nature of reference and meaning (in)variance in scientific theory-change, as well as the related threat of relativism that Putnam, like many others, repeatedly perceived in Kuhn's views. They have also been treated as equally dangerous ontological relativists, constructivists, or idealists by more traditional scientific realists defending a non-epistemic correspondence account of truth as mind- and theory-independent.[64]

Putnam's place in twentieth-century philosophy of science was so central that we must largely neglect the details of his complex views, just as we have been forced to set aside Peirce's ideas in this chapter. It will, however, be useful to note briefly how Putnam and Kuhn viewed each other's work, especially in relation to the realism issue.[65] Putnam's references to Kuhn—from his early scientifically realist phase in the 1970s through his first substantial defenses of internal realism (Putnam 1981, 1983) up to and including his later treatments of the realism issue (e.g., Putnam 1994)—are mostly highly critical: together with Feyerabend and the notorious "French postmodernists," Kuhn seems to be, for Putnam, one of those irrationalist relativists and incommensurabilists whose ideas threaten to give up the objectivity of science altogether. According to Putnam, that objectivity must be maintained also within a pragmatist understanding of science, even if metaphysically realist interpretations of it have led philosophers astray.[66] Hence, in brief, Putnam's reading of Kuhn does not significantly differ from the traditional line of criticism that pictures Kuhn as a relativist turning science into a subjective, irrational conversation[67]—even though Putnam's own views have frequently been subjected to similar antirelativist attacks (cf. Davidson 1984; Norris 2000).[68]

Kuhn's tone of voice differs from Putnam's in interesting ways. His fundamental *agreement* with Putnam is clearly visible in his 1991 essay, "The Road since *Structure*," where he says that "the relationship between the lexicon—the shared taxonomy of a speech community[69]—and the world the members of that community jointly inhabit" cannot be "the one Putnam has called metaphysical realism," because "insofar as the structure of the world can be experienced and the experience communicated, it is constrained by the structure of the lexicon of the community which inhabits it" (Kuhn 2000, 101; see also ibid., 218–221, 247). Kuhn still maintains, as he did in his main work (see especially Kuhn 1970 [1962], "Postscript"), that insofar as the notion of truth has anything to do with scientific development, it cannot be extratheoretical correspondence truth but must be intratheoretically applied (Kuhn 2000, 115, 160–162, 251). This, obviously, is a view largely (though perhaps not entirely) shared by Putnam. Kuhn goes on: "No more in the natural than in the human sciences is there some neutral, culture-independent, set of categories within which the population—whether of objects or of actions—can be described" (ibid., 220). Truth, then, may be pragmatically (rather than "externally" correspondence-theoretically) characterized, whether we are talking about natural-scientific truth or interpretive, *geisteswissenschaftliche* truth. (I will briefly get back to the notion of pragmatist truth in the humanities in chapter 3 below.)

Even so, Kuhn, as much as Putnam, rejects any naive antirealist use of the metaphors of "construction" or "invention." The world is, in some sense, "experientially given" and "solid" (ibid., 101), not anything we simply make up. Still, he speaks about the "world-constitutive role" of intentionality and mental representations (ibid., 103), thereby returning, with qualifications, to his frequently attacked view that different paradigms constitute "different worlds" and that the world "changes" when a new paradigm is adopted in a scientific revolution (cf. Kuhn 1970, 111; see also ibid., 206).[70] Kuhn replaces "the one big mind-independent world about which scientists were once said to discover the truth" by "the variety of niches within which the practitioners of these various specialities practice their trade" (Kuhn 2000, 120). This conception of practice-bound "niches" suggests a strongly pluralist view of science (ibid., 119, 249), which can also be plausibly applied to understanding the practice-embedded and hence plural ontologies of the humanities—though keeping in mind that Kuhn's own focus was always the history and philosophy of the natural sciences. Putnam (e.g., 1994) repeatedly embraces a similar pluralism, in contrast to versions of physicalism and scientific realism (still) subscribing to the "unity of science" program (albeit in a manner different from that of the logical positivists).

Here, both Putnam and Kuhn equally clearly do subscribe to a kind of pragmatism. There is an irreducible plurality of scientifically acceptable ways of representing reality—of "carving up" the world by means of scientific concepts and theories, or "humanistic" ones, for that matter—and thereby settling problematic situations; these vary according to the environment, the situations, the Kuhnian "niches" we find ourselves in (as inquirers and as human beings), and the pragmatic needs and interests that govern our attempts to deal with such situations. In this sense, no theory is, to borrow James's phrase again, a "literal copy" of reality. *All* our theories are rooted in our needs to cope with the pragmatic, concrete situations we arrive at in the course of our natural lives. Kuhn thus clearly continues a theme central in early pragmatism—and indeed, as George A. Reisch (2019, xxxii, 70, 79, 154–156, 246) importantly reminds us, Kuhn was very much inspired by his reading of James, especially *The Varieties of Religious Experience* (which he apparently read already in 1943), so we can with some plausibility trace at least some of the pluralistic ideas he later developed back to his early Jamesian influences. According to Reisch, Kuhn's *Structure* actually "turns to James to argue that paradigms are necessary for the mind to think scientifically" (ibid., 154), and the "plasticity" of the world that "changes" through a paradigm shift is an eminently Jamesian theme (see ibid., 166–167, 336). This historical fact may be regarded as highly significant for pragmatist philosophy of the humanities, given how central Kuhn is as a modern classic largely responsible for the historicist turn in the philosophy of science. Presumably the most important "Jamesian" idea carried over to Kuhn's famous theory of scientific revolutions was the one of "life-transforming conversions" (ibid., 79) that could easily be compared to the kind of *Gestaltswitch* typical of a paradigm shift.[71]

Now, the plausibility of the above-quoted constructivist-sounding statements by Kuhn (as much as the ones by James himself) crucially depends on their being interpretable from the standpoint of a Kantian construal of pragmatism (or of naturalized pragmatic realism), along the lines already very briefly indicated in the beginning of this chapter.[72] This, more generally, is the leading thought in my attempt to drive through a Kantian pragmatist understanding of the ontology and epistemology of the humanities. We should note here that the Kantian interpretation is actually supported by Kuhn's own remarks. "By now it may be clear that the position I'm developing is a sort of post-Darwinian Kantianism," he tells us. "Like the Kantian categories, the lexicon supplies preconditions of possible experience. But lexical categories, unlike their Kantian forebears, can and do change, both with time and with the passage from one community to another" (Kuhn 2000, 104). The Kuhnian "categories," accordingly, are practice-embedded and may vary, depending on the changes our practices of conceptualization and inquiry undergo. This, if anything, is a pragmatic way of viewing the world as a human construction in the Kantian sense. Both Kuhn's "structured lexicon" and Kant's "apriori" (in an historically relativized sense) are "constitutive of *possible experience* of the world," without dictating what that experience must be (ibid., 245), that is, without telling us *which* experiential objects and events we in fact encounter in the world (or, by extension, which theoretical objects we need to postulate to account for our experience). Thus, in an interview in 1995, shortly before his death, Kuhn perceptively described himself as a Kantian with "movable categories" (ibid., 264).[73] In an analogous way, I have suggested earlier that pragmatism should also be viewed as historicized Kantianism in a strikingly similar sense (cf., e.g., Pihlström 2003a, 2009, 2013, 2020, 2021), and this is also the understanding of pragmatism the present chapter opened with.

What Kuhn rejects in Kant is, unsurprisingly, the *Ding an sich* (see Kuhn 2000, 207; cf. also Conant and Haugeland 2000, 8), although he admits that underlying the processes of change (of lexical categories) there must be "something permanent, fixed, and stable" that is as ineffable as the thing in itself (Kuhn 2000, 104; cf. Andersen 2001, 85). This comes close to Putnam's admission that "perhaps Kant was right" in postulating a noumenal ground of experience, after all (see Putnam 1983, 226)—even though Putnam, no less than Kuhn, was always suspicious of the very intelligibility of the notion of a thing in itself. Indeed, while Kuhn's position is often described as "non-realist" (e.g., by Andersen 2001, 60), Kuhn does seem to maintain that we should somehow be able to combine realism and Kantianism (see Sharrock and Read 2002, 178). As Kant himself was not only a transcendental idealist but also an empirical realist, this should not be an impossible task, especially for the Kantian pragmatist. In any event, Kuhn is engaged in the same task of *mediating* between realism and idealism (constructivism, relativism) that the classical pragmatists from Peirce onward already carried on, following Kant in their own ways.[74]

As Paul Hoyningen-Huene (1993, especially 35ff., 267–271), one of Kuhn's best commentators, lucidly explains, the notion of a world-in-itself does play a significant role in Kuhn's conception of scientific inquiry. Science is concerned with a Kantian-like humanly constituted "phenomenal world," whereas the world-in-itself remains unknowable (cf. also Sharrock and Read 2002, 52ff., 173, 179).[75] Our phenomenal worlds are, however, "reshapings" of the world-in-itself, "substantial" and independent of human subjectivity (Hoyningen-Huene 1993, 268); reality is in this sense resistant to our activities. This is inevitable, given Kuhn's account of anomalies as formative factors of scientific crises and revolutions (ibid., 269–270). If anomalies are to occur at all, the structure of the world cannot be simply up to us. This view might be construed along the lines of the "one world" (two aspects) interpretation of Kant's transcendental idealism (cf. Pihlström 2003a, 2009). Obviously, this is no place to engage in any Kant exegesis, but it can hardly be denied that Kant is the most important background figure of both pragmatism and the realism dispute in the philosophy of science and is inseparable from the kinds of issues Kuhn (as well as Putnam) investigated.

It is not easy to interpret the key Kantian notions, as used by Kuhn, in any strictly nonmetaphorical manner, however. It therefore remains unclear what Kuhn's—or Putnam's—commitment to a noumenal reality in effect amounts to.[76] But his views, as interpreted by Hoyningen-Huene in particular, indicate how difficult it is to avoid employing the traditional Kantian vocabulary, as soon as one admits (as pragmatists tend to do) that the world as we know it is in some sense a human (transcendental) construction or dependent on the constitutive activities of our subjectivity (e.g., our scientific paradigms, practices, or practice-embedded lexicons) instead of being anything objectively ready-made, precategorized, or straightforwardly and unproblematically given in its ontological determinacy. Again, this applies, in principle, to the "humanistic" world(s) as much as to the "scientific" one(s).

Kuhn's attachment to something like a thing in itself has also led to the rather nonstandard charge that he after all seems to maintain, in an a priori manner, an invariant ultimate structure of nature (viz., something like the mind- and lexicon-independent world of the metaphysical realist) and thus precludes any epistemically realist (or, for that matter, idealist) view of the *availability* of that structure, given his historicist conception of science (Margolis 1993, 72–80, especially 74).[77] There may be a correct insight in this argument, but on the other hand it is an open issue whether any even partially Kantian approach to the realism issue can avoid *some* commitment to the *Ding(e) an sich*.[78] Among Kuhn's interpreters, Wes Sharrock and Rupert Read have perceived the central problem most clearly: while Kuhn admits that something (some sort of a "fixed nature" or "the world out there") can be said to retain "a certain constancy" in scientific revolutions, "there is no way of saying *what it is that remains constant* throughout" (Sharrock and Read 2002, 57). That is, there is no paradigm- or lexicon-independent, neutral point of reference to which one could appeal in saying something more specific about the constancy at issue.

The problems underlying the interpretation of phrases like "world changes" can, then, be claimed to be primarily semantic rather than metaphysical; they are problems concerning what we can meaningfully say in our language and what we cannot. However, this does not lead us out of the Kantian predicament but merely transforms the Kantian concern with the *limits of knowledge* (and thus with the unknowability of the *Ding an sich*) into a concern with the *limits of language*, of the sayable—and hence we are brought, through Kuhnian philosophy of science, to a largely Wittgensteinian territory (cf. ibid., 165, 169–170, 200ff.).[79] Semantically speaking, it is also possible to explicate the constitutive role that paradigms and/or lexicons play in making scientific knowledge and its objects possible by saying that it is only against the background provided by a paradigm or a lexicon that scientific statements can receive truth-values or are possible truth-candidates (and falsity-candidates) (cf. Friedman 2001, 74–75). Functioning as such constitutive presuppositions, paradigms are necessary for the empirical *possibilities* postulated in a given scientific field (see ibid., 94, 114), that is, not just presuppositions of the truth of the statements scientists make. They create a "logical space" for such possibilities to be taken seriously in scientific investigations (ibid., 95). Something essentially similar could again be said, in pragmatist terms, about the practices of inquiry.[80] In Kuhn's (2000, 249) own words, it is effability instead of truth that is to be relativized to "worlds" and scientific practices; indeed, a "pluralism of practices" (ibid.), an unambiguously pragmatist—above all Jamesian—notion, seems to capture Kuhn's ideas rather nicely here.

Using phrases like this, the Kuhnian pragmatic realist is, obviously, embedded in deeply Kantian commitments. However, as soon as we are prepared to relativize the Kantian conditions for the possibility of experience or cognition, we can, according to Friedman (2001, 2002, 2003), see Kuhn as vindicating crucial parts of Carnapian logical empiricism, too, precisely because of his profoundly Kantian approach, which he shares with Carnap and other logical empiricists. This relativization of Kant's transcendental conditions or principles is, in fact, a common theme in the early history of twentieth-century philosophy of science: in addition to Carnap and Hans Reichenbach,[81] a relativized notion of the a priori was defended by C. I. Lewis (1923), among others. Through Lewis, we can, again, somewhat more explicitly build a bridge to the pragmatist tradition, whose encounters with logical empiricism in mid-century America are thus not restricted to Quine's reaction to Carnap (cf. again Pihlström 2017c, 2018). These connections have, unfortunately, remained somewhat neglected by most of Kuhn's commentators, including Friedman, although his defense of the relativized a priori is readily applicable, mutatis mutandis, in pragmatism, too.[82]

This chapter is not, however, the right place to examine in any more detail to what extent pragmatism can accommodate insights drawn from Kantian transcendental philosophy and transcendental idealism or how a pragmatically established form of (scientific) empirical realism can be reconciled with transcendental idealism (see further Pihlström 2003a, 2009, 2021). The topic is crucial, nevertheless, because it has become clear that

Kuhn and Putnam can both be interpreted as leading neopragmatists in the philosophy of science and in the general realism discussion, and both, not despite but rather because of their pragmatism, developed robustly neo-Kantian views on the practice-laden (transcendental) constitution of empirical reality. This constitution, for both Kuhn and Putnam, is a value-laden activity, and therefore there is no principled metaphysical dichotomy between fact and value even in the natural sciences, let alone the humanities.

Neopragmatism, then, can be seen as a via media between realism and constructivism, analogously to classical pragmatism's mediating role between realism and instrumentalism. I will return to "transcendental pragmatism" in chapter 3—though only in the context of pragmatist philosophy of the humanities, not in the much broader context of assimilating Kantian transcendental idealism with pragmatism.

Pragmatic Naturalism and the Practices of Inquiry

Kuhn's true novelty in the philosophy of science has been claimed to lie in his emphasis on science as a practice and his rejection of the traditional epistemological questions of justifying scientific beliefs (see Rouse 2003). The interpretation of Kuhn as a pragmatized Kantian thinker (or even a transcendental idealist), as developed above, is compatible with this suggestion, provided that (i) the view of "science as a practice" amounts to a form of pragmatism and (ii) pragmatism itself can receive a Kantian reinterpretation (as I have emphasized and will continue to emphasize throughout this book).[83] Joseph Rouse's reading of Kuhn is helpful, however, in spelling out clearly what a truly pragmatist reading should *not* look like: after correctly noting that Kuhn leads us toward a description of science as an activity (rather than as the completed product of an activity), Rouse says that paradigms should be understood as "exemplary ways of conceptualizing and intervening in particular situations" instead of being understood "as beliefs (even tacit beliefs) agreed upon by community members" (ibid., 107). Now, a pragmatist, as pointed out earlier, should construe beliefs themselves as (literally) habits of action, as famously done by Peirce and the other classical pragmatists;[84] it is precisely in virtue of being ways of conceptualizing and intervening that paradigms are also, *eo ipso*, beliefs, or perhaps rather networks or Quinean "webs" of beliefs. It is in our activities and practices themselves that our ontological construals of the nature of the world are to be found—and once again, this holds as much for the humanities as it does for the natural sciences. Thus, Rouse's dichotomies between "practitioners" and "believers" (ibid., 109) and between beliefs and forms of life (ibid., 112) are far too *un*pragmatist to be helpful in what might be labeled a "transcendentally pragmatist" rereading of Kuhn as a philosopher of scientific practice.

Rouse, however, comes closer to a transcendental interpretation when proposing that Kuhn should be seen as a critic of scientific realism, as someone who denies that science aims at correct representations of a concept- and practice-independent world (ibid., 117), and especially when pointing out that "the realist can posit a world 'beyond' language and culture only by mistakenly thinking that we can have a definite language and culture distinct from how we engage the world" (ibid.). What he misses is only that a form of scientific realism (just like Kantian empirical realism) can be maintained within the overall position of transcendental pragmatism.[85] Of course, it is perfectly legitimate to offer a nonpragmatist account of Kuhn as a "philosopher of scientific practice"; it just needs to be acknowledged that a pragmatist way of putting the matter is also available and might strengthen Rouse's point by linking it with the transcendental concerns raised by Friedman and others. Certainly we should *not* simply read Kuhn as an opponent of scientific realism, especially if the issue is the existence of unobservable theoretical entities. In Kuhn just as in Dewey, we find resources for a much more sophisticated pragmatism that refuses to be reduced to the simple oppositions between realism, on the one side, and its antirealist alternatives like instrumentalism, idealism, or relativism, on the other.[86]

If, as I suggest, we approach Kuhn as a pragmatist (or pragmatic realist), should we also acknowledge Feyerabend (1993 [1975])—the anarchist and archrelativist—as a pragmatist, in some sense? Probably we should, inasmuch as we also acknowledge, say, Rorty's entitlement to the word *pragmatism*. Feyerabend avoids committing himself to the pragmatist (or any other) tradition, but he does speak about "pragmatic philosophy" when referring to people or groups "participating in the interaction of traditions"; such pragmatic philosophy is required for the "open exchange" between people and traditions that is, in turn, needed to transcend simple relativism (cf. ibid., 217–218, 226–228). Accordingly, Feyerabend's pluralism, antiessentialism, and antifoundationalism are also clearly put forward in the spirit of pragmatism, especially Jamesian pragmatism.

Here our survey, arriving closer to our own day through Kuhn, must end up with recognizing a plurality of quite different neopragmatist philosophies of science and inquiry. It will suffice to mention a couple of examples in order to give an impression of the richness and variety in the field. A very important pragmatically oriented philosopher of science—very different from Kuhn and Feyerabend—is Ian Hacking, whose emphasis on experimentation, "intervening" instead of representation, has partly set the tone for later empirically informed work in science and technology studies (Hacking 1983). While Hacking agrees with Dewey's (1960 [1929]) rejection of the spectator theory of knowledge (Hacking 1983, 130), the chapter he devotes to pragmatism (ibid., chapter 4) is located in the context of his treatment of the philosophies of science oriented to representing rather than intervening.[87] Although his "historical ontology" (Hacking 2002) is not formulated in explicitly pragmatist terms, it might—as briefly speculated in chapter 1 above—also receive a pragmatist reinterpretation, given Hacking's somewhat Deweyan (though more obviously Foucauldian) historicism about practices and discourses. Indeed, in a manner not unlike Dewey's pragmatic naturalism, Hacking's historical ontology "is concerned with objects or their effects which do not exist in any recognizable form until they are objects of scientific study" (ibid., 11).

Furthermore, other late twentieth-century philosophers of science in some ways close to pragmatism include, for example, Mary Hesse, who also wishes to steer a middle course between realism and relativism;[88] Larry Laudan, a leading critic of "convergent realism" (see Laudan 1981) who has come to favor a version of pragmatism in the "four-cornered debate" among pragmatists, realists, relativists, and positivists (see Laudan 1990); and Nicholas Jardine, whose theory of the "scenes of inquiry" is characterized as a "pragmatist" one, and is even compared to James's pragmatist theory of truth, by Jardine himself (see Jardine 2000 [1991], 232–233).[89] Laudan's "pragmatist" joins Kuhn in, for instance, rejecting the (naively) realist view of scientific progress as cumulative (Laudan 1990, 17) and in characterizing science as a problem-solving activity (ibid., 28), with the pragmatist qualification that we should be primarily interested in "whether a theory will be a reliable guide to the future" (ibid.). Moreover, Laudan's pragmatist joins Quinean naturalists in asserting that "philosophy can, and should, make use of any of the forms of reasoning appropriate to scientific research" (ibid., 99), and in urging that explaining the empirical success of science requires paying attention to our interaction with nature (ibid., 165–166). In a Deweyan experimentalist fashion, the rules for theory-choice should be accepted or rejected on a "trial and error" basis:

> There is a fact of the matter which our rules reflect, namely, that inquiry in this particular world works better using these rules [viz., the ones that have produced successful theories about the natural world] than it does using a host of rival rules which humanity has devised for getting a valuable knowledge. [. . .]
>
> The justification for our theories about the world and for our methods (which, for me, are simply theories about inquiry) are precisely the same: our theories are worthy of acceptance precisely because they work; our rules are worthy of acceptance because they have shown themselves able consistently to pick out theories which work with a pretty high degree of reliability. It's all a matter of finding the right tools for the job. (Ibid., 103, 105–106)

Thus, as Laudan already argued in his 1984 book, theories, methodological rules, and the values or aims of science ought to be brought into harmony with one another. None of these is more fundamental than the others. As far as I can see, a moderate realism—even about truth, pragmatically understood—is compatible with this view, as clearly as it is with Dewey's or Kuhn's conceptions of inquiry. Again, the pragmatic realism we have arrived at here can be smoothly extended to the philosophy of the humanities. For example, in White's (2002) terms, this could be seen as a version of holistic pragmatism: we have to continuously assess the harmonious equilibrium of theories, methods, and values as a totality, and there is no reason to restrict this idea to the philosophy of science narrowly conceived, as the same kind of holistic harmony is applicable to the theory-construction of the humanities, too.[90]

For Kuhn (and Putnam), as we have seen, the world as investigated by science is an elaborate human construction, not absolutely independent of paradigms, theories, descriptions, conceptualizations, or (scientific) practices and traditions. In this sense, but only in this sense, we "construct" the world. This neopragmatist and neo-Kantian view—which bears close resemblance to the idea of the human constitution of empirical reality, or phenomena, that Kant himself defended—is easily visible in what the classics of pragmatism, especially Dewey, had to say about scientific objects (cf. above). Neopragmatism in the philosophy of science too often overlooks these important philosophical predecessors. For example, Dewey remarked that thinking—or, more specifically, inquiry—does not set out with the object of knowledge already in place but ends up with it: the object is "an achieved triumph," "something which the processes of inquiry and testing, that constitute thinking, themselves produce," something essentially practical, as "it depends upon a specific kind of practice for its existence—for its existence as an object of knowledge" (Dewey 1916, 334).[91] Furthermore, while the classifications of things we construct for our pragmatic purposes can in some sense be objectively evaluated, "a classification is not a bare transcript or duplicate of some finished and done-for arrangement pre-existing in nature," but instead "a repertory of weapons for attack upon the future and the unknown," classifying things so as to promote "successful action for ends" (Dewey 1957 [1948], 153–154). Clearly, there is no reason not to extend this account to "humanistic objects," which can—presumably even more obviously than scientific objects—be taken to ontologically depend on our practices of conceptualization and inquiry.

Similar formulations that today remind us of Kuhn's or Laudan's pragmatism can be found in James (1975 [1907], especially Lecture VII), who repeatedly affirmed that the world is not ready-made but still "in the making," constantly made and remade by us, by inquiring human beings purposefully acting in the world. However, while Dewey's pragmatist articulation of the way in which scientific objects are constructed in and through inquiry, or emerge out of inquiry, can be usefully compared with later accounts—especially within science and technology studies—about the "constructed" nature of scientific objects and facts, James was not as much interested in the *scientific* construction of reality. He focused, rather, on human beings' individual constructions of meaningful objects, situations, and experiences through their moral and religious lives. Therefore, while he wrote relatively little explicitly on the humanities, his pragmatism may in the end be more relevant to a (transcendental) pragmatist philosophy of the humanities than the more naturalized and science-oriented currents in pragmatist philosophy of inquiry.

Insofar as a pragmatic realism is a possible outcome in Kuhn's case, it should be possible also in Dewey's (and the other classical pragmatists'). But I believe we just cannot get rid of the tension we have analyzed. Recalling Quine's pragmatist tension—that is, the fact that his "robust realism" is clearly a realistic account of mind-independent nature, yet his philosophy of science has often been criticized as antirealist, both in the sense of relativism and in the sense of instrumentalism—we ought to take seriously the claim (by Rouse 2002, 133) that even Quine is guilty of "first-philosophical" assumptions, offering "an alternative candidate for first philosophy: an implicit metaphysics of nature as the already determined object of what natural science *can* be about, and the already unified subject of knowledge in the physical bodies of individual human organisms." While I was a moment ago somewhat critical of Rouse's reading of Kuhn, I fully approve of his criticism of Quine. The pragmatist (the true naturalist) should not engage in the kind of postulation of prior metaphysical conditions that Quine seems to engage in but should let the practices of inquiry through which we encounter the world we live in themselves determine the proper conditions and postulations that are needed for those encounters to make sense.[92]

Recent Deweyan philosophy of science, as developed by John Shook (2002, 2003b) agrees in interesting ways with such pragmatic naturalism. Shook's position is a relatively rare example of an explicit use of classical pragmatism for the purposes of a novel philosophy of science seeking to avoid the obscurities of the realism issue (see also Shook 2022). Where Shook differs from pragmatic realists like Putnam, or more constructivist thinkers like Kuhn, is in his requirement that pragmatist philosophy of science must, above all, be *empiricist*: the object of scientific knowledge must be experienceable in some way, though not necessarily directly. However, Shook's Deweyan pragmatism is also *naturalistic*, claiming that scientific knowledge is directed toward natural objects. Furthermore, his pragmatism is, as he says, *productionist*, viewing those objects as "technologically created." Yet, they are *real* objects; hence, pragmatism is, for him, a form of scientific realism (Shook 2003b, 331). What such a pragmatic realism denies is, first, "transcendent realism,"[93] according to which scientific knowledge aims to describe an experience-transcendent reality; secondly, "scientific idealism," which does not view scientific knowledge as a relation to naturally existing objects; and thirdly, "objectivism," which claims science to be aiming at an understanding of reality in the absence of human intervention (ibid., 332). In these respects, Shook's Deweyan realism is very different from, say, Leplin's (1997) or Niiniluoto's (1999) forms of scientific realism,[94] although Shook is obviously right to insist that his realism is more realistic than positivist instrumentalism or van Fraassen's (1980) constructive empiricism, which too restrictively limit experimental evidence to directly observable infallible data (Shook 2003b, 342). As Shook summarizes his view,

> Pragmatism offers an empirically naturalistic and moderately realistic philosophy of science. Pragmatism's expansive concept

of interactive evidence harmoniously complements a naturalism wary of the transcendent. Philosophy of science should embrace pragmatism's view that the proper object of scientific knowledge is the technologically created natural object in human experience. Pragmatism offers the most realistic interpretation of the growth of scientific knowledge that is consistent with both actual scientific practice and experimentally confirmed results. (Ibid., 343)

The emphasis on technological creation or production should bring pragmatism into a natural dialogue with recent science and technology studies (see, e.g., Sismondo 2004), in which such a "productionist" attitude is often present, though again without explicit pragmatist influences—and without detailed attention directed to the realism issue. Thus, "Deweyan" philosophy of science can be expected to have a bright future in the growing interdisciplinary work on science as embedded in its social and technological surroundings.

What slightly worries me, however, is not so much Shook's demand that scientific objects be (indirectly) observable but his failure to emphasize a point that Rouse (2002) discusses at considerable length, namely, the *normativity* of scientific practices. By being (of course rightly) wary of the *transcendent*, Shook's Deweyan pragmatic realism may end up rejecting the legitimate *transcendental* concern about the practice-embedded conditions for the possibility of science (of scientific knowledge and experience) that Kuhn investigates. The "production" of scientific objects, as Shook calls it, would be better interpreted as transcendental constitution. As such, it would not actually amount to a constitution of objects, or facts, at the first-order level but to a constitution of the very possibility of scientific objects (or, by extension, objects of humanistic inquiry, which can be considered "technologically" created only in an extremely broad and inclusive sense of "technology").[95] The pragmatist tradition, when carried forward in general philosophy of science and inquiry, as well as in the philosophy of the humanities, should definitely not overlook or hide such transcendental concerns (cf. Pihlström and Siitonen 2005; Pihlström 2012b), and this is one of the reasons why I have found both Kuhn's and Putnam's neo-Kantian forms of pragmatism promising, though not unproblematic.[96] This does not mean that all forms of pragmatist philosophy of science and inquiry must be reduced to transcendental pragmatism; of course there are also nontranscendental ways of developing pragmatism and pragmatic realism. But I hope to be able to provide, in chapters 3 and 4, some further reasons for the transcendental account of pragmatism loosely sketched here that I find indispensable for the pragmatist philosophy of the humanities.

Pragmatism, Realism, and Naturalism (Again)

It remains a further task for pragmatist philosophers of science and inquiry to investigate what nonreductively naturalist views (e.g., Rouse's) of scientific practices and the "normativity of nature" might ultimately come down to in explicitly or implicitly pragmatist terms and how this kind of naturally emerging and evolving normativity of human inquiries could be invoked to constrain the "production" of scientific objects Shook regards as essential to a pragmatist account of science. Furthermore, it is still an open issue exactly in what sense a form of scientific realism can be based on these ideas. The only thing that is clear is that pragmatism, as such, is no enemy of (moderate) scientific realism at all. Again we see that pragmatism, as developed in the heterogeneous directions we have surveyed, can avoid simplified commitments to the traditional dichotomies between realism and instrumentalism or realism and idealism.

It is through the kind of complex developments I have highly selectively reviewed in this chapter that we ought to, again and again, take a fresh look at the pragmatist classics—especially James and Dewey—in order to evaluate their role as the (largely implicit) background figures of today's "pragmatist philosophy of science," and, mutatis mutandis, of the humanities. It is only by so doing that we can defend the key claims of this chapter—namely, that pragmatism need not amount either to an empiricist instrumentalism (opposed to realism about unobservables) or to radical relativism and constructivism (opposed to realism about objectivity)—and apply those claims to our development of a pragmatist philosophy of the humanities. It was Kuhn in particular, I wish to suggest, who smuggled pragmatist ideas into the mainstream discussions in the philosophy of science, making possible a (Deweyan) historicist pragmatic naturalism, a view in the end much more pragmatist than Quine's. Possibly partly as a result of Kuhn's influence, several thinkers, both realistically and relativistically inclined, emphasize the central role played by scientific practices in the construction of scientific knowledge (and, with a constructivist twist, even its objects) and thereby carry this task forward, usually without explicitly linking their views with the pragmatist tradition, though.[97] Others, like Laudan and Shook, offer more explicitly pragmatist views, though in Laudan's case the possibility of defending a pragmatic *realism* may in the end be sacrificed (cf. Niiniluoto 1999)—depending on how exactly his central concept of "problem-solving" is interpreted.

The fact that the tradition of pragmatism suffered a period of decline, roughly between the 1930s and the 1960s, as logical empiricism arrived and was established in the United States, being soon overshadowed by both scientific realism and Kuhnian constructivism, might be explained not only by reasons internal to philosophy but also by external, social ones: perhaps the fact that pragmatism, Dewey's in particular, was a form of "social philosophy" made it suspicious in the strongly anticommunist post–World War II America (cf. Giere 1996, 346–348).[98] The new rise of pragmatism since the 1970s might, conversely, be explained by the fact that the academic community has become increasingly dissatisfied with the applications of exact scientific modes of thought and strict, narrowly conceived principles of rationality in human life at large. Pragmatists have traditionally argued that we can never have enough rational, critical discussion (within and outside science) concerning not only the means by which to pursue our ends but also those ends themselves, and this seems to be precisely what is urgently needed in our current situation, including our academic contexts of developing the humanities. The developments within (both pragmatist and nonpragmatist) philosophy of science have themselves brought us to a situation where the need for a philosophy of the humanities is more pressing than ever.

The pragmatist tradition in the philosophy of science and inquiry, I conclude, provides an example of the complexities involved in any attempt to write the history of this discipline, a case in which several issues are intertwined. These include the issues of (i) realism versus antirealism (that is, in their various forms, instrumentalism, relativism, constructivism, idealism, etc.); (ii) logical versus sociohistorical and practice-oriented approaches to science in general and to theory-choice and scientific change in particular (as manifested, for instance, in the opposition between traditional scientific realists and their Kuhnian opponents); and (iii) "hard" versus "soft" naturalism (as epitomized in the conflicting accounts of naturalism we find in Quine and more relaxed naturalists, e.g., Rouse). A reconsideration of pragmatism as an identifiable, albeit somewhat indeterminate and inevitably open, tradition in the philosophy of science may thus deepen our understanding of the historical transformations of these—and many other—issues, only (i) among which has been discussed in some detail here. There is no reason why the historian of the philosophy of science (and, by extension, of the humanities) should treat this (or any) tradition as fixed and closed once and for all; keeping the tradition open for constant reevaluation and redescription is itself a most pragmatic attitude.[99]

So how to write the history of pragmatist philosophy of science and inquiry? It is easier to say, on the basis of the somewhat scattered reflections of this chapter, how it should *not* be written. It should not be assumed that pragmatism is, on the whole or inevitably, committed to some particular standard view, such as instrumentalism—or realism, for that matter. The pragmatists' problems and tensions surrounding the realism issue, beginning with Peirce, are much more complicated; none of the pragmatists, classical or modern, can be said to have simply defined their positions in terms of traditional oppositions, such as realism versus antirealism. But precisely for this reason, tensions do remain, and it should not be assumed that pragmatism can avoid tackling the disputes between realism and its alternatives, or the various metaphysical and epistemological problems connected with these disputes.[100] These classical issues are, then, well and alive in pragmatism, despite some pragmatists' (e.g., Rorty 1991, 1998, 2004; Fine 1996 [1986], 2004) claims to have overcome the entire realism debate.

If anything, I hope the present chapter has contributed to our need to see, *pace* Rorty and Fine, the realism issue as a genuinely pragmatic, and even pragmatist, one. Pragmatist philosophy of science can, therefore, be regarded as a middle ground position in several ways, also metaphilosophically: it aims at synthesizing the healthy naturalist (Quine-inspired) rejection of all foundationalist forms of "first philosophy" with an equally healthy and humble respect for the depth of philosophical issues, such as realism, that we cannot simply brush aside, if we wish to understand our practices of inquiry—scientific or humanistic. The task of the next chapter is to say something more specific about the realism issue—and the pragmatist or pragmatically realist approach to it—in the philosophy of the humanities.

Chapter 3

Developing Pragmatist Philosophy of Literary Theory, Historiography, and Religious Studies

Having described the main philosophical approach of this book as well as the general history of pragmatist philosophy of science and inquiry in broad strokes in the first two chapters, I will in this chapter and the next one move on to more specific treatments of selected research topics that a pragmatist philosopher of the humanities needs to explore. I will take up a number of (related) issues only briefly, pointing toward further work that will have to be done, should anyone start more systematically developing a pragmatist philosophy of the humanities. Most importantly, I will suggest that we ought to apply the basic issues and tensions of pragmatist philosophy of science identified in chapter 2 to more detailed questions concerning the ontology of the humanities. In particular, the transcendental nature of the constitution of the objects of inquiry in and through practices of inquiry—with the concepts of "transcendental" and "constitution" understood in their originally Kantian meaning with a key pragmatist twist, namely, the practice-embeddedness of any such constitutional activities—is an extremely important idea to be carried over from general philosophy of science to the philosophy of the humanities. This notion of constitution will crucially shape the kind of pragmatic realism available to us in this area.

This form of transcendental pragmatism, discussed in the previous chapter on the basis of the neopragmatist views of philosophers of science like Kuhn and Putnam, in particular, emphasizes that the value-embedded constitution of objects through inquiry is not a causal process of "producing" those objects (some pragmatists' more straightforwardly constructivist or "productionist" ways of speaking notwithstanding) nor any empirical or factual process at all. Instead, it is a process of making certain ontological postulations *possible* within our practices of inquiry, and this takes place at a transcendental level. On the other hand, that transcendental level itself must be understood as emerging from our entirely natural practices of inquiry in the natural world we live in.[1] Therefore, we will also have to further examine the relation between naturalistic and transcendental approaches (in relation to pragmatism but also more generally) in chapter 4 below.

Selected Pragmatist Themes in the Philosophy of the Humanities

Let me begin this chapter by identifying a few highly general themes that I find ineliminably present in pragmatist philosophy of the humanities, particularly insofar as they need to be addressed in any serious and comprehensive consideration of pragmatism and realism. I will comment on each of them only briefly here and will later explain how they are related to my case studies and the more specific research hypotheses that may be ventured.

First, *realism, truth, and "post-truth"* constitute a set of interrelated concepts and issues that pragmatists need to consider very carefully—both in general epistemology or theory of inquiry and the philosophy of the humanities. As explained in chapters 1 and 2 in some detail, the problem of realism (as contrasted with various forms of antirealism, relativism, constructivism, or idealism) runs through the tradition of pragmatism, from its earliest pronouncements to latest neopragmatisms. The concept of truth is obviously highly central in any examination of pragmatism and realism—all the way from Peirce's account of truth as the ideal limit (the "final opinion") of scientific inquiry via James's notorious "pragmatist conception of truth" to Putnam's internal realism and its epistemic concept of truth as idealized epistemic justifiability, as well as, eventually, Rorty's radical neopragmatism dropping the notion of truth as relatively uninteresting. The current "post-truth" era (epitomized by extreme populist political developments) might be critically regarded as a result of cultural and philosophical developments such as postmodern relativist philosophers' and also possibly some radical pragmatists' repudiation of the realistic correspondence theory of truth.[2]

In this context, one question that needs to be further discussed, in particular, is *to what extent, and in what sense exactly, we may say that theories and hypotheses formulated in the humanities are true or false*. We already saw that pragmatism need not be opposed to scientific realism in the sense of embracing any instrumentalist (radically empiricist) views according to which scientific theories lack truth-values (but are, rather, mere calculatory devices of prediction and systematization of observations, as it were). But is this the case regarding theories and hypotheses in the humanities as well? That is, to what extent is humanistic scholarly discourse "*truth-apt*"? Are there relevant differences among the different fields of the humanities in this respect? For example, is historiography in some sense "more truth-apt" than literary criticism, and if so, why? If there is such a difference, could it be explained by the fact that literary criticism is even more deeply dependent on subjective interpretive perspectives (for instance) than historical inquiry that can, with some objectivity, be anchored in documents of the past serving evidential functions? Does the pragmatist articulation of truth tackle these questions better than, say, the traditional correspondence theory of truth? My initial proposal is that it does, but this needs to be critically investigated.

In particular, the pragmatist philosopher of the humanities may argue that there is no need whatsoever to resort to any analogy of instrumentalism. Just as the pragmatist does not have to follow instrumentalism in denying truth-values to scientific theories, the pragmatist philosopher of the humanities need not, and should not, reduce the contents of humanistic theories to their merely "instrumental" role in helping us cope with the world we live in (including its history). Just like the sciences aim at delivering (humanly speaking) objective knowledge about the deep structures of reality, insofar as those structures are available to us through our normatively guided practices of inquiry, the humanities may be seen as engaging in the business of providing knowledge and understanding about the deep structures of humanly constructed cultural reality—instead of, say, merely ideologically biased interpretations or perspectives. The mere fact that the humanities deal with a human-made world by no means motivates an antirealist or instrumentalist assessment of the truth-aptness of the discourses through which we encounter that world.

What is needed, however, for this realistic account of the truth-aptness of humanistic discourse to work is something like the pragmatist conception of truth. Our very notion of truth in the humanities needs to be articulated in such a manner that truth is by definition a *value* we aim at in our practices. This is basically what William James (1975 [1907], especially Lecture VI) proposes when telling us that truth is a species of the good (see also Pihlström 2021, especially chapters 1–2). This does not mean that truth would not be a relation of "agreement" or "correspondence" with the ways things are, as realist correspondence theoreticians would prefer to put it. Rather, the pragmatist conceptualization of truth as a valuational concept inextricably tied to our purposive inquiries emphasizes a certain way of understanding this agreement between our beliefs or theories and the elements of the world they are about.[3]

The ontological question concerning the reality of the objects of humanistic inquiry needs to be examined in close relation to the realism issue in its diversity—again not only in the context of the realism versus instrumentalism opposition and the truth-aptness question but also in the context of the distinction between realism and constructivism and the related account of the transcendental constitution of objects of inquiry (cf. chapter 2). While the natural sciences study (according to scientific realists) objects, processes, and laws existing and obtaining in the natural world itself, independently of the human mind and of our scientific concepts and theories, and while the social sciences seek to explain and understand humanly created social reality, such as social structures and institutions, it may be suggested that the humanities primarily examine humanly created *meaningful* objects (e.g., texts and historical documents) as well as their historically contextual meanings and representational relations to whatever they may be taken to be "about." However, scholarship in the humanities also in a sense focuses on other portions of reality beyond such texts, namely, things and events that those documents themselves may refer to, such as historical events that "really" took place. Thus, for example, a war historian may examine archival documents and by using them ask (and answer) questions about the historical events those documents may be taken to represent. Accordingly, the "object" of research is not simply the document, nor simply the event the document may be thought to (accurately or nonaccurately) represent, but this representational relation itself, as well as, critically, its purported accuracy. The question concerning what the humanities are actually "about" is therefore much more complex than it might prima facie seem. Humanistic inquiry may be "about" historical and meaningful objects and events, but it may also be "about" (the meanings of) documents that purportedly themselves refer to such objects and events, and about those referential links. To provide another example, literary criticism may focus on the way a historical novel refers to both historical reality and fictional characters, which makes the ontological status of the objects of interpretation rather complex.[4]

The question about the objects of humanistic inquiry is, as we have seen, intrinsically related to the question about realism and truth: in what sense exactly are these objects—including literary meanings, events and actions in our human past, or religious doctrines manifested in a certain institutionalized practice—"real" as objects of study and thus even potentially available for true or false scholarly or theoretical representation?[5] As noted above, it may also be asked whether there are "theoretical entities" in the humanities comparable to the theoretical entities postulated in natural-scientific theories (e.g., electrons and genes), that is, unobservable entities whose existence explains observable phenomena that would otherwise be very difficult or impossible to explain.[6] My general proposal is that pragmatists about humanities should take a basically realistic attitude to the ontological postulations of humanistic theorization, in the same spirit of pragmatic realism in which they would approach the realism issue in general philosophy of science—without, however, claiming such theoretical entities to exist in any "ready-made" world that would be "there" independently of the scholarly perspectives motivating those theoretical postulations. Both the postulation of theoretical entities and the conception of truth involved in the realistic account of such postulatory theoretical discourses as "truth-apt" must be subordinated to pragmatism.

Rationality in humanistic scholarship may not be the most central theme in a pragmatist philosophy of the humanities that focuses (as I am doing) mainly on ontological and epistemological issues, but this topic certainly needs to be invoked whenever investigating the epistemology of the humanities, as any theoretical postulations within the humanities should obviously be considered from the point of view of their rational justifiability. While the natural sciences with their sophisticated methodologies might seem to be the paradigm of universal human use of reason, the question concerning rationality arises in the humanities in a more historically and culturally relative and contextualized manner. There may be "local," perspectival, and context-specific traditions of humanistic scholarship in a sense in which it would be inappropriate to speak about local traditions of scientific research. Philosophers thus need to ask whether there is an ineliminable degree of *relativism* in our understanding of the use of reason in the humanities or whether it is rationally possible to arrive at (relatively) objective truths about the dimensions of reality studied by the humanities. Is rationality always necessarily embedded in culturally local social practices, or are there transculturally and transhistorically valid criteria of rationality (not only in the natural sciences but also in the humanities)?[7] This large question cannot be resolved here, of course. But it is in one way or another present in almost everything a pragmatist philosophy of the humanities will engage in, and it is clearly related to the realism issue in its various aspects, too. For the pragmatic realist hoping to avoid the pitfalls of radical relativism and to defend a broadly realistic view on humanistic truth, the challenge remains that all truth claims and all ontological postulations may seem to take place only within local practices with their own, mutually incommensurable criteria of rationality.[8]

Furthermore, as related to the issues concerning rationality and relativism, the distinction between *explanation and understanding (Erklären* vs. *Verstehen)* names a traditional controversy in the philosophy and methodology of the human sciences.[9] It is a cliché to suggest that the natural sciences seek to objectively (and typically causally) *explain* natural events with reference to universally obtaining laws of nature, while the humanities, such as historical and literary studies, aim at *understanding* unique meaning-carrying objects and phenomena, such as texts and other documents, or individual and social actions, and their cultural and historical significance. This opposition is presumably in many ways outdated. Yet we do need to analyze, again from a pragmatist perspective, why this is the case and how the tasks of explanation and understanding might still be weighed differently in different frameworks of humanistic inquiry, especially in relation to the ontological presuppositions concerning the relevant objects of inquiry. For example, some scholars in religious studies (e.g., within the "cognitive paradigm" utilizing the findings of cognitive science and evolutionary psychology for explanatory accounts of religious representations) may argue that religious studies can be properly scientific only by adopting the "external" perspective of, say, evolutionary explanations of the emergence and spreading of cognitive representations of supernatural agents.[10] Others (e.g., more "hermeneutically" oriented scholars)[11] might argue, in contrast, that in order to explain any phenomenon—say, a cultural practice—as religious at all we first need to adopt an "internal" perspective of understanding that practice from its practitioners' standpoint; the concept of a "religious representation" of supernatural agents might itself be problematic from such an internal point of view at the basic ontological level. The issue, then, is not merely methodological but heavily ontological.

A pragmatist philosophy of the humanities should be able to offer tools for a critical overcoming of this opposition, integrating the plausible ideas from both extremes. In this way, pragmatism may here crucially facilitate dialogues between apparently conflicting scholarly approaches, analogously to the way it bridges opposite extremes in the realism discussion. Again, this is something that cannot be done in a single book, but as already emphasized, I am merely sketching a program of pragmatist philosophy of the humanities rather than any final product.

Further questions concerning *the value-ladenness of objects of research— and the value of the humanities themselves*—come up when the valuational ontology of humanistic inquiry is characterized along pragmatist lines. Pragmatism might be prima facie regarded as an "instrumentalist"[12] philosophy focusing exclusively on the practical utility of (say) the humanities (as well as, of course, the sciences) instead of their inherent worth that would be independent of any considerations of useful applications. One of the aims of my discussion is to demonstrate the utter falsity of such a naïve conception of pragmatism. On the contrary, a pragmatist philosophy of the humanities should be able to account for the very special and distinctive value of the humanities based on the human interests, aims, and goals they (and they only) are able to pursue. This value is not reducible to, for example, the benefits in social welfare that people's appreciation of literature or their engaging in religious practices might bring about (or, perhaps more plausibly, the social value created by our more profound understanding of the mechanisms of such welfare-producing habits and processes of appreciation and engagement), nor to the cultural and political stability that a sound appreciation of the facts of history (including the darkest hours when those facts were created) may bring to societies—even though these are all clearly valuable outcomes. Whatever value there is in humanistic scholarship, it must at the deepest level be understood as value based on what is truly characteristic of such scholarship qua humanistic.[13]

A fundamental idea to be explored by the pragmatist philosopher of the humanities, as indicated above, is the value-embeddedness of the very ontology of the humanities, and understanding this ontological (or, perhaps rather, metaontological)[14] feature of humanistic inquiry is necessary for understanding the value of the humanities in a broader sense. This ontological focus on value is also crucial for recognizing what is distinctive in the pragmatist conception of truth as (in James's memorable phrase) a "species of good" (see above). At the same time, the nature of values themselves may be a topic for pragmatist investigation. It may be suggested that values are elements of the cultural reality that humanities (as well as social sciences) are in the business of studying. All the fields of the humanities examined in this book are in their distinctive ways concerned with the nature of values and human value commitments in their own specific areas. Values, in short, are humanly natural social and cultural constructions, but they also play a transcendental role in *enabling* any ontological postulations and truth claims we are capable of making in the context of our practices of inquiry. In principle, this value-embeddedness also concerns the ontologies of natural-scientific inquiries, and in this sense there is no fundamental philosophical dualism between the two types of inquiry. Even so, our focus here is, of course, on humanistic inquiry as a *value-laden yet realistic* process aiming at *truths* about our human condition.

Three (Plus One) Case Study Areas

My general hypothesis is, unsurprisingly, that all the philosophical problem areas briefly described above (which should also be seen as mutually entangled and by no means as exhaustive) can be crucially enlightened by adopting a pragmatist approach, especially a Kantian pragmatism embracing a form of pragmatic realism within a transcendental framework.

As explained in the introduction, the philosophy of the humanities has up to now been only relatively marginally recognized as a field of research in its own right. It arguably needs to be more widely acknowledged as comparable to, say, the philosophy of social science. Therefore, I am in this chapter trying to identify the kinds of questions that the (pragmatist) philosopher of the humanities needs to ask in some of the central subfields of the philosophy of the humanities. As also explained above, a comprehensive pragmatist philosophy of the humanities would fill another major gap, too: while pragmatism has been extensively studied and creatively developed since its initiation in the late nineteenth century and ever more actively since its reemergence in the 1970–80s in general philosophy of science and theory of inquiry, as well as in the philosophy of social science, both by historians of philosophy and systematic philosophers, relatively little has been done to explicitly develop a pragmatist philosophy of the humanities (to the extent that this very phrase has, as far as I know, not been used previously, at least not in any systematic way). Through the kinds of questions asked above and the hypotheses to be formulated in what follows, I am hoping to establish pragmatist philosophy of the humanities as nothing less than an acknowledged research program and a philosophical approach in its own right. I am thus sketching a philosophical project that would fill two rather wide lacunae in existing scholarship, while of course appropriately recognizing the massive scholarly work that has been done in specific contexts, such as (pragmatist) philosophy of historiography.

I am, thus, now somewhat programmatically proposing that we may establish a general pragmatist philosophy of the humanities by approaching this theme via relevant case studies with their own specific questions, representing some of the central traditional fields of scholarship in the humanities, all of which may be fruitfully investigated in a pragmatist context. Note that the general research themes just listed above run through all the following case study areas. My three case study areas were already mentioned: the philosophy of literary theory and criticism, the philosophy of historiography, and the philosophy of theology and religious studies. These are distinct but can be entangled; for example, one may study both the writing of history and religious texts as literature, and obviously both literary theory and theology have their historiographies (as do, of course, philosophy as well as historiography itself). Indeed, no contemporary phenomena or practices can be studied humanistically without serious awareness of their historicity.[15]

Philosophy of Literary Theory and Criticism

Taking up the philosophy of literary theory and criticism first, the realism issue explored above may be formulated in terms of the question concerning the objectivity (vs. subjectivity) of literary interpretation. Are there objective criteria for "true" or correct interpretation of literary works of art, or are literary interpretations always thoroughly relative to contexts, perspectives, and/or traditions? Is the concept of truth applicable here, and if so, in what sense exactly? Are there, ontologically speaking, objectively existing meanings of texts (in any reasonable sense of "objectively")? In what sense, moreover, can scholarly investigations of literature by literary theorists and critics determine whether literary works of art are themselves "about" the nature of the world, for example, about contemporary society or historical events (and again, if so, in what sense exactly)? Questions such as these receive distinctively pragmatist answers when the practices of literary study as well as their representational relations (or, as the case might be, scholars' claims that no representational relations exist) are analyzed from the perspective of a pragmatist philosophy of the humanities.

Pragmatists and other scholars dealing with the philosophy of literary theory and criticism may also focus on a literary analysis of how *metaphorical* (and hence, in some sense literary) language has been or can be used to characterize the production of knowledge in the humanities (see, e.g., Kivistö and Pihlström 2017). It is, arguably, important for our understanding of the impact of science and scholarship, as well as academic freedom, to examine the metaphors used to describe the acquisition of knowledge in general; this of course applies to the knowledge-seeking practiced within the humanities, too. We may also identify distinctively pragmatist metaphors, Dewey's (1960 [1929]) rejection of the "spectator theory of knowledge" being one of the most famous among them (cf. chapter 2). Many of such pragmatist metaphors relevant here express a general commitment to fallibilism and antifoundationalism in inquiry.[16] A somewhat different yet related pragmatist metaphor is James's hotel corridor: James (1975 [1907], Lecture II) argued that the pragmatic method is like a corridor in a hotel leading to very different rooms in which different intellectual activities (e.g., scientific experimentation, prayer) are going on. The corridor metaphor might be seen as a special case of the prevalent metaphors of map and navigation: seeking knowledge, or inquiring into the ways the world is, especially from a pragmatist perspective, is like finding one's way around in the world. Again, unlike metaphors of looking, seeking, or spectating, this emphasizes human beings' active role in inquiry.[17]

Another matter to be potentially illuminated by pragmatist philosophy of literary theory is the complex relation between philosophical and literary discourses themselves. This can be explored by examining to what extent scholars *can* theorize about literature without losing something of the sui generis value of literature as literature (cf., e.g., Danto 1984; Edmundson 1995; Mikkonen 2013; Cascardi 2014). Questions such as these go beyond the scope of this volume, but it is not implausible to suggest that they might also in interesting ways be related to the issues of pragmatic realism and truth that the pragmatist philosopher of literary theory and criticism needs to emphasize. Literary-theoretical investigations of meaning and interpretation can also extend beyond literature proper to, say, scholarly language needed in the (other) humanistic discourses themselves.[18]

Literature, or at least good and serious literature, can presumably be claimed to examine "the human condition," or as Milan Kundera (1986) puts it, "human possibilities." Accordingly, even fictional literature is "about" the world in an important sense: while depicting merely imagined people, situations, and events, it does seek to tell us something about what human life or existence in general terms is like, considered in the light of some specific and in many cases extreme human possibilities. It can rather plausibly be suggested that it is one of the tasks of literary theory and criticism to investigate how—that is, by means of what kind of stylistic, textual, narrative, symbolic, metaphorical, and other techniques—literature does, or is able to do, this. The philosophy of literary theory and criticism (as a special field within the philosophy of the humanities) then investigates, at a metalevel, the theoretical and interpretive ways in which literary theory and criticism are able to accomplish such a task. Therefore, the philosophy of literary theory and criticism takes as its objects of study the various theoretical and interpretive constructions of literary theory and criticism, as well as the complex representational (or, as the case might be, antirepresentational) relations such constructions might bear on the literary works analyzed as well as their real or alleged relations to the world (or "human possibilities") they are claimed to be "about." A formulation like this is certainly not unique to pragmatist philosophy of literary theory and criticism, but the pragmatist twist to the discussion can in this case be introduced by emphasizing that a pragmatist philosophy of literary theory and criticism approaches both literature itself (its production and reception) and the theoretical and critical projects of its scholarly interpreters as human practices through which we continuously critically construct our understanding of what the human condition and our human possibilities are. Whatever is taken to be real in the object of study of literary theory and criticism is available to us only within such interpretive practices, and pragmatist philosophy of literary theory and criticism seeks to better understand this "availability."

Philosophy of Historiography

As mentioned earlier, when proposing a pragmatist philosophy of the humanities, I am primarily investigating not any detailed methodological questions of any particular field, such as historiography (though such questions are certainly not irrelevant to my overall considerations), but, rather, the general realism issue as applied to the study of the historical past from a pragmatist perspective. The following questions are therefore central for this subfield of pragmatist study: Can historical truth be construed in terms of pragmatist conceptions of truth? In what sense can the pragmatist philosopher of historiography claim that truth is what is satisfactory for us to believe (with reference to our future aims, values, interests, goals, and concerns) when the object of study is the past? Can the pragmatist even claim the historical past to really exist, given that the pragmatist conception of truth always assesses our truth claims in terms of their future experiential significance?[19] If we do endorse a pragmatist understanding of historiography, does this mean that writing history is ultimately indistinguishable from the writing of literature, as Hayden White (1973) controversially suggested?[20] Does the pragmatist conception of truth ultimately commit us to a view of historical truth comparable to the view held by O'Brien, the Party torturer in George Orwell's *Nineteen Eighty-Four* (1949), who maintains that truth is completely dependent on the contingent opinion of the Party (cf. also Pihlström 2021)?

This Orwellian example is highly relevant in this context also because one of the classes of truths considered in the novel is, indeed, the class of historical truths.[21] Winston, the protagonist of *Nineteen Eighty-Four*, claims to remember that there were airplanes already before the Party came to power. O'Brien, however, denies this: if the Party claims that there were no airplanes before the rule of the Party, then there were no airplanes before the rule of the Party. Truth, according to O'Brien (and the Party), is just what the Party claims to be true; indeed, this "theory" of truth itself is, at the metalevel, something that the Party claims to be true, too. This thoroughgoing historical contingency—what the Party contingently says just is the case—creates an equally thoroughgoing metaphysical instability to the Orwellian world, as the opinion of the Party could change randomly, and along with it any truths or facts whatsoever would change as well. Presumably even the view the Party holds about what truth—historical truth or truth in general, including mathematical truth—*is* could change randomly. Even if the Party suddenly declared that it no longer maintains that truth depends on its opinion, *this* allegedly realistic or perhaps correspondence-theoretic account would be dependent on the Party authority. This shows that when an absolute dictator starts to meddle with truth, there is no easy return to any ordinary understanding of truth; indeed, truth can be genuinely destroyed, which seems to happen in *Nineteen Eighty-Four*.

It should be perceived that the totalitarianism imagined by Orwell is considerably more radical than any real-life totalitarianism has ever been. For example, in the Soviet Union, it was (as it is in today's China) extremely important for the ruling Communist Party to control what people believe, with the intention of hiding the "real" truth from them (e.g., by manipulating historical photographs by wiping out unwanted characters from them). This, however, presupposes that (historical) truth itself remains important: truth is respected precisely in the attempt to hide it. In the Orwellian context, however, the Party's use of extreme violence succeeds in abolishing any distinction between what is true and what the Party claims to be true—to the extent that Winston, when horribly tortured, not only says that he believes that 2+2=5 but really comes to believe that 2+2=5.[22] Similarly, historical truths about, say, airplanes, or anything else, are dependent on what the Party says, and there is no external control for checking the Party's opinion against any objective fact.[23]

Orwell's novel has been regarded as a defense of realism and the objectivity of truth (also by pragmatists: cf. Mounce 1997), but on the other hand, Rorty's (1989) reading of *Nineteen Eighty-Four* emphasizes the concept of *freedom* in contrast to the concept of truth (see Conant 2000 for an insightful critique).[24] The basic claim that I believe the pragmatist philosopher of historiography may argue for here is that it is (again) only within a pragmatist account of the humanities that we can successfully counter the absurd reduction of pragmatist conceptions of truth to O'Brien's extreme antirealism while acknowledging the dependence of historical truth on our contemporary and future-oriented pragmatic value-laden perspectives. Indeed, a plausible starting point for a pragmatist account of historical truth can be found in William James himself, particularly in *The Meaning of Truth* (1978 [1909]), where he seeks to show that pragmatism can very well accommodate a robust conception of historical truth, as well as of the existence of historical persons and events (his example is Julius Caesar).[25]

Truth is pragmatically—vitally—needed in historiography also in order to make sense of the very idea of historiographical disagreement. If there were no truth to be found (however fallibly and insecurely), there would be no point in disagreeing with anyone else's interpretation of history; all interpretations would then collapse to mere subjective preferences. Emphasizing this point should not be taken to entail an implausible commitment to the naïve idea that historians would primarily disagree about whether a certain event took place or not. Usually (as, again, various constructivist and/or narrativist contributions to the philosophy of historiography have insisted) their disagreements concern broader accounts and interpretations of history instead of any simple or straightforward "facts." Yet, the very idea of disagreement—even about plausible interpretations of whatever facts there might be—presupposes that we in some sense are engaged in the practice of pursuing truth and objectivity. This can be generalized into a pragmatic argument for the truth-aptness of humanistic discourse more inclusively, including not merely historiography but also literary studies and religious studies. However, it may also be argued that a pragmatist conception of truth is sufficient for this role: historiographical constructions do not refer to ready-made facts "out there" in the metaphysically given historical past but to complex historical realities constituted (at the pragmatic-transcendental level) by our interpretive practices.[26]

Furthermore, how should we understand the relation between the rationality of historical scholarship, on the one hand, and the historicity of human existence (including the inevitable historicity of any idea of rationality we may have)[27] and the historicist critique of teleology in the philosophy of history, on the other? This kind of metalevel questions also need to be tackled by the pragmatist philosopher of the humanities seeking to reflexively account for the historical contingency and mutability of our scholarly perspectives on history. It is itself a historically contingent matter that we are able to consider issues of historical contingency in the ways we do. We *could*, after all, live in an Orwellian dystopia, with no methods of or even capacities for rational thought whatsoever remaining at our disposal.

Pragmatists have fortunately not simply agreed with the Rortyan deflationary attitude to truth but have developed a wide array of accounts of truth, realism, and rationality in the philosophy of history and historiography, ranging from Peircean realism to historicist antirealist "narrativism" and "postnarrativist" forms of "rational pragmatism" indebted not as much to the classical pragmatists as to, for example, Robert Brandom's (one of Rorty's students and critics) inferentialist version of pragmatism.[28] Jouni-Matti Kuukkanen's (2015, 2017) carefully crafted postnarrativist pragmatism deserves brief comments here as an up-to-date major contribution to pragmatist philosophy of historiography. My views come in many ways close to his, especially regarding the need to find a balanced combination of realism and constructivism (or objectivity and subjectivity) and the commitment to historiography as a rational practice of inquiry; Kuukkanen plausibly develops these ideas by taking a critical move beyond the (partially correct) narrativist insights of Hayden White and Frank Ankersmit (among others). He correctly claims that historiography must be considered both subjective and objective at the same time (Kuukkanen 2015, 175, 200). Narrativists, antirealists, and postmodernists are right to maintain that historiographical writing does not correspond to any definite "entities in the past" in the sense of "mirroring" historical reality (ibid., 9),[29] but it does not follow that historiography cannot be distinguished from fiction-writing.

It seems to me that Kuukkanen's pragmatism, though rightly opposed to the antirealist extremes of narrativism, remains unstable in its attempt to avoid claiming that historians are in the business of discovering truths (see, e.g., Kuukkanen 2015, 11, 2017, 90) and in suggesting that truth could be replaced by, for example, "warranted assertion" (Kuukkanen 2015, chapter 7, 2017, 95). He proposes to "reject absolute truth-functional standards and replace them with a cognitively authoritative rational evaluation without implying that there are absolutely correct interpretations" (Kuukkanen 2015, 2). Historiography, he maintains, is a discursive and argumentative practice of reasoning for or against theses (ibid., 66–67, 198–199), and this makes it a rational practice answerable to critical normative standards (see further ibid., especially chapter 5). Yet this does not, he argues, make it a search for the truth.

His argument for rejecting the truth-functionality of historiography is basically that no historical entities in the past exist as truthmakers for historical interpretations (ibid., 11). Pragmatist "redefinitions" of the meaning of truth are not helpful, either (ibid., 138–142); Kuukkanen finds it more promising to give up the very idea that historiography aims at truth, replacing it with the Deweyan notion of "warranted assertion" and justification (ibid., 143ff.). However, as soon as we embrace a richer pragmatist conception of the historical past as ontologically dependent on historians' value-guided selections of relevant facts, this problem with truth and historical reality will cease to trouble us.[30] Combining pragmatically understood truth with a sophisticated, ontologically serious pragmatic realism helps us accept that historians, too, do engage in the practices of pursuing the truth. Nor do I find it necessary to reject what is sound in "representationalism" (another philosophical interpretation of historiography criticized by Kuukkanen; see ibid., chapter 4). A relatively ordinary pragmatic notion of an historical text being "about" something "real" in the past is sufficient to account for the moderate realism needed for the pragmatist; moreover, the problem of representationality is analogous across academic disciplines, certainly not confined to historiography. There is no need for specifically historiographical "nonrepresentationalism" just in order to reject the implausible idea that historiographical writing would refer to "unique corresponding entities" (cf. ibid., 64).

In addition to Kuukkanen, one of the most balanced recent pragmatist responses to the challenges of realism, truth, and objectivity in the philosophy of historiography has been formulated by Marek Tamm (2014). He is, as a pragmatist should be, mostly interested not as much in applying some pregiven theory of truth to historiography as in the question which conceptions of truth and objectivity are "practised within the discipline of history" (ibid., 266). Utilizing the theory of speech-acts (like Kuukkanen 2015, 158–161), he proposes to analyze this in terms of what he calls a "pragmatic 'truth-pact'": "the conditions of historical truth depend on the illocutionary force of historical utterance," and this "pact" is "'guaranteed' by fellow historians" and thus by a "disciplinary consensus as to the methods of inquiry, cognitive values and epistemic virtues" (Tamm 2014, 271). Truth thus becomes an epistemic notion, as the "truth-pact" is based on a "critical analysis of the available evidence" (ibid.).

The "truth-pact" is an implicit agreement between the historian and their addressees, according to which the historian's intention is to tell the truth. It presupposes "rules"—that is, in my preferred pragmatist terms, normative principles structuring our practice of pursuing the truth in historiography—according to which, for instance, the historian making historiographical assertions must be able to provide evidence and reasons for their truth claims, and the asserted propositions must not be "obviously true." The historian must also be sincere in the sense of believing in the truth of what they claim to be true (ibid., 274–275). In brief, we could say, in Bernard Williams's (2002) terms, that the historian needs to be *truthful*.[31] As Tamm (2014, 275) reminds us, following such rules obviously does not guarantee truth, but these normative principles "form the necessary grounds for an historical assertion to be considered as true." They could, therefore, be viewed as transcendental conditions for the possibility of historical truth—and, indeed, conditions based on how our historiographical practices function.

One of the implications of Tamm's view, like Kuukkanen's, is that historiography must be carefully distinguished from fictional narrative-writing that does not purport to be true (ibid., 277). Hence, narrativist philosophy of historiography must be firmly rejected.[32] On the other hand, the "truth-pact" does not involve any correspondence theory of truth, as the obtaining of a correspondence between the historian's claim and the historical fact would be "impossible to check" (ibid., 278). At this point, the critic might want to ask why this would be any easier to "check" in the natural sciences or in any other practices dealing with truth. Why, then, wouldn't Tamm's "rules," or the "truth-pact" in general, be applicable within *any* practice of inquiry pursuing the truth? Accordingly, while I find Tamm's discussion lucid and helpful in many ways—and I also strongly agree with his pragmatic analysis of objectivity as "a way of *doing* things" (ibid., 281), a practice-embedded epistemic virtue rather than a mysterious property that the objects of our inquiries could enjoy independently of those inquiries—I am not sure whether his epistemic construal of truth in terms of the truth-pact really helps us in capturing any distinctive pragmatic core of historiography as a pursuit of truth. I would be happy to retain most of what he says about truth and objectivity being practical pursuits within our fallible practices of historiographical inquiry, while insisting that we still need to link the pursuit of truth with the *ontology* of historiography, understanding that ontology itself along the value-laden lines suggested here. Truth would then fall in its place as a pragmatist "species of good."

In sum, then, Tamm's version of pragmatism lies somewhere between Kuukkanen's and mine. Without being able to develop a comprehensive philosophy of historiography that would thoroughly engage with their positions, I hope to have provided some reasons for defending a slightly more robust pragmatic realism. In any event, as the recent active discussion of pragmatist philosophy of historiography is already growing rather voluminous, there is no need for me to go into any greater detail here—except regarding pragmatic realism and ontology, my main concerns in this work, which I will continue to dwell on in the next section.

Philosophy of Theology and Religious Studies

Insofar as, arguably, academic theology and religious studies cannot examine the nature of God (because we cannot, in an academic context, make any commitment to God's existence or any other supernatural matters),[33] what exactly *is* the object of study of theological inquiry? Does the ontological status of the objects of research vary considerably across the various theological subdisciplines, such as systematic theology, biblical studies, church history, practical theology, and comparative religion? To what extent are these fields of research reducible to more general disciplines independent of theological contexts, such as the history of ideas or social and political history? How, moreover, can pragmatist philosophy of the humanities be applied to the study of religion in such a way that both "external" (causal, objective) explanations of religious practices and "internal" (hermeneutic or possibly Wittgensteinian) ways of understanding them might be plausibly synthesized?

In formulating this type of questions, it is important to keep the discussion focused on the philosophy of theology and religious studies instead of philosophy of religion itself, that is, not primarily aiming to understand what religion, religious belief, and religious language are like, but what theologians and religious studies scholars are doing (or what they should be doing) when studying religious ideas and activities. On the other hand, it would also be important to draw attention to the ways in which scholarly work in, say, literary theory and criticism may illuminate, and benefit from, theological perspectives (see, e.g., several essays in Felch 2016). It is, furthermore, a relevant question—coming closer to the philosophy of religion proper—how humanistic inquirers' own religious or nonreligious background assumptions may (or may not) affect their inquiries into religious beliefs and ways of life (cf. chapter 1). The ontological issues surrounding humanistic scholarship in theology and religious studies are thus complicated.

Pragmatist philosophy of theology and religious studies needs to distinguish between the different levels at which the realism issue becomes a problem in this area.[34] We may speak about realism (and its alternatives) in relation to religious practices and vocabularies themselves, about theological interpretations of those practices and vocabularies, about the metalevel interpretations of various theological frameworks and religious orientations within comparative religion and religious studies, as well as, finally, within the philosophy of religion seeking to understand what religious and theological thought are all about. I have dealt with these different forms of religious and theological realism elsewhere (Pihlström 2020, chapter 2), so I will not pay more attention to these distinctions here. I will, however, explore a kind of pragmatist transcendental argument in the context of the "naturalization" debate concerning religious studies in chapter 4 below.

The claim that theology is a humanistic discipline might still be resisted by suggesting that theology does deal with, for example, Christian (or other religious) dogmas concerning the metaphysical nature of the divinity. Insofar as, say, Christology (within Christian theology) is understood as a study of the nature of Christ, it may not be clear that we are dealing with a humanistic discipline. More generally, theology, and especially analytic theology utilizing concepts and arguments drawn from analytic philosophy in the service of an articulation of (say) Christian dogma (cf., e.g., Vainio 2020), could thus be claimed to be at least in principle involved in the study of the fundamental nature of reality as such instead of being confined to human cultural meanings (as a humanistic discipline). *If* theology is not subordinated to any religious creed or institution, the various theological disciplines, including even dogmatics and analytic theology, can be interpreted as investigating the ways in which human beings have developed religious meanings in their thoughts, actions, and institutions.[35] In this sense, theology is a discipline pursuing truth about human culture and its history, just as any other humanistic discipline. The fact that theologians' own (possible or actual) religious commitments might affect the ways in which they view their own scholarly endeavors is contingent regarding those endeavors themselves; in principle, similar "ideological" commitments could affect our inquiries in any discipline, as scholars are inevitably human beings with their own extraacademic interests and pursuits.

The only specific theology-related subdiscipline that could with some legitimacy be claimed to be in the business of finding metaphysical truths about the way the world is in general, beyond human cultural reality, is, presumably, the philosophy of religion, insofar as the metaphysical question concerning God's existence is taken to be a proper object of study in that field. However, this would already presuppose construing philosophy of religion as a metaphysically realistic investigation of the nature of reality independently of human culture- and value-embedded conceptual categorization. Insofar as we view not only the humanities but philosophy as well along the Kantian-cum-pragmatist lines outlined in this book, even philosophy of religion—at the most fundamental metaphysical level of investigation available to us human beings—is a critical study of human conceptual categorizations of reality instead of aiming at a fundamental theory of the precategorized ontological structures of reality "in itself."[36]

Metaphilosophy (and the History of Pragmatism Again)

This brings us to a metaphilosophical discussion of philosophy itself as a humanistic discipline. There is a reflexive metalevel question to be asked in addition to the three case study areas and their typical research issues distinguished above. What exactly should we think about the scholarly (and ontological) status of philosophical inquiry, both generally and when (as here) applied to the study of the humanities? How should we characterize philosophy as a humanistic inquiry, for example, in comparison with the sciences or formal methods of inquiry (cf. Williams 2006)? What actually is *its* object of study: Is it the human world (as in the other humanities), or is it in some sense reality in general?[37] Are philosophical claims or theories themselves true or false—and if so, in what sense exactly, if not quite in the sense in which, say, scientific or humanistic theories can be regarded as true or false? Furthermore, is the pragmatist conception of truth also applicable to philosophical "truths" (along with other truths), if any, within a pragmatist philosophy of the humanities placing philosophy among the humanities? Instead of seeking a direct answer to these questions, we might consider the possibility of developing a critical *agnosticism* not only with regard to our being able to know which philosophical theories are true but at the metalevel regarding the truth-aptness of philosophical discourse itself (cf. Pihlström 2021, chapter 6).

This metaphilosophical discussion raises reflexive questions the (pragmatist) philosopher of the humanities may ask about the nature of their inquiry. Such questions can be particularly fruitfully discussed from a pragmatist perspective, because it is natural for the pragmatist philosopher to draw critical attention to their own *practices* of philosophical activity.[38] We may, I argue, remain critically agnostic about the truth-aptness of philosophical discourse itself in a sense different from the truth-aptness of, for example, historiographical or literary-theoretical statements (within which, as suggested above, we do need to commit ourselves to a moderate form of pragmatic realism involving truth-aptness). Accordingly, philosophy is not straightforwardly a field within the humanities among others. In some contexts of philosophical inquiry, we may be pragmatically justified to apply the concept of truth to philosophical claims, while in other contexts this hardly even makes sense (and this context sensitivity must be duly recognized). Reflexively, we may also ask whether *these* metaphilosophical claims are, or even can be, true or false in a pragmatist (or any other) sense. A critical form of agnosticism arguably prevails, at least prima facie, when we climb onto a metalevel. Philosophical discourse verges on the limit of cognitive meaningfulness and meaninglessness and must critically, reflexively, examine that limit itself.

Furthermore, while I am proposing pragmatism as a central framework for the philosophy of the humanities, including reflexive investigations of philosophy itself as a humanistic discipline (albeit different from other humanistic disciplines in its constant uncertainty about its own truth-aptness), its own history with regard to the philosophy of the humanities remains mostly unwritten.[39] It would be the task of another comprehensive project to write such a history; this book has been and will be able to offer only some tentative proposals in this regard. A fresh look should be taken at the entire tradition of pragmatist philosophy (and pragmatism in a more interdisciplinary sense), not only from the perspective of general philosophy of science (as in chapter 2) but also from that of the philosophy of the humanities. The views of the classical pragmatists, and those of their followers and interpreters, on the nature of the humanities remain largely implicit in their work, and therefore it would be a matter of careful historical research to make these ideas more explicit. This kind of research would also have to involve comparisons between pragmatists' ideas and some of the best-known historicist views in the philosophy (and history) of science—not only Kuhn's (1970 [1962]) famous theory of paradigms and scientific revolutions but also, for example, the earlier and less well-known account of the emergence of scientific facts by Ludwik Fleck (2012 [1935]). The general history of pragmatist philosophy of science as laid out in chapter 2 is only a beginning in this respect.

Finally, one might also propose—again in a more comprehensive undertaking going far beyond the scope of this book—a number of more concrete case studies for further investigation. For example, a somewhat less philosophical and more practical research within the philosophy of the humanities could analyze how scholarly and administrative humanities networks, institutes, research centers, and other organizations and their public declarations about the nature and value of the humanities today may be understood in terms of the pragmatist philosophy of the humanities.[40]

In all the case study areas described in this section, special attention needs to be drawn to the relations between the relevant fields of humanistic inquiry (i.e., literary theory and criticism, historiography, theology and religious studies, and philosophy) and the practices and/or areas of culture they investigate (i.e., literature, historical—including political—events in the past, religion, and philosophy itself), thus addressing questions concerning their relevant objects of investigation, examined with a special focus on developing a plausible version of pragmatic realism. In addition, more practical engagements with "politics of the humanities" could and should also be analyzed in relation to all these fields, paying attention to the ways in which the value of the humanities is affirmed or possibly questioned by various social actors, including political decision-makers.

Note also how inherently all these case study areas are connected with the question concerning realism and the objects of inquiry, as well as the very possibility of those objects as objects of inquiry—an issue we have been and will continue to be preoccupied with both in the previous chapter and this one. The interplay between transcendental and naturalist approaches within pragmatism is, furthermore, ineliminably present in any serious inquiry into pragmatist philosophy of literary theory, historiography, or religious studies. Inevitably, we need to somehow reconcile *natural* human activity with its necessary or constitutive *conditions*.[41]

Some Research Questions and Hypotheses

The following more detailed research hypotheses, understood as responses to particular research questions, may be taken up for further investigation throughout all the case study areas sketched here. They can all be claimed to deepen and concretize the general themes described above and to provide partial and tentative specifications of and responses to the kind of research questions identified in the previous section. Thus, this catalogue of research problems and hypotheses may serve, I hope, as a step toward a further articulation of what a pragmatist philosophy of the humanities might look like when more fully developed.

Let me begin this discussion with *the aims and values of humanistic inquiry*. Like any values, they can, as already indicated, be subjected to a pragmatist analysis. In particular, pragmatism is well placed to examine the vexing question of the intrinsic value of humanistic scholarship in relation to the various instrumental societal "utilities" that the humanities may involve. Scholars in the humanities often argue that the humanities are inherently valuable in themselves, without reference to any external benefit (and this may be claimed to distinguish them from the natural sciences involving a "technical interest" in controlling nature);[42] on the other hand, deepening our understanding of human culture and its past is also "useful" for human beings and societies in many ways. From a pragmatist standpoint, there is no need to draw any essentialist dichotomy between intrinsic values and instrumental values. Many human values can be both, as Deweyan "ends-in-view," when achieved, always open up novel ends-in-view to be pursued.

Pragmatism, seeking to understand and evaluate human practices in terms of the value-laden interests and goals they pursue, may therefore also lead us beyond too easy oppositions between "basic research" (allegedly motivated by a disinterested pursuit of truth as valuable "in itself") and "applied research" (motivated by some human values or goals external to the research itself). *All* research is value-guided, value-embedded, and value-oriented, simply because it is humanly conducted, and any humanly conducted activity pursues some value, but no research—either in the humanities or in the natural sciences—needs to be understood as *merely* instrumentally useful. In particular, we may live better lives by developing our capabilities of understanding more profoundly, by means of humanistic scholarship, what human culture in its inevitable historicity is like, without any immediate concern with practical benefits or applications. This nonutilitarian amelioration of our lives and practices—without any specific practical application driving the inquiry—can, from a pragmatist point of view, be considered essential to humanistic scholarship.[43] Again, this rejection of naïve instrumentalism is also related to the rejection of instrumentalism in the more technical sense familiar from the philosophy of science: inquiry is about reality itself—albeit pragmatically constituted—not just about observations or empirical data, nor about the mere practical effects reality may have on us (cf. chapter 2). While all of our inquiries to a considerable extent draw their motivation from our practical needs of living on in this problematic world, no serious pragmatist views humanistic or scientific inquiries as simply reducible to immediate concerns of instrumental utility.

This brings us, again, to one of my major themes: *pragmatic realism about the humanities*. As already tentatively argued, it is possible to develop, from a pragmatist perspective, a plausible and sophisticated version of scientific realism applicable to the humanities. This form of realism about the humanities pertains to their theoretical objects of study (and the mind-dependent yet qualified theory-independent existence of those objects), the truth-aptness[44] of their theoretical discourses, their aims and goals of inquiry, and their criteria of rational theory-choice. Pragmatist philosophy of the humanities is well placed to carry out the promise of, for example, Niiniluoto's (1999) critical scientific realism with regard to the humanities:[45] the objects of study of the humanities are, according to such realism, human-made entities belonging to what Karl Popper memorably called "World 3," that is, the "world" of relatively autonomous cultural entities that emerge from their material and psychological bases (viz., Popper's "World 1" and "World 2," respectively) but are ontologically irreducible to the latter.[46] Realism then prevails—but this is *not*, for the pragmatist, any metaphysical realism committed to the task of uncovering the privileged ("ready-made") ontological structure of the world as it is in itself but a form of realism that pragmatically conceptualizes any ontological commitments made within human practices of inquiry as based on human values, qua constitutive conditions of inquiry. Even though Paisley Livingston (1988) fails to deal with pragmatism, his defense of scientific realism as applied to humanistic inquiry must be acknowledged as a relative of the view I am here developing.

The specific character of the pragmatic realism available for pragmatist philosophy of the humanities also needs to be considered from the point of view of the question concerning scientific (or scholarly) *progress*: If the scientific realist defines scientific progress as convergence toward the truth (or, more technically, as an increase in the truthlikeness of successive theories; cf. again, e.g., Niiniluoto 1999), is there any analogy of this concept of progress in humanistic inquiry? Another specific question concerning realism about the humanities is the existence of *values* themselves (as "theoretical entities" postulated in humanistic scholarship): If inquiry is value-guided, in what sense are values real as objects of study? The first step in any pragmatist attempt to deal with such issues is to investigate the values (e.g., truth, as a "species of good" à la James) in relation to which any claim to progress must be evaluated. The progress of humanistic scholarship may not be measurable in the sense in which scientific progress might (though that is no trivial matter, either), but it could nevertheless be characterized as a progress of approximating the human values such scholarship seeks to serve, including truth. At least it would, clearly, be misguided to venture any claim to progress that would be taken to be completely independent of the concept of truth.[47]

My main hypothesis concerning this set of questions is that pragmatism is able to provide us with a plausible version of realism that takes seriously the ontological autonomy and irreducibility of human culture as an objectively available, albeit never "ready-made," sphere of reality to be investigated in the humanities. A related hypothesis (which would also require more critical assessment than is possible here) is that we may argue for pragmatic realism about the humanities *by elimination*: both overly strong metaphysical realism (committed to a "ready-made world") and radical forms of relativism, constructivism, and irrealism lead to implausible or even absurd conceptions of the humanities. *Either* the (human) world becomes ultimately inaccessible due to its being ready-made independently of our contribution and hence completed or "closed" in its fundamental nonperspectival and theory-independent ontological structure (metaphysical realism), *or* it becomes both ontologically and epistemically entirely unstructured and arbitrary, with no rational criteria constraining the diverse shapes it may take from a potentially unlimited number of perspectives (relativism, irrealism).

This eliminative argument for the plausible middle ground position has roots in the tradition of pragmatism itself, because pragmatism has at least since James[48] been regarded as a critical middle path between various extreme options (not only realism and antirealism but also, say, empiricism and rationalism), and in the Kantian tradition, because the argument can also be considered transcendental: pragmatism turns out to be a necessary condition for an overarching philosophical conceptualization of the possibility of epistemically accessing the human world by means of valuational humanistic inquiry.

This general argument takes somewhat different forms in the different case study areas outlined above. For example, what is the "reality" studied in literary theory or criticism, pragmatically analyzed? It is not the fictional world "made" by the author of a literary work, but it may be the process of *fingere* itself, that is, the way the work or its author creates such a world out of the meagre input of words and phrases.[49] This process itself emerges from the structures of the work, and the scholar's interpretation may focus on the reality of such processes in addition to the underlying structures. Reality is dynamic, changing, and (in James's words) "in the making," but this does not prevent a pragmatist conception of the relevant kind of realism from being applicable to it; on the contrary, it highlights the significance of *pragmatic* realism in the humanities.

"Real Generals"

It needs to be acknowledged—as an important special case of the realism issue, as applied to the humanities—that humanistic inquiries do not merely focus on concrete particulars, such as literary texts or unique historical events. They may also take more abstract entities and phenomena among their objects, such as historical tendencies of development, interpretive possibilities, as well as general traits of religious practices irreducible to any particular rituals.[50] These can all be analyzed in terms of Peirce's realism about "real generals" (e.g., habits, dispositions, laws), which has rarely if ever been developed in the philosophy of the humanities in any detail.[51] I will next explain why I believe that such general entities can be, and often are, among the ontological postulations of humanistic theorization and interpretation. Without a proper account of such generality, our conception of the ontology of the humanities would remain hopelessly inadequate.

This seemingly abstract philosophical issue is directly relevant to more concrete ones, such as the methodological questions of historical explanation. For the historian, it is decisively important to be able to explain why a certain event or chain of events (i.e., a historical process) took place at a certain time, and explaining this typically involves explaining why some *other* event(s), among the countless number of events that *could* have taken place, did *not* take place; therefore, counterfactual questions ("what if . . . ?") and contrastive counterfactual explanations ("why did X happen instead of Y?") are part and parcel of historical scholarship and have obviously been thoroughly explored by philosophers of historiography.[52] Thus, the historian does not merely seek to find out what exactly happened ("*wie es eigentlich gewesen*") and why. Their focus is on the fact that something happened rather than something else. This fact must be taken not only *explanatorily* seriously (in terms of contrastive and counterfactual explanations) but also *ontologically* seriously; it is a fact requiring interpretation and thus the entire value- and purpose-oriented scheme of inquiry through which we conceptualize historical reality. In this sense, the ontological status of historical facts as "general" facts (in addition to their being in an obvious sense "particulars," too) is fundamentally connected with their value-laden character. It is only in the context of value-based selection that they (can) ontologically emerge as the kind of general facts they are.[53]

A historical example can illustrate this. A war historian may ask not only why Finland ended up in two wars against the Soviet Union (i.e., the Winter War in 1939–1940 and the so-called Continuation War in 1941–1944) during World War II—in contrast to the counterfactual possibilities of having ended up in no war at all or, say, only one. They may also ask, and have indeed asked, whether Finland *could have avoided* these wars, proposing different answers to such a question concerning historical possibilities. Clearly, if questions about possibility such as this one can be among the kind of scholarly questions asked by historians, history is not merely concerned with what actually happened in the past. It is deeply concerned with modally complex questions about what happened in the context of possibilities that failed to actualize, and this set of questions may include various specific questions about how exactly, say, the Continuation War might have been avoided (or not). Questions like these presuppose that historians investigate a modally complex reality. They may not primarily view their efforts as aiming at the truth but only at a plausible interpretation with some degree of objectivity and support by evidence (cf. Tamm 2014; Kuukkanen 2015), but it seems to me that in the absence of the pragmatically realistic idea of a modally complex world of "real generals" being "there"—though available only through our practices of inquiry aiming at the truth—the historians' practice would be incomprehensible. The normative context of inquiry within which it is possible to ask general questions about possibilities (such as the ones in our simple war-historical example) presupposes that historical inquiry is not just a matter of telling the most plausible story but about discovering truths about the real world and its real possibilities.

It is, therefore, we might argue, only within a Peircean realism of generality that we can really make sense of the idea that even though only the actual historical events really "exist" in the past (to the extent that anything that is past can be said to "exist"),[54] historical scholarship can also study real generals, such as unactualized historical possibilities, that is, things that could have existed but did not and do not, and also study the reality of what did exist in the context of what could have existed. This is also crucially related to the role played by historical representations in the study of history. As has been suggested, historical facts, as well as the facts investigated within all the other humanities, ontologically (transcendentally) depend on our purposive practices of representation. There is a *reflexive* structure that needs to be appreciated here: through those practices, we examine not only the objects to be represented but representations and representational relations themselves. A pragmatist philosophy of the humanities investigates how representational relations develop within our practices, that is, how (ontologically, epistemically, ethically) we represent, not just what we represent, and how it is possible for us to arrive at such representations.[55]

Another context within which historians can be argued to need the ontology of real generals is their use of what have been called "colligatory concepts" (see Kuukkanen 2015, chapter 6). By using such synthesizing concepts, the historian interpretively organizes the past and makes it intelligible. The antirepresentationalist suggests, again, that historiography should not be regarded as referential or representational because it crucially employs such concepts that do not refer to any corresponding entities in historical reality—as, for example, the concept of "renaissance" does not refer to any clearly identifiable object or event in the past. The proposal to interpret historical ontology in terms of real generals resolves this problem by making our ontology rich enough to provide reference, and even truthmakers, for colligatory concept-use and theorization.[56] Whatever colligation in historiography refers to, this referentiality can be accounted for in terms of pragmatic realism analogously to the way in which scientific realism deals with the referentiality of theoretical concepts.

Analogously, the literary critic may be claimed to study not only the actual meaning(s) of a literary text but also the possible meanings it could take under a plurality of different, possibly conflicting interpretations (even in the event that s/he does not consider all those meanings to really "exist" in the work itself). A related question is what exactly it means to say that a literary (or more generally artistic) work *can* be interpreted in a number of different ways. In this sense, pragmatic realism about generality is also directly relevant to a philosophical analysis of the semantic openness of literary works, which may be regarded as an essential component of their literary value. Furthermore, analogously, scholars of religion may examine general traits of religious ways of life and practices without claiming that they are always, or perhaps ever, actualized as concrete ritual behaviors. Peircean realism of generality is valuable for making sense of these ideas, too, because it draws a clear distinction between the concepts of existence and reality: the former applies to concrete particulars and events, while the latter applies to "real generals," including historical tendencies and habitualities, but also "real possibilities" that fail to concretely actualize as existing particulars. General patterns of thought and action can be real without being always concretely realized in particular, contingently existing objects or events.

Accordingly, interpretive *possibilities* can be regarded as Peircean real generals, and for this reason pragmatism is able to make sense of the openness of such possibilities—or, in other words, the reality of open questions of interpretation—as theoretical entities of humanistic inquiry within our practices of interpretation. Indeed, there is a clear analogy between unactualized historical possibilities and possible literary interpretations that may not be actually claimed by anyone to capture the meaning(s) of the work interpreted. Not all possible readings of a novel, for instance, are plausible or even anyone's actual readings, just as not all historical possibilities actualize in the course of real-life events. Yet they can be among the scholar's "real" objects of study. The Peircean pragmatist philosopher of literary theory[57] could go as far as to claim that, for instance, *merely possible irony* in a literary (or other artistic) work is, qua real, a genuine part of the ontology of the work, albeit dependent on our interpretive practices claiming the merely possible truth of an ironic reading of the work.

We could, for example, consider the *possibility* (sometimes actually suggested) of interpreting Stanley Kubrick's classical horror film *The Shining* (1980), based on Stephen King's novel, as antiracist and post- or anticolonialist (as well as, presumably, feminist), while recognizing what many viewers of the film would consider the artificiality of such an interpretive suggestion. (Yes, the hotel in the film is called *Overlook*, and the only black character is brutally killed, and yes, the main protagonist Jack loses his mind—in a sense all this could be regarded as an attempt to remind us, against our temptation to "overlook" this, that our unbearable responsibility for the sufferings of various "others," especially the indigenous peoples all over the world, cannot be faced without our losing our minds.) The possibility of ironically viewing *The Shining* through these general antiracist (and related) ideas could be argued to remain "real" even though we would not actually subscribe to such an interpretation as a "correct," "true," or even remotely plausible account of the meaning(s) of the film. "Correct" or plausible interpretations are put forward against the field of various possible interpretations, just as historical facts are "selected" out of potential facts in terms of their relevance. Most "mere possibilities" are trivial and uninteresting, but their reality needs to be postulated in order to make sense of humanistic inquiry as a process of investigating reality—especially the reality of value-laden facts and interpretations taken to be relevant in the context of an enormous field of implausible mere possibilities. It is a part of the reality of the work itself that *it* has all the interpretive possibilities it has, including the wild and implausible ones. Real generals thus need to be postulated in order to account for the very value-ladenness of humanistic ontology the pragmatist needs to defend. They are not merely epistemic possibilities for interpretation; they are ontological features of the reality investigated.

Alternatively, consider an example from the literary canon of my home country Finland:[58] Väinö Linna's novel trilogy, *Täällä Pohjantähden alla* (1959–62), translated into English as *Here Under the North-Star*, is a massive family saga depicting the sufferings of poor peasants throughout approximately a century of Finnish history, especially the bloody Civil War of 1918, as well as the enormous sacrifices the (fictional) family has to go through during World War II.[59] In today's terms, it could be suggested that Linna's profound social critique in the novel presents a powerful artistic case for something like intersectional feminism. Linna (who died in 1992) would not have recognized such a concept, and he was not an academically learned intellectual, but he did examine very carefully and with unparalleled historical insight the various ways in which people in multiply precarious social positions are made to suffer.[60] Again, we might say that the interpretation of the novel as representing or at least sympathizing with intersectional feminism is an open, yet real, possibility in the scholarly practices of appreciating Linna's work.[61]

Of course, not *all* possibilities are *relevant* at all. For pragmatists, interpretive relevance is a value-laden ontological criterion of real possibility. The point of invoking real generals is not to make the trivial claim that, for example, an ironic interpretation of something perceived or depicted would always be a "possibility," though in a sense it certainly always is. To engage in humanistic scholarship at all is to engage in normative interpretive practices that constantly try to draw and justify boundaries between relevant and irrelevant possibilities, or plausible and implausible interpretations, weighing their credentials, and thereby continuously creating the reality of meanings that is being studied. This is an investigation of human reality, with relevance as a (but not *the*) criterion of the real.[62] The pragmatist philosopher of the humanities, operating at an abstract metalevel, need not determine which historical or literary interpretations are relevant or plausible; her/his task is to clarify the ontological structure of the scholarly endeavors that seek to determine this.

Furthermore, Peircean real generals are extremely important in this context also because they can be reflexively applied to make sense of some of the fundamental ideas of pragmatist philosophy of the humanities itself: while humanistic ontology is value-dependent, it may be argued that values are Peircean real generals, too; they do not exist as particular objects but are, rather, "real" as general patterns guiding our thought, inquiry, and action. Moreover, insofar as humanistic inquiry investigates possible interpretations of, or possible ways of explaining, a historical fact (or a historical possibility, for that matter),[63] it may be argued that the kind of real possibilities that Peirce postulated along with other "real generals" need to be assumed in order to make sense of the type of pragmatic ontology of the humanities that I have proposed we need. Appreciating the nature of scholarly problems (open questions, conflicting interpretive possibilities, etc.) may thus, again, require a view like Peirce's realism about generals; it is a major advantage of pragmatist philosophy of the humanities to be able to take ontologically seriously this very openness—and also the related vagueness—of our open questions and problems. Nor do we have to stick to the merely Peircean terminology of real generals here; a pragmatist understanding of possibility is considerably richer. We could also invoke the Deweyan notion of a *problematic situation*, suggesting that a humanistic scholar seeks to resolve a problematic situation a given literary work, theological interpretation, or historical fact to be explained presents them with, that is, to render such a situation nonproblematic. In Jamesian terms, it could be further suggested that a choice between two (or more) different interpretive possibilities (understood as real generals) can be—or can fail to be, for that matter—a "genuine option" for the scholar, roughly in the sense analyzed by James in "The Will to Believe" (see James 1979 [1897]; cf. Pihlström 2021, chapter 4).[64]

It is often maintained—to the extent that this intuitively simple idea has turned into a cliché—that humanistic scholarship widens our thought and shows us new perspectives on reality. This idea is made philosophically more precise and ontologically robust when it is spelled out as a pragmatist account of open interpretive possibilities as elements of the reality studied within humanistic disciplines. This is a truly integrated pragmatically realist account of our scholarly practices and their representational relations to reality.

Furthermore, the pragmatist ontology of real possibilities is valuable regarding the need to illuminate the otherwise vague and unclear philosophical question concerning the inevitably potentially open issue about the categorization of the relevant research questions of any given humanistic inquiry.[65] Why, for example, is it important to study precisely questions A, B, and C (and not, for instance, D) when examining a given problem X? Because these questions play a pragmatically *relevant* role in our coming up with potentially relevant responses and/or solutions to X. They are *contingent* in the sense that both X and the triad of A, B, and C could always be different from what they are. (Tradition is also obviously important here: certain questions, and their subquestions, are given to us as something we inherit from earlier scholars, though this gradually, or in some cases suddenly and unexpectedly, changes in the course of history.) One may further ask why, in particular, a certain body of sources or literature (e.g., A, B, C) *is* relevant to X. There *could* always be more—or some of the sources included in the study could turn out to be irrelevant, after all. This is all contingent, and pragmatism duly recognizes such contingency. The choice of the relevant questions to be studied, and the relevant sources to be used, depends on the pragmatic interests and purposes of the research in question. Pragmatist philosophy of the humanities can fruitfully approach *both* the conceptual (or even ontological) question of the categorization of the research problem and its relevant source materials *and* the epistemic question concerning the criteria in terms of which certain given items (A, B, C) fall under the category examined (X). There are always fuzzy borderline cases; there is real vagueness involved, to be taken ontologically seriously.[66]

The openness of interpretive possibilities also reminds us why humanistic research should not be regarded as simply "paradigmatic" normal science in Kuhn's (original) sense (see chapter 2 above for some remarks on Kuhn in relation to pragmatist philosophy of science). There is no such openness in research that moves on by applying well-defined methods to solving well-defined problems, as "normal science" does. The humanities, rather, are in a perpetual crisis, because they are, and must remain, "open." Therefore, there is also a much more explicit need for philosophy in (and of) the humanities than there is in the (mature, paradigmatic) sciences; it is a clearly Kuhnian idea that it is at the time of crisis that a discipline turns to a philosophical questioning of its fundamentals (see also, e.g., Reisch 2019, 127).

One more example should be provided. Real generals can be argued to be needed also for making sense of the idea of "religious possibilities" in theology and religious studies (including the philosophy of religion), as well as, by extension, "existential" possibilities as well as necessities. These are not ordinary logical or metaphysical modalities, of course, but modalities shaping and coloring our lives, or emerging from the actualities of those lives and their historical contingencies. For an individual, a certain religious or existential belief may be a "genuine option"—again, in a sense familiar from James's "The Will to Believe" (1979 [1897])—and thus a real possibility for them, no matter how exactly that possibility is understood in terms of the metaphysics of modalities. Such possibilities of individual (or communal, for that matter) faith decisions, including Jamesian will-to-believe decisions, may be among the objects of religious studies and theology, and thus among the kind of theoretical entities that we may see the humanities as engaging with. Real possibilities of religion are, then, not merely general features of religious rituals, for instance, but also what individual religious believers (or nonbelievers)—that is, human beings whose thoughts and actions can be seen as "objects of study" in religious studies—are *able to* choose to believe as their highly personal decisions of faith. Here a pragmatist philosophy of theology and religious studies will reach a point of cooperating with pragmatist philosophy of religion analyzing such existential modalities of faith on the basis of, for example, the Jamesian will-to-believe argumentation.[67]

Does this analysis more metaphysically extend to the "merely possible" existence of God—or to the "reality" of *this* possibility as an object of study in theology or the philosophy of religion? More specifically, is this "real possibility" real as a cosmic metaphysical possibility (concerning the real possibility that God might exist) or as an interpretive possibility regarding human thought and culture (concerning the possibility of theism as a "genuine option" in the pragmatist sense)? A lot depends on this question, as it largely shapes our understanding of theology, religious studies, and the philosophy of religion as either humanistic inquiries into human meanings or more general metaphysical inquiries into (nonhuman) reality. As pointed out earlier, this choice depends on our prior philosophical choice between a metaphysically realistic account of the relation between human conceptualization and the world "in itself" and a more pragmatist account (drawn from Kant) according to which any reality, even the reality of generals and possibilities, is for us inevitably a human reality. The pragmatist ontology of real generals I have proposed here as a necessary condition for the possibility of (much of) humanistic scholarship with open interpretive hypotheses (for instance) only requires the latter, that is, a pragmatist understanding of real generals as among the value- and practice-embedded postulations depending on our human inquiries (while also enabling them).

Finally, even the research results of philosophical inquiry may be understood in terms of real generals. If we characterize philosophy (including the philosophy of the humanities) as, for example, a practice of demonstrating, in Kantian terms, the necessary applicability of certain concepts to a certain subject matter insofar as the latter is available to us as a possible object or topic of inquiry or cognition (or, e.g., moral consideration) at all, these multiple modal structures could be understood as real generals in the sense of being real modal structures of our philosophical practices of inquiry. Peircean real generals may thus be employed to articulate Kantian transcendental modalities, while conversely their necessity for making ontological sense of our practices of interpretation and inquiry may itself be analyzed transcendentally.

What is philosophically crucial is the metalevel question concerning which purposes are relevant enough to structure our ontologies and why. Our critical reflection on such endlessly negotiable issues can never be finally concluded, and it is this (metalevel) openness that pragmatism, again, fully acknowledges. This also serves as a reminder of why we need a *pragmatist* theory of real generals (subordinated to what may be described as a more general transcendental pragmatism; cf. Pihlström 2003a, 2009), not just any metaphysical account (based on, e.g., metaphysical realism) of modal realism, such as a possibilist theory of "really existing" possible worlds. Real generals are postulated in order to make the processes and practices of (humanistic) inquiry possible—from within those practices themselves, not from outside them, or from an imagined purely metaphysical vantage point, or a God's-eye view.

As the realism discussion both in this chapter and the previous one indicates, we may, from a pragmatist standpoint, *overcome and critically synthesize a number of standard dichotomies* that stand in the way of developing a plausibly holistic philosophy of the humanities and to replace them with entanglements. These include the oppositions between, among others, naturalism and humanism, objectivism and relativism, *Erklären* and *Verstehen* (explanation and understanding), basic and applied research (see above), as well as, obviously, realism and antirealism (constructivism, idealism), including questions of realism concerning both generality and particularity. For the pragmatist, the world may be regarded as both "natural" and "human"; it is *both* objectively real *and* always only perspectivally accessible and constituted by us. It can be studied and explained without any immediate practical applications in mind, but any inquiry into the nature of reality is also (always already) practically relevant merely by being based on human value-laden practices. The distinction between "naturalist" and "humanist" methodologies is particularly relevant in the study of religion, where the objects of study themselves (e.g., religious ideas and practices) involve supernatural postulations not available to the academic scholar in their academic role; in pragmatist scholarship on religion, issues concerning naturalism therefore remain hotly debated.[68] However, humanistic inquiry by no means precludes (nonreductive) naturalism but should arguably honor the generally naturalistic worldview of modern science (cf. Faye 2012).

Pragmatist philosophy of the humanities is challenged to find a middle course between, for example, causal-externalist explanations of religious phenomena and hermeneutic-internalist attempts to understand religious practices "from within" them. This may yield a strongly critical evaluation of very different types of one-sided methodologies, such as both "positivist" attempts to restrict humanistic methodology to objective causal explanation[69] and autoethnographical methods claiming to understand one's object of study (only) from an imagined "internal" imaginative participation.[70] The overcoming of such dichotomies follows from the fact that pragmatist philosophy of the humanities is based on a general theory of inquiry available in the pragmatist canon from Peirce to Putnam and beyond (see chapter 2). The basic form of the pragmatist conception of inquiry was already outlined, but its concretizations in real-life contexts of humanistic scholarship require more detailed attention. It is an essential feature of the pragmatist theory of inquiry that inquiry is a *critical* process acknowledging, and reflecting on, its own perspectival and fallible status. The pragmatist philosopher of the humanities should, moreover, follow Dewey's (1986 [1929], 354) characterization of philosophy as "the critical method of developing methods of criticism." Accordingly, it should be reemphasized that the interpretation and further development of pragmatism as a naturalized and historically relativized reconceptualization of Kantian critical (transcendental) philosophy is highly central to this entire discussion (cf. again, e.g., Pihlström 2003a, 2009, 2012b, 2013, 2015b, 2016, 2020); certainly no principled dichotomy or opposition should be presupposed between pragmatist and transcendental approaches.

To clarify this general commitment to Kantian pragmatism, the question whether the kind of ("scientific," humanistic) realism—either realism in general or realism about generality, including real possibility (see above)—that needs to be defended in the philosophy of the humanities can be accommodated within a more comprehensive transcendental pragmatism, analogously to the way in which empirical realism, according to Kant, depends on transcendental idealism, can itself be interpreted as an instance of the naturalism–humanism entanglement or integration. It may be further asked whether these forms of realism can (perhaps only?) be defended by means of a Kantian-styled transcendental argument.[71] If so, the naturalism–humanism integration itself emerges as a transcendental condition for the possibility of our inquiries.

The ontology of value-laden objects of inquiry within practices of inquiry, as transcendentally articulated, deserves further clarification.

As already pointed out, the transcendental account of the constitution of objects of inquiry within value-guided practices of inquiry is not to be conflated with a causal process of making any objects come into being. Transcendental constitution is no causal production, and it is particularly important for the pragmatist to emphasize this difference. It would be absurd for the pragmatist philosopher of historiography, for instance, to claim that the objects of historical inquiry, such as past events and processes, would be causally produced into the past by the present valuational activities of the historians, and it would presumably be equally absurd to suggest that the theologian's objects of inquiry—the structures of religious practices of dealing with what their practitioners take as spiritual realities—would simply be constructed by the scholars of religion. (The latter could also be ethically extremely problematic as a way of nonrecognizing the religious practitioners' own perspectives on the lives they are leading.)[72]

The relation between pragmatic realism and the Kantian account of pragmatism, as applied to the philosophy of the humanities, is in any event intimate. The pragmatist philosopher of the humanities should appreciate the *diversity* of the various issues of realism in the different fields of philosophy, while insisting on the need to investigate the realism question in the distinctive context of the humanities, too. We may also propose specifically pragmatist ways of dealing with such realism issues. A case in point would be Putnam's internal realism (which he later said he should have called "pragmatic realism").[73] Yet a "Putnamian" conception of pragmatic realism in the philosophy of the humanities acknowledges, more or less as we just did a moment ago, that scholarly fields like literary theory and criticism, historiography, and theology and religious studies may postulate—as real objects of inquiry—such things as, say, interpretive possibilities and potential meanings of texts. Putnam's internal realism (pragmatic realism) emphasizes pluralism in ontology by admitting objects like texts and their meanings among the "real things" there are in the world, as objects of inquiry. Indeed, Putnam (2004, 82–84) maintains that there is "something *mad*" in the scientific view that "passages which are difficult to interpret" do not exist in the world in itself.

However, we still need, *pace* Putnam, a Kantian transcendental account for such realism: pragmatic constructivism (invoking a human-made world) functions at the transcendental level, enabling "first-order" empirical realism about the objects whose postulation is made possible by our engagement in practices of inquiry. Mere pluralism in ontology, however pragmatic, is far from sufficient for the purposes of pragmatic realism without a transcendental account of how the plurality of ontological postulations is possible for us within our practices of inquiry. Thus, my version of pragmatist philosophy of the humanities suggests that pragmatic realism itself needs to be given a Kantian-like transcendental articulation. Pragmatic constructivism insisting on the human-made character of the world of objects postulated in our inquiries thus operates (only) at the transcendental level. This is, then, one way of articulating the inextricable entanglement, again at the transcendental level, of the natural and the human (or cultural)—without denying, of course, that the natural and the cultural are also empirically entangled in multiple ways.[74]

Holistic Pragmatism

The form of pragmatism in my view most valuable for a plausible overall philosophy of the humanities is not only inspired by Kantian transcendental philosophy but also based on the holistic pragmatism proposed by Morton White (e.g., 2002, 2005).[75] Holistic pragmatism is not restricted to the humanities but may in its own right function as a general theory of inquiry; at any rate, it is particularly well suited for a critical pragmatist philosophy of the humanities especially because it enables us to transcend the boundary between *the factual and the normative*. This, arguably, is essential in humanistic scholarship, both in formulating research hypotheses and in their critical evaluation. According to White, our beliefs—factual and normative beliefs included—constitute a holistic totality in the sense that any critical testing of them inevitably amounts to the testing of such a conjunction of beliefs as a whole.[76]

White (2002, 79) clearly wishes to preserve a form of historical realism in the sense that the historian, in his view, "seeks to tell the truth as natural and social scientists do," even though the primary aim is not generalization but (usually) something like the construction of a historical, and often explanatory, narrative, with the *explanandum* and the *explanans* both guided by human interests (see further ibid., 89ff.). Following the classical pragmatists, White plausibly rejects any "picture or copy view" of history (as much as a picture or copy view of science) (ibid., 101). No truths, as James already reminded us, can be usefully regarded as mere copies of an independent reality. White also refers to the plurality of interests at work in historiography, as constrained by the "ethical rules of the historical game" (ibid., 106): "It seems to me that we should recognize that the interests of the historian determine (a) his *terminus a quo* and his *terminus ad quem*, (b) the entrenched and the major intervening items in his chronicle, and (c) the items he selects as causes from his varying points of view. In that case, we should also recognize that his construction of a history is determined not only by the historian's interest in telling nothing but the truth but also by his other interests" (ibid., 102).

Whatever our "interests" are, they are, in any event, value-laden. This makes even the causal truth claims of a historiographer value-laden: "Although a historian tries to present causal truths about some subject in a narrative, he chooses *what* truths to link causally on the basis of value judgments that a fellow historian may not accept when telling a true story about the same subject" (White 2005, 40; see 49–50). White rejects full-blown or radical relativism, however, as well as a straightforwardly pragmatist view he associates with James; we cannot, he maintains, "do" anything with the "dead and buried" historical past with regard to our "practical aims" (ibid., 45–46). Here I would propose a more subtle understanding of practical aims. Even the most antiquarian historical interest in the past must, according to (Jamesian) pragmatism, serve our future experience, our challenges of living our lives in the world we find ourselves in. Those interests need not be practical or forward-looking in any immediate sense, but there must be a dimension of future-orientation in them. Otherwise we cannot even find any pragmatic meaning in the historical concepts we use. Recall the pragmatic maxim: it is in terms of the conceivable practical effects of (the objects of) our concepts and conceptions—including the objects of our historical concept(ion)s—that we must determine what those concepts and conceptions mean for us.[77]

No matter how explicitly pragmatist White's holistic pragmatism may in the end be considered, he formulates a clear and, in my view, generally plausible account of the entanglement of truth and interests as his conclusion:

> A historian's total judgment of what should be recorded in a history, and by implication in a chronicle, is a blend of two judgments: one of truth and one of memorability. Truth may be the stronger claimant and the more objective, but memorability is always a factor in spite of being subjective. The absence of an objective criterion of historical importance makes it very difficult to show that historical truths about a society's

economy or politics are more memorable than those about its philosophy. It also shows that there are more historical truths than are dreamt of by historians. (Ibid., 50)

Accordingly, the holistic pragmatist following White's lead must admit that value judgments about what is more or less "memorable" or historically interesting play a key role in the historian's choice of "facts"—even causal facts—to be included in a historical account of a phenomenon to be explained; accordingly, when examining not only the methodology but also the ontology of historiography, values are inescapably relevant along with "mere facts."[78] Moreover, when evaluating an argument with a normative conclusion, the holistic pragmatist maintains, we may revise or reject not only its normative but also (one or many among) its factual premises, provided that relevant adjustments are then made elsewhere in the overall belief system.[79] In the context of holistic pragmatism, philosophical and metaphilosophical ideas and arguments also constitute a single holistic totality and can only be critically evaluated as elements of such a whole. These holistic epistemological principles play an obvious role in the philosophy of historiography, but they are equally relevant in the philosophy of literary theory and of theology and religious studies. They are—if not according to White's own holistic pragmatism, at least according to a more strongly historicist and constructivist pragmatism such as Margolis's (e.g., 1995, 2012)—equally relevant in the natural sciences as well, since there is no inquiry, however objective, that would be immune to the influence of values and interests guiding our purposive practices. Even the natural sciences do not simply register ready-made objective facts, as pragmatists philosophers of science have of course always acknowledged (cf. chapter 2). However, the fact that the humanities, including history, do not do so is not, for pragmatists, a reason to claim that they would not be in the business of realistically capturing humanly speaking objective truths.

When holistic pragmatism and the transcendental characterization of the ontology of the humanities sketched above (or, more precisely, a metalevel transcendental account of what such ontological pursuits are and can achieve) are woven together, the picture of the ontological postulations of, for example, historiography may become clearer. The result is a comprehensive pragmatic realism based on a transcendental account of the necessary dependence of the possibility of historical facts and truths on our normative perspectives guiding our choice of relevant facts and truths—that is, on the (themselves historically mutable) value-laden relevance criteria embedded in our normative practices of inquiry. The pragmatic holism espoused by White comes to the picture here again: when critically evaluating our beliefs and theories (in the humanities or anywhere else), we are always simultaneously evaluating the entire system of normative principles, including our interests, needs, and values, that structure our inquiries into objective facts. Truth and objectivity are not sacrificed—not at all—but their transcendentally necessary embeddedness in normative interests and values is incorporated in the methodology of holistic belief fixation and assessment. What White calls historical "memorability"—that is, something's being valuable or relevant enough to be historically remembered—is itself an object of value-laden yet objectivity-pursuing inquiry. There may be no *fully* "objective criteria of historical importance" (in the superhuman sense of "objectivity" demanded by the metaphysical realist), as White says, but there is no reason to suppose that we could not engage in a value-guided rational discussion on such criteria within our practices of inquiry. A truly reflexive conception of holistic pragmatism presupposes that such pragmatic inquiry into values themselves, as guiding our choices of what is historically relevant and thus real, is possible for us. Hence, we may discuss the rational criteria of historical "memorability" or related relevance considerations as objectively as we can discuss any value-laden issues of the human world, as studied by the humanities and analyzed by the philosophy of the humanities.

We may on this basis briefly return to a critical examination of the kind of antirealistic ontology and truth-theory (as applied to historical statements) that, for example, Orwell's dystopic figure O'Brien espouses. As noted above, Winston claims to remember that airplanes existed already before the Party came to power, while O'Brien denies this and claims that if the Party says it is true that airplanes have only existed during the era of the Party, then this is true; there is, he maintains, no contrast whatsoever between what the Party believes or claims to be the case and what "really" is the case. At the face of it, this is obvious antirealism, and Orwell's novel has been taken to defend realism and the objectivity of truth (cf. Mounce 1997; Conant 2000). However, a holistically pragmatist analysis would be able to settle the matter in a philosophically illuminating way, without being carried away by the Rortyan claim that truth is unimportant in contrast to freedom (Rorty 1989). The claim that the opinion of the Party, or any other contingent context or framework, partly or entirely constitutes the truth about the airplanes is already to apply a certain value-laden framework to this particular issue. Insofar as normative statements about value are in principle to be critically tested as elements of one and the same totality together with factual statements, then we are never merely testing the truth claim about the airplanes (for instance) but an entire conjunction of statements about airplanes *and* the value framework within which it becomes so much as possible for us to claim any truths (or falsehoods) about them.[80] If we really take holism seriously, we are inevitably testing our very conception of truth itself when testing any particular truth claims, as that conception ultimately belongs to the same totality of our beliefs facing the "tribunal of experience" as a corporate body. Only pragmatism can, I would be willing to claim, really make sense of this reflexivity as a structural element of our practices of inquiry.

Carried to its logical conclusion, this conception of holistic pragmatism eventually yields a holistic conception of the relation between the transcendental and the empirical as well. Whenever testing any empirical claim or ontological postulation—whether in history or any other area—that a certain normative framework of inquiry makes possible for us, we are testing the entire conjunction of the claim or postulation *plus* the framework. That is, our entire conception of transcendental pragmatism is always at stake, holistically, whenever we set out to discuss any particular ontological postulations within our philosophical account of literary theory, historiography, or theology and religious studies (or any other field, for that matter). For the pragmatist philosopher of the humanities, it is fundamentally important to take this kind of holism very seriously.

Having elaborated on pragmatic realism and holistic pragmatism as well as their relation to "transcendental pragmatism," I wish to add a few remarks on *methodological* and *ethical* issues concerning the humanities within the overall position we are developing.

Methodologically, pragmatism enables us to avoid at least the naïve versions of what we may call "immersive" approaches to the humanities, such as the Collingwoodian conception of historical understanding as "re-enactment" of past thoughts or actions,[81] accounts of literary understanding in terms of the reader's "immersion" in the text, as well as participatory or (auto)ethnographical conceptions of understanding in religious studies, while contributing to critical research on how, say, historians or literary theorists "think," that is, what kind of cognitive mechanisms (of, e.g., imagination) historical or literary scholarship involves (cf., e.g., Koposov 2009). Once again, these issues are not merely methodological but involve ontological aspects, as they are related to the very reality that scholars in the humanities are in the business of investigating. Pragmatism, in short, is needed for the proper kind of *critical distance* between the scholar and the object of study in the methodology of the humanities—recognizing *both* the shared humanity of the scholar and the object or topic of research *and* the impossibility of ever truly sharing (reenacting, immersing in) other human beings' experiences. This methodological discussion has also clear ethical significance, at it concerns our relations, as human beings and scholars, to the individuals and their cultural productions that our humanistic scholarship takes as its research objects.

While pragmatism incorporates its own methodology, especially the pragmatic maxim (see chapter 2), we can also say that pragmatism sets itself "against method" in the sense of emphasizing that the humanities are not, or at least need not be and should not be forced to be, "paradigmatic" in Kuhn's sense. That is, the humanities need not be regarded as applying certain definitive paradigms of problem-solving as quasi-mechanical algorithms, hoping to make humanistic inquiry look "scientific" and less unclear or indeterminate. A Kuhnian strategy of analysis in the pragmatist philosophy of the humanities should thus not amount to a loose application of "paradigms" to humanistic research (as in phrases such as the "Chicago paradigm" of pragmatism) but to a critique of the idea of humanistic inquiry as "paradigmatic" normal science (in Kuhn's original sense of "paradigm" as an exemplar of puzzle-solving).

A distinctive pragmatist ethics of humanistic research should thus also be developed in relation to methodological and ontological questions concerning appropriate critical distance. In relation to this overall set of issues, it might also be more practically considered how the research practices in the humanities may have changed or may be changing, as more and more research is conducted in groups rather than individually.[82] Pragmatist philosophy of the humanities ought to be able to find a critical balance between individualist and collective research practices in a manner that honors the ethical requirement of maintaining a proper critical distance. Again, however, these themes cannot be included in the present programmatic inquiry.

Let me close this chapter with some further (in a broad sense) *metaphilosophical* remarks. First, pragmatism yields a distinctive account of the possible analogies in the philosophy of the humanities of the opposition between *naturalism and antinaturalism* in general philosophy of science and epistemology (for more details on this issue, see chapter 4).[83] As a first approximation, this distinction may be compared to the one between *historicism* and *antihistoricism*, more central to the humanities than the naturalism issue as such. For the philosophical naturalist, normative issues in epistemology and (general) philosophy of science or theory of inquiry cannot be sharply distinguished from, or regarded as autonomous in relation to or as more fundamental than, factual (naturalistically discernible) issues that concern the nature of human beings and their scientific practices of inquiry as knowledge-producing agents. The antinaturalist denies this and claims that epistemology and philosophy of science must irreducibly autonomously maintain a normative standpoint to such issues.

Now, an analogous problem in the humanities concerns our historical existence. Due to our irreducible historicity, there is no ahistorical formulation of historical explanations or literary interpretations, for instance, nor of philosophical problems or, for that matter, their solutions. Unless we are full-blown naturalists about philosophy itself, we also need to problematize the idea of directly applying the concept of truth to philosophical theories (cf. above), as if those theories could be ahistorically true or false. Indeed, only a very straightforwardly naturalized conception of philosophy would explicitly maintain that philosophical theories are truth-apt exactly in the sense in which scientific theories are. Philosophy thus needs to be understood as in certain respects comparable to literature rather than science,[84] while maintaining its argumentative rigor. This is, again, possible on holistically pragmatist grounds. In relation to this metaphilosophical moral, pragmatist research may develop an increased awareness of the historicity of humanistic scholarship itself, while avoiding both ahistorical views on the nature of research (arguably typical of narrowly conceived mainstream analytic philosophy) and overly radical historicism (which tends to lead to uncritical relativism), as well as the reduction of the aims of historical scholarship to a mere antiquarian interest.[85]

It is fully in accordance with this (in itself historicist) way of thinking that pragmatism can make sense of the idea that even when inquiring into the human past, or into the meanings of texts written in the past, we are inevitably doing so with reference to our future concerns and interests defined by our values. Those past objects and events are relevant to us now and in our lives unfolding toward the future, and the truth claims we make about them need to be assessed within this dynamic valuational practical framework (cf. again Tamm 2014). More strongly, *only* a pragmatist philosophy of the humanities, it might be argued, is truly able to make sense of this idea.

A further ethically relevant metalevel hypothesis at this point is that the frequently discussed conflict between *humanism and anti- or posthumanism* can also be examined and resolved in pragmatist terms. It would, however, have to be examined in detail how exactly this opposition is related to the nature of the humanities. Today many scholars in the humanities argue against classical humanism and the traditional Enlightenment subject, proposing to replace these by an allegedly both ethically and politically superior posthumanist understanding of human existence as not in any essential sense different from, say, the existence of nonhuman species. This is, again, an immensely large topic not to be covered here. However, it can be maintained that developing a pragmatist philosophy of the humanities is also highly relevant to developing a distinctive pragmatist humanism critically encountering at least the most radical versions of post- or antihumanism (cf. Pihlström 2021).[86] A pragmatist examination of the humanities and humanism also involves an ethical exploration of *our relations to other human beings*—including historical and contemporary figures that may be or become our objects of study in the different humanistic disciplines.

It may be suggested, moreover, that a certain kind of critical distance in inquiry is an ethical requirement for humanistic scholarship with obvious metaphysical, epistemological, and methodological relevance; indeed, it can be regarded as an important value guiding our metaphysical, epistemological, and methodological pursuits. My hypothesis is that it is, again, holistic pragmatism that (only) can make sufficient sense of the continuous search for a balance between the extremes of "too much distance" and "too little distance" in our inquiries. Pragmatist humanism is essentially about the right kind of distance we should take from other human beings within our human practices, including the practices of inquiry.[87] The necessity, both epistemic and ethical, of keeping a critical distance from others does not entail, however, that we would not have to be constantly concerned, also when engaging in humanistic scholarship, with how to respond to and recognize, or acknowledge, other human beings.

We may ask, metaphilosophically, whether philosophy is autonomous and/or foundational in relation to the (other) humanities—for example, literary theory and criticism, historiography, and theology and/or religious studies—that is, what is the appropriate critical distance between philosophical inquiries and the practices of inquiry within such humanistic fields. Is philosophy in some sense the "ground" of these (and other) disciplines, somehow over and above them? (This issue is closely related to the questions concerning naturalism and historicism, and their denials; see above.) Very different philosophical orientations, such as logical empiricism and phenomenology, have suggested that it is indeed such a ground. However, holistic pragmatism rather argues that philosophizing inevitably begins in medias res: philosophical and humanistic inquiries constitute, again, a web to be holistically evaluated. There is no imagined state of presuppositionlessness from which philosophical investigations could get started, as a Cartesian foundationalist, for example, would assume.

Philosophy, then, is only *relatively* autonomous, certainly not reducible to literary criticism (though Rorty might have suggested it is), to historiography, to theology, or to anything else, but not over and above them, either, in the sense of being able to fully ground their ontologies and methodologies, or in the sense of being able to "dictate" their proper norms of conduct. A pragmatist philosophy of the humanities must walk the thin line of not claiming to set up any philosophical foundation for the disciplines it studies and of not claiming philosophy to be superfluous or irrelevant with regard to them, either. As outlined here, a pragmatist philosophy of the humanities can examine the general traits of humanistic ontologies, for instance, but it must leave specific ontological commitments and postulations of theoretical entities to the detailed investigations conducted within the humanistic disciplines themselves. This is analogous to the way in which a pragmatist philosopher of science must, in emphasizing the practice-ladenness of scientific inquiry, avoid telling the physicist what kind of specific particles or energy fields to postulate, that is, to avoid intervening in the physicists' own practices from a philosophical perspective. This moderate naturalism is actually a corollary of holistic pragmatism, if we really take seriously the kind of holism briefly sketched above.

In his critical dialogue with Putnam, Bernard Williams (2006 [2000], chapter 16) interestingly defended the idea of philosophy itself as a humanistic discipline,[88] investigating both our attachment to and our ability to detach ourselves from certain historically contingent (local, nonabsolute, nonscientific) concepts, such as liberalism and human rights, for example. Our historical understanding of the contingent emergence of such concepts is crucial. Rorty (1989) famously took such historicity to a certain extreme, emphasizing, in terms of his *ironism*, that we should adopt a fully self-conscious historicism, acknowledging the radical contingency of our "final vocabularies." Williams argues, however, that there is no need for the problem that ironism is intended to solve. Now, pragmatism, in my view, should approach this issue by drawing attention to our practices of using concepts, our being committed to them by our engagement in practices.[89] We need an active interplay of a pragmatist understanding of the "natural" history of our concept-use[90] and transcendental analysis and/or reflection on what it means for us ("from within" our concept-use) to be committed to those concepts in a sense in which we recognize their constitutive role for the very structure or even possibility of our practices, while being aware of their historical contingency. There is, in Williams's (2006 [2000], 195–196) terms, something in our constitutive concepts, or in what Rorty called our final vocabularies, that can be characterized by the German term, "*Unverhintergehbarkeit.*" We cannot back them up with anything more fundamental and cannot thus "go behind" them. It is this feature of them—whatever it is that makes them constitutive for our practices—that a philosophical analysis of our conceptualizing activities should focus on. Yet, this "not-being-able-to-go-behind" is, despite its contingency, itself a transcendental feature of our practices of organizing our lives and world in terms of those concepts; it is *not* a feature of those concepts independently of our ongoing practices.

Williams, in my view, offers an ample defense of the humanistic project of "trying to understand ourselves" (ibid., 198) that takes fundamentally seriously the contingent historicity of the concepts in terms of which we structure our world and lives, with the recognition that some of those concepts are—for us, from our practitioners' perspective—so basic that they cannot be justified in terms of any more fundamental concepts. I do share Putnam's worries about Williams's (also in my view) unfortunate notion of the "absolute conception" of the world, but one may also appreciate Williams's willingness to resort to a "contrastive 'we'" in the sense of the community of us human beings, "humans as contrasted with other possible beings" (ibid., 187). Therefore, the point Williams wishes to make about philosophy as a humanistic project of understanding ourselves in my view requires a robust conception of a "transcendental we" (cf. Lear 1986)—though developing that point further is no longer a task of this inquiry (see also Pihlström 2003a, 2020, 2021).

Yet, there is also an element of pragmatic pluralism in this picture that cannot be neglected.[91] We have to develop a pragmatic understanding of our own selves—of ourselves as inquirers, or as philosophers—as being able to switch the perspective between the "natural-historical" account (acknowledging full contingency) and the transcendental (including ethical as well as metaphysical) commitment focusing on constitutive necessity, that is, between detachment and attachment. Philosophy as a humanistic discipline must develop a rich diet of both pragmatist and transcendental methodologies. The perspective-switching transcendental self (cf. also Pihlström 2016) may be an "object" of philosophical inquiry, though it is precisely not an object at all but, by definition, a subject to whom objects can be given, or in Wittgensteinian terms, a "limit of the world" instead of any "thing" in the world. At this point, a pragmatist philosophy of the humanities, enriched by Kantian transcendental concepts and methodology, will already move on to the area of fundamental transcendental questions of epistemology and ontology—questions concerning the availability of the world as an object of inquiry for us in the first place—and therefore a further articulation of this aspect of pragmatist philosophy of the humanities will have to refer to the foundational work done on transcendental pragmatism in general (cf. again Pihlström 2003a, 2009, 2016, 2020, 2021).

Yet another "humanistic" benefit, or pragmatic value, of the pragmatist philosophy of the humanities lies in its ability to make sense of the potential *impact* of the humanities (and arguably all the humanistic and social-scientific fields of inquiry) while maintaining a commitment to the irreducible inherent value of humanistic learning, scholarship, and *Bildung*.[92] There should be no reduction either way. The relevant kind of impact may be enormously diversified: whenever discussing the potential impact of the humanities, we should remember that such impact can take place within the academia itself (and even there highly diversely, e.g., within our "own" field as well as across other disciplines) and outside the academia in environing society. It is typically also a very long-term matter. In particular, a pragmatist analysis of the impact of humanistic inquiry should always duly recognize that such impact may take place across an enormously (humanly speaking) long time scale. Only an extremely naïve form of pragmatism will seek to reduce academic impact to a narrowly conceived immediate or short-term benefit.

I have not developed, nor will I here develop, any substantial account of the impact of humanistic scholarship in the academia or in society. It is nevertheless important for us to realize that pragmatism is highly valuable in this more practical and "political" respect as well. For a holistic pragmatist, all this is ultimately entangled: metaphysics, epistemology, ethics, methodology, as well as societal and political relevance considerations concerning the value of the humanities all need to be examined as an interpenetrated set of normative value issues concerning the amelioration of our practices.

Finally, our understanding of the basic philosophical character of the humanities matters tremendously to what kind of "human world" we take ourselves to be living in—that is, whether it is a world of a thoroughly "disenchanted" scientific picture of reality (a notion we owe to Max Weber; cf. Joas 2017; Schlette et al. 2022; Pihlström 2021, chapter 4) or a world partially "re-enchanted" through a pragmatic acknowledgment of the meanings, values, and other normative and interpretive structures that the humanities are in the business of examining and that we may view as irreducible to mere "matter in motion" as understood by the natural sciences. No humanistic ontology entitles us to any wild speculation going beyond the broadly naturalist account of the universe based on our most advanced science, but taking the pursuit of truth seriously in the humanities—as articulated in pragmatist terms here—may help us view the natural sciences as one aspect among others of our human constitution of meaningful reality. In order to deepen this dialogue between naturalism and philosophical attempts to account for irreducible normativity, the next chapter will be devoted to the complex relations between naturalized and transcendental approaches to the humanities.

Chapter 4

Pragmatic Naturalism and Transcendental Arguments in the Philosophy of the Humanities

The previous chapter was, as this entire book is, somewhat programmatic in outlining potential case studies as well as general research themes and more specific questions and hypotheses that would all have to be explored in much greater detail in a more substantial investigation of pragmatist philosophy of the humanities. I do hope, at any rate, that it sketched out what *a* plausible pragmatist philosophy of the humanities might approximately look like, which problems it would have to tackle, what kind of ideas it could develop further, and how it might proceed in approaching the various open issues in the field. The purpose of this book, as explained, is only to outline such a project (to offer a "prolegomenon" to it, as it were). In this chapter, I will examine more closely a fundamental philosophical issue that I take to be common to the potentially diverging case study areas—the relation between naturalism and transcendental arguments in the philosophy of the humanities—again seeking to argue that a pragmatist approach can crucially enlighten such topics. Indeed, the prospects of entangling naturalism and transcendental reflection[1] are, I will show, highly relevant to pragmatist philosophy of the humanities. While the previous chapter laid out the overall ontological nature of humanistic disciplines from a pragmatist standpoint, this more metaphilosophical chapter primarily investigates philosophy itself as a discipline in its naturalized and transcendental shapes, and thus its potential relevance to our understanding of humanistic inquiry.

The main motivation for turning to a more detailed critical examination of transcendental and "naturalizing" projects in this chapter is the nagging question concerning the credentials of the philosophical point of view itself for understanding the nature of the humanities. Why, someone might ask, do we need a *philosophy* of the humanities in the first place? Wouldn't it be sufficient to treat the relations between the humanistic disciplines and their objects (for instance) from a theoretical standpoint lying within the humanities themselves? This proposal would be analogous to what is known as naturalism (or naturalized epistemology) in general philosophy of science and theory of inquiry (cf. chapter 2).

Whatever (pragmatist) philosophy of the humanities is, it is surely a subcategory of philosophy. In order to become clearer about how exactly a philosophical investigation of our scientific and scholarly activities can yield any warranted account of the kinds of issues tentatively and inconclusively discussed in the previous chapter, we also need to examine some conflicting conceptions of the possibility of what can be called "philosophical knowledge." This chapter will thus first focus on the tension between naturalist and anti- or nonnaturalist approaches to human epistemic pursuits in general, and philosophy in particular, thus investigating the basic nature of the cognitive project of the philosophy of the humanities. There are several areas of discourse that could be examined as exemplifying the contrast between philosophical knowledge and the kind of knowledge that is the goal of the special disciplines—both the natural sciences and the humanities. A key question is whether philosophy can teach us any new truths about its subject matters (e.g., morality, science, or religion—or the humanities) that cannot be taught by the various scientific and scholarly disciplines, including humanistic disciplines, investigating those same subject matters.[2] If our answer to this question is affirmative, then the next questions are obvious: Why and how is philosophical knowledge different from special-scientific knowledge? More specifically, insofar as we are willing to understand the nature of the humanities, how exactly should we try to do this—by engaging in what I have called the philosophy of the humanities, or perhaps by just developing the humanities themselves, or possibly even simply by providing natural-scientific (e.g., neurophysiological) explanations of human beings' actions as they pursue humanistic scholarship? What kind of truths, moreover, are the new truths that we may learn by investigating philosophically the kinds of topics—for example, realism—that were discussed as central for the philosophy of the humanities in the previous chapter? I will, indeed, begin this examination by returning to realism, the key issue of this entire volume, in relation to the project of naturalization (of the philosophy of science and inquiry generally and of the humanities in particular).

Addressing such questions is also necessary if one wishes to say anything significant about the more general program of naturalism that any pragmatist needs to take a stand on. After having explored naturalization and its problems at some length, I will toward the end of this chapter return to transcendental philosophy and transcendental arguments within pragmatism. The discussion as a whole, implicitly creating a critical dialogue between naturalizing and transcendental perspectives on our epistemic activities, is intended to enhance our understanding of what it means for us to inquire into the nature of the human world. For the philosophy of the humanities, it is vital to come to terms with the program of naturalism in philosophy generally and in epistemology and theory of inquiry in particular; therefore the metaphilosophical explorations of "philosophical knowledge" in contrast to various naturalization programs proposing to reduce human epistemic normativity to merely natural matters of fact need serious attention in a pragmatist articulation of what kind of cognitive projects the humanities can and should be conceived as. In short, a pragmatist philosophy of the humanities may propose to acquire (practice-embedded) philosophical knowledge about the nature of the humanities, and it is this type of knowledge claim that radical naturalization projects call into question.

No comprehensive treatment of either naturalism or transcendental arguments, or their mutual relations, is possible in this chapter, of course. My discussion will be confined to points that I believe ought to be taken into consideration when developing a pragmatist philosophy of the humanities.

The "Natural Ontological Attitude"

The Quinean rejection of aprioristic "first philosophy" (briefly discussed in chapter 2) might be captured as the slogan, "Wherever science will lead, I will follow" (Keil and Schnädelbach 2000, 22)—even though this slogan itself, as presumably any formulation of naturalism, is philosophical rather than simply scientific. This maxim contains, *in nuce*, the naturalist's central metaphilosophical idea: there are no philosophical problems concerning reality, existence, truth, or knowledge prior to, or independently of, the various scientific problems to be encountered and resolved within the special-scientific disciplines themselves. It nicely captures Quine's basic "naturalizing" position, as well as, for example, Wilfrid Sellars's (1963) conception of (advanced, best-explaining) science as the "measure" of what is and of what is not.[3] Applied to the humanities, these views could claim, for example, that there are no philosophical questions concerning the ontology of meanings or the historical past over and above questions that can be studied by the humanistic disciplines themselves.

Arthur Fine's (1996 [1986]) "natural ontological attitude" (NOA), already mentioned in chapter 2 above, can be regarded as an extreme example of naturalism in the philosophy of science. It is tempting to say that Fine's NOA—the view, roughly, that science will take care of itself without needing help from any philosophical conceptualizations and interpretations—is where Quine's naturalistic repudiation of "first philosophy" ultimately leads us—even though Quine may, in the end, have left more room for the autonomy of philosophy than Fine, as he arguably did preserve elements of rather traditional metaphysics in his philosophical system, seeking to explicate the broad categorial features of the world that science reveals to us (see Koskinen 2004). On the other hand, Fine hopes to disentangle himself from more radical naturalists' views on "scientistic naturalization" and from any essentialist idea that science itself is a "natural kind" or subject to universal laws (Fine 1996 [1986], 177). It is not clear that Quine would be guilty of scientistic naturalization in this sense, although he would obviously be willing to grant that the same natural (ultimately physical) laws that, according to our best theories, govern whatever takes place in the universe govern science itself as well. Fine, in any case, explicates the "wherever science leads us" maxim in a pure form. It will thus be useful for us to take a somewhat closer look at his position.[4]

Fine is famous for the critique of abductive defenses of scientific realism presented in his seminal 1984 paper, "The Natural Ontological Attitude" (reprinted in Fine 1996 [1986]). In that essay and many subsequent ones, he argues that realism—which he characterizes as the view that scientific theories and hypotheses, even when they are about unobservable entities or processes, are true or false independently of our abilities to know their truth-value and that science aims at truth about the mind- and theory-independent world—cannot be defended by means of an inference to the best explanation (that is, as the supposedly best explanation of our scientific practices) without begging the question against instrumentalist antirealists, since the abductive defenders of realism simply assume that good explanatory hypotheses legitimately can, or ought to, be taken to be true. Nor does Fine accept any antirealist (e.g., constructive empiricist, instrumentalist, or "internal realist")[5] interpretation of science, however. On the contrary, like Rorty, he prefers a thoroughly deflated, "no-theory" account of truth (ibid., 9)—and thus of the scientific or scholarly pursuit of truth. There is no philosophically interesting relation between our theories and the world they are about (a relation labeled "truth") that would have to be invoked in a systematic interpretation of science and inquiry. Both realist and antirealist attempts to interpret science philosophically are, according to Fine, "unnatural." We should simply stop worrying about typical philosophical (essentialist, ahistorical) questions concerning science, truth, reality, existence, and related notions. Instead, we ought to accept the ontological commitments of science (and of common sense) "naturally," without any extrascientific philosophical justification or problematization. We should, that is, take science "on its own terms," without attempting to make sense of it philosophically. This can be understood as a natural outcome of the kind of naturalized epistemology Quine (1969) famously defended (cf. chapter 2).

While Fine mostly discusses the physical sciences, the naturalized stance of the NOAist can in principle be extended to an account of the humanities as well: we should *not*, a NOAist philosopher of the humanities could argue, seek to interpret the humanities in the kinds of terms proposed in chapter 3 above—not, that is, in terms of the controversies between realism and its various alternatives (let alone any Peirce-inspired conceptual machinery of "real generals") or of any other systematic philosophical notions, however pragmatic, that might yield an interpretation and evaluation of humanistic practices of research from a philosophical point of view beyond those practices themselves. Instead, we should just take whatever entities the humanities postulate "at face value," believing without any philosophical problematization in theoretical objects such as the meanings of texts or historical facts and events. A philosophy—even pragmatist philosophy—that finds these problematic in any sense not available within the research practices that postulate them in the first place is to be rejected as something "unnatural," an unnecessary layer attached to the solid core of humanistic research itself. Whether there are literary meanings, for instance, is a question to be asked by literary theorists, not by philosophers, and whether there are past events independently of historians' interpretations is to be discussed by those historians themselves.

Fine's position in his 1996 postscript to the second edition of *The Shaky Game* (first published in 1986, and many of its articles earlier than that) is perhaps slightly less radical than his earlier statements. He does not seem to reject philosophy for good but only the sort of bad, worn-out philosophical questions that need no longer be asked as soon as we have adopted the relaxed and open-ended attitude of the science-sensitive NOAist. What he still regards as mistaken is the idea that we should "add distinctively philosophical overlays to science in order to make sense of it" (ibid., 188). Presumably, any claim to "philosophical knowledge" (about either science or the humanities) would, according to Fine, amount to such an "overlay" that has no use in genuine inquiries.

Fine's NOA has, unsurprisingly, been attacked from various philosophical perspectives, especially by scientific realists.[6] The typical critique can be summarized as follows: the NOAist *either* rejects philosophical questions about science altogether (in which case their position is not philosophically interesting and there is no reason for a realistically inclined philosopher to subscribe to it) *or* embraces some form of scientific realism after all, precisely because the ontological commitments of our accepted scientific theories are to be taken at face value (in which case NOA provides no threat to realism at all and in fact turns out to be a philosophical interpretation of science, after all, namely, a realistic one). Why, most critics seem to ask, shouldn't scientific realism, which postulates a mind- and theory-independent reality "out there" as the object of our scientific research, be our "natural attitude" to science? We may find it necessary to heavily modify such a realism, for example, along the lines of pragmatic realism (see chapters 2 and 3 above); even so, Fine's arguments against realistic philosophy of science do seem to be inconclusive. The same could, moreover, be argued, mutatis mutandis, in the context of the realism discussion concerning the humanities, should anyone propose a humanistic analogy to NOA.

Still, Fine has made a very important point. It is not clear, at least not without further argument, that there *is* any specific philosophical knowledge to be achieved through traditional analysis of issues such as realism (as applied to the sciences or to the humanities). It might indeed be the case that all the knowledge we can legitimately hope to obtain is scientific and scholarly knowledge and that our knowledge about scientific or humanistic inquiry itself, insofar as it can be considered knowledge at all, is scientific and/or humanistic, too, rather than philosophical. Thus, Fine, like all naturalists, presents a challenge for those who believe in anything like "philosophical knowledge." His challenge is parallel to, and in a way even more extreme than, someone like Quine's, even though he does not share the latter's scientism and physicalism.[7] Both appear to hold that insofar as concepts such as realism, truth, existence, and reference can be spoken about at all, they should be spoken about *within* science, not in any prior philosophy of science. The same would be the case regarding the use of these notions within the humanities. There would be no privileged access by anything like the philosophy of the humanities to the ways in which theories formulated in humanistic scholarship can be said to have truth-values or refer to existing realities.

On the other hand, philosophers defending the possibility of philosophical knowledge may argue that we cannot really enjoy the kind of philosophical neutrality that radical naturalizers of philosophy like Fine dream about. We always already stand on a philosophically committed ground. Thus, one cannot completely avoid the issue of realism, for example, neither in the sciences nor in the humanities. If one takes the commitments of science—or of the humanities—at face value, or maintains, with Quine or Sellars, that science determines the correct ontology of our world, one *is*, in a sense, a scientific realist, postulating an independent, scientifically explainable reality. (Quine, after all, used to describe himself as a "robust realist.") If, on the other hand, one declares that there is no objective "world" out there for science or the humanities to study, then one should rather be called an antirealist. It is not always clear how Fine's (or Quine's) views should be classified in this respect.

What is more obvious is that both Quine and Fine, qua naturalists, differ in crucial respects from more traditional metaphysical naturalists or physicalists like David Armstrong (1997). The latter's naturalism is not metaphilosophically as radical as the formers', since Armstrong believes that general ontological questions, such as the question of whether there are universals or whether the world ultimately consists of states of affairs or not, ought to be decided by means of philosophical analysis prior to any scientific investigation. Still, science, according to Armstrong, ought to determine our ontology in the sense that it will eventually decide *which* universals, if any, really exist—indeed, this is the task of the natural sciences, according to Armstrong, rather than the humanities. In this way, science is, again, epistemically speaking, the measure of what there is, although there are abstract and general philosophical issues underlying any scientific account of the world. We may say that Armstrong subscribes to ontological naturalism but not to anything like the "natural ontological attitude" in Fine's sense. Nor is his naturalism metaphilosophically as holistic and empiricist as Quine's. Armstrong might be willing to say that we can *know*, in some philosophical—albeit fallible and scientifically revisable—manner, that, for example, universals exist and are instantiated in states of affairs (that is, we can have philosophical knowledge about their existence, although this knowledge will have to be supplemented by genuinely scientific knowledge about which universals are actually instantiated). Still, insofar as even Quine engages in something like *metaphysica generalis* (see Koskinen 2004), one might suspect that the distance between someone like Quine and someone like Armstrong is not as great as it first seems. Clearly, the former rejects the existence of properties, and the latter believes in universals—but that is a difference at the level of their "first-order" philosophical views, so to speak, not (at least not primarily) one concerning the *status* of such views. Both Quinean nominalism (should that be a correct label to be attached to his rejection of properties, intensions, meanings, etc.) and Armstrongian realism are philosophical commitments made, in Quine's terms, within the most abstract and general part of our holistic scientific enterprise.[8] Similar commitments more clearly relevant to the philosophy of the humanities might include ontological postulations of, say, past states of affairs or textual meanings—or values themselves as "real generals" guiding our ontological commitments (cf. again chapter 3).

It seems that there is no analogous role for philosophical knowledge to play in Fine's view. Instead, Fine tells us, philosophizing should not disturb the natural advancement of scientific knowledge. We have seen that Fine launches a fundamental attack on the very idea of there being specifically philosophical knowledge about science—or, more broadly, about any normative practices of inquiry, including the humanities. However, a reflexive question arises: if NOA is a plausible position, is this because it is *true*—and *knowable*? Could NOA, or naturalism generally, itself be "made true" by the way things naturally are?[9] What exactly would such an attribution of (any) truth-value to NOA mean, and how—within what kind of inquiry—could we determine whether this is a correct account of NOA and its relation to reality? Would it even make sense?

Seeking a Truly Natural Attitude

Naturalism can, as we have seen, be subjected to philosophical scrutiny at a reflexive metalevel through a critical examination of Fine's NOA (which, of course, is only discussed as an illuminating example here). According to the (in one sense) extreme naturalism Fine advocates, science should simply be investigated and explained scientifically, without recourse to philosophical speculations or interpretations.[10] *But why?* If we carry naturalism into its natural extreme, claiming that there is only a scientific perspective available for us for pursuing a fair and reliable account of science (or analogously of the humanities), shouldn't we also claim, equally "naturalistically," that *religion*, for instance, should not be explained scientifically (since *that* would amount to a step outside the "natural attitudes" adopted *within* religious practices themselves) but *religiously*? Wouldn't a religious study of religion, instead of any scientific or scholarly approach,[11] be the only fair option for the one who has adopted a truly natural ontological attitude? Shouldn't we, then, believe what religious practices ontologically postulate, without engaging in any "prior philosophy"—or any prior science seeking to understand or explain what religion "is" or how it is generated by some allegedly more basic mechanisms?[12]

James Robert Brown (1994, 17–18) touches a similar issue in what I find a simple but convincing argument against NOA. The "theological analogy" of NOA, he says, would be "to take the Bible at face value."[13] While such an unreflective, "natural" reading might be our initial reading (both in the case of science and of religion), it can hardly be our final one, since rival interpretations (of the Bible or of science) quickly arise. As Brown points out, both religious fundamentalists and atheists usually read the Bible realistically, disagreeing about the truth-value of (at least some of) its statements and assuming, as realists do, that those statements do have truth-values independently of whether or not we can determine what those truth-values are. Liberal believers may step closer to antirealism, as they are willing to interpret religious or Biblical statements nonliterally, symbolically, or metaphorically. Now, NOA, in the case of either religion or science, leads us nowhere in such controversies.[14] It is a conversation-stopper rather than a return to genuine "naturalness." The notion of "naturalism" itself becomes rather elusive here.

Consider, furthermore, the analogous case of "taking at face value" the postulations made in a work of literature. Wouldn't that also be a (radically) NOAist way of thinking about the relation between literature and reality? How could one even determine, from within the work itself taken at face value, that it is a fictional work? In order to determine that—and in order to focus one's interpretation on, say, the representational relations the work bears on the world around us, conscious of its fictional characteristics—we need to take a step out of the work and maintain a critical distance to it. That is, we have to approach it as a critical reader does, from the point of view of literary criticism rather than literature itself. I do not see why this would be an unfair analogy. In a corresponding sense, the philosopher willing to understand science and the humanities cannot simply remain "within" them but must take a philosophical step to a "critically distant" position of interpretation and analysis. To take such a step within an overall pragmatist framework is, I am trying to argue, a way of maintaining critical distance while not going too far, that is, while appreciating the fact that the practices of inquiry and interpretation are indeed practices, human ways of being in the world.

What, furthermore, would it mean to naturalize the issue of realism in this context? For naturalist philosophers of science like Quine or Fine, this means, as we have noted, that notions such as "reality," "existence," "reference," and "truth" are internal to science rather than being the private property of philosophers seeking to interpret science in an a priori fashion. In general philosophy of science, we may distinguish between the opposition between realism and antirealism (1) at the level of scientific practices and language-use themselves, (2) at the level of philosophy of science seeking to interpret those practices from an "internal" point of view, attempting to render them significant to the people who engage in them, and (3) at the level of purportedly neutral science studies, approaching scientific practices from an "external" point of view, in which no philosophical commitments are made. Now, which of these levels is the relevant one in the naturalization of the realism issue? It is not obvious that a naturalistic philosopher of science should simply adopt level (3), if they follow their naturalistic faith. It is equally plausible to suggest that the naturalization should occur at level (1), within the "natural" practice of science itself. If so, then the charge that the normative dimension of scientific language and practices qua scientific has been ignored becomes all the more pressing. To adopt level (3) for the framework of one's naturalizing project is already to make a value-laden commitment, to choose a philosophical perspective, albeit one broader than the "purely" philosophical one of level (2). It is *not* simply to do science, as distinguished from all philosophical interpretations and problematizations. The kind of naturalism capable of justifying, say, level (3), presupposes philosophical commitments and *is* a philosophical commitment. Again, a similar argument could be presented in the philosophy of the humanities against an analogous program of thoroughgoing "naturalization"—say, historicization—of the normative.[15]

NOA might look similar to the kind of pragmatic pluralism about ontology I have defended in this book: there *are* entities such as literary and religious meanings postulated within the humanistic disciplines, just as much as there are entities like electrons, genes, and social group pressures postulated in the natural and social sciences. Operating (in the philosophy of the humanities and more generally) within such a general understanding of pluralism is, of course, well in harmony with both classical pragmatism, especially Jamesian pragmatic pluralism (cf. again James 1975 [1907], Lectures IV-V), and neopragmatism, for example, Putnam's internal or pragmatic realism (see, e.g., Putnam 1981, 1990). These versions of pragmatic pluralism, just like NOA, are opposed to reductionisms that try to narrow down, following metaphysical realism, a privileged class of entities that the world "in itself" is taken to be composed of, an ultimate furniture of the world. However, pragmatic pluralists do not rest content with the NOAist relaxed acceptance of whatever entities the sciences or the humanities contingently happen to postulate. They observe, on the contrary, that the price of such a relaxed attitude is an uncontrolled proliferation of pluralistic ontology beyond any reasonable limits. Would pragmatic pluralists then also have to endorse ("take at face value") the indefinitely numerous wild ontological postulations that are, for example, made in the historical documents the humanities are concerned with? Where would the (or any) limits be drawn?

A key idea in truly pragmatic pluralism—unlike NOA—is that ontological postulation is always based on, and takes place within, critically and self-critically engaged normative practices of inquiry. *No* ontological postulation whatsoever—in the sciences or in the humanities, or, for that matter, in any other human area of discourse, such as religion or everyday life—should be "taken at face value" in the sense that no philosophical problematization or critique would be relevant. *All* our ontological postulations, however "natural" and plural, need to be subjected to careful critical scrutiny—not merely within the practices making those postulations but within a critical philosophical metalevel analysis of those practices.

The problem we are facing might, accordingly, now be diagnosed as follows. Extreme naturalism, such as NOA, does not provide a sufficiently rich normative framework for critically distinguishing any specific practice (or its ontological commitments) from any other or for favoring one such practice (or its commitments) rather than another. We should follow "good science" without pursuing ontological questions beyond the postulation of the entities that good science itself postulates (Fine 1996 [1986], 184), but how are we to determine the criteria of good science? The question of why science and not religion (or even some pseudoscience) cannot, any more than the realism question, itself be answered in *scientific* terms or in religious ones, for that matter. There can be no purely scientific justification for a scientific study of *anything*, even science itself, or for a realistic (or antirealistic) interpretation of such a study; indeed, more precisely, any such justification is hardly stronger than a religious justification for a religious study of religion. What is required is an irreducibly philosophical account of normative issues, especially methodological and axiological ones. As E. P. Brandon (1997) also argues, NOA may be a good attitude to adopt *within* science, as far as only science itself is concerned, but it is unable to tell us why we ought to prefer science to, say, astrology or religious fundamentalism.[16] Similarly, it is unable to tell us why we ought to prefer a serious academic historical inquiry into our human past to other possible approaches, such as an "inquiry" based on ancient myths or stories, or pseudoscientific nationalist or authoritarian memory politics.[17] Furthermore, it cannot tell us why we should not simply view historiography as fiction-writing. It fails to acknowledge the differences between the normative structures of these different human practices. Accordingly, it also prevents us from truly *engaging with* the kind of philosophical issues explored in chapter 3 above.

Belief systems and doxastic practices themselves (science, the humanities, religion, and others) are, we may say, essentially *contingent* in the sense that it is not necessary for us to adopt any particular system or operate within any particular normatively organized practice. We have found some reasons to think that it is only at a genuinely philosophical level that normative questions related to the justification of such systems can be adequately discussed. In this way, perhaps, a philosophical attitude enables us to distinguish between what is contingent or can conceivably be thought to be "otherwise" and what is (at least contextually) necessary or noncontingent.[18] If NOA, or any form of naturalism, were a *correct* conception of science, then it would be a philosophical conception, after all (which in a sense renders it self-refuting). It is an *addition* to whatever the ontological postulations of scientific theories contain, although its main point is that no such (philosophical) addition should be made. As Geert Keil and Herbert Schnädelbach (2000, 35) point out in introducing a volume of essays on naturalism, the naturalist ends up with a dilemma resembling the situation in which Wittgenstein finds himself at *Tractatus* §6.53: insofar as everything that can (or should, according to naturalism) be said belongs to the totality of scientific propositions, there is no room for the naturalist thesis itself. It is not a scientific proposition but a philosophical one (an "addition," as it were). Conversely, if this thesis *is* added, its advocate has taken the crucial step beyond what they are entitled to claim according to the asserted thesis itself (see also Janich 2000, 291 and passim; Keil 2002, chapter 5).

Naturalism will, accordingly, have to react to the following dilemma: either naturalism, declaring that the world is wholly natural and is to be studied by means of the empirical sciences, is not included in or justified by empirical science, in which case it is self-defeating, or it depends on "a special reformulation of the 'proper understanding' of empirical science," in which case it is philosophically harmless, hardly convincing for those who do not already share the naturalist's picture of science (Moser and Yandell 2000, 13).[19] There is, then, no way of avoiding normative discussion concerning the basic orientation of naturalism itself. After all, the naturalist, even the NOAist, is a normatively engaging agent—at least when arguing for the naturalistic position or treating it as a correct or at least well-established one rather than just stating it without argument (in which case naturalism would hardly be philosophically interesting). Any extreme naturalism that eliminates the possibility of normative debate concerning the very criteria of acceptability of naturalism itself is self-destructive.[20]

Furthermore, the emergence of normativity as a pervasive feature of human life need not be accounted for in any nonnaturalist or supernaturalist manner, since we can see normativity simply as being grounded in our *human nature*, in our being the kind of creatures we naturally are and the practices we naturally engage in (see Pihlström 2021, chapter 5; cf. Niiniluoto and Pihlström 2020). But we do need to reconsider what "human nature" amounts to: in order to accommodate normativity into our picture of the world and ourselves, we presumably have to think of humans as reflective, autonomous, "self-legislative" beings along broadly Kantian (cf. Korsgaard 1996b) or pragmatist lines, the roots of which could in this respect be seen as lying in the Kantian conception of the primacy of practical reason in human affairs. Qua humans, but entirely naturally, we occupy "two standpoints": the one picturing us as creatures of the natural world, to be fitted into the natural-scientific worldview, and the other conceptualizing human life as value-concerned, free, and responsible (see Korsgaard 1996a). It is of course the latter that humanistic disciplines primarily seek to explain and understand.

More generally, from a Kantian perspective, we are both rational and animal (sensible) creatures. In Kant himself, this conception of human beings as, on the one hand, animals subject to laws of nature and as, on the other hand, finite rational creatures capable of autonomous legislation irreducible to mere facts of nature runs through the entire critical philosophy. Unlike purely rational (nonanimal) creatures such as angels (if they existed), we have a sensible intuition instead of an intellectual intuition; analogously, human beings need a moral law—that is, the categorical imperative—because our will does not automatically follow the requirements of practical reason, again unlike the will of (say) angels who, if they existed, would have a "holy will" that would inevitably accord with the moral law. Nonreductively naturalist philosophers, such as pragmatists, may share this Kantian idea by conceptualizing human rationality as (not simply grounded but) embedded in our natural habits of action. The normativity of epistemic, scientific, ethical, and aesthetic "rules" (or, more broadly, normative expectations and considerations) lies in the relevant practices themselves and their historical development, instead of being imposed on those practices from a "higher" point of view, let alone a Platonic "God's-eye view." While not being reducible to *mere* facts of nature, the practice-embedded manifestations of normativity can be philosophically examined in terms of (nonreductively naturalized, historically relativized) transcendental arguments seeking to show that we are necessarily constrained by certain conditions, rules, or principles insofar as we are able to engage in certain practices at all (see below). Given that such philosophical investigations are ultimately investigations of our specifically human (instead of, say, purely rational) ways of engaging in, for example, scientific, scholarly, ethical, or artistic practices, we may follow Kant in understanding the fundamental questions of philosophy as being ultimately synthesized in the question, "What is a human being?"[21]

What we have arrived at amounts to a transcendental argument against the plausibility of any radical non- or postphilosophical naturalism such as NOA (even if we were not willing to employ the explicitly Kantian route that philosophers like Christine Korsgaard adopt when explaining the emergence of normativity).[22] A normative framework provided by the philosophy of science and of the humanities—as irreducible subdisciplines of philosophy rather than as "naturalized" elements of science or the humanities pure and simple—can, if my argument is sound, be shown to be a necessary condition for the possibility of any intelligible, reflexively justifiable decision to pursue science or humanistic scholarship, as distinguished from other human practices, in relation to any given problematic situation (to use a Deweyan term) we might arrive at.[23]

In contrast to reductive naturalism, a Wittgenstein-inspired "social naturalism" or "naturalism of second nature" (see McDowell 1996 [1994]) has been argued to be able to preserve normativity—in semantics, epistemology, ethics, and elsewhere—in a sense not available to Quinean scientistic naturalism. In a series of papers, José Medina articulates this critique most lucidly. He argues that Wittgenstein's "pragmatic contextualism" differs significantly from the scientific naturalism we find in Quine (Medina 2004a, 556). For Wittgenstein,[24] the relevant context for the meaningfulness of our language is human action in general, the practices and/or forms of life within which language is used, whereas for a more extreme naturalist like Quine (or Fine), the relevant context is, simply, science. Thus, Quinean holism is "theoretical," not action-oriented, social, and "anthropological" as in Wittgenstein's case (ibid., 555–556).[25] Medina further argues against Quine by appealing to Dewey—often seen as a precursor of Quinean naturalism—from whom he borrows the term "*spectator view*," which he ascribes to Quine's conception of language (ibid., 557). In contrast, Wittgenstein's (pragmatist) view of language is a "*participant view*," emphasizing the perspective of "a social agent engaged in practices" (ibid.; original emphases; see also 565, as well as Medina 2004c, 83).[26] This applies to our language-use in general and to such specific uses of language as natural science and humanistic scholarship.

As both Wittgenstein and Dewey in their different ways argued, our tacit agreement in action is a (nonfoundationalist) precondition for the possibility of meaning and normativity, constraining the contextual determinacy of meanings (see Medina 2004b, especially 345, 364–365). There seems to be no room for such a precondition or even constraint in more radical naturalism, for instance in Quine, for whom (despite his behaviorism) language is *not* tied to real-life human action or practices but is viewed, from a "spectator view," as a theoretical device of formulating (primarily scientific) sentences about reality. Moreover, the irreducible normativity of the Deweyan-Wittgensteinian account of language and meaning, required by the adoption of "the situated perspective of a competent practitioner" (Medina 2004a, 558), is simply missing from Quine's picture, which therefore ultimately, Medina argues, leads to meaning skepticism. When Medina concludes that a pragmatic "anthropologism" should be preferred to Quine's naturalism as a framework for the study of language (ibid., 551), it is easy to agree with him, especially on behalf of pragmatist philosophy of the humanities.

Quinean naturalism, then, remains within the *skeptical* framework that arises as a result of Quine's famous indeterminacy arguments. There is no place for a contextually determinate, normatively constrained meaningfulness of human language—not, at least, if the relevant context is human action in a broad, inclusive sense (including, indeed, the humanities and their representational relations to their objects of investigation), instead of mere natural-scientific theory formation.

Medina's anti-Quinean polemics seem to be essentially similar to Putnam's (1994, 2002)—even though Medina (2004c, 84) problematically classifies Putnam as an "anti-naturalist," thus contrasting him, too, with Wittgensteinian and pragmatic nonreductive "social naturalism."[27] Both argue against Quine's excessive naturalism *pragmatically*, drawing attention to our actual practices of language-use, which should be described in a richer way than Quine's scientism allows. Their arguments can also be reconstructed as transcendental ones, insofar as they examine the preconditions of meaning, that is, conditions without which no meaning (or, a fortiori, knowledge about the natural or human world) would be possible for us. Thus, these criticisms of excessive (normativity-debunking) naturalism are examples of the way in which pragmatic nonreductive naturalism can be reconciled with quasi-Kantian transcendental argumentation.[28] Moreover, even though Medina, for instance, nowhere explicitly comments on Fine's NOA (as far as I know), his criticism of nonnormative naturalism in general should be taken seriously by anyone willing to extend NOA into a naturalistic program in any field. Again, through his work, we may appreciate the possibility of advancing a pragmatic critique of naturalism, while endorsing a softer conception of naturalism.

Let us, before concluding this engagement with naturalism, return to the nagging reflexive question concerning the status of philosophical naturalism. Is naturalism itself—in any of its specific versions, reductive or nonreductive, including NOA—a piece of philosophical knowledge? Can or could it be? Is it knowable, if true? And is it, if true, "made true" by natural facts alone? This can hardly be the case. For if mere natural facts sufficed as truthmakers for the truth of naturalism (let alone NOA), then we should be able to determine the truth-value of such positions by mere empirical inquiry into such facts. To suppose we could do this would, however, beg the question against nonnaturalism. There is no way of escaping the conclusion that the fate of naturalism (including NOA) in its various versions must be settled—if it can be settled at all—at a philosophical, normative level irreducible to (though not isolated from) empirical inquiry. Again, this holds for whatever analogy of naturalism one might propose regarding the humanities.

The (nonreductively naturalized) transcendental yet pragmatist philosopher of science and of the humanities is largely concerned with the meanings of scientific and/or scholarly ideas, beliefs, and theoretical systems in the contexts in which those meanings are possible and of the ontological commitments those systems make. If there is any philosophical knowledge at all, as distinguished from special-scientific or discipline-internal humanistic knowledge, it concerns, presumably, transcendentally necessary conditions for the possibility of humanly given actualities of meaningful practices and their value-laden ontological commitments rather than any specific objects of inquiry. This general status of philosophical knowledge about the humanities must be duly kept in mind also when investigating, at the philosophical level, the ontology of humanistic disciplines (as was done in chapter 3).

For the pragmatist philosopher of the humanities, it is essential to explore the conditions for the possibility of philosophical knowledge in a nonreductively naturalistic setting in which the divisions between philosophy and empirical disciplines have been softened, even though the relative autonomy of philosophical investigation has not been given up. A transcendental reflection, by definition, focuses on the questions concerning the conditions for the possibility of some given phenomenon. Nonreductively naturalized transcendental philosophy, or even, say, Husserlian transcendental phenomenology, need not presuppose any inherently nonnaturalizable "first basis" à la Husserl (cf. Haaparanta 1999, 37–38). The kind of transcendental inquiry that can be viewed as compatible with naturalism and (holistic) pragmatism can very well begin in medias res, from within the dynamically evolving system of scientific and humanistic thought we (always already) have at our disposal, seeking to understand in most general terms how that system hangs together. Such a naturalized transcendental inquiry into the conditions for the possibility of philosophical knowledge (about, say, the normative grounding of science and the humanities, the possibility of historiographical representations of the past, or the meanings of literary or religious language-uses) maintains the *critical* project of philosophy, the idea of philosophy as a "discipline" in its own right, assessing the foundations, limits, and enabling conditions of our ontologies, methods of inquiry, and reason-use—albeit not from any external, "first-philosophical," point of view.

Any philosopher of science and inquiry attempting to understand the nature of scientific and scholarly methods and the rationality of inquiry (and thereby also the possibility of naturalizing perennial epistemological issues) from within the rational and normative practices of inquiry, hence reflexively, can, mutatis mutandis, be described as a transcendental philosopher in my loose pragmatic sense (cf. Pihlström 2004b, 2016, 2021).[29] If we are willing to employ such Kantian notions in our reaction to the naturalism debate, we do have some room for "philosophical knowledge" in our metaphilosophical scheme and thus also for philosophy itself as an autonomous—though not fully autonomous—humanistic discipline. Therefore, the prospects of straightforwardly nonnormative naturalisms such as Fine's NOA look dim, while the prospects of Quine's naturalism may not seem rosy, either.

We have, thus, reached a limit to what the naturalist program can legitimately hope to achieve. In sum, normativity—as the object of philosophical knowledge in the philosophy of the humanities as well as more generally—cannot be either eliminated or reduced to nonnormative, "purely" natural (or social, or historical) facts and processes (cf. Pihlström 2020, 2021). Yet maintaining the normativity of philosophical inquiry requires no pure philosophy, either. A reasonable interplay and overlap, without reduction either way, between philosophy and empirical inquiry is sufficient. This result should be relevant to our understanding of the humanities as naturally emerging human activities of investigation both focusing on irreducibly normative matters and remaining themselves inescapably normatively structured and guided.

Enriching Naturalism:
Transcendental Arguments and the Humanities

The critical examination of naturalism in the previous sections culminated in what might be called a "humanist" defense of transcendental reflection as a strategy of seeking "philosophical knowledge" about the ways in which both scientific and humanistic inquiries not only contingently do but *are able to* ontologically and epistemically structure their subject matters. Such transcendental reflection focuses on the conditions for the possibility of inquiry as well as of the objects of inquiry (scientific as much as humanistic). The very task of understanding how the world is "constituted" through inquiry (cf. chapters 2–3) can be regarded as a transcendental challenge. Therefore, we should take a further pragmatist look not only at naturalization strategies but also at transcendental arguments, which constitute a very important type of argumentation in post-Kantian philosophy. While these arguments have mostly been employed in general epistemology, often in attempts to overcome skepticism about the external world or other minds, they are also directly relevant to philosophical explorations of the humanities.

The second half of this chapter will therefore first briefly sketch the basic structure of transcendental arguments and then provide examples of their use in the philosophy of science in general and the philosophy of the humanities in particular. Toward the end of the chapter, I will also (again) examine the use of transcendental arguments in the philosophical debate over realism (insofar as it is relevant to the philosophy of the humanities) and in a more concrete case illustrating the philosophy of the humanities, namely, the debate on how exactly the study of religion ought to be conducted. I find this investigation crucial for our ability to critically consider the reductive tendencies of "naturalization" referred to in the previous sections, in which I already resorted to a transcendental mode of argumentation in order to defend the inescapable normativity of our practices of inquiry. We will now more explicitly discuss this argumentative strategy and some concrete ways of employing it.

As we will see, it is in many cases debatable whether a given philosophical argument or piece of reflection should be classified as "transcendental" or not. The current debate over transcendental arguments is an indication of the difficulties in strictly separating transcendental philosophies from nontranscendental ones (cf. Pihlström 2004b, 2021). There may be no single essential criterion that distinguishes the two; the context of philosophical inquiry is decisive. This also constitutes a problem in historical interpretation, as we may ask whether a particular philosopher—say Wittgenstein, Husserl, or Peirce—actually presented transcendental arguments and, if so, whether those arguments were similar to Kant's original ones (and, furthermore, whether they are valid or sound arguments). Such historical matters do not primarily concern us here, however.[30] What I will aim at in the rest of this chapter is a sufficiently lucid understanding of transcendental argumentation enabling us to determine in what sense the philosophy of the humanities can be claimed to reach (or even aim at) results of philosophical inquiry (and hence "philosophical knowledge") that can be used to analyze the necessary conditions for the possibility of both the epistemic practices of the humanistic disciplines and the objects of those practices—thus continuing in this metaphilosophical manner the preoccupation with the ontology of the humanities of the previous chapters.

Although Kant himself only rarely used the term *transcendental argument*, this type of argument is largely based on the *Critique of Pure Reason* (Kant 1990 [1781/1787]). After Kant, philosophers of quite different persuasions—for example, Husserl, Peirce, and Wittgenstein—have engaged in transcendental inquiries, though it is often controversial how exactly a certain argument available in their works should be interpreted. In contemporary philosophy, a novel debate over the nature of transcendental arguments, to some extent still going on, was launched by P. F. Strawson and Barry Stroud in the 1950–60s (see Strawson 1959; Stroud 1968). I have earlier proposed that these debates, as well as their Kantian background more generally, have enormous influence on how we ought to view the structure of pragmatist philosophizing, too (cf. Pihlström 2003a, 2020, 2021), and this also concerns the pragmatist project in the philosophy of the humanities.

Generally, a transcendental argument seeks to demonstrate that something is a *necessary condition* for the *possibility* of something else, namely, something whose actuality is taken for granted or considered indubitable in our practices. The historical paradigm case is Kant's project of demonstrating the necessary applicability of the forms of intuition (space and time) and the pure concepts of the understanding—that is, the categories (e.g., causality)—to all objects of humanly possible experience. Kant (1990 [1781/1787]) tried to show through his complex argumentation that for sensible rational beings like us, these sensible and intellectual conditions must obtain insofar as there can be any cognitive experience of a structured, nonchaotic reality. As we undeniably do have such experience, the argument concludes that the relevant conditions must indeed obtain, that is, for instance, that all experienceable objects and events are spatiotemporal and subject to the law of causality.

A transcendental argument can be schematically presented as follows:

1. Necessarily, if A is possible, then C (must be presupposed).
2. A is possible (because actual).
3. Therefore, C (must be presupposed).[31]

As such, this schema does not essentially differ from an ordinary *modus ponens* inference. There is, of course, an aspect of *necessity* involved here: necessarily, if A is possible, as premise (2) says, and if premise (1) holds, then the condition C indeed does obtain, or at least it must be presupposed by us as obtaining. But it is far from obvious whether this is anything more than the logical and/or conceptual necessity of any deductively valid argument. Importantly, necessity cannot be attached to the obtaining of C itself, because this is contingent; C just obtains given the truth of premises (1) and (2). According to Kant himself, it is clearly contingent that there *is* any (human) experience whatsoever; a fortiori, it is also contingent that its conditions obtain, if they do. The relevant kind of necessity in a transcendental argument is *presuppositional*: *if* there is (or can be), say, cognitive experience (and, hence, any objects of experience), *then* its conditions must (be taken to) obtain. Typically, this presuppositional necessity is considered a powerful weapon against the epistemological skeptic: even skeptics cannot coherently doubt that there is experience; by allowing that, they must allow that experience and its possible objects have a certain conceptual (categorial) structure. Or so the Kantian argues.

However, insofar as this argumentation works against skepticism, it might be said to only work in an ad hominem manner against the (real or imagined) Cartesian or Humean skeptic who claims to entertain doubts about experience being about spatiotemporal and/or causally connected objects and events. Transcendental arguments can hardly be expected to provide any overall theoretical demonstration of the falsity of skepticism as a general philosophical position. It was hardly Kant's intention to overcome Hume in that sense.[32]

Mere argumentative form does not, then, provide us with the "essence" of transcendental arguments. It may be suggested (in a quasi-Wittgensteinian vein) that transcendental arguments—and, more generally, transcendental philosophy employing such arguments—have a "family-resemblance" character (cf. again Pihlström 2003a, 2004b). There can be quite different uses of transcendental arguments depending on the contexts of inquiry in which they are placed. For example, Kant's own employment of transcendental reasoning must be understood with essential reference to his transcendental idealism, according to which the spatiotemporal world structured by the categories is not the world of "things in themselves" but a humanly constructed phenomenal world.[33] Pragmatists, in turn, insofar as they have any use for transcendental arguments, may wish to avoid any form idealism, but they might nevertheless find transcendental argumentation vital for articulating how, for instance, the objects of (humanistic) inquiry do not exist independently of inquiry but are constituted through it (as suggested in chapters 2–3).[34]

In contrast to Kant's idealism, in the modern epistemological debate, Stroud argued in his "Transcendental Arguments" (1968) that it remains unclear whether transcendental arguments can overcome skepticism without presupposing idealism (or some close alternative, e.g., verificationism). His criticism was primarily directed at Strawson's use of transcendental arguments in *Individuals* (1959). Despite their disagreement about the success of these arguments, Strawson and Stroud agreed that they should be disconnected from transcendental idealism. Others, including Kant scholars like Henry Allison (2004), have suggested that such a connection is vital to whatever success those arguments may have. Why, after all, *should* transcendental arguments avoid idealism? The pragmatist can settle this matter precisely by making pragmatism itself play the role of idealism: transcendental conditions are not provided by the (individual, psychological) mind but by our practices of inquiry.[35]

Furthermore, while many philosophers insist that transcendental arguments, in order to be interesting at all, should be inherently antiskeptical, others acknowledge more moderate types of transcendental argument, aiming at clarifications of our conceptual commitments instead of any knockdown of skepticism (cf. Stern 1999). Few philosophers maintain that transcendental arguments can reach conclusions about reality as it is independently of the conditions of experience. Whether this means that those arguments fall short of what they should achieve or whether this is, rather, something to be expected depends on one's overall philosophical commitments, especially regarding realism and its alternatives. In particular, we should take seriously the embeddedness of transcendental arguments in practices and contexts of inquiry—and this is, again, part and parcel of any pragmatist approach to the philosophy of the humanities.

Philosophers of science have, however, only rarely explicitly explored transcendental arguments, even though several key positions in twentieth-century philosophy of science relied on broadly Kantian assumptions. The logical empiricists, especially Rudolf Carnap (1950), presupposed a version of the distinction between the empirical and the transcendental in distinguishing between existence questions "internal" and "external" to linguistic frameworks. Carnap's suggestion that external questions concerning the choice of a linguistic framework are ultimately practical questions not to be decided theoretically but in terms of the fruitfulness of the framework contributed not only to integrating pragmatism with logical empiricism but also, indirectly, to setting transcendental philosophy (of science and inquiry) on a more pragmatic path (cf. chapter 2 above).[36]

A slightly different classical position in the philosophy of science (also discussed in chapter 2), Kuhn's (1970 [1962]) theory of paradigms, is, again, not explicitly transcendental—indeed, given Kuhn's historicism, it appears to be contrary to Kantian endeavors—but Kuhn may, as we have seen (with the help of commentators like Hoyningen-Huene 1993), be interpreted as claiming that, at a normal-scientific stage, a shared paradigm is a necessary condition for the possibility of there being any relevant scientific entities or truths about them. Scientific representations of the world would be impossible without socially shared frameworks of ontological and methodological commitments (paradigms); such representations are possible, because actual. Hence, science is (mostly or even essentially) an activity taking place within paradigms, and those paradigms constitute the world (for us) in a way comparable to Kant's categories. An additional Kuhnian insight, based on his extensive empirical documentation, is that paradigms change historically, that is, scientific revolutions do occasionally happen. The contexts making scientific representations possible are thus not fixed once and for all. The variable C in the transcendental argument schema is, then, truly variable; similar historical relativizations of the Kantian a priori have been proposed by philosophers of science and inquiry coming from quite different orientations, including Reichenbach and Foucault (cf. Pihlström and Siitonen 2005).

As discussed in chapter 2, Kuhn is famous (or notorious) for having advanced a kind of Kantian "constructivism": paradigms in a sense constitute the reality they are about (or the reality the scientific representations that are possible within the paradigm *can* be about), and the world in some sense itself "changes" as the paradigm changes in a scientific revolution. This view is also something that still needs to be revisited in relation to the more general realism issue in the context of the philosophy of the humanities (see the next section). Although transcendental arguments seem to have their "timeless" deductive form, they can, then, be operative within historically and pragmatically relativized contexts; this, indeed, is vital for the success of such arguments in the philosophy of the humanities. The use of transcendental arguments need not be based on ahistorical and essentialist conceptions of philosophy, such as traditional Kantian transcendental philosophy. This is why they can be useful also in contemporary practice-oriented philosophy of science and in a pragmatist philosophy of the humanities. Moreover, as transcendental arguments seem to lack any unifying essence, it may be more appropriate to describe philosophical approaches, methodologies, argumentative strategies, or traditions—instead of isolated arguments—as transcendental.

An obvious place to look for transcendental arguments in the philosophy of the humanities in particular is hermeneutics, which traditionally seeks to establish conditions for the possibility of meaning and/or communication. Discussions of the necessary presuppositions of communicability and intelligibility can be found in very different philosophies of meaning and understanding, including Heidegger's and Gadamer's hermeneutics examining understanding as a human mode of being in the world, Karl-Otto Apel's and Jürgen Habermas's discourse ethics and theories of communicative action, and Donald Davidson's theory of triangulation. These and other thinkers have offered a variety of "repositionings" of the idea of the transcendental (Malpas 2003). Transcendental arguments in the philosophy of the humanities, in particular, thus seem to cut across the unfortunate analytic versus Continental divide—just like transcendental arguments generally do, given their prevalence in, say, logical empiricism and phenomenology alike (as well as pragmatism).

Just as the paradigm case of *epistemic* transcendental arguments is Kant's argumentation for his theory of the categories as necessary conditions for the possibility of experience—itself modified and reconceptualized in various ways both in the analytic epistemological discussions following Strawson and Stroud and in the post-logical-empiricist and post-Kuhnian developments in the philosophy of science referred to above—the paradigm case of *semantic* transcendental arguments focusing on meaning and understanding is, presumably, Wittgenstein's "private language argument" in *Philosophical Investigations* (1953). Wittgenstein himself never attached this label to his attempt to demonstrate that there can be no such thing as a private language—in the strict sense, namely, a language that only the individual speaker or user could understand—and scholars have debated not only what the private language argument exactly seeks to show and what it possibly succeeds, or fails, in showing but also whether there is such an argument in the *Investigations* and even whether there are any traditional philosophical arguments or theses to be found in Wittgenstein at all.[37]

The private language argument can be seen as straightforwardly transcendental (though the scholarly controversies on this issue must be skipped here): it is, according to Wittgenstein, a necessary condition for the possibility of meaning (or meaningful communication, or meaningful use of language) that meanings are public, that is, at least in principle publically available; meaningful communication (or use of language) is actual, hence possible; therefore, meanings *are* public (or at least non-private). Thus, necessarily, insofar as there can be any communication of meanings or any normatively constrained language-use at all, or insofar as *we* can see ourselves as engaging in such activities, linguistic meaning cannot be entirely private to the speaker even when we use language to express our private experiences. Language need not be essentially social, as we may imagine Robinson Crusoe using a solitary language in isolation, but it *must* be public in the sense that the meanings of its expressions are in principle open to others. It must also be normatively structured, and arguably the public nature of language must be presupposed for the relevant kind of normativity to be possible. Otherwise it is no language at all, because grammatical rules are needed precisely for the public availability of meaning. Rules, as Wittgenstein says, cannot be followed privately. However, this obviously does not commit us (or Wittgenstein) to the dubious conception of meanings as mysteriously existing abstract entities. Meanings are public precisely in the sense of being, or being embedded in, public rule-governed human activities—what Wittgenstein called language-games.

As human social and cultural action is largely a matter of constructing, communicating, and sharing historically developing meanings, arguments of this kind, referring to the possibility of meaning and communication, are highly relevant to the philosophy of the humanities (as well as the philosophy of the social sciences, for that matter). Following Wittgenstein, Peter Winch (1958) challenged "positivistic" social sciences by arguing that social practices—or Wittgensteinian "forms of life"—should not be externally causally explained but internally understood by learning to understand their rules, just as we learn to play a language-game by learning to follow its rules. Many critics maintain that Winch went too far in embracing a form of relativism, suggesting that social practices (or cultures, traditions, perspectives, etc.) are only intelligible and rationally discussable in their own terms, "from within."[38] At least in its radical form, this view seems to make any critical dialogue across practices impossible, because even the meanings of our concepts would, strictly speaking, be available only from an internal participant's perspective. Yet the transcendental character of Winch's and other Wittgensteinians' arguments can be appreciated without drawing their somewhat extreme conclusions. Even in order to engage in causally explanatory social-scientific or humanistic inquiry, one must *first* understand the phenomena to be explained, and transcendental arguments and analyses may play a significant role in clarifying the conceptual networks underlying those phenomena, as well as our conceptual commitments and "pre-understandings."[39]

Transcendental arguments are, thus, also connected with the *Erklären* versus *Verstehen* (explanation versus understanding) debate over the methodology of the human and social sciences (cf. von Wright 1971; see chapter 3 above), a debate that may have lost its urgency since the 1960s and 1970s but that may still characterize important divergences among different approaches in the humanities. There is no consensus available about the philosophical relevance of transcendental arguments, or even about their nature, but they continue to attract not only scholars interpreting Kant or Wittgenstein but also those systematically working on issues in knowledge and meaning. Certainly transcendental arguments are not a major trend in, for example, contemporary empirically oriented practice-based philosophy of science (or interdisciplinary science and technology studies), but many of the philosophical ideas and debates in such fields can be reconstructed and further illuminated in terms of this conceptual machinery. Even more importantly, pragmatist philosophy of the humanities can crucially employ transcendental arguments in attempting to account for the ways in which humanistic scholarship constitutively depends on practice-laden and value-directed conceptions of human reality. I have already tried, to some extent, to do so in the previous chapters and in the first half of this chapter (encountering excessive naturalism), and I will continue to engage in a transcendental examination toward the end of the chapter as well.

Transcendental Arguments and Realism

Having offered a brief sketch of transcendental arguments and their (potential) use in the philosophy of science and of the humanities at a general level, I will next take a look at two philosophers who have argued transcendentally for a certain kind of realism, the first (Nicholas Rescher) in metaphysics and philosophy of science generally and the second (Roy Bhaskar) in the philosophy of the human sciences in particular.[40] The potential implications of all this for the humanities should be clear. The problem of realism is, after all, *the* key issue for the philosophy of the humanities I am preoccupied with in this volume. While standard analytic debates on transcendental arguments (manifested, as we briefly saw, in Strawson's and Stroud's work, as well as their many followers' and critics' contributions) usually start from realism as a premise, struggling to avoid idealism—or, conversely, argue *against* realism by reminding the realist that transcendental arguments presuppose transcendental idealism (cf. Allison 2004)—Rescher and Bhaskar argue *for* realism (instead of arguing *from* realism for some other philosophical thesis) on transcendental grounds, as do those somewhat controversial Kant scholars (e.g., Westphal 2004, 2014) who believe that Kant's own work provides a powerful case for realism rather than transcendental idealism.

Rescher is, indeed, one of the relatively few philosophers today employing explicitly transcendental considerations in the debate over realism and its alternatives in the philosophy of science and in general metaphysics and epistemology (see especially Rescher 1992–94, 2000; cf., however, also Westphal 2014; Pihlström 2017b). He labels his basic view of reality metaphysical realism, defined as the doctrine that "there indeed is a real world—a realm of mind-independent, objective physical reality" (Rescher 2000, 126; see also 147), that is, that "the world exists in a way that is substantially independent of the thinking beings that inquire into it, and that its nature—its having whatever characteristics it does actually have—is also comparably thought independent" (Rescher 1992–94, I, 255). A critic of realism might question the notion of (mind-)independence here, problematizing statements such as the one about objective things existing and functioning "in themselves," "without specific dependence on us" (ibid., I, 131). In the terms of Rescher's earlier conceptual idealism (see Rescher 1973), the objective world might still be regarded as "conceptually" dependent on us; moreover, not everybody, at least not every transcendental philosopher, maintains that conceptual and (say) existential or ontological (in)dependence can be sharply distinguished from one another.

Be that as it may, realism is, in Rescherian pragmatism, a deeply human commitment, not a description of the world in itself or of things in themselves from a God's-eye view. It is "a commitment that we presuppose for our inquiries rather than discover as a result of them" (Rescher 2000, 126). We cannot discover, on the basis of evidence, that such a general thesis as realism is true; we can only presuppose realism as something that makes sense of and regulates our inquiries and other practices. It is right here that transcendental arguments come into the picture. Realism can, from the Rescherian point of view, be supported by a transcendental argument as a necessary precondition for the possibility of inquiry and communication (ibid., 134–135). It is not to be defended on the basis of evidence but to be postulated in order for us to be able to collect any evidence for any view (or better, to be able to *make sense* of our "given," unproblematized practice of gathering evidence for any other view). In this sense, Rescher's realism is a transcendentally grounded commitment arising from what seems to be a transcendentally idealistic (Kantian) conception of the necessary conditions for the possibility of certain given actualities of human life (i.e., inquiry and communication).

While Rescher's realism primarily concerns the independent existence of the natural world, it can be extended to a claim about the (qualified) independence of cultural reality as well, when it comes to realism as a thesis about the independence of the objects of inquiry from the inquirers' beliefs, theories, and perspectives. Moreover, it could be argued that Rescher defends realism about the world in general as a transcendental presupposition for the possibility of inquiry also covering humanistic inquiry: we cannot inquire into anything, not even into humanly created (and thus causally mind-dependent) culture, unless we presuppose that *something* (the world in general) remains largely independent of our inquiries, that is, that our inquiry just does not produce its objects ex nihilo even though it may (as pragmatists have argued; see again chapters 2–3) play an ontologically relevant constitutive role in their emerging *as* the objects they are.

It is not clear without further investigation, however, that the transcendental mode of argumentation (in favor of realism or anything else) can be employed entirely independently of transcendental idealism or some of its equivalents, such as transcendental pragmatism. A key issue here is the relation between Rescher's peculiar form of pragmatism and his transcendental argumentation, since realism, transcendentally defended, is also for Rescher "ultimately a principle of practice," justified because "we need it to operate our conceptual scheme" (ibid., 134), that is, a principle of inquiry pragmatically "retrojustified" (ibid., 145–146). The very same principle is treated simultaneously as a transcendentally necessary condition for the possibility of certain purposive human activities and as a pragmatically useful postulate enabling us to engage in those activities efficaciously—that is, as a postulate itself pragmatically validated. A pragmatist conception of human activity is both a presupposition of realism (understood as a practical commitment) and something that itself requires, as its presupposition, a realistic conception of the world in which human beings act. In this sense, we may say that the transcendental cuts both ways: something can be a transcendental precondition of something else while also being itself "conditioned." In this context, also the question concerning the relation between transcendental arguments and inferences to the best explanation could be raised (cf. Pihlström 2003a). Rescher, in any case, provides an important (though not unproblematic) account of the interplay of pragmatist and transcendental considerations in relation to the realism issue—and this is as relevant in the philosophy of the humanities as it is in general epistemology and philosophy of science.[41]

In the philosophy of social science, Roy Bhaskar (e.g., 1979, 1991), in turn, has made significant use of transcendental arguments. He argues in a transcendental manner for the reality of *causal powers* in particular. Labeling, like Rescher, his view metaphysical realism or even transcendental realism (in contrast to Kantian transcendental idealism), he maintains that only a transcendentally grounded realistic philosophy committed to the reality of both causal structures in general and social structures in particular can really make sense of the social sciences, or of science generally. According to transcendental realism, "it is the nature of objects that determines their cognitive possibilities for us," and it is human knowledge that is contingent and accidental rather than the world and/or objects that knowledge is about (Bhaskar 1979, 31).

One of the immediate critical targets of Bhaskar's transcendental criticism is Winch's philosophy of social science (which, as we saw, can itself be interpreted as employing a form of transcendental reflection). According to Bhaskar, Winch commits a typical neo-Kantian epistemic fallacy in its linguistic form, failing to appreciate the way in which the ontological structures of the independent world itself must—for transcendental reasons—be regarded as primary to the epistemic and linguistic perspectives constructed by human beings (see ibid., 169–195). Another major philosopher Bhaskar attacks on similar grounds is Rorty. Like Kant and his followers, Rorty fails to appreciate the metaphysically realistic concern to "ask what the *world* must be like for certain characteristic (practical and discursive) social activities of science to be possible" (Bhaskar 1991, 27). The transcendental realist begins their analysis "from within human being," and especially from human achievements like knowledge, but finds the conditions for the possibility of such achievements in the nonhuman world, thus criticizing all anthropomorphisms and anthropocentrisms (ibid., 32–33). Moreover, not only Rorty and Winch but also philosophers like Habermas remain, according to Bhaskar, "ensnared in the antinomy of transcendental pragmatism: nature cannot both pre-exist and be constituted by society" (ibid., 142).[42]

Here, I suppose, we may locate one of the fundamental issues of this entire controversy. There are transcendental philosophers (of science, but also more generally) who are happy to acknowledge the mutual *co-constitutivity* of nature and humanity, nature and society, nature and language, or nature and human experience. In particular, many philosophers of pragmatist persuasion could be regarded as endorsing (at least implicitly) such co-constitutivity, which could itself be transcendentally examined. Then there are transcendental realists, idealists, and constructivists of various stripes claiming that the direction of transcendental constitutivity can only run one way, either from the human to the nonhuman (Kant, Wittgensteinians) or from the nonhuman to the human (Bhaskar, Rescher). Here we need not take any final stand on this matter, but it should be obvious that our views on this issue will be crucial for our understanding of the nature of humanistic inquiry. Let me just note that a pragmatist approach to metaphysics, epistemology, and the philosophy of science and inquiry might make us more open to a *pluralistic* conception of transcendental constitutivity itself, just as it might make us responsive to the idea that there is no essence of transcendental argumentation but a family-resemblance-like plurality of transcendental reflection. Indeed, I have in the previous chapters tentatively proposed to view the transcendental constitutivity of the ontology of the humanities in terms of the value-ladenness of the objects postulated in humanistic practices of inquiry. The human reality investigated by humanistic scholarship *is* what it is because of our value commitments. Had we (significantly) different values through which we viewed the world, also the human reality as the object of inquiry in the humanities would be—ontologically, not just epistemically or semantically—different. Yet, this value-embedded activity constitutive of our ontologies is itself humanly natural.

We should now examine these issues in a somewhat more "applied" manner by drawing attention to an example that may, I hope, further illuminate the role of transcendental arguments in the philosophy of the humanities, at the same time continuing the case studies preliminarily introduced in chapter 3 above.

Another Case Study: Transcendental Arguments in the Philosophy of Religious Studies

The study of religion—or, rather, the philosophical debate over its proper ontology, epistemology, and methodology—is not only one of the case study areas that I suggested a pragmatist philosophy of the humanities may focus on (see chapter 3) but also a particularly interesting example to be illuminated by considering the relevance of transcendental arguments in relation to projects of naturalization. I will refer to some selected discussions in this field as an example in my investigation of the role of transcendental arguments in the philosophy of the humanities, though their relevance extends to more broadly social studies of religion as well. Therefore, I will now take a slightly more detailed look at a specific debate in the philosophy of religious studies, while my main goal in this chapter as a whole is to draw a more general moral on the availability of transcendental arguments in the philosophy of the humanities.[43]

There is a rich methodological diversity in the study of religion, yet it seems that the methodological and philosophical discussions in the field rarely contain substantial references to either pragmatism or realism (see, e.g., the essays in Orsi 2013). In the current methodology discussion, there is, rather, a clear—perhaps excessive—focus on cognitive psychology, the cognitive sciences generally, and their methodologies, as contrasted with the traditional "softer" hermeneutic methods of interpretation. For example, Daniel Dennett (e.g., 2006) and other leading philosophers of mind and cognition have found naturalistic approaches relevant to the study of religion. To a certain degree, such a psychological orientation goes back to William James and the "science of religions" (cf. Proudfoot 2004a) that we may take his interdisciplinary studies of religious experience to have established. Indeed, Jamesian investigations of religious experience remain vitally important both in the philosophy of religion and in the study of religion more generally, in addition to being classical contributions to pragmatism. As Wayne Proudfoot (2004b, 39–41) explains, James himself (in *Varieties*) was not satisfied with fully naturalized explanations of religion qua religion, especially insofar as it is seen to bring meaning and value into human experience. Proudfoot also reminds us, highly importantly for this inquiry, that when James speaks about "moral order" (again, especially in *Varieties*), he means this in the sense of the "moral sciences" (i.e., the humanities and social sciences): the issue is whether to understand reality, including religious responses to reality, and even religion itself, as a mere collection of ultimately meaningless material processes and contingent natural facts or as "shaped to," or perhaps even shaped *by*, human thought and action (cf. ibid., 32). The issue is, then, to what extent religion is a topic for *humanistic* inquiry that may, pragmatically, focus on its "fruits" in our lives and practices rather than natural-scientific inquiry focusing on its causal origins (ibid., 37).[44] Clearly, for James and Jamesian pragmatists, it is also *ethically* significant whether we view disciplines such as religious studies as (partly) humanistic or as purely scientific.

In a Jamesian spirit, it might be argued (see above) that religious practices ought to be first "humanistically" *understood as religious*, taking into consideration whatever humanly valuable "fruits" they might purportedly teleologically involve, in order for any, say, social-scientific (or, for that matter, natural-scientific, causal) *explanations* to be so much as possible. Thus, those who seek to causally (e.g., evolutionarily and/or cognitively) explain religious beliefs—their emergence and social spreading and maintenance, for instance—would commit the kind of "positivistic" vices that Winch (1958) challenged in his broadly Wittgensteinian philosophy of social science. While authors engaging in these debates rarely label their arguments transcendental, this discussion can be viewed from that perspective.[45]

In the beginning of this chapter, we considered naturalized analyses of science and inquiry, especially Fine's NOA. It is possible to maintain that both scientific and religious worldviews are naturalistically explainable, in analogous if not identical ways, because both enable us to cope with the nature in which we live and of which we are a part. (Analogously, it could also be suggested that historical events could in principle be purely causally and naturalistically explained, if we just knew their background conditions and the laws governing them sufficiently well—and any historian would admit that such a "positivist" explanatory perspective would in most cases just miss the point of historical study.) Well-known naturalistic explanations of religious experiences and religiosity generally have been proposed within cognitive science, comparative religion, and cultural anthropology. Insofar as the general (by itself moderate) naturalist proposal that empirical inquiry is not insignificant for philosophical purposes is taken seriously, we should obviously consider such explanations of religion relevant to the philosophy of religion as well as the philosophy of social science and humanities.[46]

Some decades ago, "cognitivist" study of religion emerged as a major orientation in the field. Such research can be referred to here as an example of naturalized study of religion—which, however, according to its critics leaves too little room for an understanding of religion *as* religion ("from within"). The cognitivist approach (cf., e.g., Kamppinen 1997, 2001; Lawson 1998; Boyer 2001; Guthrie 2001; Pyysiäinen 2001a, 2001b; Dennett 2006) is of course only one example of a naturalist, reductionist, and methodologically atheist line of thought within this discipline.[47] Reductionist attempts to explain religion in terms of something that is not religion appear not only in the cognitivist framework but also in various social-scientific approaches (see Segal 1994); consider, for instance, the classical reductionisms of Marxist and Freudian accounts of religion. Here we need not pay any close attention to the differences between diverging reductive approaches within the study of religion; a fundamentally philosophical motivation for using transcendental arguments may emerge from the problems of both natural-scientific and social-scientific reductionisms.

Cognitivist scholars of religion purporting to explain religion naturalistically sometimes try to capture the specific sense of "rationality" that can be found in religious worldviews by construing religious conceptions of the world as "models," "structured internal representations of environments" (Kamppinen 1997, 85), enabling their subjects to orient themselves in the world they live in and solve various problems they encounter in their lives. Religious models thus form a subset of "cultural models," and their central characteristic, even their essential feature, is their reference to "superhuman powers or agents" (ibid.). Religious belief systems and institutions are, then, "cultural means of problem solving" (ibid., 88).

One may be tempted to immediately ask whether invoking supernatural entities as a hallmark of religious "models" is intended as a definition of religion and, if so, whether an empirically informed scholar ought to take it seriously as such. Not all religions necessarily postulate superhuman ontologies. Be that as it may, it may be argued, more importantly, that the very concept of rationality constitutes a challenge for our understanding of religion, as religious beliefs about superhuman agents seem to be flatly irrational from the standpoint of at least standard Western conceptions of scientific rationality (cf. ibid., 96–97). Still, they ought to be "incorporated into the cognitivist paradigm," since superhuman entities "are still entities, and faith as a foundation of belief is still a foundation of belief" (ibid., 87). Now, from the point of view of "Wittgensteinian" philosophy of religion in particular, a statement like this is clearly a misunderstanding. Those philosophers, D. Z. Phillips (e.g., 1986) most prominently, could respond that religion is primarily a matter of faith, not a matter of belief based on any epistemic foundation, and that it is inappropriate to talk about faith itself as a "foundation of belief" in the sense in which ordinary beliefs have (e.g., perceptual) "foundations." This character of religious faith as irreducible to and undefinable in terms of any evidential foundation should be *understood* in order for us to even ask any explanatory questions about religious phenomena, and it is at this point that "humanistic" understanding will have to enter the research process even if natural-scientific or social-scientific explanations were pursued. Again, understanding and explaining are not opposed to each other but mutually supplementing processes within inquiry into religion (cf. chapter 3). However, the typically cognitivist description of "religious models" as "theoretical models" is also at variance with Wittgensteinian, pragmatist, and many other views that take religion to be something quite nontheoretical—a cultural practice rather than a theoretical commitment to an ontological picture of the world.[48]

Indeed, the claim, intended as an introduction to the cognitivist approach, that "religious thinking and doing is generic human functioning and does not differ from other modes of cognition and action" (Kamppinen 2001, 193) may, in the eyes of both religious believers and humanistic scholars of religion, appear to be a problematic starting point for any attempt to understand what religion is. Certainly religion must differ *somehow* from other modes of cognition and action if there is anything special in it for us to understand and explain. There have to be differences at the (irreducibly) normative level of meanings and values. Otherwise, why should we study religious experiences and practices at all rather than just everyday perceptual experiences and practices? Why should we be interested in God or other supernatural entities as the objects of religious believers' propositional attitudes instead of being merely interested in people's postulations of tables and chairs—or electrons and genes? We might think, as many reductionists do, that the *differentia specifica* of religious models of reality is their reference to supernatural powers. But this view treats the objects of religious belief on the model of the ontology of the ordinary objects we encounter in the physical and social world, picturing the "superhuman" world as a mysterious realm unknown to us yet somehow ontologically arranged in a way analogous to the world we live in. It is unclear whether such objects of religious models could have any *religious* status in the lives of the people who postulate them. On the other hand, it is obvious that reductionists are not impressed by the (typically Wittgensteinian) argument that religious studies should begin from an acknowledgment of the specifically religious character of the objects studied: on the contrary, it is an open issue what "religious" means, how it should be interpreted, and how its manifestations should be explained (Segal 1994). No philosophical preunderstanding should dictate the scholar's answers to such questions. We can, perhaps, see the above-discussed NOA raising its head in such naturalizing ways of thinking and talking.

Cognitivists may admit that their approach is "reductive," because it views religious phenomena as "related to more fundamental mechanisms," seeking causal explanations in terms of origins (Kamppinen 2001, 193–194; cf. also Andresen 2001, 1; Boyer 2001). Such reductionism can, however, be claimed to be only epistemological, not ontological (Kamppinen 2001, 195). In religious studies, a distinction is typically made between reductionists (including modern cognitivists but also more classical critics of religion to be found, say, in the Marxist and Freudian traditions), according to whom religion is "nothing over and above" some other more basic phenomenon of human life, and antireductionists (such as phenomenologists of religion, as well as Wittgensteinians), according to whom religion is in some sense a sui generis phenomenon, never to be adequately accounted for in nonreligious terms. This opposition has sometimes been understood as the one between "social scientists" and "religionists" in the study of religion (cf. Idinopoulos and Yonan 1994; and especially Segal 1994). The problem, in brief, is whether the first group of scholars can offer us any understanding of *religion* and whether the second group of scholars can really engage in scientific or scholarly *research* of religion at all.[49] Insofar as the study of religion is just a branch of the humanities and social sciences along with all other branches, the philosophical and methodological problems its practitioners have to deal with are similar to the problems belonging to those other disciplines, even though the problem concerning the possibilities of understanding religions and religiosity from a nonreligious, scholarly point of view is unique to this particular field of humanistic inquiry.

"Nonreligionists" usually try to understand religion naturalistically (and, of course, purely secularly),[50] as a naturally evolved psychological and social structure, based upon the human cognitive machinery with its long evolutionary history, yet a social and cultural formation that typically contains supernatural claims that cannot be supported by science. Such causal explanations of religious phenomena arguably run the risk of missing the point, however, as they do not approach religious phenomena as religious at all (but as something else, allegedly as something more "basic"), and thus they ultimately fail in explaining what they were designed to explain. The contested notion of explanation, however, needs further elaboration here. When cognitivists claim that religious models themselves exist in order to explain observable facts or to make them intelligible to us and that religious studies explains this explanatory function of those models by its evolutionary development, ultimately based on our brain structure (for instance), one may argue that they either deliberately or accidentally conflate scientific explanation with *religious* attempts to make things intelligible to religious practitioners. Certainly religious worldviews try to make the world intelligible to those who hold them. But they are hardly simply reducible to any scientific form of explanation; on the contrary, one of their purposes may be to highlight the unexplainable. Therefore, naturalistic accounts seeking to explain religious ways of thinking on the basis of the assumption that *they* explain, through their models, their practitioners' experiences, may be doubly misleading.

Religious ideas indeed often deal with *unexplained* and *unexplainable* objects and events—miracles,[51] for instance. Ineffability and mysteriousness—the sheer inapplicability of any scientific canons of explanation—are what could be regarded as making religious experiences religious in the first place. From a religious believer's standpoint,[52] one offers a simplistic and scientistic account of religion if one supposes that religious ontologies are primarily intended to explain empirical events. Cognitivism may, from such a standpoint, in the end amount to little more than a conflation of religion and science. Discussions of the cognitive and/or social roots and contents of religious phenomena provide, of course, *one* perspective on religion, but a narrow one indeed. The critic can argue that such a perspective does not help us understand religious phenomena any more than an eliminatively physicalist conception of human agency, conceptualizing actions as processes that are merely redistributions of microphysical states, helps us in understanding our actions qua actions (that is, as something normatively constrained and meaningful, distinguished from mere causally determined bodily movements or behavior). These same remarks would apply, mutatis mutandis, to other naturalized accounts of religion, including the most famous ones, such as Marx's and Freud's.

Reductionism in religious studies has been criticized from a wide range of philosophical perspectives over the past decades. Instead of paraphrasing any of the best-known antireductionisms (e.g., within theological hermeneutics), we may briefly compare what has been said here to David Wisdo's (1993) attack on the adequacy of reductionism in understanding the nature of religious belief. Wisdo, influenced by both pragmatism and Wittgensteinian philosophy of religion, argues that religious beliefs and worldviews cannot be examined as isolated claims that a subject (or a community) just happens to hold about the world—that is, as "models," as cognitivists tend to view them—but must be seen as "holistic interpretations about the meaning of life that enables us to make sense of our emotions and desires as well as our attitudes about suffering and death" (ibid., 5). Our intellectual or even "scientific" attempts to understand religion should be able to take this into account far more seriously than standard naturalizing reductionisms seem to do.

Inspired by Kierkegaard, James, and Wittgenstein, among others, Wisdo points out that religious beliefs, as inseparably intertwined with our deep personal cares and concerns, organize or structure "the facts" that we take to belong to the world we live in rather than picturing any novel facts (ibid., 45). From the point of view of religions themselves, no scientific "organization" of the facts is needed; religious experiences, for instance, require no further scientific explanation from the point of view of the believer (ibid., 118)—although, of course, there are nonreligious contexts in which the need for explanation is entirely legitimate. Drawing on Wittgenstein's "Remarks on Frazer's *The Golden Bough*" (Wittgenstein 1993 [1967]), Wisdo seeks to show, furthermore, that the chief failure of reductionism is *ethical* rather than epistemological. Although we may have to reject certain relativistic excesses in Wittgensteinian thinkers like Winch (1958, 1972) or Phillips (1986),[53] naturalized reductionist approaches to religion offer a seriously impoverished perspective on human life, blinding us to the profound significance that religion may have for some individuals, the essential role it plays in their lives, that is, in "the human form of life" or in "our natural history as human beings," by (for example) seeking causal explanations in terms of the origins of beliefs and practices (see Wisdo 1993, 9, 113, 119–123, 129). Such approaches are thus, arguably, research failures both in an epistemic, or intellectual, sense and in an ethical sense—and the pragmatist, we may add, should here acknowledge this essential entanglement of the factual and the valuational.[54] Wisdo writes:

> Our capacity to understand religious beliefs and rituals [. . .] is not primarily a matter of our ability to explain their origins for the simple reason that such explanations could never account for the depth of our impression and the claim such forms of life make on us. What is needed to understand religion, rather, is [. . .] first of all [. . .] the kind of practical interpretative skills and capacities that enable us to describe the practices and rituals in a meaningful way. [. . .] The task then is *not* to offer an explanation, but to assemble the facts in a certain way in order to *see* what kind of pattern might emerge [. . .]. (Ibid., 121)

This task to "see" the meaning of a pattern, to be able to structure or organize "the facts" in a particular meaningful way, is, according to Wisdo, an irreducibly ethical task, not simply a scientific or epistemic one (although these two dimensions may be inseparable). Reductive naturalists tend to suppose that some privileged, scientifically rational organization of "the facts"—natural facts, such as evolutionary ones, or more broadly natural and social facts—of the world is already at our disposal, overlooking the compelling (metalevel) fact that religious attitudes to life are relevant and interesting for some people precisely because no such ontologically privileged organization of the facts exists.

Hence, whatever the merits of Wisdo's and other antireductionists' contributions to the debate over the rationality of religious belief are, we should take seriously their arguments concerning the ethical and personal significance of religious commitments as something that cannot be ignored by the scientific or scholarly study of religion (and, by extension, of other relevant commitments people both studied by and engaging in humanistic scholarship might have). Moreover, the reductionist's attempt to find an allegedly fundamental, naturalizable cognitive or social mechanism underlying religious beliefs, experiences, and practices could lead, from the ethical point of view, to a profound misunderstanding of the place of religion in the lives of the people for whom religion *is* (experienced as) religion in the first place. Thus reductionists, in a sense, violate a necessary condition for the possibility of making sense of religion. They can, then, hardly offer us any substantial "understanding" of religion, although they can undoubtedly produce sophisticated scientific knowledge about the functioning of certain humanly natural and perhaps culturally universal cognitive and social mechanisms. This, roughly, is one way in which the antireductionist can try to counter reductionist views on religion (without dogmatically rejecting naturalism, either).

The relevance of all this to our overall concerns is the following. What we have arrived at amounts, presumably, to a transcendental argument against the plausibility of any scientistic reductionism in this special case study field—and by extension in other fields, for example, against reductive accounts of literature as ultimately something else and "more fundamental" (say, mere psychological activity taking place in reading and writing) or of historical events as something else (say, mere causal processes or what have you). A normative framework provided by pragmatist philosophy of science and the humanities, drawing serious attention to the normative practice examined, can, if this argument is on the right track, be shown to be *a necessary condition for the possibility* of any intelligible, reflexively self-engaging decision to pursue inquiry (into religion or into anything else) instead of some other human practice in relation to some particular problem of human life. Reductionists seeking to understand religion through *mere* scientific explanations tend to overlook the need for an irreducibly normative dimension in our assessments of people's religious outlooks. The danger is that naturalizing reductionism misunderstands not only its object of study but also its own normative commitment to inquiry.

This should motivate us to take seriously the kind of pragmatist philosophy of (general) inquiry as well as (specifically) the humanities that I have defended. In the nonreductively naturalized framework of pragmatism, the aim to understand both scientific and scholarly inquiries as well as their objects of study, such as religious practices and institutions, as first and foremost human practices with their inbuilt normativity and constitutive methods and goals emerges as a natural or even unavoidable way of accounting for the very possibility of scholarly understanding and scientific explanation of a complex human practice such as religion. This can, perhaps, be seen as a quasi-transcendental argument (at a metalevel) for the pragmatist approach itself.

In the case of religion, the situation is, however, complex. Even though the proper scientific and/or scholarly attitude obviously does not allow the results of interpretation to be determined by anyone's religious demands, it is quite clear that religious practices themselves are not strictly separable from the "scientific" attempts of a community of scholars (theologians, biblical scholars, comparative religion scholars, and others) to study—to interpret and reinterpret—religious texts, especially in monotheistic religions like Judaism, Christianity, and Islam that are essentially based on sacred writings preserved in the community. Religion itself, then, requires theology, not only vice versa. Where would reductionism leave us—in religion, theology, or academic interpretive study of religious texts and practices? The point of this discussion has been that no satisfactory answer to this question is forthcoming on "first-order" scientific principles alone. The equivalent of NOA in religious studies is simply insufficient. We need "second-order" normative criteria, which, it seems, can only be established (and debated) on philosophical grounds, though of course in close relation to the actual interpretive and explanatory work that is done in the special disciplines that those criteria are intended to govern. There is no end to normative questions concerning the criteria we use to assess that kind of work, or, indeed, our criteria of assessment themselves. To admit the availability of such questions is already to open the door for transcendental considerations.

Indeed, some typical antireductionist arguments can—in relation to religion and in other contexts, too—be reconstructed as transcendental ones, insofar as they examine, say, the preconditions of meaning and understanding, that is, conditions without which meaning (or, a fortiori, knowledge) would be impossible for us. Thus, Wittgensteinian, pragmatist, and many other criticisms of scientism, reductionism, or radical naturalization are examples of the ways in which something like pragmatic nonreductive naturalism can be reconciled with quasi-Kantian transcendental argumentation (cf. Pihlström 2003a, 2004b, 2009, 2012b, 2013, 2021).

Putting the matter in terms familiar from phenomenology, we might suggest that, remaining within the "natural attitude," reductionism about religion only offers us scientific knowledge and explanations from an external perspective from which the *inner meaning* of religious practices, as appreciated by the practitioners as they identify themselves as participants of those practices, can hardly be revealed.[55] It is doubtful whether religious phenomena are thereby "understood" and whether any critical comparisons between, say, religion and science (or other social practices) can be carried out on such a basis. What we might propose, then, in contrast to reductionism, is an account of humanistic inquiry into religion as something like transcendental inquiry into the preconditions of certain kinds of experiences that some of us naturally seem to go through within certain historically rich traditions in the context of which certain texts are constantly read, studied, interpreted, and (re)produced. We are now in a position to conclude that such transcendental inquiry cannot be *replaced* by mere scientific explanation, although we need not assume any sharp, historically unchanging contrast between the scientific (naturalistic) and the humanistic or philosophical perspectives, either. Truly antireductionist understanding of religious phenomena construes those phenomena as religious in the first place. To study religiosity on the basis of, say, "methodological atheism" (cf. Pyysiäinen 2001b) is, moreover, already to make a philosophical commitment; it is not clear that such a methodological starting point can be sharply distinguished from atheism *tout court* (see also Wiebe 1994, 112). Certainly it is not a neutral starting point that one may simply embrace irrespective of any philosophical problems. Its alleged philosophical neutrality is as illusory as that of radical reductionism.[56]

Accordingly, reductive explanations of religious phenomena may be criticized (though of course not excluded) not as false but as at least partly irrelevant, even though a broadly secular (religiously noncommitted) approach in our understanding of the development of religious worldviews must obviously also be maintained in any serious research. The interesting and compelling task we are invited to work on is to make room for *both* secular, scientific explanations *and* attempts to understand religious ways of thinking "from within" the practices that (only) make them possible for their practitioners, and it is in this task that transcendental arguments can be extremely helpful. Exploring such arguments may thus be vital for opening the critical space for any genuinely humanistic inquiry into religion. This result has obvious ontological relevance, because ultimately what is at issue here is our understanding of what religious phenomena at the ontological level *are*.

However, as any ontological inquiry within pragmatism, what we have arrived at is ethically relevant, too. I do not only mean simply that religious studies is subject to the same kind of ethical norms and considerations as any research involving human beings and groups of people as its objects. Rather, the need to understand religious practices *as* religious—along the lines explored here by means of pragmatist-transcendental considerations—could be regarded as distinctive in the ethics of religious studies. What this involves is the need to draw appropriate attention to developing proper attitudes to the "reality" examined. The methodological dispute between "external" (e.g., causally explanatory) and "internal" (e.g., hermeneutic or Wittgensteinian, practice-involving) approaches is thus not only ontologically but also ethically significant.[57] In addition, religious studies also focuses on religious people's own ethical views and ideas—and clearly no such research can ever be completely ethically neutral. Nor is the need to draw and redraw the boundaries between religious studies, theology, and religious practices themselves ethically neutral. Again, pragmatism is well suited to make sense of these complexities.

Why Transcendental?

Let us finally address an obvious worry: why insist on the need to employ transcendental arguments at all, or even use the complex vocabulary of transcendental philosophy, given the evolving nonfoundationalist historicity of human reason (including science and humanistic scholarship)? Not all historical conditions of actual human phenomena are transcendental conditions. Should the term *transcendental* be reserved for strictly a priori conditions and arguments? In philosophy of science and the humanities, in particular, couldn't we just replace transcendental arguments with empirical historical, sociological, anthropological, and other inquiries? Wouldn't this precisely be the way the pragmatist should view the matter, refusing to "transcendentalize" the naturally human or to adopt any age-old aprioristic philosophical methodology?

One reason that we may want to maintain the transcendental vocabulary, approach, and argumentative strategy is that this makes better sense of the "constructivist" views according to which the world is not simply there for us to discover but to a large extent a human (social, cultural) "construction," albeit in a historicized sense (see again chapters 2 and 3). In nontranscendental versions of such constructivism, the danger is that the construction process is considered causal or factual, a process of "production." This makes little sense of the way in which our practices of thought and inquiry can seriously be claimed to "constitute" the objects of thought and inquiry. Kant himself avoided this danger with his transcendental versus empirical distinction. We may see various constructivist, pragmatist, and historicist positions as versions of Kantian transcendental idealism in this regard, but as already argued in the preceding chapters, their plausibility in my view essentially depends on their being available for a transcendental interpretation. The constitution of the objects of the humanities (as well as of the sciences) is not a causal but a transcendental process. This also holds for the constitution of the peculiar kind of "reality" studied within the academic field(s) explored in the previous section—religious studies. *Its* objects are (transcendentally) constituted through a value-laden pragmatic understanding (itself practice-embedded) of certain human activities and meanings as irreducibly religious.

Even so, the status of the a priori is certainly a problem here. Fortunately, there are historically relativized notions of the a priori available,[58] and when the transcendental is "pragmatized," "naturalized," or "historicized" (as suggested here), we have to work with such a softened and contextually relativized notion of the a priori (cf. Pihlström and Siitonen 2005). It may, admittedly, be to some extent a terminological matter whether we then still want to call it a priori or transcendental. Nevertheless, the transcendental and/or the a priori even in this culturally relativized and historicized sense is stronger than a mere empirical social condition, because we are also dealing with (again admittedly culturally relative and historically changing) *limits* to what is *thinkable* or *conceivable* by us. The modal structure of transcendental arguments (as briefly explored above) is thus still there. We do need to admit that any such limits are continuously transformed, redefined, rearticulated, and occasionally overcome; yet there are, inevitably, some such limits in place at any given time (as, e.g., in the case of Kuhnian paradigms), and this makes a fundamental difference when it comes to interpreting certain practices as religious (or nonreligious, for that matter).

How exactly this is compatible with nonreductive, pragmatic naturalism in the philosophy of science and the philosophy of the humanities needs to be spelled out in much more detail.[59] These issues are also obviously related to the question of what kind of nonreductive naturalism can be developed on pragmatist grounds in the philosophy of science or the philosophy of the humanities. Can our philosophical naturalism really be so nonreductive that it accommodates transcendental (historically relative) a priori arguments? I must leave this question open here, but my tentative response in this chapter has been moderately positive. If we wish to make sense of the idea that transcendental constitutivity (transcendental grounding, transcendental conditioning) could run in two (or more) directions, that is, from nonhuman nature to human culture but also vice versa, we might want to seriously pursue the option of pragmatist transcendental philosophy in contrast to both orthodoxly Kantian transcendental idealism and non-Kantian transcendental realism. The latter unfortunately dominates most of the mainstream reductive naturalizing projects in religious studies but also more generally.

With these characterizations concerning the transcendental constitution of objects of inquiry, we have, I hope, taken some important steps toward better understanding and appreciating the dependence of the reality we are engaged in studying—and its very possibility of being studied and understood, or even ontologically postulated as "real"—within the humanities (as well as, by extension, the sciences) on those processes of inquiry themselves. A considerable amount of further work, historical and systematic, would, however, be needed in order for us to arrive at a substantial pragmatist philosophical theory of the humanistic processes of inquiry being enabled by transcendentally constitutive structures of value-embedded ontological postulation discernible by transcendental argumentation and reflection.

Chapter 5

Conclusion

The Values and Limits of the Humanities

I have in this book argued that philosophers should take seriously the task of developing a systematic philosophy of the humanities—in comparison to and partly based on general philosophy of science and inquiry (cf. chapter 2), yet with a distinctive and autonomous status comparable to, for example, philosophy of social science—and that they should seek to do so in a broadly pragmatist framework. As such, my book has only offered a prolegomenon to such a project. No comprehensive or systematic philosophy of the humanities has been formulated here. Rather, I have only argued that a project like this is important and worthwhile and that pragmatism is a truly promising philosophical basis for such a project. Thus, my discussion has, I duly acknowledge, been rather programmatic. I have tried to argue for what ought to be done in this field rather than actually doing what I think ought to be done. I have thus offered (especially in chapter 3) a catalogue of relevant topics of investigation as well as some central research questions and hypotheses, with slightly deeper case studies illuminating, for example, the interplay of naturalizing and transcendental strategies of argumentation (see chapter 4).

Despite the tentative nature of my endeavor, I hope to have been able to convey a sense of the urgency of exploring these issues. Not only do I find it an inherently interesting academic philosophical task to understand more deeply what the humanities are like as epistemic practices and how their ontologies ought to be (metaontologically) construed, but I also find it more generally culturally important that we value the humanities by taking them philosophically seriously in this way. While I have argued for a pragmatist way of doing this, my defense of the philosophical significance of the humanities is definitely not restricted to pragmatist accounts of this significance. In a world troubled by all kinds of old and new threats to human meanings and values, we should—pragmatically—employ all the philosophical resources we can to defend the humanistic practices that enable us to better understand how such meanings and values can be studied as elements of the human world, constantly keeping in mind that this "human world" is not only a "positive" realm of meanings and values but also a world in which the fragmentation and loss of meaningfulness is a painfully real possibility. The humanities are as important for analyzing the collapse and destruction of meaning as they are for understanding the emergence of meaning. Only in a "human world" ontologically dependent on valuational activities can meanings be, or become, real, and only in such a world can their loss be a genuine loss; moreover, only in such a context of possible loss, a world with "real chance" and genuine risk, as William James (e.g., 1975 [1907], Lecture VIII) described it, can human beings *fail* to realize a meaningful world, and it is a task of the humanities to make such a world intelligible to us.

Final Thoughts on Pragmatic Realism

Despite the provisional nature of my discussion, I have relied on a certain identifiable historical line of thought extending through the pragmatist tradition, especially when it comes to developing a form of pragmatic realism hoping to secure a balanced and critical middle path between strong forms of realism and relativism/constructivism. This form of realism has above been tentatively applied to the philosophy of the humanities. I have suggested that we may take a pragmatically realistic attitude to the ontology of the humanities (without making any specific ontological commitments that must be left to the humanistic disciplines themselves) and that the notion of truth in these fields can also be (roughly) understood along these moderately pragmatist lines.

I want to note, by way of conclusion, that the problem of realism is by no means easier in the philosophy of the humanities than it is in the philosophy of the natural or social sciences. It may even be more difficult, as the question is about how to maintain a plausible form of realism regarding a humanly created and maintained reality. This reality is of course not independent of the human mind, thought, and language in general, yet it needs to be understood as (empirically and factually speaking) independent of any particular inquirers' thoughts, opinions, and theories, while being at the same time transcendentally constituted by our human practices of inquiry and their embedded values. What is more, the complex objects of inquiry in the humanities about which we should, in my view, be (pragmatic) realists are themselves, in many cases, representational objects (e.g., texts and documents of various kinds) purporting to refer to other parts of human and nonhuman reality—or, as the case might also be, complex properties of such objects (including their meanings or meaningful structures) which play a role in our scholarly interpretations of them, a role analogous to the role played by explanatory postulations of theoretical entities and properties in natural-scientific inquiries.

I have not sought to provide any final solution to this problem but have primarily wanted to give the reader a sense of its complicated character while also rendering pragmatism a well-motivated perspective on the realism issue. I do think that a form of pragmatic realism can be maintained across the board—in the philosophy of the humanities as much as in the philosophy of science more generally—but this requires that we subordinate the realism discussion to a pragmatist approach viewing *all* human ontological postulation as a deeply value-laden and interest-driven practice. In this respect, all ontological postulations are in the same boat, whether they are scientific or humanistic (or something else). Furthermore, in the spirit of holistic pragmatism (cf. chapter 3), we should be able to critically test our commitment to scientific realism (in the humanities and more generally) as a commitment *within* the overall totality of our philosophical views regarding the humanities, including holistic pragmatism itself. This entails that there is no way of ever finally concluding the discussion concerning pragmatic realism in the humanities (or generally) from any privileged and stable standpoint. Our realism needs to be constantly revisited and reexamined; it is as open-ended and as open to continuous critical renewal as any other philosophical, scientific, or scholarly view. And so is pragmatism, only within which, I have claimed, realism is viable.

I have interpreted this pragmatic realism in a (broadly) Kantian framework of "transcendental pragmatism." Thus, when speaking about the constitutive dependence of the objects of inquiry (in the humanities and more generally) on our practices of inquiry, I hope to have made clear that I have not intended that notion of dependence to be taken in any factual or directly ontological sense, let alone the sense of causal production of entities through research practices. On the contrary, the relevant kind of (ontological) dependence is, I have suggested, transcendental in a quasi-Kantian sense. The objects of inquiry of the humanities are possible for us as the objects they are only in certain practice-embedded contexts of inquiry.

These general philosophical and inquiry-theoretical ideas have been briefly, and only tentatively, applied to the case studies that I hope pragmatist philosophers of the humanities will pursue further. I have (though only briefly) focused on the philosophy of literary theory and criticism, the philosophy of historiography, and the philosophy of theology and religious studies as exemplary cases of humanistic study. In all these areas—with all their similarities and differences—we can, I believe, carry through a pragmatist articulation of their ontologies, for instance, in terms of pragmatic realism and Kantian critical transcendental pragmatism. Toward the end of the book (chapter 4), I included a substantial discussion of the dialectics of naturalism and transcendental argumentation (in an exemplary way applicable to the debates over the nature of religious studies), which I take to be significant for any adequate development of transcendental pragmatism.

I have also suggested, though again only tentatively and in passing, that the pragmatist philosophy of the humanities developed here can help us understand and appreciate the kind of impact the humanities are able to make in contemporary academia. The ways in which our projects of inquiry can make an impact also depend on the ways we philosophically understand those projects and even the ways in which we—to some extent metaphorically (cf. Kivistö and Pihlström 2017)—describe and articulate them. A pragmatist account of the philosophy of the humanities may, arguably, accommodate a sophisticated conception of the nature of humanistic inquiry also in relation to the partly metaphorical notions of the vertical and horizontal dimensions of knowledge, as well as change and stability in research practices and institutions.[1] The latter distinction may be concretely manifested in the tension between scholarly traditions and their renewability. Humanistic research is, to a significant extent, a matter of continuing traditions of scholarship.[2] When understanding our own scholarly point of view within a certain tradition, we contribute to shaping the framework in terms of which the objects of the inquiry that scholarly point of view opens up may become possible as the objects they are. Our ways of describing our own scholarly perspectives and their practice-laden contexts are thus never completely neutral; they are essential to the very emergence of the objects those perspectives enable us to inquire into.

One aspect of pragmatism that has repeatedly albeit not always explicitly been at work in this volume is *pluralism* (cf. Pihlström 2013, 2020, 2021). It could be suggested (cf. again, e.g., Kivistö and Pihlström 2017) that forms of monism narrowing down our conceptions of scholarly identities and conceptions of inquiry as well as research environments usually constitute the *proton pseudos* leading to a deterioration of academic life, especially in the humanities but perhaps also more widely. From a pragmatist point of view, it is natural to emphasize our need for a rich pluralism of methods and ontologies as well as, by extension, academic administrative structures—a pluralism recognizing *genuine otherness* in various contexts of inquiry yet highly critical of any naïve relativism that would render critical discussion impossible by declaring that "anything goes." It is right here that pragmatism is fundamentally important for the future of our academic life in the humanities and more broadly. We should duly recognize the pragmatic plurality inherent in our practices of knowledge production and knowledge acquisition, acknowledging that there is no single correct let alone practice-independently privileged way of conceptualizing knowing and research.[3]

Finally, while I have sketched (though indeed only sketched) a version of the pragmatist conception of truth that I hope could be widely attractive in the philosophy of the humanities, let me reemphasize that I am not at all proposing to follow those pragmatists (e.g., Rorty) who prefer to replace the concept of truth by something else or allegedly more interesting (such as freedom, as essential to our understanding of human life as it is). Nothing I have said about pragmatism, truth, realism, and the humanities should lead anyone to believe that I would be willing to replace the pursuit of truth by any other pursuit or to view it as subordinate to something else. It is fundamental in the humanities—as elsewhere—that we pursue the truth about the world we live in. Nothing can compensate for this. Yet this is a pursuit of truth internal to our practices themselves and guided by our historically developing values. It is never a "pure" pursuit of truth in the sense of being intended to "copy" or "mirror" a practice-independent reality "out there," just waiting to be represented by us, but it is, indeed, a pursuit of truth about the world that *we*, human beings, *live* in. Pragmatist truth is not a static relation of correspondence but a practice-laden and dynamic structural feature of our processes of inquiry.

This practice-embeddedness of truth entails, as Rorty (1989) argued, especially in the context of his reading of Orwell, that truth constitutively depends on human freedom, as our engagement in the practices of pursuing the truth involves free and responsible human action (though, *pace* Rorty, we may also say that our freedom depends on our honoring truth). Academic freedom can never guarantee that the scholarly community will achieve the truth or even progress toward it, but insofar as truth and the pursuit of truth matter to us at all, then we must organize that pursuit in a framework taking academic freedom very seriously. Again, pragmatism can make sense of this inescapable commitment to maintaining freedom—a commitment that we may even see as itself having a transcendental status in the sense that it (only) enables us to create practices of *inquiry* at all. Truth and freedom, then, interconnect in profound ways that (again) only pragmatism in my view sufficiently strongly appreciates. This is not at all to follow Rorty in claiming that "if we take care of freedom, truth can take care of itself" (ibid., 176) but on the contrary to affirm that we need to take care of *both* freedom *and* truth, and their inextricable entanglement, in order to be able to take care of any human reality worth inquiring into. This is a fundamental characteristic constitutive of the humanities, in particular, conceived as inquiries into the ways in which human beings have freely created and continue to create and maintain their cultural world.

This pragmatically realist attitude to the pursuit of truth (cf. Pihlström 2021), including the pursuit of truth in humanistic inquiry in particular, does *not* signal any simple return to a nonpragmatic realistic correspondence theory, however. Truth, especially in the humanities, remains deeply value-laden, a "species of good" in a Jamesian phrase. Pursuing historical truth (e.g., about past atrocities, but in principle about more mundane matters as well) is never an ethically neutral project. Nor is the pursuit of truth about literary or religious meanings. Any truths and any inquiries into the world that makes our truths true depend on what *we* find relevant and valuable in our lives.[4] We encountered this valuational account of the dependence of objective facts and truths on our interests and practices particularly in the context of the holistic pragmatism developed by Morton White (explicitly in the philosophy of historiography, for instance, as articulated in chapter 3), but at a general level this way of thinking runs through (at least the Kantian versions of) pragmatism and characterizes not only pragmatist accounts of the humanities but the general pragmatist conception of inquiry.

Inhumanity, or Representing the Nonrepresentable

Humanistic scholarship investigating our human representations of reality—and the philosophy of the humanities analyzing such representational activities—can also bring us to the limit of what can be represented. Various human experiences of the transcendent (as distinguished from the transcendental) could mark such limits, challenging what humanistic scholarship can achieve. There could, for example, be individual religious outlooks that can only be understood in a very limited way by means of any scholarly or scientific contribution (cf. chapter 4). There could be "limits of language" and meaning that are challenged in serious literature investigating by artistic means what language can express (think about Samuel Beckett's methods of literary expression, for instance). In some cases, transcendental argumentation could show the need to postulate, or at least verge toward, such manifestations of the transcendent, but this would still remain a scholarly postulation "at the limit," so to speak, never a full-fledged step toward the transcendent itself in a metaphysical sense. The transcendent would, then, remain a "limit concept," a *Grenzbegriff*, as no humanistic or any other scholarship, qua rational research, can transgress its transcendental limits.

As a special case of the limits of inquiry and understanding, concluding our discussion of the philosophy of the humanities, we may take a brief look (brief, indeed, in its inevitable inconclusiveness) at what may be called the problem of representing the Holocaust—standing here as a metonymy for all historical atrocities that defy human thought.[5] Literature, historiography, as well as theology and religious studies may all make their own efforts to represent the Holocaust. Our representational activities in those fields, my pragmatist analysis suggests, are crucially dependent on our values, and thus we may say that there are, for instance, ethical constraints for historical representation. However, the Holocaust, arguably, is not a mere "historical fact" but a metaphysical disruption violating such ethical constraints or even the very idea of ethics, shattering our ordinary value categories. It is a fundamental challenge to representability itself and to the ontology of meanings and values in the "human world" (see above), not just another further fact that ought to be scholarly represented (and whose representations could be philosophically analyzed). It also needs a pragmatist elaboration in the sense that even facing this thought-defying limit to any representation, we still do need to move forward in our own historical environment, yet without the false hope for any final reconciliation with historically real suffering. We have to acknowledge the humanity at the core of inhumanity or the interplay between the human and inhumanity. This is an unending scholarly task for anyone (the historian, the literary critic, the theologian) seeking to understand the Holocaust (which thus cannot be thoroughly understood), as well as for the philosopher seeking to understand such attempts at understanding.

No straightforward realism is, then, possible about an event such as the Holocaust. It disrupts our world-categorization, so even the kind of pragmatic realism I have advocated in this book arrives at its limits.[6] Categorization and representation presuppose comprehension or at least comprehensibility, and to claim to comprehend the Holocaust is to make an unethical attempt to appropriate this historical "fact" (in a sense overlooking the fact that it is not just a fact).[7] We are thus brought to the limits of any ethically possible (say, historical, literary, or religious and/or theological) representation of such a limit of humanly intelligible factuality and representability. We are, accordingly, dealing with transcendental limits and conditions of our very humanity here. It is, arguably, an unethical transgression of those limits to claim to simply "know" what happened in the Holocaust or to thoroughly understand the event. The Holocaust is an extreme example in terms of which we may reflect on our pragmatist philosophy of the humanities in general, combining history, literature, and theology or religious studies, as well as philosophy. All these human activities are silenced at this limit, and the inevitability of this metalevel silence must be duly recognized by anyone seriously pursuing the humanities. Any humanistic (or any other) research can only be seriously pursued within the transcendental limits that this kind of transcendence—inhumanity—sets to our human endeavors. The world is indeed not the same "after Auschwitz"; its very representability must be, repeatedly, rethought in the light of that historical event.

"Representing the Holocaust," or rather taking seriously its utter nonrepresentability (cf. Patterson 2018), can thus be regarded as an ultimate challenge (though using the everyday word *challenge* is problematic here) for both the humanistic disciplines pursuing historical, literary, or theological representations and the philosophy of the humanities pursuing a pragmatist-cum-transcendental understanding and appreciation of this problem of representation. This is an ethically pregnant outcome of a transcendental analysis of processes of reflection and (non-)representation taking us to the limits of transcendence. However, here I just wish to point out that this ethical finitude of humanistic understanding needs to be acknowledged as a way of acknowledging the victims of history (and inhumanity); pursuing such issues further is a task for another investigation.

Nor is the ethical significance of the humanities restricted to the kind of extreme dimensions of the human world (or history) that escape our understanding and representation—such as, paradigmatically, the Holocaust. Rather, such significance, and the question concerning possible ethical significance, extend to all the "normal" scholarly activities that humanistic scholars engage in. Appreciating the scholarly practices of the humanities may have enormously rich ethical, educational, and societal significance even with regard to the more mundane aspects of those practices (see also, e.g., Olafson 1968). Accordingly, the philosophy of the humanities has a multifaceted future agenda to work on, and this also demonstrates that the humanities, as well as the philosophical project of understanding them ever more deeply, are ultimately in the service of the humanistic defense of human value and dignity even when exploring considerably less dramatic topics than (say) the Holocaust. For scholars in the humanities, including philosophers seeking to deepen our understanding of the humanities, there is no neutral place to stand outside ethical concerns and judgments in our problematic world; however, this responsibility to engage in moral reflection on the subject matter of one's research does not, of course, entail any subordination of scholarship to any predetermined ideological standpoints. On the contrary, as I hope this book has made clear, pragmatist philosophy of the humanities emphasizes the duty, both ethical and epistemic, to engage in continuous self-critical reflection on one's fundamental presuppositions in research. Those presuppositions can always be challenged, for both epistemic and ethical reasons.

Motivation and Duty

Leaving, inevitably, such *Grenzbegriff* issues as the representation of the Holocaust unresolved, let me conclude with brief remarks on the fundamental values and motivation of humanistic inquiry. *Why* do we pursue humanistic (or any) research at all, and why *should* we? For a pragmatist drawing attention to the purposiveness of all of our practices, why to engage in the practice of scholarship—or why, indeed, to do anything at all—is always an open question. In the case of the humanities, we may distinguish between a number of different senses in which it may be reasonable or well motivated to pursue scholarship.[8]

First, one might have a purely selfish and thus thoroughly instrumental interest motivated by money, fame, social media presence, or personal "branding." Secondly, one might base one's motivation on one's employer's (e.g., one's university's) demands and expectations; this would in a sense be a heteronomous version of the first motivation, but hardly less instrumental. Thirdly, one might in some sense have, or claim to have, an obligation to engage in (humanistic) research that is not reducible to one's duty toward the university one is affiliated with, for instance. Rather, one might experience an ethical duty toward one's object of study itself. This could be a particularly strongly experienced obligation, especially if one, say, inquires into the lives and experiences of historical people and wishes to raise them from their marginalized position and let their "voice" be heard. Alternatively, one might also experience a duty not toward one's employer but to the academic community as a whole, or even to humankind in toto. Humanistic scholarship enriches our shared life on this fragile planet. By engaging in such scholarship, one might thus also in a sense strive for immortality in a secular sense. One could do this out of vanity, hoping that one's books will survive even a devastating catastrophe in a nuclear-strike-proof library basement, or perhaps self-ironically, realizing that one is mortal but recognizing that the best possible use for one's finite time in this world of inescapable death is pursuing (in vain) immortality by writing books about human life, human culture, and human beings. It is, indeed, as close to immortality one may get in this life.

In addition to these (selfish or nonselfish) purposes motivating one's scholarly activities, one might, fourthly, also be motivated—at an essentially deeper level, one might say—in a qualitatively different sense. This would be a motivation arising not out of any specific internal or external goals reflecting a definite purpose or interest but simply out of a fundamental, irreducible, and perhaps unexplainable—in a sense ethical but more broadly metaphysical or existential, or possibly even quasi-religious—need or duty. To quote Oiva Ketonen's (1992) words on his great teacher Eino Kaila and *his* ultimate motivation for philosophizing: "One must." There is no way of grounding *this* motivation in anything allegedly more fundamental. A humanistic scholar's being motivated for their scholarly work in this manner is in the end just "there—like our life" (to borrow Wittgenstein's memorable phrase). There is nothing else such a person could do and still remain who they are. Being a scholar is at this level not merely being engaged in a certain activity for which we get paid by our universities, for instance. It is an existential choice in one's life—a deep vocation, as one might say.[9]

For the pragmatist, there is always an element of sheer *contingency* involved in any such duty and motivation. If one asks why we should seek deeper understanding about some particular object of study, A, one may answer that we need to know A (better) in order to do B. But why should we do B? Because . . . And so it goes. It's all thoroughly contingent—but all our purposes and their contingencies can themselves be pragmatically scrutinized. The door is always open for further critical inquiry. A deep contingency and a continuous consideration of relevance pertain to our research questions, sources, categorization of objects, and so on, as well as to our motivation for asking those questions and pursuing those sources and objects of study in the first place. This, however, is not the shallow kind of contingency that might resemble, for example, a strategic "list of values" a university (like a business corporation) might choose as a kind of motivational basis for its employees. True scholars do not pursue values such as truth, freedom, or *Bildung* in the interest of fulfilling the strategic goals of their universities but because such values, as contingent as they are, constitute their identities as scholars in an existential sense. Any serious philosophy of the humanities, as much as any serious philosophy of science, must be able to make sense of this fundamental—constitutive—characteristic of academic values, while acknowledging their contingency.[10]

At the same time, a serious philosophy of the humanities must appreciate the individual uniqueness of the way a humanistic scholar, through their deeply personal habits of viewing the human world under investigation, is committed to cherishing those values. This, indeed, is to appreciate the existential vocation of scholarship as the deepest motivation for the scholarly pursuit. I hope to have been able to argue in this book that such an understanding of the humanities as real human individuals' practices of inquiry need not at all conflict with the (pragmatically speaking) objective character of the pursuit of truth those individuals engage in through their scholarly practices. The humanities, including the fields of scholarship analyzed here via several case studies, are capable of truth and objectivity as long as these concepts are understood pragmatically, and they are capable of delivering objective (albeit always fallible and revisable) answers to the scholarly questions posed by scholars, answers grounded in the ways the human world is, as long as the critical spirit of truthfulness remains a guiding norm of our inquiries (cf. again Pihlström 2021). What is more, the precise ways those questions are posed, and which questions are found interesting and valuable in the first place, are what is distinctively personal in humanistic scholarship, shaping not only the practices of inquiry in these fields but the very reality those practices aim at representing and interpreting. No matter how strongly we pursue objectivity in humanistic research, there is no way to overcome the contingently personal, even existential, points of departure of our inquiries. One major attraction of humanistic scholarship may indeed be the entanglement of the rigorous objectivity of research with the irreducibly value-laden personal perspectival nature of humanistic (as well as philosophical) inquiries into meanings and values themselves. On the other hand, this does not create any essential dualism between the humanities and the natural sciences; both are human activities and as such dependent on human processes of valuation.

Pragmatist philosophy of the humanities is, I believe, uniquely able to address the contingency of *everything* in our human lives and human world, moving from conceptual categorization and our practice-laden purposes and perspectives to the ethical and existential questions about why we have the purposes and perspectives we do in academic life, while also analyzing the constitutive features of these value-guided processes of world-categorization, representation, and inquiry in strictly transcendental terms. We are thus invited to ever new self-critical reflections at increasingly reflexive metalevels, and those reflections will always make additions to human culture to be studied by new generations engaging in philosophy and humanistic scholarship.

Notes

Preface

1. My earlier publications most relevant to the themes of this volume include my writings on pragmatic realism and Kantian pragmatism (including Pihlström 2003a, 2009, 2013, 2014, 2015a, 2020), my works directly addressing pragmatist philosophy of science and the nature of the humanities (including Pihlström 2003a, 2011b, 2012b, 2015a), and my more recent work on pragmatist truth and the pursuit of truth (Pihlström 2021).

Chapter 1

1. See, however, Faye 2012; Leezenberg and de Vries 2019—as well as Fitz-Hugh's (1897) old book, which I have been unable to access. Leiden University in The Netherlands hosts an MA program in the philosophy of the humanities (see https://www.universiteitleiden.nl/en/education/study-programmes/master/philosophy-120ec/philosophy-of-humanities), while the University of Amsterdam has a similar program in the philosophy of the humanities and social sciences (see https://www.uva.nl/en/programmes/masters/philosophy-humanities-social-sciences/philosophy-of-the-humanities-and-the-social-sciences.html?cb). I am pleased to note that at my home institution, the University of Helsinki, some junior colleagues, Inkeri Koskinen and Tomi Kokkonen in particular, are working on the philosophy of the humanities (entirely independently of my research in this area and coming from a different tradition in the philosophy of science and the social sciences). Faye (2012, 6) polemically speculates that "there is no such discipline as philosophy of the humanities," because "continental philosophy stole any such discipline a long time ago by claiming that there existed an essential ontological distinction between objects studied by the natural sciences and those studied by the humanistic sciences."

2. The field of investigation I am focusing on could in German be labelled "*Philosophie der Geisteswissenschaften*." To the extent this expression is used in German, the context is typically a hermeneutical approach examining the methods of humanistic scholarship: see, e.g., Kimmerle 1978. Note, furthermore, that I am not providing any explicit definition of "the humanities" here; the boundary between the humanities and the social sciences (and in some cases, other forms of inquiry as well) is inevitably somewhat fuzzy, but this does not prevent academics generally from understanding very well what we mean by the humanities. Ostensively, we may characterize the humanities as whatever it is that people affiliated at faculties of arts as well as many other faculties, including law and theology, are typically engaged in at universities all over the world. Moreover, there are interdisciplinary fields such as gender studies, East Asian studies, or Holocaust studies that can be taken to include both humanistic and other (e.g., social-scientific) dimensions. There are also borderline cases within traditional disciplines like psychology that can be practiced "humanistically" but also scientifically. Furthermore, it is not easy to define the key concept of "discipline," either. Here it suffices to note that well-established humanistic—as well as scientific—disciplines typically have a historical tradition of research, both national and international institutional organization (including professorships, journals and other publication forums, conferences, etc.), widely used (and sometimes controversial) methods, a shared (though again sometimes controversial) understanding of normative standards of research, as well as shared aims and goals that the academics within the discipline believe ought to be pursued and believe their colleagues to pursue as well. Kuhn's (1970 [1962]) notion of "disciplinary matrix" is useful here. For an illuminating discussion of literary studies as a "discipline," also in relation to its interdisciplinary prospects, see Olsen 2016.

3. For a comprehensive report on the global status of humanities, see Holm et al. 2015. While Holm and his colleagues also interestingly discuss the nature and value of the humanities, their approach is not *philosophical* in the sense in which this book aims at a philosophy of the humanities. See also online resources on the humanities, such as the HERA website: http://heranet.info/. For a proposed list of "big questions" that humanities scholars should focus on, see Jarrick 2016. Martha Nussbaum's (2010) defense of the value of liberal humanistic education for democracy is well known; what the pragmatist tradition can add to this discussion on the significance of humanistic education is, for instance, an exploration of the contemporary relevance of William James's 1907 [1987] essay, "The Social Value of the College-Bred": see, e.g., Hall 2012; Goldman 2019.

4. While radical relativism will be criticized through my defense of pragmatic realism in chapters 2–3, radical naturalism will be subjected to critical scrutiny in chapter 4. To anticipate: both lose track of the irreducible normativity we must ascribe to human practices of inquiry.

5. The "myth of progress" has been a major theme in critical philosophy of culture and history not only within the Frankfurt School (e.g., critical theorists' such as Theodor Adorno's and Max Horkheimer's elaborations on the "dialectics of the enlightenment") but also in works by analytic philosophers (e.g., von Wright 1993; Bouveresse 2017). Generally, we may see pragmatist meliorism—steering a middle course between optimistic and pessimistic interpretations of history—as an approach criticizing naïve views on progress (cf. also Pihlström 2020, 2021), and this could have an implicit influence on how we think about historiography within pragmatism (cf. chapter 3).

6. See, e.g., Tucker 2009 for a major reference work covering these themes and many more; cf. Kuukkanen 2015.

7. Even so, I think my job as professor of philosophy of religion, involving collaboration with colleagues representing various fields of theology and religious studies, provides a suitable background for engaging in a research like the present undertaking. Let me note, moreover, that even though my own current main area is the philosophy of religion (for my recent work in this field, see, e.g., Pihlström 2013, 2020; Kivistö and Pihlström 2016), I actually started my academic career by primarily teaching philosophy of science in the 1990s and early 2000s.

8. Both realist (e.g., Livingston 1988) and (broadly) pragmatist (e.g., Faye 2012) critics have in my view convincingly shown why radical postmodern relativism is detrimental to a serious appreciation of humanistic inquiry. Regarding Faye's comprehensive discussion, in particular, I here simply wish to signal my agreement with him concerning nonreductive "normative" naturalism (cf. ibid., 37; see, however, chapter 4 below for my critique of excessive naturalisms); the pragmatist philosopher of the humanities can safely rely on, for example, Faye's careful criticism of the tendencies toward relativism in hermeneutics, due to an overemphasis on interpretation. He convincingly shows us that the humanities need not be any less "scientific" and "objective" than the natural sciences and that we need to overcome the "methodological dualism" between these fields of inquiry (ibid., 6; see also 46, 176, and passim), to the extent that even a "naturalized hermeneutics" is, according to him, possible and desirable (ibid., 144). However, while he advances a pragmatic view of the humanities in the sense of considering our concepts and theories "as representational tools, and not given as mere passive reflections on the unchanging constituents of the world or fixed by necessary and universal categories of the cognizing mind" (ibid., 31), he fails to engage with the pragmatist tradition in any detail, as witnessed by his highly misleading, textbook-like summary of the "classical pragmatic theory of truth" as the claim that "truth is equivalent to usefulness" (ibid., 182). Nor does he devote any extended discussion to the varieties of realism (in general or in the humanities). Thus, there is still a lot to be done even after his in many ways important contribution. (Note also that pragmatists realized long ago that we

need to move beyond "postmodernism": see, e.g., Hickman 2007 on Dewey's pragmatism as "post-postmodernism.")

9. The main reason for Kant's importance in the development of the modern humanities is that, for Kant, human freedom and action cannot be studied scientifically—as free agents we are not simply parts of (deterministic) nature but, in Kantian terms, "things in themselves"—and therefore "another kind of science" would be needed for such studies (Leezenberg and de Vries 2019, 69). This could be regarded as *one* philosophical root of the humanities. As Leezenberg and de Vries emphasize, there are many other such roots, both intellectual and institutional. It was not just the Kantian understanding of the human being but also the rise of nation states and the Humboldtian conception of *Bildung* (leading to a major renewal of universities) that led to the emergence of what we now know as the humanities around 1800 (see ibid., 31–32, 152–155; see also, e.g., von Wright 1993, chapter 9. I will skip these historical developments in my discussion. (For Humboldt's important *Bildung* writings, see Humboldt 2017.)

10. Yet the authors by no means accept any full-blown relativism about interpretation (see Leezenberg and de Vries 2019, 25–26), and they generally avoid strong philosophical commitments. Their textbook is certainly highly recommendable to anyone interested in the philosophy of the humanities.

11. Note that when proposing to study "humanities in general" (through some representative examples), I am of course not saying that we should not develop specific philosophies of the humanities, such as philosophy of historiography, philosophy of anthropology, or philosophy of linguistics. Perhaps that kind of specification trend will be the future of the philosophy of the humanities. My discussion focusing on the realism issue, in particular (to be motivated and further explained below), will highlight certain themes that are arguably shared by all the humanities and, to a certain degree, by the natural sciences as well.

12. This should be kept in mind both by humanistic scholars themselves and university administrators, both of whom may—for different reasons—have mistaken expectations (and fears) concerning the future of the humanities.

13. When speaking about methodology, I am not taking any clear stand on the question of whether there is such a thing as "the" humanistic research method or whether the specific methodologies scholars use are irreducibly context- and discipline-dependent. Often there seems to be no clear method in the humanities: the scholar might just sit down to read an enormous pile of books and start thinking about them as carefully as possible, trying to find their own voice to say something interesting about those books—and I do not think there is anything wrong with such a "method." On the other hand, there are, of course, also very specific methods that scholars use. For example, systematic theologians sometimes speak of "systematic analysis," but I have always wondered what exactly this means (as opposed to something like "unsystematic analysis").

14. Incidentally, it may be pointed out that Lovejoy (1913) was one of the early critics of pragmatism, and many of his arguments may still be relevant in the critical assessment of pragmatism today. (On Lovejoy in the context of pragmatist philosophy of history and historiography, see Niklas 2016.) Hintikka, in turn, identified a pattern of thought that could ironically be regarded as *his* central "unit idea," namely, the distinction between language as a "universal medium" and language as a reinterpretable "calculus" (cf. Hintikka 1997), and applying this distinction to the history of modern philosophy may yield important insights concerning pragmatism, too (especially when it comes to interpreting Peirce, if not James and Dewey).

15. On the other hand, some philosophical ideas that have been investigated—also in the pragmatist tradition—such as Peirce's conception of "real generals" (see chapter 3 below) may have immense relevance to our understanding of what general unit ideas would be, if any such were to be postulated, and how their historical development could be accounted for. Moreover, it can be easily admitted that "narrativist" philosophers of historiography like Hayden White (1973) and Frank Ankersmit (e.g., 2001, 2009) are right in maintaining that there is nothing—no metaphysically "ready-made" "thing" or object "out there" in the historical past—that such ideas would correspond to; historiography is, indeed, close to literature in inventing or constructing such ideas in order to interpret otherwise chaotic historical experience. Yet this is not at all to join these anti-realist philosophers in claiming that there would be no objective historical past that would not constrain our conceptualizing history in terms of such general ideas (cf., e.g., Kuukkanen 2015). The challenge for the pragmatist is, precisely, to interpret this historical objectivity—and historical realism—in pragmatic terms.

16. Clearly, the question of "what really happened" is philosophically more complex than the simple slogan, "*wie es eigentlich gewesen*," associated with Leopold von Ranke's famous program of "scientific" study of history launched in the nineteenth century (on Ranke's importance for the development of historiography, see, e.g., Leezenberg and de Vries 2019, 169–171). Neither naïve realism nor naïve historicism is plausible, according to a pragmatist conception of historiography. See chapters 2 and 3.

17. Let me note that I will, throughout this book, use the word *theology* in the way it is customarily used in my home country Finland and other Nordic countries (e.g., at faculties of theology of the universities in this region): theology is a religiously noncommitted and nondenominational academic study of religion. I am of course aware of the fact that this is not the way theology is understood in many other academic contexts and traditions; both in the English-speaking world and at traditional German universities, theology is often taken to be denominational. Nothing crucial depends on these differences in meaning as long as we are always clear about the sense in which the word is used. Further

specifications regarding, for example, the relations between theology and (comparative) religious studies will be made later to the extent they are relevant to my discussions. For a highly useful discussion of how to facilitate the dialogue and cooperation between theology and the study of religion, see Helmer 2013. Both philosophically and historically, the question concerning the status of theology in relation to the other humanities and philosophy is complex; one important philosophical source of these issues is Kant's famous 1794 essay on the "conflict of the faculties" (on theology and philosophy in this regard, see, e.g., Jüngel 2005).

18. Specific questions concerning ontology must, of course, be left for the various humanistic disciplines themselves to settle—in a pluralistic spirit. My focus on the ontology of the humanities in this book must not be misunderstood as a claim to know what specific ontological postulations should be made by scholars but as a general pragmatist analysis of what it is to make them. (Pragmatic pluralism in ontology is thus perhaps better characterized as "metaontological.")

19. William James's (1975 [1907], Lecture IV) defense of pluralism as opposed to monism is the central historical point of reference for this kind of pragmatically pluralistic ontology, which I find necessary for any adequate philosophy of the humanities. On pragmatic pluralism in metaphysics generally, both historically and systematically, see Pihlström 1996, 2009.

20. On the other hand, this can be regarded as a basically Kantian and/or pragmatist interpretation of even the natural sciences, including physics. "All sciences are human sciences," as Joseph Margolis (e.g., 1993, 1995, 2012) repeatedly emphasized.

21. As this is primarily a question to be pursued in the philosophy of religion—rather than the philosophy of theology and religious studies—I will mostly set it aside here, though (but see, e.g., Pihlström 2020).

22. Authoritarian rulers, such as Xi Jinping in China and former president Donald Trump in the United States, as well as Vladimir Putin in today's Russia and the former communist leaders of the Soviet Union, typically use history very selectively for their ideological purposes—and this tendency could be described as "vulgar pragmatism" (see Pihlström 2021, chapter 1). An extreme case is Putin's version of the history of Ukraine, intended to destroy the legitimacy of Ukraine as a sovereign state. These examples should not be overhastily compared, though: Trump, during his shameful presidency, was fortunately unable to destroy American democracy, though he did try, while China with its communist rule clearly has no democratic institutions to begin with, and any such totalitarian rule is a threat not only to universal human rights but also to historical truth. Moreover, these threats are often combined: just think about the way in which the communist leaders of China have tried to entirely wipe out of its citizens' historical memory how hundreds if not thousands of students were ruthlessly murdered by their own government and military on the Tiananmen Square in

May and June of 1989. On the other hand, sometimes even the "good" people willing to, for example, tear down racist statues and memorials, may run the risk of going too far in the "cancel culture" in the sense of letting some historical facts slip out of our view. It is another matter entirely that such a view, or any responsible way of viewing our history, must always be inherently self-critical.

23. Nonrealists like Arthur Fine (1996 [1986]) and Richard Rorty (1991) prefer to reject this entire question, defending a nonphilosophical "natural ontological attitude" simply taking "at face value" whatever postulations science makes—but this is hardly a philosophically (or pragmatically) sustainable solution, as I will argue below (see chapters 2 and 4).

24. While I do not share Faye's (2012) "naturalizing" program in every detail, I do agree with him that a philosophical reconstruction of the humanities ought to start from a generally naturalistic worldview, which has no serious rivals in contemporary academic practices of inquiry. (Religious practices could be another matter, but they are not what is at issue when we are concerned with academic inquiry—including inquiry into religion itself.) Yet what naturalism exactly is remains debatable (cf., e.g., Pihlström 2003a, 2003b, as well as chapter 4 below).

25. Recall here what was noted about the nature of my ontological approach in this book: I am not hoping to settle any specific ontological questions but only discussing what it means to make ontological commitments in the humanities.

26. For example, philosophical issues in historiography have been extensively discussed by major scholars over the decades (e.g., Mandelbaum 1977; Dray 1980; Murphey 1994), while the status of literary theory and literary criticism as a scholarly discipline has been explored by Paisley Livingston (1988), among many others. These studies do not deal with pragmatism, however.

27. The obvious fact that the philosophy of history is itself historically conditioned and contextual has of course been recognized by scholars: see, e.g., Thyssen's (1954)—obviously in many ways dated—history of the philosophy of history.

28. In addition to Spengler, Arnold Toynbee is presumably one of the best-known speculative philosophers of history (see Toynbee 1946). Incidentally, it may be noted that Georg Henrik von Wright, whose views on explanation and understanding are clearly relevant to the pragmatist philosophy of the humanities (cf. von Wright 1971), wrote semipopular essays on Spengler and Toynbee at an early stage of his career in the late 1940s (those essays are, I'm afraid, available only in Swedish and Finnish); he repeatedly returned to Spenglerian pessimistic topics in his later writings (see, e.g., von Wright 1993). On the concept of freedom in relation to historical semantics, see McKeon's (1990) presumably slightly forgotten analyses; McKeon reminds us that his views on freedom and pluralism in historical interpretation do not sacrifice historical objectivity or lead to irresponsible relativism (see ibid., 144, 157). It deserves

to be mentioned that McKeon, with his pragmatist and pluralist sympathies, was an influential background figure of Richard Rorty's later neopragmatist historicism (see Gross 2008).

29. Another relatively recent work with a wide impact on the ethics and politics of historical memory is Margalit 2002.

30. The basic idea of the practical syllogism, as formulated by von Wright (1971), is that human actions are to be explained as resulting from the agent's intention to realize a certain state of affairs and their beliefs about the necessary conditions for bringing about such a state of affairs. For an extended discussion of explanation in the humanities, see Faye 2012, chapter 3.

31. Von Wright, of course, was no pragmatist, but his theories of action, causation, and explanation do bear some relevant analogies to pragmatist ideas (cf. Pihlström 2019).

32. Thus, to the extent that I will offer a qualified (pragmatist) defense of realism in this book, its primary context is indeed the kind of realism issue explored (via an analogy to scientific realism) by Livingston (1988), addressing realism about literary theory (and analogously realism in the other fields of the humanities to be explored) rather than, say, the kind of realism Tallis (1988) defends, namely, realism as a mode of writing fiction, in contrast to postmodern antirealism. But I am not claiming these to be entirely distinct forms of realism, either. For a pragmatic realist about literature, it may be natural to be a realist about literary theory, too, and vice versa. For a wide array of perspectives on the relation between the study of literature and the philosophy of literature, see Selleri and Gaydon 2016.

33. Clearly, therefore, the various philosophical investigations of how our thoughts and linguistic expressions can so much as be "about" the world at all are at least potentially relevant to the philosophy of the humanities. This concerns philosophical ideas as different as, for example, phenomenologists' analyses of the intentionality of consciousness as "aboutness," analytic philosophers' of language theories of reference, and Wittgenstein-inspired philosophers' articulations of meaning in terms of the use of expressions within language games.

34. In the latter special issue (Kuukkanen et al. 2019), Margolis is among the contributors. See also Kuukkanen 2015, and chapter 3 for some more detailed references.

35. See also Richardson 2014. For a wider array of perspectives on pragmatism in various areas of culture and the human and social sciences, including law and the arts, see Dickstein 1998. Furthermore, William James is very interestingly explored in relation to literary and cultural modernism in Evans 2017. Among the classical pragmatists, James is presumably the one most often interpreted in contexts of literary scholarship (see also, e.g., Strohmaier 2019). In addition to Strohmaier's work on James's relation to a historical classic like Goethe, it is

interesting to examine literary writers' Jamesian influences: for example, Jorge Luis Borges was inspired by James and even wrote a preface to a Spanish translation of James's *Pragmatism* (see, e.g., Nubiola 2000; for Borges's take on James, see several references in Borges 1999). Wallace Stevens's Jamesian influences are the most widely known and discussed (cf. Evans 2017). While I will not explore these lines of interpretation here, James's own literary influences and his reception among writers could provide an interesting case study on interpretive and historical possibilities (cf. chapter 3), as well as the pragmatist concept of truth as applied to humanistic inquiry. Literary influences might be crucial for our understanding of the historical development of James's own pragmatist views, and the notion of pragmatic truth might need literary applications in order to be interpreted in its historical and philosophical richness. It could, furthermore, be investigated why a thinker like James was *not* influenced by some writers or thinkers he could have been influenced by. All such questions at the interfaces of philosophy, history of ideas, and literary criticism are examples of humanistic research topics whose philosophical dimensions can be illuminated by means of a pragmatist philosophy of the humanities.

36. Rorty's academic career is interesting from the point of view of the philosophy of humanities: his first major job was as professor of philosophy at Princeton University; he then became professor of the humanities at the University of Virginia, before completing his career as professor of literature at Stanford University. On the formative years of Rorty's philosophical development, see Gross's (2008) brilliant intellectual sociology.

37. Reactions to Rorty's work by scholars of pragmatism increasingly take up his literary readings in addition to his more purely philosophical ideas. See especially Conant 2000, as well as Auxier et al. 2020. On Rorty as a "humanist," see Bernstein 2010; Schulenberg 2015; Višňovský 2020a. For Rorty's own remarks on reading books that "help us become less cruel," see Rorty 1989, 141–149, and chapters 7–8 passim.

38. Cornelis de Waal (2021) offers an excellent account of how pragmatism can be regarded as internal to the very concept of inquiry. However, I do not view pragmatism as a *rival* to any of the just mentioned philosophical orientations (cf. also Pihlström 2015a). Pragmatism is certainly not opposed to analytic philosophy, for instance, but shares its expectations of conceptual and argumentative rigor (while usually avoiding *unnecessary* formalism, though). In particular, the debate over realism in the philosophy of science and of the humanities—a key issue to be elaborated on in this volume—is equally important, I think, for both pragmatism and analytic philosophy. On the other hand, pragmatism shares with phenomenology an emphasis on the significance of the concept of experience and the philosophical commitment to analyzing its structure, especially insofar as both approaches are interpreted transcendentally as investigating the necessary

conditions for the possibility of experience (again, this theme will be revisited in due course). For a recent collection of essays exploring the relations between pragmatism and phenomenology, see Luft et al. 2019.

39. I am not at all opposed to Taylor's (e.g., 1985) defense of the irreducibility of the human sciences, hermeneutically conceived, to any naturalized accounts of human beings (see also chapter 4 below). I fully agree with Taylor that our self-understanding involves what he calls "strong evaluation" and that as human beings we noncontingently exist "in a space defined by distinctions of worth" (ibid., 3)—to the extent that the "human sciences" (or "moral sciences," as they have historically been called) cannot be regarded as value free (ibid., 57). Indeed, in earlier work I have explored the availability of a Taylor-inspired transcendental argument within a generally pragmatist framework, hoping to integrate pragmatic naturalism with the kind of transcendental considerations Taylor advances (see Pihlström 2003a). For a more comprehensive engagement with Taylor's views on "strong evaluation," normativity, and philosophical anthropology, see Laitinen 2008. I do, however, question the need to draw any principled dualism between the natural and the human sciences (see also, again, Faye 2012; Shook 2022)—hence my preference for pragmatism rather than hermeneutics (even of the relaxed and scientifically sensitive kind defended by Taylor).

40. For relatively recent contributions, see, e.g., several articles collected in Shook 2003; Frega 2011; Knowles and Rydenfelt 2011; Westphal 2014; Pihlström 2015a, 2017a.

41. The role played by the problem of realism in this volume is so central that the book could have been titled, for example, "Toward a Pragmatically Realist Philosophy of the Humanities." However, I have chosen to use the somewhat broader title in order to avoid giving the misleading impression that *only* realism would be investigated—even though this issue is implicit in virtually all the questions to be dealt with. It is, I believe, one of the virtues of the pragmatist approach that the systematic entanglements of realism with other philosophical problems across the humanities (and other fields) can also be made explicit. Note, however, that there is no way in which this book could take into consideration the enormous literature on the problem of realism in general or even scientific realism (generally and in the philosophy of science). I have earlier (Pihlström 1996) comprehensively discussed pragmatism in relation to the realism literature up to the mid-1990s. Regarding scientific realism, I mostly rely on Niiniluoto 1999; see, however, also Psillos 1999; for a pragmatically informed account of scientific realism, see Kitcher 2012. General discussions of realism rarely comment on the realism issue in the humanities (see, however, Bonino et al. 2014; though again pragmatism is not included in the discussion there). Realism has of course been intensively debated in the philosophy of social science and its subfields, including the philosophy of economics (see, e.g., Bhaskar 1979; Mäki 2005, 2007), but again pragmatism is usually not part of those debates, either.

As far as I know, my investigation here is the first comprehensive attempt to examine the problem of realism from a pragmatist perspective in the philosophy of the humanities.

42. In the critique of scientism and reductionism, pragmatism may of course find allies from philosophical approaches not based on pragmatism. For insightful critical examinations of the problems of scientism and for defenses of a more pluralistic understanding of humanity, see, e.g., Sorell 1991 and Dupré 2001.

43. The very concept of *relativism* itself needs to be carefully specified from a pragmatist point of view, and again this is an enormous task that cannot be generally taken up in a single volume. There are very different relativisms—for example, conceptual and epistemic—available, and for the pragmatist philosophy of the humanities it is vital to determine which among them may be benign and which ones need to be firmly abandoned. The pragmatist would thus have to deal with, say, Peter Winch's (1958) and other Wittgensteinians' "language-game relativism" in the study of other cultures, Thomas Kuhn's (1970 [1962]) and Paul Feyerabend's (1993 [1975]) "incommensurability" relativisms in the philosophy of science (cf. chapter 2), French poststructuralists' and their followers' views on historical relativism (e.g., Michel Foucault, Francois Lyotard, Jean Baudrillard, and others), Bruno Latour's and many others' relativism in interdisciplinary science and technology studies, as well as the kind of interpretive anthropological relativism associated with, say, Clifford Geertz (e.g., 1973)—to name just a few of the most prominent ones. Moreover, pragmatist philosophy of the humanities needs to ask in what sense some key (neo)pragmatist thinkers, such as Hilary Putnam and Richard Rorty (or earlier pragmatists, especially William James), may themselves have embraced relativism. Some of these forms of relativism (and many others) are criticized under the rubric of "framework relativism" by Livingston (1988, 5, 23–26, 172–174), who argues for a resolutely realistic philosophy of literary theory (and by extension humanistic inquiry). Incidentally, while I agree with many of Livingston's criticisms and while I also wish to defend a pragmatist version of realism as applied to the humanities, I find his straightforward categorization of Foucault as a framework relativist among others somewhat overhasty (see ibid., 150–152). However, there are also pragmatists explicitly defending relativism, e.g., Margolis 1991. For a highly useful overview of the discussion of relativism from the point of view of the philosophy of the humanities, focusing on anthropology, see Koskinen 2019; for a now classical collection of essays, see Hollis and Lukes 1982.

44. I realize that it may be somewhat unclear what the concept of *valuational* means. My key motivation for using this term—often replaceable by *value-laden*, *value-guided*, or *value-directed*, for example—is the need to emphasize that our practices of inquiry are irreducibly committed to values. They are activities with human values at their very core. In this sense, *valuational* does not simply mean "evaluative," for example, because also activities (including inquiries) that do not

explicitly evaluate something can be valuational in the sense of being inescapably committed to pursuing certain values and to being assessed in terms of values.

45. Several contributions to Tucker 2009 (e.g., chapters 14–16) address this basic question of realism about historical facts. When speaking of values here, I intend that notion to be taken in a broad sense, in principle including not only ethical but also epistemic and, at least potentially, also aesthetic (and other) values. Pragmatist theory of values and valuation is an important field in its own right, but cannot, obviously, be engaged in here in any detail. (For a consideration of how "subjective" factors may have an effect on the objective pursuit of historiography, see the discussion of the "limits" of objectivity in Mandelbaum 1977, chapters 6–7; for a more recent analysis, see Kuukkanen 2015.)

46. Note that, being no specialist in the philosophy of historiography, I make no claim to correctly interpret such famous narrativist or constructivist thinkers in any detail; my pragmatist aims in this discussion are more general.

47. As Margolis (1993, 25) aptly puts it, even when it comes to interpreting "alien people," objectivity "is a matter entirely *internal to our own practices of objectivity*." On objectivity in the humanities, see, e.g., Faye 2012. For example, there is no reason to presume that the undeniable underdetermination of correct interpretation(s) by textual evidence in humanistic inquiry would be a threat to objectivity in any more dramatic or principled sense than the familiar (Quinean) underdetermination of theory by evidence is such a threat for scientific explanation. Whether any of these versions of underdetermination is a problem for the objectivity of our inquiries and theory formation depends on a host of other philosophical assumptions.

48. The concept of emergence cannot be theoretically explicated in this book, but in some of my earlier work I have examined this concept, too; definitely, it should be recognized as potentially highly important for pragmatic naturalism (see, e.g., Pihlström 1996, 2003a).

49. Recall, however, that I am not proposing pragmatism as a rival to these philosophies. Rather, a critical dialogue on the abilities of all these approaches to sustain a critical philosophy of the humanities ought to be encouraged, and this book will seek to make a contribution to enhancing such dialogues.

50. On the compatibility of humanism and pragmatic naturalism, see Ryder 2013, especially 287–295.

51. I am *not* claiming, of course, that pragmatism would be uniquely able to philosophically account for the humanities. Establishing such a claim would require a considerably more comprehensive investigation than is possible in a single volume; the pragmatist philosophy of humanities developed here would have to be carefully compared with its relevant rivals representing different philosophical traditions. That is a discussion I must leave for the broader community of philosophers of the humanities. I just hope to be able to outline *a* form of pragmatism plausible enough to be regarded as a distinctive approach in this field.

Whether it might be literally uniquely plausible as such a philosophy deserves to be discussed in more detail. Thus, I am proposing *a* pragmatist philosophy of the humanities, and I am happy to invite both representatives of other versions of pragmatism and nonpragmatist philosophers to enter into dialogues with this proposal.

52. Whenever speaking about the "philosophical foundations" of the humanities (or anything else) in the context of pragmatism, this should be understood as a reference to a philosophical articulation of foundational questions regarding these fields of inquiry instead of any commitment to foundationalism in an epistemological or any other robust philosophical sense. Pragmatism generally avoids all forms of foundationalism—both in epistemology and in the philosophy of the humanities in particular.

53. We should recognize that philosophical methodology is a constantly contested matter. What would, for example, a research funding agency say about an application claiming to use the "philosophical method" of magically realist imagined scenarios that philosophers in the Wittgensteinian tradition proposing thought experiments—such as Wittgenstein's image of a goldfinch suddenly quoting Virginia Woolf (cf. Uschanov 2006)—may claim to employ? Philosophical methods themselves can be radical, even extreme and wild, but methods of philosophical scholarship must also honor the cool rationality of humanistic thinking about the world and human beings.

54. I do think of my earlier work on pragmatism as at least partly metaphilosophical in the sense that the very attempt to advance a pragmatist argument—for example, in the general realism discussion or in the philosophy of religion (cf., e.g., Pihlström 2020, 2021)—can also be seen as a metalevel defense of the significance of that argumentative strategy in philosophy generally.

55. Pragmatism of this type is a relative of what Ian Hacking calls *historical ontology*, because the latter emphasizes the dependence of not just truths or objects but the *candidates* for truth and falsehood on historically developing "styles of reasoning" (see Hacking 2002, 160–161). The most significant philosophical background for this idea is, presumably, Foucault's (1970 [1966]) concept of *episteme*; on Foucault's major role in the emergence of the understanding of the nature of the humanities, see again Leezenberg and de Vries 2019, 133–139.

56. From the Kantian point of view, the distinction between the transcendental and the transcendent is obviously extremely important. See, e.g., Pihlström 2020, 2021 for further discussion.

Chapter 2

1. There is no way of even summarizing the historical development of the pragmatist tradition here. As this is not primarily a historical study on

pragmatism, I will only minimally cite the classical works of the pragmatists in detail. For relevant sets of collected works of the classical canon, see Peirce 1931–58, 1992–98; James 1975–88; Dewey 1967–87. The reader is also referred to the Pragmatism Cybrary (http://www.pragmatism.org/), a comprehensive online resource through which detailed information and bibliographies of both primary and secondary literature can be found. For a collection of articles on various aspects of pragmatism, including its history, see Pihlström 2015a; for useful, up-to-date introductions, see de Waal 2021; Shook 2022.

2. See, e.g., Pihlström 1998, 2003a, 2004b, 2009, 2013, 2020, 2021.

3. Obviously, the term *transcendental* must be understood in its Kantian meaning here. Even many pragmatists—including classics like James and Dewey—have notoriously confused the transcendental with the transcendent. In brief, whereas a transcendental investigation inquires into the necessary conditions for the possibility of something that we take for granted within our practices (e.g., linguistic meaning or cognitive experience), transcendent speculation goes beyond the limits set by such conditions. For a pragmatist who, in a general, naturalistic spirit, avoids any commitment to the transcendent, it is perfectly fine to engage in transcendental argumentation concerning such constitutive conditions and limits. See further chapter 4.

4. This general pragmatist position may not be very far from views such as Ricoeur's (2004) on historical facts as critical (and often narrative) interpretive constructions based on empirical facts.

5. I would not go as far as Margolis in his theory of flux and historicity, that is, to a wholesale rejection of any (natural) invariance. I would, rather, admit that it is always a matter of historically situated and developing human practices to make sense of any (tentative, revisable) invariances there might be (for us), and to remain open to further interpreting them in the course of inquiry. The *concept* of invariance need not be abandoned: we do need, for example, to make sense of natural-scientific attempts to understand the "dynamic invariances" in nature (lawlike dependencies of variables on other variables), to use terminology introduced by Eino Kaila (cf. also Niiniluoto 1999).

6. In addition to his historicism and (moderate) relativism, Margolis's complex position incorporates a nonreductive form of naturalism and a resolute rejection of any forms of "transcendentalism" (whether Kantian or Husserlian, for example); see, e.g., Margolis 2012, 2019. Clearly, no comprehensive discussion of Margolis's historicism is possible here; that would be a topic for a study of its own. See Grube and Sinclair 2015 for a collection of essays on his metaphysics of culture. It should be added that though Margolis has made lasting contributions to the philosophy of art, too, he never seems to have been deeply interested in the philosophy of religion or theology. Presumably the best-known pragmatist philosopher engaging in aesthetics—and largely responsible for the emergence of pragmatist aesthetics as a distinctive tradition in contemporary philosophy

of art—is Richard Shusterman (e.g., 1992); however, his more recent work on "somaesthetics" is relatively far from my concerns.

7. I do believe that Margolis's overall project is compatible with (and even represents) a moderate, historically relativized form of transcendental pragmatism, though (cf. Pihlström 2015b).

8. Olesen (2013, xi) intends his notion of "transcendental history" to be taken in a "full ontological sense," referring to the historicity of human existence, not merely human knowledge acquisition. In my view, pragmatist philosophy of the humanities can very well agree with the idea that all humanistic inquiry presupposes human existence as historical, while studying that historicity itself. This could be understood as a version of the reflexive structure Olesen refers to by claiming that "history presupposes itself," appearing "both as constituted and as constituting" (ibid., 105). Even our attempts to understand our own historicity already presuppose that historicity as something that must, and can only, be explicated and appreciated from a historicized—that is, human—standpoint.

9. One obvious specific question that would also, in a more comprehensive investigation, have to be settled is to what extent it is possible to defend realism (even pragmatic realism) about *time* and *temporality* within an overall Kantian framework, given that time is a pure form of our sensible intuition (*Anschauung*)—instead of being a property of things as they are in themselves—in Kant's own transcendental idealism. This is a key issue to be considered not here but in broader articulations of Kantian pragmatism; in outlining the present project, it is sufficient to note that the Kantian transcendental approach is manifested in the way I am asking *questions* about the necessary conditions for the possibility of humanistic inquiry into the past (or anything else, for that matter) and about the ways in which our practices of inquiry constitute the objects of inquiry (arguably not only in the humanities but in any inquiries we might engage in).

10. Throughout the discussion of pragmatic realism, we should keep in mind that Peirce, in particular, was careful to distinguish between existence and reality. This distinction will be specifically made whenever it is relevant to our discussion.

11. Yet, even natural-scientific postulations ultimately serve our future-oriented practices and their interests; see the discussion of pragmatist philosophy of science later in this chapter.

12. In Putnam's (1981, xi) memorable phrase, "the mind and the world jointly make up the mind and the world." Something similar, yet slightly more specific, is the main content of my claim about our practices of humanistic inquiry "making" their objects. Nelson Goodman's (1978) constructivist (and arguably implicitly neopragmatist) theory of "worldmaking" is obviously also relevant here, though it goes too far into the constructivist direction, giving up even moderate realism (even about the natural world).

13. I will get back to this idea in the context of White's holistic pragmatism in due course.

14. More historically speaking, it has been a major question on the agenda of pragmatists working on the problem of realism to determine how exactly pragmatism (e.g., Peirce's or James's) can avoid sliding into the radical constructivism that F. C. S. Schiller called "humanism," that is, the view that we human beings create the world and any truths there are about it (see the essays collected in Schiller 2008). A Jamesian pragmatism, for instance, does not, I believe, entail Schillerian "humanism" (despite James's numerous sympathetic pronouncements on Schiller), but this is an issue that needs to be scholarly investigated in more detail (see also Honnacker 2018). Another in my view problematically radical (nonpragmatist) form of pluralism is defended by Prickett (2002), who interestingly examines science and theology from the perspective of literary criticism but arguably exaggerates when suggesting not only that theology has become increasingly aestheticized but also, for instance, that modern science has turned essentially "ironic." "Irrealist" philosophy of history and "ironic" philosophy of science are, of course, readily comparable to the narrativist philosophy of historiography mentioned in chapter 1 (e.g., White 1973; Ankersmit 2001, 2009) that reduces historiography to literary narrative rather than construing it as epistemically constrained objective research.

15. Accordingly, I am in agreement with, for example, Kitcher's (2018, 74) account of Deweyan pragmatic naturalism as "partly realist, partly constructivist" (see also Kitcher 2012)—and this same synthesis of realism and constructivism should in my view characterize pragmatism generally. (For some comparative remarks on Kitcher's and Margolis's versions of pragmatism and realism, see Pihlström 2015b.)

16. These and many other relevant writings by the pragmatist classics are available in Peirce 1992–98; James 1975–88; and Dewey 1967–86, respectively. For a rich collection of early texts by the original Metaphysical Club members (including Peirce and James) whose work in the 1870s was instrumental for the emergence of pragmatism, see Ryan et al. 2019.

17. For Peirce, the paradigmatic practical effects to be considered here were experimental effects in a scientific laboratory, whereas for James, the range of applications of the pragmatic maxim were considerably wider, encompassing human ethical and religious experience. See, e.g., Pihlström 2013, 2015a for further discussions of this major difference between the two founders of pragmatism, often taken to be the key division within the pragmatist tradition.

18. Clearly, the objects of humanistic inquiry do *not* exist independently of human minds, precisely because they are (typically) humanly created cultural entities of some kind. Characteristically, these objects may not exist theory-independently, either, because it may be meaningful to discuss their existence and their properties only within a certain theoretical framework (though in a sense—albeit perhaps not exactly in the same sense—this can also be claimed to be the case with natural-scientific theoretical entities). However, whatever theoretical entities

are postulated in the humanities, they may still be, realistically, independent of the researchers' individual or collective opinions, beliefs, and wishes: they are not simply subject to any of our contingent, subjective ways of thinking or talking about them. Moreover, realism does not depend on any particular objects' existing; both scientific and humanistic realism are fully compatible with the progress of inquiry continuously correcting our picture of *which* theoretical entities exist.

19. Famously, Peirce, in "How to Make Our Ideas Clear" (1878, in Peirce 1992–98, vol. 1) and elsewhere, characterized truth as the "final opinion" toward which inquiry *would* converge if it were continued indefinitely long. Cf., e.g., Misak 2013. For a comprehensive interpretation of Peirce's views on history and historiography emphasizing his realism (as a key element of his pragmatism, or pragmaticism, as well as semiotics), see Viola 2020 (particularly his concluding chapter).

20. My pragmatic realism is most deeply indebted, in addition to the classical pragmatists, to Putnam's (e.g., 1990, 2016) struggles with realism over the decades. Putnam, however, never seems to have explicitly (apart from scattered remarks here and there) applied his "internal realism" (his view in the 1980s) or his later versions of pragmatic realism to the humanities.

21. See, e.g., Popper 1972 [1963], 99, 223, 382; 1994, 118, 154, 171–174. Because of his evolutionary epistemology, Popper may, however, have been unable to avoid some sort of pragmatist commitments (see Campbell 1974, especially 447ff.). Lakatos (1970, 99) was as critical as Popper: according to him, James denied "the possibility of any kind of objective knowledge," and pragmatism is, in James as well as Quine, a philosophy of mere "psychological comfort" (ibid., 185). Even in contemporary discussion, pragmatism is sometimes equated with instrumentalism and/or constructive empiricism (and thus with one or another form of empiricist antirealism): see, e.g., Leplin's (1997, 132ff.) way of contrasting the pragmatic virtues of theories with the realist's key virtue, truth. Niiniluoto (1999) is more careful, but as a proponent of scientific realism, he does count pragmatism—at least in its typical versions—as one of the positions he opposes, if not as downright instrumentalism, at least as an attempt to replace the correspondence theory of truth (which Popper also defended) by an epistemic "surrogate" (see ibid., 11–12, 101–103).

22. For a collection of essays on the complex historical relations between pragmatism and logical empiricism, see Pihlström et al. 2017. While that relationship is to a certain degree relevant to my historical story in this chapter, I won't here venture any new interpretation of how logical empiricism was indebted to pragmatism but will primarily focus on the realism issue in pragmatist conceptions of inquiry.

23. In addition to Putnam, the most important neopragmatist for the purposes of a pragmatist philosophy of the humanities is Morton White, whose holistic pragmatism develops Quinean themes further (cf. Pihlström 2021);

however, I will postpone more detailed discussions of holistic pragmatism to the next chapter.

24. Cf. Bernstein's (1995, 2010) reflections on the "argumentative telling and retelling" of the story of pragmatism.

25. Peirce figures largely in, e.g., Burks's (1977 [1963]) pragmatic theory of probability (see especially 165–178), though Burks finds Peirce's pragmatic principle of meaning "essentially the same" as the logical empiricists' operationalism and verifiability principle of meaning (ibid., 167), complaining (!) that pragmatism fails to reduce general theoretical statements to statements directly verifiable by observation (ibid., 174). Given the later developments in pragmatism, it is ironic that anything like this has ever been seen as something that pragmatism ought to achieve. Suppe (1989, 112), referring to Burks, also claims Peirce to have anticipated Bridgman. The Peircean conception of abduction is also highly central in Niiniluoto's (2018) way of developing a scientifically realistic philosophy of abduction as a method of scientific inference and explanation.

26. I am, of course, (again) referring to Peirce's famous essays, "The Fixation of Belief" (1877) and "How to Make Our Ideas Clear" (1878), available, e.g., in Peirce 1931–58, vol. 5, and Peirce 1992–98, vol. 1. On the realism versus idealism tension in Peirce, see also, e.g., Pihlström 1996, 2004a, 2008, 2009.

27. Nagel (1961, 129) cites both Peirce and Dewey as advocates of the what he calls the "instrumental view of theories." For a sympathetic discussion of Peirce's place in the history of verificationism, see Misak 1995.

28. See Niiniluoto 1999, as well as Levi 1991. Theorists of truthlikeness, such as Niiniluoto, need not share Peirce's conception of truth as the ideal limit of inquiry, or the "final opinion" of the scientific community, but the basic idea—the gradual approximation of truth through a succession of strictly speaking false theories by means of an investigation employing scientific methods—is closely similar.

29. See, for variations of this idea, several papers in Leplin 1984, as well as Leplin 1997 and (again) Niiniluoto 1999; for criticism of this "explanationist" line of defending realism, see Fine 1996 [1986] (to be revisited in chapter 4 below). De Regt (1999, 376–379) notes, however, that the concept of abduction employed in this discussion is not Peirce's, who eventually came to view abduction as "the First Stage of Inquiry" instead of an explanatory inference. De Regt (ibid.) also interestingly considers Peirce's extreme scholastic realism about "real generals" as a form of scientific realism (see also Haack 1998; Pihlström 2003a; as well as chapter 3 below) and finds Peirce's views less relevant to the contemporary challenges to realism based on the underdetermination of theory by data than has sometimes been supposed (de Regt 1999, 385–391). For earlier, still influential discussions of Peirce's relation to scientific realism, see Almeder 1980, 1983, 1989 and Skagestad 1981; for discussions of Peirce as a precursor of

Popper's scientific realism and pursuit of scientific objectivity, see Freeman and Skolimowski 1974; Niiniluoto 1984.

30. For Peircean contributions to the philosophy of historiography and attempts to clarify Peirce's complex views in this area, see, e.g., Colapietro 2016; Topa 2016; Viola 2020.

31. The purpose of this chapter is not to evaluate James's "pragmatist conception of truth" (see James 1975 [1907], Lecture VI) in any general way. For some discussion and references, see Pihlström 1996, 1998, 2008, and 2021. In the next chapter, I will have something to say about the pragmatist conception of truth in the context of a pragmatist philosophy of the humanities, though.

32. Philosophers of historiography typically reject—even when trying to defend the objectivity of historiography—the naïve idea that historians could just "copy" historical reality. See, e.g., Kuukkanen 2015 (to be revisited in chapter 3).

33. See the editors' notes to James 1975 [1907], 153–154.

34. One of the classical figures of logical empiricism, Carl Hempel, employs an example drawn from Dewey when discussing his famous model of deductive-nomological explanation (see Hempel 1965, 235ff.) but fails to consider pragmatism. See, however, Hempel 1992 for a brief account of a view on scientific progress that does not invoke the concept of truth: Hempel argues that the idea of science as a quest for truth is fundamentally mistaken and that a "strictly pragmatist and non-realistic" conception of scientific inquiry replaces the mistaken goal of truth by that of "epistemically optimal worldviews" (ibid., 48–51).

35. According to Peirce's "extreme scholastic realism," generals do not *exist* but are *real*. According to Dewey (1936, 532), such Peircean generals perform a vital function as "formulae of operations," guiding us in our inferences; thus, their status is logical, not metaphysical (in Dewey's broad sense of "logical," as related to his "theory of inquiry": cf. Dewey 1938). For some remarks on Peirce's and Dewey's differing views on these matters, see Pihlström 2004a, 42–44. In chapter 3 below, I will argue that Peircean generals play an important role in the conceptualization of the ontology of the humanities.

36. Dewey here seems to allow for probabilistic laws merely.

37. For Dewey's instrumentalism about laws, see also, e.g., Dewey 1989 [1929], 121–123. Shook (2003b, 328) connects the Deweyan view of laws as revisable "working hypotheses" with the more recent position among philosophers of science, such as Ronald Giere and Nancy Cartwright, that scientific realism need not be committed to the truth of exact laws of nature.

38. The entire chapter 4, "Nature, Means and Knowledge," of *Experience and Nature* (Dewey 1986 [1929]) is essential to Dewey's views on the status of scientific objects.

39. Thus, in a sense, there seems to be hardly any significant problem of reality (or of realism) in Dewey. Reality is simply what is given—or, better,

"taken"—in experience. Here Dewey disagreed with the "new realists" of his time (cf. his exchanges with his critics available in Morgenbesser 1977). Compare also the following: "The world as we experience it is a real world. But it is not in its primary phases a world that is known, a world that is understood, and is intellectually coherent and secure. Knowing consists of operations that give experienced objects a form in which the relations, upon which the onward course of events depends, are securely experienced. It marks a transitional redirection and rearrangement of the real. It is intermediate and instrumental" (Dewey 1960 [1929], 295). On the importance of distinguishing between knowledge and experience in Dewey's naturalism, see, e.g., Hildebrand 2003 (a study that is also one of the best accounts I know of Dewey's relation to the realism issue).

40. See Dewey 1916, 331, for his characterization of instrumentalism as a "logical version of pragmatism," according to which "knowing is literally something which we do." On this intimate relation between knowledge and action, see especially Dewey 1960 [1929], passim. Given Dewey's lifelong effort to avoid unpragmatic dichotomies between these two, it is odd indeed to note that a relatively early French critic and further developer of pragmatism, Gaston Bachelard, has been interpreted as criticizing James's and Dewey's pragmatism for a model of instrumental or practical rationality in which reasoning (intellectual work) is separated from practical work (Tiles 2005, 172). Bachelard's antireductionist emphasis on the richness and diversity of reality, to be encountered in a variety of historically developing ways, is obviously close to pragmatism, but his view that pragmatism failed to seek a "detailed understanding of particular conditions" and discuss the use of technology in experiments (ibid., 160) is narrow, if not downright false. Dewey, in particular, devoted a life's work to such issues. Perhaps Bachelard's major novelty in relation to pragmatism was his insistence on the processual dynamics of science, coming close to views later known as Kuhnian (see below).

41. Talking about "antirealism" here is prima facie highly misleading, because idealism as such certainly entails no antirealism. For example, Peirce can clearly be interpreted as an idealist, especially in his cosmic metaphysics, but it would be entirely inaccurate to call him an "antirealist."

42. See Kivistö and Pihlström 2017 for a discussion of both pragmatist and nonpragmatist metaphors of knowledge, among which the conception of knowledge as "spectation" of course belongs to the latter camp.

43. French's response to these scientific antirealisms draws from Peirce rather than Dewey, but I believe that an essentially similar response can be made on the basis of Dewey's naturalism, which is as antiskeptical as Peirce's pragmatism.

44. See, however, Shook's (2003b) version of pragmatically realist philosophy of science, which rejects an "extreme" realism about entirely unobservable entities. I will briefly return to Shook's views below.

45. For such a strong conception of scientific realism, see Sellars 1963 and Tuomela 1985; for some criticism, see Pihlström 1996. According to Rorty (1997, 92–93), scientific realism and religious fundamentalism are "products of the same urge," the pursuit of an absolute conception of reality. It is this pursuit that the pragmatist who follows James's and Dewey's pluralist insights should abandon; and one certainly need not be a Rortyan in order to be able to appreciate these insights. On James's defense of pluralism against monism, see James 1975 [1907], Lecture IV; cf. also Putnam's (1981, 1983, 1990, 1994, 1995, 2012, 2016) analogous rejections of absoluteness and the "God's-eye view."

46. I am grateful to one of the anonymous reviewers of my book manuscript for the emphasis on the importance of Mead. One reason for the neglect of Mead among pragmatist philosophers (including, I admit, the present author) may be the widespread tendency to view him as primarily a social theorist instead of a philosopher. However, as Erkki Kilpinen, among others, convincingly reminds us, this is a mischaracterization of Mead's essentially philosophical project. Mead, probably most famous for his distinction between *I* and *me*, can be said to have developed a general philosophical theory of intersubjectivity as something that makes human sociality and communication possible. See, e.g., Kilpinen 2002. On Mead's and Dewey's interaction within the school known as "Chicago pragmatism," see, e.g., Feffer 1993.

47. See, e.g., "Empirical Realism," "Scientific Objects and Experience," and "The Objective Reality of Perspectives," available as "supplementary essays" in Mead 2002 [1932].

48. This section is partly based on (my part of) Koskinen and Pihlström 2006 (a paper offering a more detailed examination of Quine's place in the pragmatist tradition).

49. In comparison to Quinean naturalism, Faye's (2012) "naturalistic reconstruction" of the humanities (already briefly commented on in chapter 1) is considerably modest, as it basically amounts to the view that human meanings, values, and normativity have their grounding in natural evolution and the thereby evolved human mind and cognition. No pragmatist needs to reject that even when criticizing stronger forms of naturalism that fail to acknowledge the irreducibility of normativity (cf. chapter 4). On the relevance of Quinean naturalism (or pragmatism) in the philosophy of historiography, see, however, Gorman 2016.

50. See Creath 1990 for rich historical materials concerning the relation between Carnap and Quine. Cf. also, e.g., Holton 1993 and Sandbothe 2004.

51. Carnap's (1950) distinction between internal and external questions of existence was an important milestone in pragmatism (or the synthesis of pragmatism and logical empiricism), as he held that the latter kind of questions are only pragmatically decidable, concerning the utility of choosing a particular linguistic framework, such as the "world of things" or the system of natural

numbers. Carnap, clearly, was more a positivist than a pragmatist, although his famous distinction did influence, among others, Putnam's neopragmatist "internal realism" (cf. Putnam 1981, 1983, 1990). It is a noteworthy historical fact that Carnap engaged in a dialogue with Dewey on meaning and the nature of philosophical problems in the first volume of *Philosophy of Science* in 1934 (see Shook 1998, 462). C. I. Lewis, whose views in many ways resembled Carnap's, endorsed roughly at the same time a pragmatist conception of meaning and experience in contrast to a strictly positivist one (Lewis 1934). Recent historical scholarship duly recognizes the connections Carnap and the other major logical empiricists had with the pragmatist tradition (see also the next note).

52. In addition to Carnap's and Lewis's contributions, Charles Morris was instrumental in the 1930s in emphasizing the complementarity and even the possibility of "convergence" of pragmatism and logical empiricism (see Morris 1937, 1938, 1979 [1937]; cf. Stadler 1997, 401, 869ff.). Later Morris (1963) returned to the topic in his contribution to Carnap's *Library of Living Philosophers* volume. According to Morris, one may hold on to the requirement of excluding meaningless expressions—both in the logical and the "biological-empirical" senses—even if one broadens the logical empiricists' original strongly individualist verifiability principle by reinterpreting it pragmatically, in order to make sense of social cooperation in scientific experience. In his response to Morris, Carnap (1963, 860) emphasized Morris's and Ernest Nagel's role in the exchange between pragmatism and logical empiricism. Like Morris, Nagel (1940) highlighted Peirce's role as a precursor of "modern empiricism" already soon after the collapse of the Vienna Circle. A paper on "Charles S. Peirce, Pioneer of Modern Empiricism" was presented by Nagel at the Fifth International Congress for the Unity of Science at Harvard in September, 1939 (Stadler 1997, 430). Another major bridge builder who might have been more influential, had he lived longer, was of course Frank Ramsey, whose 1927 article, "Facts and Propositions," bears important resemblances to Peirce's and James's views: Ramsey held that the meaning of a proposition lies in the activity the stating of the proposition would lead to. Ramsey's role in the pragmatist tradition has been emphasized by Misak (e.g., 2013), in particular. An even earlier connection between the traditions of pragmatism and logical empiricism can be found in Otto Neurath, who reviewed the German translation of James's *Pragmatism* (by Wilhelm Jerusalem, 1908) in *Der Kunstwart* 23 (1909) (Shook 1998, 116) and whose collected papers (Neurath 1983) include various references to Peirce, James, and Dewey, though no systematic discussion of pragmatism. Neurath's importance as an early naturalist and pragmatist in the philosophy of science—as a precursor of a number of ideas later associated with Quine, Kuhn, and others—has been emphasized by Uebel (1991, 1992, 1996); cf. also Stadler 1997, 434. In his authoritative, highly detailed historical documentation of the origins, development, and influence of logical empiricism, Friedrich Stadler notes the classical pragmatists as one important source of ideas

(ibid., 97). For more recent work on the relations between logical empiricism and pragmatism, see Pihlström et al. 2017 (a volume emerging from the activities of the Vienna Circle Institute, led by Professor Stadler for decades).

53. It is an open question whether Quine's "scientism" (a word the use of which he endorsed himself, when I had the opportunity to interview him for a Finnish philosophy quarterly at Harvard in 1995) ought to be classified as "reductive" or, perhaps better, "eliminative." Quine does, after all, eliminate from his scientific ontology many kinds of entities that others, including most pragmatists, would accept, e.g., mental, intensional, and normative ones. Such an elimination may be seen as one of his major projects, especially in *Word and Object* (Quine 1960) and subsequent writings.

54. See Rorty 1979, 1991, and 1998. Rorty himself prefers to talk about "ethnocentrism" and "antirepresentationalism," refusing to be a "relativist." Rortyan views do, however, represent relativism in, e.g., Laudan 1990, and elsewhere. As the issue is about the very possibility of transhistorical and transcultural normativity, relatively little hangs on terminology here. In any case, as important as he is for the philosophy of the humanities, we can safely ignore Rorty's neopragmatism for the purposes of this chapter, because his contributions to pragmatist philosophy of science and theory of inquiry have been scarce—unless one wants to emphasize his claim that science is in no closer contact with "reality as it is in itself" than, say, poetry. For a pragmatist critique of representationalism that differs significantly from Rorty's in maintaining both realism and the possibility of normative inquiry, see Rydenfelt 2019.

55. For several contributions examining the prospects of pragmatic realism in relation to (primarily Deweyan rather than Quinean) pragmatic naturalism, see Shook 2003a. It must be noted that there are also those who deny that the reception of logical empiricism in the United States—a process led by Quine and others—was a turning away from Deweyan pragmatism, as it has often been described: see Richardson 2002. For references to Dewey as a precursor of Quine, see also Sleeper 1986.

56. Some of the relevant literature is cited in Koskinen and Pihlström 2006.

57. For other pragmatist criticisms of Quine, see Nevo's (1992) defense of the holistic pragmatism of James against both Quinean and Rortyan misconceptions, Capps's (1996) Deweyan rather than Quinean version of "naturalized epistemology," and White's (1986, 2002) "holistic pragmatism," in which Quinean holism about empirical testing is extended to the normative—a version of which was already proposed in White 1956. For Quine's stubborn response to White's suggestions, see his 1986; cf. Quine 1992 [1990], 1995. For pragmatist philosophy of the humanities, it is essential to adopt White's more inclusive, less reductive version of pragmatic holism than Quine's, though it must be recognized that the holism Quine defended in early works, especially "Two Dogmas," had a crucial influence on the development of White's holistic pragmatism. (We will return to

White's holism in the context of pragmatist philosophy of historiography in the next chapter. For my appropriation of White's ideas, see also Pihlström 2021.)

58. I have examined the development from classical pragmatism via logical empiricism to neopragmatism in considerable more detail in Pihlström 2017b and 2018. As logical empiricism generally was not very significant in the historical development of the humanities, the brief account of Quine in this section suffices in this context.

59. It is often difficult for philosophers of science to appreciate the unique position pragmatism enjoys as a middle path between scientific realism and empiricist instrumentalism. Compare Tiles's (1988, 7) words: "When pragmatists suggest that correspondence is a misleading notion to use when trying to give an account of what makes a good scientific theory, they sound to realists like confused positivists, for they insist that the role of theory is as an instrument to guide experimental and observational practice. But as they deny that we can make a sharp separation between our theoretical and observational claims they sound to positivists like muddled realists."

60. Appeals to scientific practice have become more and more usual among thinkers not directly associated with pragmatism (see, e.g., Rouse 1996, 2002; cf. also the reflections on Rouse's 1996 book in Pihlström 1998, chapter 9)—not only among relativist sociologists of science and researchers within science and technology studies, but even among scientific realists (cf. Kukla 1994). Some of the pragmatism-inspired work by historian of science Hasok Chang is also highly relevant in this regard (see, e.g., Chang 2011).

61. Thus, there may be pragmatically significant doubts about, say, the reality of certain textual or literary meanings or historical causal claims *within* the relevant humanistic practices of inquiry.

62. Despite my frequent appeals to the concept of normativity, this book makes no effort to theorize this concept as such in any comprehensive manner. For a recent collection of essays on the various aspects of normativity, see Niiniluoto and Pihlström 2020; for my own reflections on how a pragmatist understanding of truth and truth-seeking should incorporate the concept of normativity as fundamental, see Pihlström 2021, chapter 5.

63. The next few paragraphs touch upon themes more fully discussed in Pihlström and Siitonen 2005.

64. See, e.g., Niiniluoto 1999 and Norris 2000; cf. also the well-known attack on conceptual relativism, as represented by Kuhn, Quine, and others, in Davidson 1984. On the historicity of reference itself, see Margolis 1993, chapter 5.

65. Despite his frequent discussions of Putnam, especially in the essays collected in Kuhn 2000, Kuhn hardly ever refers to the earlier pragmatists. See, however, Reisch 2019 for a highly relevant examination of the intellectual and political contexts of Kuhn's philosophical development—including Kuhn's early readings of James.

66. For a brief account of Kuhn's and Putnam's controversy over realism and the reference of scientific terms, see Andersen 2001, 56–60; see also Gupta 2002, chapter 6, for the suggestion that Putnam's internal realism is a synthesis of Popper's scientific realism and Kuhn's "relativism"; and Niiniluoto 1999, chapter 7, for a critical comparison between internal realism and Kuhn's post-*Structure* views. Putnam's accusations that Kuhn is a relativist are, of course, relatively standard; this has been the usual charge among Kuhn's critics from early on (see, e.g., Scheffler 1982 [1967]; for a more recent version of the same line of argument, with a link to today's "science wars," see Sokal and Bricmont 2003, 67–73). Cf. also Livingston 1988.

67. Such an impression of Kuhn as a relativist "conversationalist" may have been strengthened by Rorty's (1991, 1998) frequent rhetoric addressed to "us Kuhnians," coupled with his insistence on there being only conversational constraints for inquiry, as distinguished from objective ones.

68. My discussion of Putnam and Kuhn here focuses on the issues of realism versus idealism and realism versus relativism, not on the issue of realism versus instrumentalism. I take it as obvious that Putnam never denied, any more than Kuhn, the existence of unobservable theoretical entities postulated in scientific theories, although both may have denied the independent, unconstructed, "absolute" existence of *any* entities (scientific, humanistic, and commonsensical alike). Thus, Putnam writes: "Electrons exist in every sense in which chairs (or sensations) exist; electron talk is no more derived talk *about* sensations or 'observable things' than talk about sensations or chairs is derived talk about electrons. Here I *am* a 'scientific realist'" (Putnam 1994, 495).

69. This can be regarded as a successor notion to Kuhn's (1970 [1962]) famous (or notorious) concept of a paradigm. I will, however, freely speak about both paradigms and lexicons, without attempting any careful definition of these notions. Both could be translated into a more pragmatist jargon by speaking (as I did earlier) about "scientific practices."

70. See several essays addressing this theme in Horwich 1993, and see especially Sharrock's and Read's (2002, 50–58) illuminating discussion. Sharrock and Read set out to show that Kuhn is, in using phrases like *world changes*, much less radical than both his friends and foes have thought he is.

71. However, in a sense Kuhn comes close to even agreeing with an "Orwellian" view on the paradigm-relativity of history. (In this sense, the ways in which Rorty—in many of his works—cites Kuhn approvingly and even speaks about "us Kuhnians" are also significant for our appropriation of the Kuhnian legacy, which should definitely not be embraced uncritically.) The tension between a Jamesian and an Orwellian understanding of pluralism and the paradigm-dependence of historical (and other) facts may be seen as a key issue for our hopes to articulate pragmatist philosophy of science and the humanities by means of Kuhnian ideas. On Kuhn's debt to Orwell's *Nineteen Eighty-Four*,

particularly the idea that (scientific) revolutions are made "invisible" from the winners' perspective, to the extent that scientists are typically "misled" by a false history of their own tradition, cf. Reisch 2019, xxxi, xxxix, 129–130, 167, 212–213, 225. See also Pihlström 2021, chapter 1, on the potentially threatening slippery slope from a Jamesian pragmatist conception of truth all the way to Orwellian fragmentation of truth. Where Reisch exaggerates, in my view, is in associating James's and Dewey's pragmatisms with "anti-'truth'" thinking—though again it is extremely important to note that Kuhn's reservations regarding the concept of truth may have a pragmatist background (see again Reisch 2019, 211). Moreover, while it is a fundamental Kuhnian point that the dogmatism of "normal science" itself results in "revolutionary advances," as the paradigm is pushed to its "epistemological limits," yielding anomalies and eventually a crisis (ibid.), it should be kept in mind that in a truly Orwellian world (whether scientific or political) there is really no place for revolution, no pushing of anything to its epistemological limits—but only limitless power and suffering. In the humanities, the logic of "crisis" must, I suppose, be somewhat different from the Kuhnian model, especially due to the diversity of individual voices that can (and should) never be fully accommodated within a dominant paradigm. I would not ban the word *paradigm* from the humanities, but I would urge extreme caution in employing it beyond Kuhn's own original territory.

72. Conversely, it could very well be argued that the plausibility of Kantian transcendental philosophy today depends on *its* being reinterpretable within a naturalized and historically relativized framework such as pragmatism.

73. Nickles (2003, 5), in his introduction to a volume of essays on Kuhn, also describes Kuhn's view as a "'historical Kantian' relativism," claiming that, for Kuhn, (shifting) scientific traditions "constitute the basis for intelligibility" (ibid., 7). Hacking (2002, 5) similarly acknowledges the link between Kuhn's paradigms and the "historical a priori" we associate with Foucault and others. While Reisch does not explicitly deal with Kuhn's Kantianism (despite his admirable reading of Kuhn's pragmatist sources), some of his characterizations do invoke, implicitly, the idea that paradigms come to replace the transcendental self: for example, nature itself, according to Kuhn, is made to conform to our preexisting scientific beliefs (Reisch 2019, 264). For Kuhn's role in accounting for the historicity of science and inquiry in a manner comparable to Foucault (indeed, the concept of a paradigm can be regarded as analogous to the concept of an *episteme*), that is, as dealing with the *possibility* of truths and objects of inquiry, see Leezenberg and de Vries 2019, 115, 121–125, 133–139.

74. It must be kept in mind, however, that Peirce's idealist, speculative metaphysics, as articulated in his cosmological theory of a spontaneously evolving, indeterminist universe (see several writings in Peirce 1931–58, vol. 6, and 1992–98, vol. 1), is an "objective" form of idealism and thus broadly Hegelian in contrast to Kantian idealism. Hegel, of course, also greatly influenced Dewey (see, e.g.,

Shook 2000); accordingly, my Kantian reconstrual of pragmatism, both classical and modern, is inevitably one-sided. It is not my purpose to downplay Hegel's influence but to offer an (in my opinion) pragmatically useful reconceptualization of pragmatism applicable to the main task of this book.

75. "Peircean realism" is one of the positions Hoyningen-Huene (1993, 56ff.) contrasts with Kuhn's views.

76. For both, the issues of realism and truth, theory and observation, and so on, were in any case *profound* and significant, genuine ones: "It's always been clear to me [. . .] that the two people I was sure were taking the problems I was looking at seriously were me and Hilary" (Kuhn 2000, 312; interview in 1995).

77. For Margolis's own complicated pragmatist, relativist, and historicist elaborations, see, e.g., his 1993, 1995, 2002, 2003, 2012, and 2019; cf. also chapter 3 below.

78. This broader issue must obviously be set aside here, as I am not engaging in Kant scholarship in this book. For an attempt to develop a pragmatic interpretation of the *Ding an sich*, see Pihlström 1996, chapter 4.

79. The influence of Wittgenstein's (1953, 1969) later philosophy on both neopragmatism and the developments in the philosophy of science in and after the 1960s would obviously require another study. On Wittgenstein and pragmatism, see, e.g., Pihlström 2012a.

80. Other related notions include, at least, Jardine's (2000 [1991]) "scenes of inquiry" and Hacking's (2002, chapters 11–12) "styles of scientific reasoning."

81. The pragmatist aspects of Reichenbach's *Experience and Prediction* (1938) have sometimes been emphasized—already by Ernest Nagel in his review of the book upon its appearance (see Shook 1998, 503; cf. Siitonen 1997). Reichenbach (1939) also contributed to the exchange between pragmatism and logical empiricism by criticizing Dewey's reasons for denying the reality of scientific objects.

82. A related issue is Peirce's debate with the other classical pragmatists, especially Dewey, on the normative status of logic (cf. Pihlström 2004a). Dewey obviously rejected traditional (especially Kantian) views of the a priori, but as he may be claimed to have adopted something like a revision of apriority in terms of "cultural entrenchment" (with notable similarities to the kind of position Nelson Goodman defended in mid-1900s), he might be seen as having sympathized with a pragmatically relativized conception of the a priori.

83. The idea of science as a "cultural practice" is indeed central in any pragmatist conception of science (cf. Višňovský 2020b). However, the obvious pragmatic turn in Kuhn's account of science does not prevent a highly influential contemporary pragmatism scholar, Murray G. Murphey (2003, 294), from describing his view as "one of the most bizarre theories of science ever propounded." He says that Kuhn leaves unexplained why scientists after the revolution come to believe in one new theory (or paradigm) instead of a chaotic proliferation of alternatives (ibid.). This may be a problem in Kuhn, but for our purposes of placing

Kuhn's work in the pragmatist tradition, Murphey's criticism is not an obstacle. Certainly the pragmatist interpretation is not, as such, *sufficient* for rendering Kuhn's ideas fully acceptable or unproblematic. (Murphey, by the way, is one of those pragmatists or pragmatism scholars who have written comprehensively on the philosophy of historiography: see Murphey 1994.)

84. See again Peirce's "The Fixation of Belief" (1877), cited earlier, available in, e.g., Peirce 1992–98, vol. 1.

85. A more radical formulation would maintain that it is *only* within a transcendental pragmatism that *any* scientific realism is possible at all. While Margolis (as noted above) prefers not to formulate his pragmatism and historicism in transcendental terms (see, e.g., Margolis 1993, 204), he in my view perceptively suggests that while "*the reality as well as the realist structure of the cultural world presupposes the reality of the physical world,*" as embodied in it, conversely (and asymmetrically) "*it is the realism rather than the reality of the physical world that presupposes the human*" (ibid., 180; original italics). I would find an explicitly transcendental formulation more natural: the cultural is, admittedly, naturalistically speaking embodied in the physical (the nonhuman), but this embodied and physically realized (and arguably emergent) character of the human cultural world, and even the ontologically independent nature of its physical emergence base, can be made sense only from within the interpretive practices of the latter.

86. Moreover, as observed above, in this sense a pragmatic (or "internal") realist like Putnam can also be regarded as a scientific realist.

87. It is worth noting that Hacking was one of those who relatively early recognized Putnam's (1981) connections with pragmatism (see Hacking 1983, chapter 7); it was only later that Putnam himself (1990, 1994, 1995, 2002) started to elaborate on these connections.

88. Hesse's (1980, xviii–xix, 190–201) "pragmatic criterion" for empirical science is the requirement to exhibit "increasingly successful prediction" and thus the possession of "instrumental control" of external reality. This is clearly not unique to pragmatism. But as Hesse admits that the pragmatic criterion allows for a "permanent plurality of conceptual frameworks" (ibid., xxiv), she comes close to Jamesian pluralist pragmatism, though not going as far as Feyerabend.

89. Already Laudan's earlier work (1984) contains references to Peirce and Dewey, but in his 1990 book, *Science and Relativism*, he more explicitly affirms his pragmatism. For criticisms of Laudan's attempt to avoid the concept of truth in his theory of scientific change and progress, see Niiniluoto 1999. For more recent reflections on how exactly to view the relation between realism and pragmatism in the philosophy of science, see the essays collected in Westphal 2014. In my own contribution to that volume (Pihlström 2014), I also critically engage with Rein Vihalemm's (e.g., 2012) "practical realism" in relation to pragmatism.

90. In terms familiar from Quinean naturalism, we may also speak of the "reciprocal containment" of not just ontology and epistemology (as in Quine) but

of theory and methodology: not only in the sciences but in the humanities as well, methodology is deeply theory-laden. This kind of holism entails that there are no Popperian "crucial experiments" that would determine the fate of a theory that could be falsified once and for all, as methods of experimentation—or, more generally, in the humanities the methods of testing an interpretive hypothesis on the basis of, say, textual evidence—are relative to theoretical contexts and/or traditions. Here the ongoing critical conversation of the interpretive community of scholars in the field would play the role of "experiment." What is essential here is that the basically same holistic ideas can be understood in Quinean-Whitean terms but also in Laudan's terms (which might also be regarded as vulnerable to the charge of relativism; cf. again Laudan 1990).

91. For the development of Dewey's "idealist" view of the objects of knowledge as dependent on inquiry, see Shook 2000. See also the discussion above.

92. Coming close to the conclusion of my historical survey in this chapter, I must acknowledge the obvious similarities between Rouse's views and the ones I am sketching here, without being able to do justice to Rouse's extremely rich presentation, and understanding that Rouse may have his own reasons for *not* wanting to label his position "pragmatist." For a position in some ways close to Rouse's antireductionist naturalism, see Westphal 2006. Westphal also defends, though with a Hegelian twist, a form of pragmatic realism, attacking, e.g., such empiricists as Quine and van Fraassen (see also his contributions to Westphal 1998; cf. Westphal 2014). Other—to some extent pragmatist—variations of the view that scientific practices themselves, in all their multifariousness, should be taken "at face value" and that metalevel philosophical problematizations and interpretations of them should be avoided, include, e.g., Feyerabend 1993 [1975] and Fine 1996 [1986], 2004. It is hardly surprising that Fine, who hardly ever refers to pragmatism but does subscribe to both a Deweyan "experimental point of view" (Fine 2004, 121) and a Feyerabendian "openness to many methods" (ibid., 118), is Rorty's (2004, 132ff.) favorite philosopher of science. Just as Rorty (1991, 1998) opts for solidarity instead of truth, and for democracy instead of philosophy, Fine (2004, 127) redefines objectivity as "that which in the process of inquiry makes for trust in the outcome of inquiry," characterizing objectivity as "trust-making" rather than "real-making." Both Fine and Rorty clearly attempt to transcend the philosophical controversy of realism versus antirealism altogether, arguing that it is a remnant of old-fashioned representationalism, which has not learned its Deweyan, Wittgensteinian, and Davidsonian lessons. Rorty (2004, 136–139) deplores the fact that Fine still speaks about ontological commitment (when saying that, according to his "natural ontological attitude," or NOA, we should take the ontological commitments of science at face value), and suggests that he should endorse his critics' claim that NOA amounts to a "preemption" of philosophy. See, however, Kukla 1994; Leplin 1997; Niiniluoto 1999, 18–20; and Pihlström 1998, chapter 3, for some critical reflections on

Fine. On one interpretation, Fine is just a realist in a relatively ordinary sense of the term—after all, his NOA urges us to *accept* the theoretical postulations of science at face value, without problematizing them philosophically. On Fine and NOA in the context of the naturalization of philosophy and normativity, see further chapter 4 below.

93. This terminology might be taken to be slightly misleading, because what *transcendent realism* here means is not that different from what Kant meant by *transcendental realism*—that is, approximately what people usually mean by *metaphysical realism* today—and as anyone familiar with the Kantian tradition knows, the concepts of the transcendental and the transcendent must be kept clearly distinct. On the other hand, the reference to the transcendent *is* accurate in the sense that the very idea of such realism, which Kant rejected as incompatible with transcendental idealism, is that our cognitions and theories can reach a transcendent world as it is in itself.

94. See Shook's (2003b, 341) specific comments on Leplin, denying the need to interpret theories as aiming at an accurate representation of unobservables.

95. The Deweyan pragmatist sense of "technology" *is* broad, though: according to Hickman (1990), virtually any intelligent purposive problem-solving is technological.

96. A Deweyan pragmatic realist and naturalist need not entirely abandon transcendental conditions in the sense of the historicized and relativized "pragmatic a priori" (see the brief remarks on this above). What might also be problematized in Shook's "productionism" is the tendency to view the emergence of scientific objects in terms of (intellectual and technological) production—hence as a causal and factual process rather than as a transcendental-level normative process of constitution in the sense of constituting contexts enabling the objects of inquiry to become possible for us. (See also chapters 3 and 4.) For a more strongly naturalist version of "pragmatic naturalism" about the humanities, see Faye 2012. While Faye, as we have seen, refers to pragmatism in his naturalizing program, and by emphasizing the normativity of the humanities in contrast to mere causal explanation, for instance, he avoids any overly reductive naturalisms, his version of pragmatism is very different from my Kantian one. He also fails to link his "pragmatism" with the historical classics of the tradition.

97. This makes Rouse's (2003) take on Kuhn somewhat unpragmatist (as we saw), which is unfortunate, given his otherwise strong entitlement to the label of pragmatism, indeed his strong potential for continuing the pragmatist tradition in contemporary philosophy of science. As noted, Reisch's (2019) study on Kuhn's development rightly and interestingly emphasizes his early pragmatist—Jamesian—influences.

98. See again Reisch 2019 for a detailed study on the Cold War context of the development of Kuhn's thought.

99. Let me also note that I have deliberately focused only on some truly major figures of the tradition (e.g., Peirce, James, Dewey, Quine, Putnam, Kuhn) here, as well as, specifically commented on some philosophers of science in a pragmatist framework (e.g., Laudan, Rouse, Shook). See some of my recent work on pragmatic realism (e.g., Pihlström 2012b, 2014, 2015b, 2017b, 2017c, 2018) for discussions of pragmatist thinkers (or close-to-pragmatist thinkers) such as Margolis, Rescher, Westphal, White, and Vihalemm, whose views on realism and pragmatism would also be highly relevant to a historical and systematic assessment of pragmatist philosophy of science and theory of inquiry. The only historically significant pragmatist largely neglected in this chapter but to be returned to in the next chapter is White, whose holistic pragmatism deserves a separate discussion in the context of pragmatist philosophy of historiography, in particular.

100. My historical account of pragmatist philosophy of science in this chapter should also be critically compared to other accounts of pragmatist epistemology and philosophy of science; I have merely tried to tell *one* possible story of the development of pragmatist ways of thinking about scientific inquiry here. For relevant overall discussions of these fields with emphases somewhat different from mine, see, e.g., Capps's (2015) and Hickman's (2015) contributions to Pihlström 2015a.

Chapter 3

1. To that extent, my transcendental pragmatist philosophy of the humanities is also "naturalized" (cf. Faye 2012); to be a transcendental pragmatist is *not* to be a nonnaturalist. What I find lacking in Faye's naturalism and pragmatism is, precisely, the transcendental dimension, particularly regarding the realism issue.

2. In a recent book (Pihlström 2021), I examine the pragmatist commitment to the pursuit of truth across a range of human practices (including existential or *weltanschaulichen* practices like religion), starting from Jamesian pragmatism but steering clear from excessively radical neopragmatism and the threatening "post-truth" developments we are familiar with in our political environments. While neither that book nor the present one is an investigation of the complex phenomenon known as postmodernism, it is characteristic of thinkers described as "postmodernists" that they tend to view even science and rational inquiry generally as just language-games among others, in no sense privileged in relation to other language-games. Even though I am throughout this book emphasizing a pragmatically pluralistic understanding of inquiry, it should be clear that pragmatism and pluralism must be carefully distinguished from radical relativism. Certainly my pragmatist philosophy of the humanities lends no support to forms of postmodern relativism claiming that humanistic inquiries (e.g., the

writing of history) are just, say, stories no more rational or representational than fictional novels. However, I am unable to engage in any detailed discussion of, say, social-scientific methodologies that (controversially) dispense with the ideas of shared objectivity and rationality, such as ethnomethodology examining social phenomena as they seem to the "insiders" of a social practice, which could be regarded as a methodological version of relativism. I do think that sound forms of pragmatism should keep a critical distance to such methodologies despite their practice-oriented character.

3. The pragmatist conception of truth is of course intended to be applied across the board, not merely to humanistic discourse. It is, however, particularly important to embrace this conception when we wish to make sense of our truth-pursuits in the humanities that themselves deal with valuational matters.

4. A historical novel typically sets fictional characters and events in "real" (or "truthlike") historical circumstances. However, in a somewhat more complex case, fictional characters can be set in a counterfactual historical situation that retains some elements (e.g., people) from "real" history, as in Philip Roth's *The Plot Against America* (which adds the further complication of integrating fictional events with a semiautobiographical background).

5. Realism about the past is a large issue not restricted to the human historical past but also relevant to the much more distant past investigated by, say, paleontology and cosmology. For an application of scientific realism to the study of history by means of an application of the "inference to the best explanation" strategy for the postulation of the mind-independent existence of the past, see Murphey 1994; for a classical pragmatist account of the availability of the past only in relation to the (or a) present, see Mead 2012 [1932].

6. For a lucid discussion of the reasons to postulate theoretical entities, see again Niiniluoto's (1999) defense of scientific realism. Cf. also, e.g., Psillos 1999. For my own early pragmatic realist attempt to argue for an analogy between the postulations of theoretical entities in the sciences and the humanities, see Pihlström 1996.

7. This question of cultural relativism obviously not only concerns the criteria of rationality but also other normative criteria, including ethical ones. Therefore, relativism must be seriously engaged with in any attempt to understand human nature and normative human practices. See, e.g., Pihlström 2003b; Niiniluoto and Pihlström 2020.

8. This is a major issue in the historicist philosophy of science largely inaugurated by Kuhn's (1970 [1962]) well-known views discussed in chapter 2. On rationality and relativism, see also, e.g., Hollis and Lukes 1982; Koskinen 2019.

9. Instead of simply referring to the historical *Erklären* versus *Verstehen* controversy, this topic of inquiry could be interpreted as a metonymy covering various specific methodological controversies in the humanistic disciplines. Typically such controversies concern the extent to which humanistic methodologies can be

reduced to, or even informed by, methodologies familiar from the natural sciences (e.g., causal explanation). For a solid defense of methodological pluralism in the social sciences and for powerful arguments against methodological exclusivism, see, e.g., Roth 1987. See further chapter 4 below.

10. This "naturalized" methodological paradigm will be discussed as an exemplary case inviting transcendental critique in chapter 4 below. The proposal to apply methods of cognitive science to humanistic inquiry is not unique to the study of religions but has also been made by scholars of literature and history: see, e.g., Bruhn and Wehrs 2014.

11. Or, perhaps, Wittgenstein-inspired philosophers of religion and philosophers of science; see, e.g., Winch 1958, 1964.

12. Here I am assuming a more colloquial sense of "instrumentalism" referring to the *instrumental value* of research instead of the technical discussion of instrumentalism as a rival to scientific realism (as in chapter 2).

13. See also chapter 5. My pragmatist attempt to articulate the value of the humanities focuses on the value of humanistic scholarship but is of course fully compatible with emphasizing the special social and cultural value created by liberal arts education focusing on the humanities; cf. Nussbaum's (2010) important defense of the value of such education. Nussbaum's argument for the necessity of the humanities for democracy may also be backed up by specifically pragmatist (e.g., Deweyan) considerations of the nature of democracy (cf. Pihlström 2011b). See also Hall 2012; Goldman 2019.

14. When referring to features of humanistic ontologies and ontologizing, such as their value-ladenness, that characterize the nature of ontological postulations in the humanities, we are dealing with metaontological rather than "first-order" ontological issues. On the value-ladenness of pragmatist ontology generally, see Pihlström 2009.

15. Even the carpe-diem philosophy of "living in the present" is for us historicized beings irreducibly temporal, referring to the historical past as well as to the future, including death.

16. Peirce compared the enterprise of scientific inquiry to a cable consisting of threads none of which is very strong by itself—and all of which may in fact be relatively slender—but which together form a strongly interwoven system. Another Peircean simile is the picture of inquiry as walking on a bog: one can never have more than partial confirmations of hypotheses; there is no recourse to an absolutely solid "bedrock of fact," and therefore we can never stand firm but must, in order to avoid sinking into the bog, constantly move on, taking new steps forward. (See Peirce's "Some Consequences of Four Incapacities" [1868], in Peirce 1992–98, vol. 1, 29, and "The First Rule of Logic" [1898], in ibid., vol. 2, 55. The latter essay is the one in which Peirce famously suggested that the words, "Do not block the way of inquiry," should be inscribed on every wall in the "city of philosophy"; see ibid., vol. 2, 48.) Other versions of comparable

antifoundationalist metaphors include Otto Neurath's famous ship or boat—scientists are like sailors afloat on the sea, having to constantly reconstruct their vessel during the voyage itself, with no option of docking in any safe harbor—and Quine's "web of belief," according to which our system of scientific beliefs or theories is like a web anchored to reality along its edges, constantly tested as a holistic totality by means of the "recalcitrant experience" received through sensory receptors, a web in principle open to even fundamental revisions at the logico-mathematical level. See Neurath 1932; Quine 1980 [1953]. Quine (1960, 3–4, 124) approvingly refers to Neurath's ship metaphor.

17. See Kivistö and Pihlström 2017 for a more general discussion of metaphors of knowledge and their relevance to academic freedom and impact.

18. Note, however, that the proposal to study the metaphors of knowledge production and knowledge acquisition by employing methods of literary analysis does not entail that it would be plausible to analyze, say, scientific theories as "literary" narratives. *Pace* Prickett (2002, 87, 193), I am not at all convinced that it makes much sense to claim modern science to be "ironic," for instance. I am not sure what it means to claim that "any story of the world, whether scientific, sociological, psychological or religious, will also inevitably be pluralistic, literary, ironic, tentative, and multiplex" (ibid., 53). It is one thing to emphasize the contextuality of all human knowledge—a healthy pluralism also shared by pragmatism—but it is another thing altogether to extend the concept of irony (and possibly other literary concepts, including metaphoricity) out of any reasonable bounds, thus eventually trivializing it. Yet, Prickett notes, accurately, that even Rorty's radical ironism is metaphysical in its own way (ibid., 204). For a critical account of Rorty's historicism and ironism that might be effective as a criticism against Prickett as well, see Roberts's (1995, 250) worry that "a historical account becomes just another form of irony, metaphor, or strong misreading" as soon as we endorse "Rorty's inflation of the literary sphere." (For Roberts's discussion of Rortyan neopragmatism in relation to historicism and aestheticism, see ibid., chapter 9. Robert's overall argument is complex, both historically and theoretically, engaging with the development of postmetaphysical and historicist thought from Nietzsche and Heidegger to more recent writers like Rorty, but it seems to me that the pragmatist philosopher of the humanities can very well appreciate his wish to establish a middle ground between the various extremes that seem to characterize our postmetaphysical situation; see ibid., 316–318. However, one main difference, I suppose, is that the kind of pragmatist philosophy of historiography and the humanities I am sketching here is not happy with the claim that we have arrived at a "postmetaphysical" situation but insists on developing a pragmatist account of metaphysics itself; cf. Pihlström 2009.)

19. This question, in its different varieties, is explored in considerable detail by John P. Diggins (1994) in his magnificent study of the (failed) "promise of pragmatism" in relation to the modernist "crisis" of both epistemic and political

authorities. See especially ibid., chapter 6, for his analysis of Dewey's views on historical knowledge.

20. White's (1973), Ankersmit's (2001, 2009), and other "narrativist" philosophers' of historiography controversial views have raised a considerable debate whose core, arguably, is the very issue of realism that this book also focuses on (even though I am not proposing any detailed response to historiographical narrativism specifically). For various responses to White's work, see Ankersmit et al. 2009. For a different approach, inspired by Hans Vaihinger, to the role of the "fictional" in history and historiography, see Kobow 2013. As has been emphasized throughout this discussion, one of the chief merits of pragmatism in this area is the possibility of critically integrating (nonmetaphysical) realism and (some form of) constructivism. As usual, pragmatism here seeks a critical middle ground, far from succumbing to the temptations of historiographical antirealism, fictionalism, or narrativism. While several contributors to Tucker 2009 explore these issues, none of them focuses on pragmatism (nor do the essays in Ankersmit et al. 2009). See, however, Kuukkanen 2015 for plausible "postnarrativist" reflections coming close to pragmatism; I will comment on some of his arguments shortly.

21. The example is important also because Orwell's novel is, indeed, a literary attempt to critically investigate some extreme human possibilities whose mere possibility has an enormous influence on the way we understand political and historical reality.

22. How firmly the novel is actually committed to this—that is, how accurate this interpretation of Winston's character is—may be a matter of some interpretive debate, though.

23. This is not to say that dictators like the current leaders of Russia and China would not be very dangerous not only to their own citizens but also to human civilization in their disrespect for both the truth and universal human rights, even though Orwell's Big Brother is far more extreme. For example, as the general trust in truth, and especially in the authorities' speaking the truth, has been lost in Russia, many people avoid taking COVID-19 vaccines even though the Russian vaccine (perhaps somewhat surprisingly) seems to be rather effective. True, the same challenge must be faced in the United States, where people were misled by Trump's constant lying and "post-truth" attitude for years, but the difference of course is that in the US, despite all its enormous problems, there is no centralized political control or censorship over institutions of free speech, such as the media and higher education (though Trumpists, like right-wing populists and nationalists everywhere, typically claim that *their* freedom of speech is suppressed). More generally, democratically minded people everywhere should be on guard: even well-meaning antiauthoritarian movements may be tempted to adopt post-truth ideas and practices when it comes to defending their cause. A liberal democratic society does not *guarantee* that truth will prevail.

24. Cf. also Kivistö and Pihlström 2016, chapter 5, and Pihlström 2020, 2021, chapter 1, for more comprehensive philosophical discussion of Rorty, Orwell, truth, and truthfulness.

25. In cases of "historic truth," "it is but one portion of our belief reacting on another so as to yield the most satisfactory total state of mind" (James 1978 [1909], 54). For James's discussion of the real existence of Caesar as compatible with the idea of true statements having "functional workings," see ibid., 120–122 (cf. also 150–151).

26. Note also that I am somewhat hesitant, to the point of being agnostic at the metalevel, to subscribe to the claim that *religious* discourse is truth-apt (see Pihlström 2021, chapter 6). Yet, this by no means precludes a pragmatic realism about the truth-aptness of the scholarly discourses of theology and religious studies as humanistic disciplines.

27. Margolis's (e.g., 1995, 2012) historicist pragmatism (which, nevertheless, is for him also a form of realism) is, again, an invaluable source of insights for these questions.

28. While one might suppose that pragmatists would generally have defended "narrativist" and antirealist views such as Hayden White's, relatively few seem to have done so, unless one includes Rorty among postmodernist narrativists (see, however, Tozzi 2016). In particular, Peircean realism about historical knowledge has been developed by many recent contributors to pragmatist philosophy of historiography (e.g., Colapietro 2016; Topa 2016; Laas 2016), while others have been inspired by other pragmatist developments, including James's, Dewey's, C. I. Lewis's, and Quine's versions of pragmatism (see Sheehey 2019 on James; Koopman 2011 on Dewey and Foucault; Portella 2019 on Dewey; Niklas 2016 on Lewis and others; Gorman 2016 on Quine). On American historians' pragmatist sources and influences since the early twentieth century, see Kloppenberg 2004. For a substantial recent scholarly investigation of Peirce's views on history, including the significance of history and historical arguments for philosophy, see Viola 2020. Viola's book is perhaps the most detailed study so far on a pragmatist classic's (Peirce's) conception of history, emphasizing the plural sources and dimensions of Peirce's ideas (viz., history of science, history of philosophy, semiotics) and focusing on Peirce's realism about history, in particular. Taking seriously the historicity of its own approach to Peirce (and the scholarly history of interpreting his views on history), it is also relevant to the ongoing debates on realism versus constructivism regarding historical facts and their "hardness" (see also Colapietro 2021). On Brandom's importance for pragmatist philosophy of historiography, see also Gazit 2019.

29. The reference to "mirroring" can be understood as a reference to Rorty's (1979) influential criticism of realism and representationalism, in particular. Kuukkanen's (2015, chapter 3) elaborations on constructivism as one of the central

tenets of narrativism (developed with a transcendental twist), critically retained in postnarrativism, is obviously relevant to pragmatist forms of constructivism as well.

30. While I have started to develop this theme in this section, some further twists in the argument will only be provided in later sections of this chapter in the context of "real generals" and holistic pragmatism. In addition, while agreeing with Kuukkanen (2017, 114) about the primarily cognitive function of historiography, I would insist on the irreducibility of the ethical function—as in any of our value-laden pursuits of truth. (See below.) Note also that though I am criticizing Kuukkanen's rejection of truth, I find his theory of justification in historiography elegant and generally plausible (Kuukkanen 2015, chapter 9)—my only reservation being that it needs a (pragmatist) concept of truth.

31. For an attempt to integrate, within (Jamesian) pragmatism, the concepts of truth and truthfulness, see Pihlström 2021, chapters 1–2.

32. In this sense, Tamm's position is shared by Kuukkanen (2015, 2017), but the difference between the two is that Tamm still believes in the need to employ the concept of truth. Generalizing Tamm's and Kuukkanen's arguments, we might suggest that narrativists, fictionalists, and other antirealists about historiography are simply wrong in supposing that our having to invoke ethical and aesthetic criteria when "selecting" (value-laden) historical facts for interpretation would preclude epistemological and ontological considerations of such value-laden factuality. For the pragmatist philosopher of the humanities, aesthetic and ethical values are, while indeed always present in our humanistic inquiry, always also entangled with ontology and epistemology. (See below.)

33. As noted in chapter 1, my understanding of "theology" here is based on a Nordic and specifically Finnish nondenominational conception of theology, albeit with full understanding that this is not the way in which theology is understood in other cultural contexts and traditions. For the sake of clarity, it should be emphasized that engaging in academic research in theology at Finnish universities involves no religious or denominational commitment whatsoever, as faculties of theology are completely autonomous in relation to any churches and other religious institutions and committed to objective norms of research. Obviously, in other academic contexts in different countries the relation between theology faculties or divinity schools and religious institutions may be organized entirely differently. For discussions of theology and religious studies as academic disciplines, see also Helmer 2013; Vainio 2020.

34. Pragmatism still receives relatively little attention in academic debates on the methodology of religious studies. For example, in Orsi's (2013) comprehensive and up-to-date collection, there is almost nothing specifically on pragmatist philosophy of religious studies, apart from a few references to William James. See, however, Bagger 2018. For a noteworthy proposal to redefine the relations between the philosophy of religion and the study of religions (in the plural),

emphatically understood as human social practices, along broadly pragmatist lines, see Schilbrack 2014.

35. Analytic theologians, however, claim that "theology can and should make publicly accessible reality claims, which are not just about how the language is used in Christian communities" (Vainio 2020, 11).

36. This, roughly, is the picture of (Kantian) pragmatist philosophy of religion I have defended in many earlier contributions (e.g., Pihlström 2013, 2021).

37. The philosophy of religion is a relevant example here, as many of its practitioners today engage in cosmological speculations regarding the nature of the nonhuman universe. Moreover, "analytic theology" (cf. above) may use the formal tools of analytic philosophy to analyze traditional theological doctrines in order to investigate their compatibility with the results of natural science. I find these attempts rather uninteresting from the point of view of pragmatist philosophy of religion, but arguing for this view is not a task for the present study.

38. In this sense, it seems to me that pragmatist (meta)philosophy is somewhat different from the mainstream of analytic philosophy today, in particular, which often seems to treat philosophical claims and theories as in principle true or false (and to find the philosopher's job as the one of determining, to the best they can, whether those claims and theories are true or false). This seems to be the case no matter whether the analytic philosopher is committed to a naturalistic way of finding philosophical theories on a par with scientific theories or to a conception of "pure" philosophy over and above the sciences. In this respect, contemporary analytic philosophy is different from early analytic philosophy, which typically maintained (e.g., in its logical-empiricist phase) that philosophical theories themselves are neither true nor false but, rather, elucidatory attempts to investigate our use of language in the sciences and elsewhere. Again, a pragmatist inquiry into this metaphilosophical set of issues may be helpful for our understanding of the practices of philosophy itself.

39. Several papers in Gronda and Viola 2016 do discuss classical pragmatists', especially Peirce's, views on historiography (see above for relevant references), but as far as I know, no comprehensive treatment of pragmatist philosophers' conceptions of the humanities has been written. As this book only uses the classical pragmatists as sources of inspiration in developing a systematic program, this is not such a work, either.

40. Relevant networks (etc.) that could be studied include, for example, the Humanities in the European Research Area (HERA), the European Consortium for Humanities Institutes and Centres (ECHIC), as well as several funding organizations, including research councils in Europe and worldwide, particularly their humanistically focused suborganizations.

41. For further discussion of this need to reconcile—pragmatically—the natural and the transcendental, see chapter 4 below.

42. Jürgen Habermas's classical theory of "epistemic interests" is a case in point here. On the other hand, according to scientific realism, the natural sciences may also at least partially aim at truth conceived as valuable in itself regardless of any technical control of nature (cf. Niiniluoto 1999).

43. I would also be happy to argue that pragmatism is—despite popular misconceptions—in many ways opposed to utilitarianism as an ethical theory (cf., e.g., Pihlström 2008, 2011a, 2016), but that is not a topic for this book.

44. With the above-suggested exception that we might take an agnostic stance toward the truth-aptness of philosophical discourse itself, or at least some of its elements.

45. See the discussion of scientific realism above in chapter 2.

46. Popper's ontology of the "three worlds" is not among the explicit topics of this discussion; this vocabulary is only used heuristically here, and no ontological commitment to the Popperian worlds is made. For Popper's introduction of the concept of "World 3," see Popper 1979 [1972]; for his later elaborations, see Popper and Eccles 1977; see also Niiniluoto 1999 as well as Pihlström 1996.

47. Here, of course, we have to keep in mind the pluralistic and value-laden characterization of truth itself that pragmatism subscribes to (cf. again Pihlström 2021, especially chapters 1–2).

48. A crucial element of this pragmatic realism is, again, the Jamesian pragmatist conception of truth (cf. Pihlström 2021), conceived as broad enough to cover, for example, literary (artistic), historical, and possibly even religious truth about the human condition as well as humanistic scholarly truths about such attempts in various spheres of culture to find truths about our human world. The literary "truth" of, say, Tolstoy (whom James admired) can be truly (or falsely) explored by scholarship. On religious truth, see, e.g., James 1958 [1902], 261.

49. Compare this to the discussions of poetic creation, including the sound of language, as a (Jamesian) process of "truth happening to an idea" in the context of interpreting "pragmatist poetry" influenced by James, especially Wallace Stevens's work (see several essays in Evans 2017). See Geisenhanslüke 2015 for a historical examination of the notion of literary truth; on the development of the philosophical problem of truth in the arts more generally, see the historical account in Rockmore 2013.

50. Even the radically individualist James, while basing his analysis in *The Varieties* (James 1958 [1902]) on a rich array of descriptions of particular cases, aims at illuminating *general* features of (individuals') religious life, such as the religious types of the healthy-minded and the sick soul, as well as the general dynamics of mysticism and conversion. Note that when defending the reality of generals, I am not intending to downgrade the importance of individuals as objects of humanistic inquiry; the pragmatist may very well advance a pluralistic ontology of, for example, historical reality, postulating, among many other things,

individual agents, events, states, processes, and institutions. The claim I am about to make next is that *some* of these entities are best accounted for in terms of Peirce's realism of generality. On the ontology of historiography, in particular, see, e.g., Udehn 2009.

51. Relevant writings by Peirce can be found in Peirce 1992–98, especially vol. 2 (though the theme runs through Peirce's writings as a whole, all the way from the early 1871 "Berkeley review" to his late essays on pragmatism and pragmaticism). For relevant loci in the *Collected Papers*, see Peirce 1931–58, 1.15–26, 4.1ff., 5.59–65, 5.93–101, 5.312, 5.423, 5.430–433, 5.453ff., 5.470, 5.502–504, 5.528, 8.7–38. For my own more Jamesian pragmatist appropriation of Peircean realism, see Pihlström 2003a, 2008, 2009. It is worth pointing out that when Peirce in 1905 rebaptized his view as "pragmaticism," using a word he famously found "ugly enough to be safe from kidnappers," he complained about the misleading use of the term "pragmatism" in what he called "literary journals." Contrary to what is popularly assumed, it was not merely, or even primarily, James's version of pragmatism that made Peirce angry and led to his terminological innovation. (See further Pihlström 2004a, 2008, chapter 1.) Viola's (2020) above-cited study emphasizes Peirce's historical realism; my use of the concept of "real generals," though inspired by Peirce, aims at no scholarly accuracy as an interpretation of Peirce. We should feel free to employ this concept for our purposes here without necessarily subscribing to the overall position Peirce labeled "extreme scholastic realism."

52. That is, both contrastive historical explanations—explaining why something happened instead of something else (i.e., something that did not happen but could, in a counterfactual case, have happened)—and the perhaps more popular genre of writing "counterfactual histories," that is, stories about how things might have developed had they not developed the way they did, arguably need Peircean realism of generals. The Peircean perspective is missing from most standard (analytic) treatments of counterfactuals in historiography, however (e.g., Weinryb 2009). See again several papers in Gronda and Viola 2016, as well as Viola 2020, for Peircean discussions of the philosophy of historiography.

53. On the value-ladenness of history, see also, e.g., Dray 1980, 28, 42–46. As Dray puts it, when we recognize this value-ladenness, "the past as it actually was" will "coincide" with "the past as it must appear from the standpoint of a certain scheme of values—political, aesthetic, social, moral, intellectual, and so on" (ibid., 46).

54. Even though historiography is one of the main areas of scholarship examined here, it is unnecessary in this context to take any definite stand on the metaphysics of time, including the question concerning the real existence (vs. nonexistence) of past (or future) events. This is a contested matter even within pragmatism (cf. Mead 2012 [1932]).

55. This is a "transcendental how" question in the sense that we are dealing with the necessary conditions for the possibility of representations within representational practices of humanistic scholarship—and the answers that any pragmatist philosophy of the humanities can deliver to such transcendental questions need to be understood as thoroughly pragmatic. (Note again that I am not as critical of the notion of representation as Kuukkanen 2015 in developing his pragmatism.)

56. In his admirable discussion of colligation, Kuukkanen (e.g., 2015, 106, 113) is somewhat unclear in criticizing the idea that colligatory concepts would be "true"; truth, of course, cannot be attributed to concepts but only to statements or theories. Again, a pragmatist account of truth (and of real generals in historical ontology) enables us to make sense of colligatory concept-use while preserving the idea of historiography as truth-seeking. Colligation itself is in the business of truth, pragmatically understood.

57. A more detailed version of such philosophy could utilize Peirce's semiotics, which I am not doing here.

58. I hope my potential reader may forgive me this use of a "local" example, presumably unknown in the larger world. Beyond what I take to be the intrinsic interest of the case invoked here, examples like this also serve as reminders about the fact that the humanities do, even in our globalized times, explore local cultural traditions, including small national languages.

59. Unfortunately, all the scholarly studies on Linna that I am familiar with are available only in Finnish.

60. In the context of the philosophy of the humanities, it may be interesting to note that Väinö Linna, a self-learned working-class man without formal academic education, received the highest honor one may get in Finland for one's artistic, scientific, or scholarly achievements, that is, the title of an Academician granted by the President of the Republic. Unlike the other (very few) writers who have received this title qua artists, Linna received it, so to speak, on the side of the scientists and scholars—and he was thus institutionally raised "above," among others, dozens of professors of history whose research had dealt with the same historical incidents and periods. This was a recognition, on behalf of the Finnish state, of the fundamental change in the Finns' general understanding of the history of their own nation made possible by Linna's compelling work. Linna, therefore, is a case in point for considering the question whether the writing of history can be usefully compared to the writing of fiction: by writing two widely read historical—yet obviously fictional—novels, he transformed the ways in which an entire nation *was able to view* its real history. (This, however, is not a judgment about the artistic quality of Linna's work but merely about its historical impact.)

61. Another, perhaps somewhat "wild" (again Finnish) example that could be further discussed by the specialists in the relevant field, would be the

interpretation of Aki Kaurismäki's films. Especially in some of his late films, including *Le Havre* (2011), the main characters are invariably "good" in the sense of never even seeming to arrive at any moral conflict; they just know what is the right thing to do (e.g., helping the weak and the vulnerable), and they simply try to do it if they can without having to reflect on the matter. This could lead us to view the films through the concepts of "beautiful soul" (*"schöne Seele,"* derived from Friedrich Schiller) and "holy will," to which Kant famously opposes his view that human beings need the moral law. Unlike angels (if there were any), we lack a holy will that would "naturally" be inclined to will what is right. Now, Kaurismäki's characters, or some of them at least, seem to be closer to beings with a holy will, or "beautiful souls," than human beings. They are, then, fairy-tale-like characters, which is further highlighted by the fact that in the late films, in particular, the ending is a happy one. So the good will actually be rewarded, and a Kantian summum bonum is achieved—something that Kant of course thought does not happen in this world. This could yield a Kantian interpretation of Kaurismäki: through his fairy-tale-like characters and endings, the director offers glimpses of (Kantian) legitimate hope for a better future, based on what is the morally right thing to do—without claiming this to be actual or even ("really") possible in the real world, though. These Kantian notions could be employed here to sketch an interpretive possibility that could enrich our viewing of the Kaurismäki films even if the Kantian interpretation were not correct or even plausible.

62. Given this deep value-ladenness of ontology, there should be no worry about a random Meinongian jungle. It is, more generally, a basic characteristic of pragmatism that reality is not given but dynamically depends on criteria of relevance, and hence on our pragmatic purposes, as argued by James, in particular, all the way from his early masterpiece, *The Principles of Psychology* (1981 [1890]), to the late writings on pragmatism (e.g., James 1975 [1907]).

63. Compare this to the Peircean method of abduction understood as a method of creatively inventing or discovering a hypothesis, that is, as a method of discovery rather than justification. For a comprehensive account of abduction and its role in science, see Niiniluoto 2018; a full-scale pragmatist philosophy of the humanities should also include a defense of the role of abduction in the humanities, but here I cannot dwell on that topic.

64. Moreover, recall Rorty's (1989) essay on Orwell: Rorty points out that O'Brien is not "wrong" or "mistaken"—or at least there is no way we could demonstrate that he is—but that Orwell merely shows us that he (O'Brien) is "dangerous and possible." As a real general, the real possibility of a fictional figure such as O'Brien could be an object of investigation for humanistic inquiry. O'Brien himself, as a fictional character, is *not*, in my view, such an object, because scholarly investigations aim at representing reality, not the unreality of fiction, but his *possibility*, as a "real possibility," *is* an element of the world that can be

studied by means of humanistic inquiry. (As Jaakko Hintikka used to point out, in an entirely different context, "the one who only knows the actual world knows very little about it.") Somewhat paradoxically, then, O'Brien's "mere" possibility is *more real* as an object of investigation for humanistic scholarship (and the philosophy of the humanities) than O'Brien himself as a fictional character that is, by definition, unreal. In general, Peircean real generals do *not* include "existing" fictional entities, but they do include the general possibility that a particular fictional situation might be, or might have been, real.

65. Again, this is not just a matter of epistemic categorization of the kinds of questions that scholars might be willing to ask but an ontological categorization of what kind of open issues are among the objects of study in the relevant field(s).

66. For example, what exactly is (currently popular) *autofiction*, in contrast to other literary genres? Which particular texts belong to this genre, and why? How do we know? Could we be mistaken about a particular item we place under this rubric? Could there be more? Why, or why not? How fuzzy are the borders?

67. For an examination of the "will to believe" in the context of an attempt to develop a pragmatist conception of the pursuit of (existential) truth and truthfulness, see Pihlström 2021, chapter 4.

68. Cf., e.g., Bagger 2018; see also Pihlström 2005, 2013, as well as chapter 4 below. For a practice-oriented discussion of the relations between philosophy of religion and the interdisciplinary practices of the study of religion, see again Schilbrack 2014.

69. We must recognize the misleading usage of the term "positivism" in such contexts; most of the philosophers accused of positivism because of their tendency to prioritize causal explanation to hermeneutic understanding would qualify as scientific realists rather than positivists. The word continues to be used, though it might be better to entirely avoid it (except in historical contexts) today. Clearly, no reasonable pragmatist should subscribe to positivism—nor follow ideological "antipositivist" campaigns to abandon natural-scientific causally explanatory methodologies from the humanities altogether.

70. While pragmatism generally emphasizes the inevitability of (partly subjective) valuation even at the ontological level, this is fully compatible with a critical attitude toward, say, autoethnography as a method of research. It by no means follows from the pragmatist repudiation of any essentialist dichotomy between fact and value, for instance, that the humanistic scholar could legitimately refer to their own experiences in developing a theoretical account of an object of study (even if that object is "experiential" in some relevant sense). However, detailed examinations of autoethnographical methodologies in use in different fields of the humanities remain beyond the scope of my discussion.

71. I have earlier proposed an interpretation and development of Peircean realism about "real generals" as based on a transcendental argument referring to such realism as a necessary condition for the possibility of inquiry (Pihlström

2003a, chapter 4). This issue could be revisited in the context of the pragmatist philosophy of the humanities. One corollary of the integration of the Peircean ontology of real generals and the Kantian transcendental approach is that metaphysically realistic attempts to develop ontologies of generals (universals) or modalities, including, say, David Armstrong's realism about universals and David Lewis's metaphysics of "real" possible worlds, are both to be rejected as problematic ways of accounting for generality (as seen from a pragmatist point of view). When interpretive possibilities are regarded as Peircean-like generals instead of being subordinated to Armstrong's (1997, 2004) "actualist" metaphysics of states of affairs and truthmaking or to Lewis's (1986) "possibilist" conception of fictional entities as denizens of concretely existing possible worlds, it is possible to maintain the basic pragmatist commitment to accounting for existence and reality generally—including the reality of real possibilities—as something based on our ongoing practices of interpretation, reflection, and scholarly understanding. The real possibility of, say, Orwell's O'Brien (a fictional, nonexistent character) can only be grounded in our normative practices of writing and thinking; this possibility would be misunderstood if reduced, say, to Lewis-like concrete possible worlds. (Cf. further Pihlström 2009 for a pragmatist critique of Armstrong's metaphysical realism.)

72. On ethical issues in the philosophy of religious studies, see chapter 4 below.

73. Putnam also occasionally characterizes the liberal ontology of his internal/pragmatic realism by means of humanistic examples: there are, he says, not only, for example, electrons and other elementary particles in the world, but also "passages that are difficult to interpret" (see below). These could be clearly regarded as objects of humanistic inquiry. (Cf. again the discussion of real generals and interpretive possibilities above.)

74. As noted earlier, Faye's (2012) pragmatic naturalism, while being on the right track regarding nonreductive naturalism in the humanities, fails to explore realism and transcendental arguments.

75. White's earliest publications on holistic pragmatism are already from the 1950s (and so are some of his early writings on the philosophy of history; see White 2005), but we may here refer to his relatively late formulations of this idea. In some of my own recent work (especially Pihlström 2021), I follow and further develop holistic pragmatism. Interestingly, Kuukkanen (2015, chapter 2) only discusses White as one of the "early narrativists," without paying attention to his later holistic pragmatism, which I am claiming is highly relevant for defending precisely the kind of pragmatist picture of historiography Kuukkanen himself is elaborating on. Note also that the "holism" Kuukkanen criticizes (ibid., 44–49) is not to be equated with White's pragmatist holism.

76. White's (2002) discussion of the role of interests in historical explanation is also highly relevant to a pragmatist theory of historiography (on the

interest-relativity of explanation, see also Putnam 1978), but the holistic-pragmatist idea of integrating factual and normative components within a single belief system tested as a totality is even more important—though it also entails a version of "historical relativism" (for a critical discussion, cf. White 2005, chapter 6) that needs to be critically assessed in terms of holistic pragmatism itself.

77. In this regard, Tamm's (2014) pragmatist philosophy of historiography, drawing attention to the practices of historians, is more clearly pragmatist than White's. It also seems to me that Kuukkanen's (2015) postnarrativist pragmatism is in many ways very similar to White's position.

78. Again, this is not terribly far from Kuukkanen's postnarrativist historiographical pragmatism discussed earlier. Kuukkanen (2015, 187) also acknowledges that historians seek cognitive warrant for their theses about what is taken to be objectively real (in some sense), while constructivism is right to insist that "historiographical objects are dependent on the historian's activity."

79. A narrower—and better known—version of pragmatic holism is of course Quine's (1980 [1953]) view, according to which the unit of empirical testing in science is a scientific theory as a whole, or even the scientific worldview as a totality, instead of any single theoretical statement or belief; the original formulation of such a holism is often attributed, also by White himself, to Pierre Duhem. Quine leaves normative beliefs out of this picture (except for normative epistemology which he ultimately reduces to empirical psychology within his program of "naturalizing epistemology"; cf. Quine 1969), but for White (2002) irreducibly normative disciplines, such as ethics, history, as well as epistemology itself, are as firmly empirical as science, because, for example, our ethical experiences of obligation may be among the empirical "observations" requiring us to adjust our web of belief.

80. I have on earlier occasions discussed both Orwell's novel and its relation to realism and truth (e.g., Kivistö and Pihlström 2016; Pihlström 2020) and holistic pragmatism in relation to pragmatist views on truth, values, and normativity (e.g., Pihlström 2021), but I have never before proposed this link between them, a link that I now see as fundamental.

81. The Collingwoodian view that historical agents' thoughts need to be "rethought" in order to properly understand them (cf. Collingwood 1946; see also, e.g., Dray 1980; Saari 1984, 1991) is a version of the claim that understanding is possible only "from within" a practice, tradition, or framework. From the pragmatist standpoint, this influential idea too easily leads to relativism sacrificing objectively shared standards of rational discussion across practices and traditions. For a substantial pragmatist (though also relativist and historicist) engagement with Collingwood's position, see Margolis 1993, chapters 1–2. As Heikki Saari (1984, 1991) argues, the Collingwoodian theory of reenactment and "absolute presuppositions" does not, however, entail any psychologistic conception of historical understanding as empathetic reenactment but is, rather, to be understood

as a (Kantian-like) theory of the necessary conditions for the possibility of intersubjective understanding in terms of participation in shared practices and meanings. If this is correct, then Collingwood's view does not offer historians any specific methodology but amounts to a philosophical theory of what makes historical knowledge possible, also enabling a certain kind of historical realism, despite Collingwood's undeniable relativism concerning interpretation. While Collingwood is a major classic of the philosophy of history, I cannot here take any definitive stand on the correct interpretation of his influential ideas.

82. Regarding this practical issue of organizing research and research-based education, I would like to view pragmatism as an approach once again occupying a critical middle ground. It is important to support human cooperation in research groups—not only in the laboratories but also in humanistic scholarship—but it is equally important to continue to value the (Humboldtian) ideals of educating autonomous critical individuals. It is still the individual scholar that can be found at the center of the processes of inquiry, and the increasing group structures of the organization of research cannot, and must not, destroy this.

83. An obvious background for this discussion in the pragmatist tradition is the Quinean project of naturalization briefly commented on in chapter 2. I will in chapter 4 approach the relation between naturalism and transcendental pragmatism from a slightly different angle, exploring the project of naturalization in the philosophy of science as well as (as a case study) the philosophy of religious studies, in particular.

84. Compare this to Rorty's (1982) proposal to follow Derrida in viewing philosophy as "a kind of writing," and his later frequent articulations of the close relation between philosophy and literature. However, the question—a very serious and important question in its own right—whether (and in what sense exactly) literary works of art may convey philosophical ideas, insights, or arguments (see Mikkonen 2013) is beyond the scope of this inquiry, as I am only focusing on the philosophy of literary theory and criticism instead of the philosophy of literature. Similarly, pragmatist philosophy of literary theory and criticism does not, as, say, analytic aesthetics does, primarily examine (literary) "art and its objects" (cf. Wollheim 1980) but, rather, the art of literary criticism itself and *its* objects, which may include the ways in which literary theorists view the ontology of the literary works they study.

85. Note, however, that when proposing that we should beware of radical historicism, I am not at all saying that we should not take seriously, for example, the kind of highly sophisticated historicism defended by someone like Joseph Margolis (1993, 1995). The pragmatist can very well agree with him that human thinking not only has but "is a history" (Margolis 1993, 205).

86. For recent reflections on what kind of humanism best fits an overall pragmatist and pragmatically naturalist attitude to science and religion, see Hon-

nacker 2018; Jung 2019. On the roots of the humanism versus posthumanism discussion in the German idealist tradition, see the essays in Landgraf et al. 2019.

87. *Critical Distance*, my unfinished joint book project with Sari Kivistö, will, when completed, (I hope) critically examine the concepts of immersion, empathy, and reenactment (among many other things) that may be regarded as central to all the humanities disciplines investigated in the present book, that is, literary analysis, historical understanding, and religious studies. Our appropriate relations to other human beings in our scholarly activities in the humanities is at the center of ontological, methodological, as well as ethical discussion here. The ontological search for a proper critical distance to the object of study in the humanities is also an ethical quest of taking seriously the other human person (past, present, or future) as a representative of shared, yet never fully shared, humanity.

88. Putnam's (2016, chapter 2) response to Williams's essay unfortunately fails to deal with this particular issue, while providing interesting further reflections on how the two philosophers differ on the question concerning realism and the "absolute conception of the world" on which they debated already in the 1980s (see also Pihlström 1996).

89. Putnam's work on truth and reference as practice-embedded and irreducibly normative concepts is also highly relevant here (see, e.g., Putnam 2016). There is much more to be done in the theory of reference regarding the theoretical terms (and also observational terms) used in theory formation in the humanities. For example, we may say that the term *World War II* refers to World War II. But how exactly does a theoretical term in theology, for instance, refer? What is the object of a term like *kenosis*, for example? A pragmatist investigation of reference must take seriously the contingency and the purpose-dependent relevance of all referential considerations: what our theoretical (or any other) terms refer to, and what exists as their object(s), depends on our purposive human activities. A pragmatist account of the relation between (theoretical) language and the reality that language is about is distinctively able to deal with this relevance-dependence of reference (and truth).

90. This "natural history" could be compared to Wittgenstein's remarks on the "natural history" of our language-games and forms of life (see Hacking 2002, 196–197), but also to what Arthur Fine (1996 [1986]) calls the "natural ontological attitude" (NOA), to be critically discussed in chapter 4 below. In a sense, this is a version of NOA in the humanities, a natural-historical account of our contingent concepts, with no philosophical judgment problematizing or interpreting it. Precisely in order to avoid any reduction to such full-blown naturalism, pragmatism needs to be supplemented with a transcendental twist.

91. In this sense I do find Putnam's (2016, chapter 2) response to Williams relevant, even though it may not get to the main issue regarding the humanistic project as such. Putnam does acknowledge Williams's "we" as "contrastive," though

(ibid., 51). Putnam's final response to Williams is better read as an articulation of his own pragmatic pluralism and perspectivalism than as a real attempt to respond to what Williams is up to in his "humanistic discipline" essay.

92. See also my brief reference to "Humboldtian" values above; on the significance of the notion of *Bildung* in Humboldt's own writings, see Humboldt 2017.

Chapter 4

1. For relatively recent collections of essays on transcendental philosophy, naturalism, and pragmatism, see Smith and Sullivan 2011; Gava and Stern 2016.

2. For example, a "naturalized" conception of historiography might suggest that humanistic (and other) disciplines themselves—such as the history, sociology, and psychology of historiography—can tell us everything that we need to know about historiography, and there is therefore no need for any autonomous *philosophy* of historiography.

3. Following Sellars, Tuomela (1985) defends what he calls the *scientia mensura* thesis: best-explaining scientific theories are the measure of what there is. For discussions of the varieties of naturalism in the philosophy of science, see several essays in Keil and Schnädelbach 2000; Nannini and Sandkühler 2000; and Koskinen et al. (2006); cf. also Craig and Moreland (2000) and de Caro and Macarthur (2004) for critical perspectives. The "culturalist" position upon which Herbert Schnädelbach's (and partly other critics' of naturalism, such as Geert Keil's) attack on naturalism is based is more thoroughly explicated in Schnädelbach 2000. On "naturalizing" the humanities, in particular, see again Faye 2012.

4. Maddy (2000, especially 107–108) also compares Fine and Quine, contrasting their "one-level" empirical naturalism with the "two-level" view Carnap inherited from Kant's distinction between the empirical and the transcendental. But it seems that Maddy (as well as, say, Friedman 2000) overlooks the distinction between science-external transcendental principles and abstract, general, constitutive (and hence, in a sense, transcendental) principles that may be formulated *within* the evolving system of scientific thought itself. A Quinean, in order to maintain the latter kind of philosophical principles, need not step beyond science but only aspire to generality within the naturalistic and holistic project of understanding reality in the absence of any *transcendent* postulations.

5. For characterizations and critiques of these views, see (again) Niiniluoto 1999. It should be noted, in particular, that Fine's critique of realism does not entail any epistemic theory of truth, such as Putnam's one-time (e.g., 1981) account of truth in terms of idealized warranted assertibility. For an interesting but controversial argument to the effect that a scientific realist should not accept (metaphysical) naturalism, see Koons 2000; it has been more common to suggest that naturalistic arguments can be utilized in defending scientific realism, and realism in general, in an empirically informed manner (cf., e.g., Devitt 1991).

6. Among insightful critiques of Fine, following the publication of his controversial NOA writings, see Musgrave 1989; Brown 1994, 15–18; Kukla 1994; Abela 1996; Brandon 1997; Leplin 1997, 173–177; and Niiniluoto 1999, 18–20. Some of this criticism is discussed in Pihlström 1998, chapter 3. Most critics, with good reason, point out that Fine simply *dismisses* philosophical problems about science rather than arguing that we are justified in dismissing them.

7. For another nonphysicalist (indeed, "postmodern") but thoroughly deflationary and "naturalized" conception of science, see Rouse 1996, 2002. We should pause to note, however, that the very concept of physicalism raises major controversies (cf. Gillett and Loewer 2001), and it is by no means clear that even Quine could simply be classified as a "physicalist," though he does seem to believe that (rather obviously) nonphysical things and events supervene on physical ones. For a detailed attempt to carefully formulate and defend a version of physicalism (labeled "realization physicalism"), see Melnyk 2003.

8. For my pragmatism-based criticism of Armstrong's realistic metaphysics, including his theory of truthmaking, see Pihlström 2009.

9. That is, would Armstrongian realistically conceived truthmakers in the natural world make NOA true, if it were true?

10. Analogously, again, the NOAist "humanist" might urge that the humanities must be accounted for humanistically (e.g., from the point of view of history, literary studies, linguistics, etc.) rather than philosophically—in contrast to what I am doing in this book.

11. While there are several rival paradigms in the academic study of religion, including hermeneutical, evolutionary, cognitive-science-based, and so forth, none of them, of course, is a "religious" study of religion.

12. For this critique of NOA-based "religious naturalism," see Pihlström 2005. In comparison, consider what it would mean to adopt a "natural ontological attitude" to the postulations of historiography. If historians' views on what exactly happened in the past run into conflict, would the NOAist simply "accept them at face value," thus explicitly embracing a contradiction? If so, and if it is plausible to suggest that the objects of humanistic inquiry may also include propositions (about, say, the past) and the logical consequences of those propositions, it would follow that every possible proposition would be among the objects of humanistic inquiry, given that *ex falso quodlibet*. This would be a truly *inflated* form of (humanistic) realism.

13. The use of *theological* here obviously differs from my use of the term, as I am, throughout this book, including theology among the (secular) academic humanities. But you get the point.

14. Plantinga's (2000) influential theory of warranted Christian belief is a kind of theological NOA, as it treats Christian theism as warranted for those who believe it to be true, *if* it is true. (Plantinga thus grounds his externalist, epistemological naturalism in a more fundamental metaphysical supernaturalism.) His "Christian philosophy" hardly justifies Christian faith for anyone who does

not already share it. For an argument to the effect that a Deweyan naturalist can successfully pragmatically justify the use of scientific explanations (*contra*, say, creationists' supernatural ones) and thereby overcome theistic criticisms of naturalism, see Capps 2000. Plantinga-type "Christian philosophy" is, for these reasons, highly problematic and in my view seriously unsound as an academic study of religion.

15. Compare the brief discussion in chapter 3 on the analogy between the debates on historicism and naturalism.

16. It can be argued that what is *philosophically* (instead of, say, religiously) wrong in fundamentalism—of any kind, including both religious and scientific fundamentalism—is that it does not engage in genuine inquiry driven by genuine problems (or problematic situations, to employ a Deweyan expression) but rather begins from a prior commitment to some presupposed views (see Anderson and Hausman 2012, especially chapter 12). Instead, fundamentalism, in a Peircean phrase, "blocks the way of inquiry." *This*, however, is again a philosophical result, something we arrive at as a result of a philosophical reflection on what inquiry is and how genuine inquiries (in science or elsewhere) are normatively structured. It is not simply a scientific claim, let alone a naturalized theory made true by any merely natural states of affairs.

17. NOA, in short, would leave us at the mercy of authoritarian rulers like Russian Putinists or Chinese communists, whose distorted historical "ontologies" would have to be taken "at face value" just as much as serious historical accounts of what happened in the past (including the horrible crimes against humanity committed by both Russian and Chinese communists which are wiped out of historical memory in those countries). In comparison, for a comprehensive study of what happened to the humanities, including history, during the Third Reich in Germany, see Hausmann 2011 (on philosophy specifically, see Sherratt 2013).

18. I am here crucially indebted to Leila Haaparanta's characterization of what may be called the "philosophical attitude"—a theme that has been discussed at length in the phenomenological tradition but appears, arguably, in traditional analytic philosophy, for example, logical empiricism, as well. See, e.g., Haaparanta 1999. In an important sense, the entire exploration of "philosophical knowledge" in this chapter emerges from ideas I originally acquired from Prof. Haaparanta's research projects and seminars.

19. Moser and Yandell (2000, 10–13) formulate their dilemma as an argument against what they call "Core Scientism," a conjunction of "core ontological naturalism" ("every real entity either consists of or is somehow ontically grounded in the objects countenanced by the hypothetically completed empirical sciences") and "core methodological naturalism" ("every legitimate method of acquiring knowledge consists of or is grounded in the hypothetically completed methods of the empirical sciences"), a thesis that, as they point out, can hardly be a thesis of empirical science itself. They also apply this dilemma to Quine's

naturalism (ibid., 19–22). (An essentially similar dilemma is discussed by many contributions to the same antinaturalistic volume, Craig and Moreland 2000, which generally treats naturalism as a metaphysical rather than methodological or metaphilosophical thesis—although Moser and Yandell, in particular, offer careful distinctions between various forms of naturalism. For analogous insights, see the papers in de Caro and Macarthur 2004.) Yet, much of Moser's and Yandell's criticism loses its urgency as soon as we admit that even Quine's naturalism leaves room for traditional philosophy, including the metaphysics of naturalism itself (cf. Koskinen 2004).

20. For further reflections on this kind of a critique of reductive naturalism, grounded in a "culturalist" understanding of human subjectivity, yet compatible with a relaxed nonreductive naturalism, see Pihlström 2003b, 2009. The idea that the naturalist cannot fully reduce her-/himself, as a rational subject engaging in normative argumentation, to the purely physical world studied by natural science (even though such a reduction were possible in the case of all *others*) has been pursued in different ways by several critics of naturalism: see, e.g., Putnam 1994; Taylor 1995; Olafson 2001.

21. In this sense, philosophical investigations of practice-laden normative requirements belong to something that can be called *philosophical anthropology*. (See further Pihlström 2016, 2020, 2021, 2022.) The pragmatist philosopher of the humanities should take seriously the recent reemergence of philosophical anthropology in relation to debates over naturalism, in particular (see the essays in Honenberger 2016).

22. For a pragmatist approach to the debate over transcendental arguments in contemporary metaphysics and epistemology, see Pihlström 2003a, 2004b; for some of my later reflections on the matter, see Pihlström 2016, 2021, chapter 3.

23. Yet, insofar as Quine, for example, still preserves a significant part of the traditional normative role of philosophy as a conceptual activity focusing on the most abstract and general elements of our web of belief, or the logical structure of that web, it is not obvious that his views are vulnerable to this critique. Thus, we should not overhastily reject either naturalism in general or Quinean naturalism in particular on the basis of the transcendental argument provided here. According to Quinean naturalism, "reality" and "truth" are, indeed, internal to our language or theory. We may ask whether this view in effect differs much from a view propounded in one of the *loci classici* of antireductionism, Peter Winch's 1964 essay, "Understanding a Primitive Society": "What is real and what is unreal shows itself *in* the sense that language has. Further, both the distinction between the real and the unreal and the concept of agreement with reality themselves belong to our language" (Winch 1972, 12). Everything depends on what *our language* signifies here: the scientific language expressed in the regimented notation of logic (Quine) or the everyday mixture of various language-games we engage in (Winch, Wittgenstein).

24. The obvious reference is, of course, *Philosophical Investigations* (1953). In the present book, I am only loosely referring to Wittgenstein (and "Wittgensteinian" considerations) in passing in this context of transcendental inquiry into normativity. I am not claiming to make any interpretive point about Wittgenstein's philosophy. For my discussions of Wittgenstein's relation to pragmatism, see, e.g., Pihlström 2003a, 2012a. We could, I believe, plausibly develop a "Wittgensteinian philosophy of the humanities" as much as a pragmatist one, with interesting overlaps though presumably also important differences.

25. White's holistic pragmatism, briefly articulated in chapter 3, is presumably closer to the Wittgensteinian anthropological holism than the Quinean theoretical one, although Wittgenstein is not among his major sources.

26. In another paper, Medina (2004b) argues at length for the similarity between Wittgenstein's and Dewey's pragmatic contextualisms (see also Medina 2002). It is impossible to evaluate this comparison here, but I find it plausible (see also Pihlström 2003a, chapter 2).

27. Insofar as this nonreductive naturalism requires the notion of a "second nature" (see Medina 2004c), it is surprising that Medina fails to discuss McDowell's (1996 [1994]) elaborations on this Aristotelian notion (cf. Pihlström 2003a, chapter 4). For a collection of insightful essays addressing McDowell's struggle with naturalism and our "second nature," see Smith 2002. We cannot examine McDowell's influential position in any detail here, but we should acknowledge, with him, the need to continuously "rethink" our concepts of nature and naturalism—indeed, this is something I am doing in this chapter.

28. I will shortly more explicitly consider the role of transcendental arguments in the philosophy of the humanities.

29. Naturalized study of religion, to be shortly examined, is one possible example that can be used to illuminate the difficulties the naturalist must face regarding the issue of normativity. Another might be Martin Kusch's (1995, 1996) naturalized, sociological account of philosophical (not just scientific) knowledge. Kusch (1995) offers a detailed case study of the psychologism versus antipsychologism debate in German philosophy since the 1880s (in which the latter camp, led by Frege and Husserl, won the battle). According to Kusch, this sociological reconstruction of a philosophical dispute, adopting the sociology of scientific knowledge as its model, is not external to philosophy but "*potentially* made of the very stuff of which the central philosophical questions are made," "an eminently philosophical project"—especially since it questions the conditions for the possibility of a philosophical issue (ibid., 23). Hence, it bears some resemblance to a transcendental philosophical undertaking, albeit a naturalized one, which is as prepared to employ empirical material as any Quinean naturalism.

30. Admittedly, I have in this book claimed that pragmatists philosophers can be, historically and systematically, interpreted as having argued transcen-

dentally. The prospects of my own attempts to employ pragmatic transcendental argumentation in the service of the philosophy of the humanities do not depend on my getting the pragmatist classics right, though.

31. In this simple schema, *A* refers to some (human) phenomenon or activity we take to be actual (and hence possible) or whose actuality we cannot genuinely doubt, and *C* to its conditions. (In fact, it is rather important for the use of transcendental arguments in general that we consider cases where we cannot *sincerely* doubt the givens whose transcendental conditions we are seeking to identify. Therefore, this argumentative strategy can be connected with ethical and existential assessments of our practices; cf. Pihlström 2021.)

32. There is a lot of relevant discussion available that cannot be covered here: see, e.g., Stern 1999, 2000; Smith and Sullivan 2011; Gava and Stern 2016; Pihlström 2003a, 2004b, 2009, 2016, 2021.

33. However, in the Kantian tradition, the transcendental must *not* be confused with the *transcendent*: whereas transcendental philosophy examines the conditions and limits of experience, the transcendent—for example, the things in themselves—lies beyond those limits. Transcendental philosophy or transcendental arguments need not deal with anything transcendent—though, admittedly, they may: in some special cases, the postulation of transcendence may itself play a transcendental and/or constitutive role in our practices; cf. Pihlström 2011a.

34. Recall that in chapter 3 I actually used a more complex formulation in order to distinguish such a transcendental pragmatism from antirealist constructivisms: it is the *possibility* of the objects of inquiry *qua* the objects they are that constitutively depends on the contexts and/or practices of inquiry. It is this dependence that is, arguably, open to transcendental analysis.

35. A version of this view could also be read into Wittgenstein's later philosophy, where the shared human form of life that enables us to play a language-game can be argued to take the place of the transcendental subject that constitutes the reality our language can refer to.

36. One obvious question here is whether this kind of philosophical inquiry remains transcendental at all. I am not taking any stand here on the question of whether transcendental arguments are actually to be found in Carnap's (or the other logical empiricists') work; it is sufficient to note that *a* version of the transcendental versus empirical distinction can be located there (cf. Friedman 1997, 1999, 2000, 2001, 2007).

37. Again, the purpose of this discussion is not to take any stand on the interpretations of Wittgenstein, but certainly the pragmatist seeking to understand the nature of the humanities can very well employ Wittgensteinian resources for their purposes as well, as I already did earlier in this chapter when citing Medina's partly Wittgenstein-inspired argumentation against reductive naturalism. For an up-to-date collection of essays on Wittgenstein's (transcendental) concerns with the limits of language, see Appelqvist 2020.

38. This idea is also at work in Winch's above-cited "Understanding a Primitive Society" (1964; see Winch 1972). On the relativism discussion in the philosophy of anthropology, see Koskinen 2019.

39. I suppose my transcendental approach is compatible with (though not identical to) the nontranscendental position articulated (in a 2004 Finnish textbook on philosophy and the "human sciences") by my colleague Panu Raatikainen, who plausibly argues that in order to avoid the positivist or behaviorist view according to which only externally observable behavior is legitimate evidence in the human sciences, we need not maintain that the "internal" perspective of the people we are investigating (i.e., the practitioners "within" a practice or a tradition) must *always*, let alone *exclusively*, be considered. There is a middle ground position available, which we can simply label "antipositivism": in the human sciences, it is, whenever necessary, *legitimate* to consider the practitioners' own point of view. A similar pluralistic, nonexclusivist account of the methodology of the social sciences has been defended by Roth (1987), among others. One of the mistaken assumptions entangled with methodological exclusivism is, according to Roth, "meaning realism," the view that there is a "fact of the matter" regarding the interpretation of beliefs (see ibid., chapter 6); Roth employs Quinean holism and naturalism to counter this view and for thus developing a (rather non-Quinean) pluralism.

40. Bhaskar's focus is on social science, but his ideas can very well be extrapolated to the philosophy of the humanities and the realism discussion there.

41. See the essays collected in Pihlström 2017a for a number of pragmatist perspectives on Rescher's work in many areas of philosophy.

42. On a slightly analogous "pragmatist antinomy," see Rydenfelt 2019b.

43. These considerations could, mutatis mutandis, be relevant to the philosophical foundations of what Mikael Stenmark (2021) calls "worldview studies," an extension of religious studies covering also "secular outlooks on life" and other worldviews irreducible to religions. I find Stenmark's proposal a welcome enlargement of the basic idea of religious studies that needs to be further explored both by philosophers of religion and philosophers of the humanities. See again also Schilbrack 2014 for a somewhat different attempt to enlarge the scope of the philosophy of religion into something less "insular" and more relevant to the study of religions.

44. See also Proudfoot 2018, 107–108, 116. See, furthermore, Bruner 2004 for an account of James as a "constructivist" investigating the "creation" of religious experiences. On (pragmatic) realism regarding James's philosophy of religion, see Pihlström 2013, 2020.

45. Even though this is not an inquiry into the philosophy of religion as such (but a contribution to the philosophy of religious studies), I cannot resist pointing out that the natural-scientific and evolutionary explanations of the origins of religion are not the only threat to the humanistic understanding of religions and religiosity. In addition, the increased tendency to discuss religious worldviews in a cosmological setting—in relation to interpretations of, for example, the quantum

theory—in contemporary analytic theology as well as analytic evidentialist and "reformed" philosophy of religion could be seen as a manifestation of the same underlying *naturalizing* line of thought, even though analytic theologians (cf. again, e.g., Vainio 2020) are typically theists (and hence supernaturalists) while evolutionary explanations of religion harbor at least methodological if not also metaphysical atheism. No matter whether they aim at theistic or atheistic overall articulations of the place of human beings in the cosmos, they may be inherently nonhumanistic in the sense of seeking to understand human beings' relation to what they take to be the divinity as a cosmic rather than a "humanistic" issue.

46. For a classical study on religious experience carefully avoiding radical reductionism (as "the chief error to be avoided in the study of religion") while not rejecting the task of explanation, either, see Proudfoot 1985 (the quote is at xiv). With its Schleiermacherian and Jamesian inspirations and analyses, Proudfoot's examination is a paradigm of a balanced pragmatist attitude to the study of religion. On pragmatist philosophy of religion as engaging with the issue of naturalism, see again also Pihlström 2013, 2020.

47. For an important critical consideration of the claim that cognitive science of religion is committed to naturalism undermining theism, see, however, Visala 2011. I am not here taking any stand on how to evaluate the legacy of the cognitive paradigm in the philosophy of religion in this regard; again, my critical discussion is confined to an evaluation of the naturalizing project from the point of view of pragmatist philosophy of the humanities.

48. Obviously, we cannot here discuss all the delicacies concerning the ways in which cognitivist or other naturalizing approaches in the study of religion may be problematic from the point of view of various philosophical accounts of religion (e.g., Wittgensteinian or pragmatist). I am paying attention to these matters here only to the extent that this discussion is relevant to my main purpose of arriving at a sound philosophy of the humanities.

49. Unsurprisingly, I will propose pragmatism as a critical middle ground option integrating these apparently opposed viewpoints.

50. The fact that reductionism sticks to secular accounts of religion does not entail, however, that an antireductionist "humanist" approach in religious studies would or should be anything else than secular. *Any* academic account of religion should seek to render religious phenomena intelligible from a scholarly or scientific—and hence secular—viewpoint, no matter whether the researchers themselves are religiously or secularly minded in their own lives.

51. Again, this is *not* a study in the philosophy of religion, but I cannot resist adding that I find the mainstream analytic philosophical literature on miracles problematic precisely in its attempt to render the miraculous rationally explainable or intelligible.

52. Let me note that I am not at all claiming to possess such an internal standpoint. My philosophical analysis of this entire debate is supposed to occupy a neutral critical perspective outside of any religious (or antireligious) commitments.

53. There is no need, or possibility, to take any stand here on whether such excesses can be found even in Wittgenstein himself. See Koistinen 2019 for an excellent analysis on why it is mistaken to attribute any straightforward relativism to Phillips. See chapters 2–3 above for some reasons why pragmatist philosophy of the humanities must steer clear from radical relativism.

54. Note the clear analogy to pragmatist ontology, which, as we have seen, is inevitably based on values guiding our practices of making ontological commitments (see chapters 2–3).

55. It could be suggested that the same more specifically concerns the natural *ontological* attitude, NOA, explored earlier in this chapter.

56. Someone might object that I am certainly relying on a kind of methodological atheism myself in my own discussion, which of course does *not* start from any religious assumptions nor defend the plausibility of any such assumptions. I would happily admit that the pragmatist humanistic scholar's reliance on naturalism is not *merely* methodological but also (contextually) ontological, while pragmatism certainly allows for, or actually requires, ontological pluralism (cf. chapters 2 and 3). This matter requires further discussion—but not here, I'm afraid.

57. Analogously, the debate between inclusivism and exclusivism in the philosophy of religion, concerning religious diversity and pluralism, is not only epistemological (or theological) but deeply ethical—and again pragmatism is able to accommodate this entanglement of ethics and epistemology (and ontology) far better than most rival approaches in the field (cf. Pihlström 2021, chapter 2).

58. These include C. I. Lewis's (1923)—but arguably also Kuhn's (1970 [1962]).

59. See also, again, my earlier work on the integration of pragmatism and transcendental philosophy (e.g., Pihlström 2003a, 2004b, 2009, 2012b, 2020, 2021, 2022).

Chapter 5

1. These sets of metaphors of knowledge are analyzed in Kivistö and Pihlström 2017.

2. Of course, this is not to deny that there are historical research traditions in other fields of inquiry as well. Humanistic disciplines are, however, often more fully conscious of their historicity than, say, natural-scientific ones.

3. In developing pragmatist pluralism in the philosophy of the humanities and elsewhere, we should keep in mind that the relevant kind of pluralism must be *critically engaged pluralism* (see, e.g., Bernstein 2010), instead of any shallow relativism according to which "anything goes." I have emphasized that the pragmatist philosopher of the humanities must resist monistic (e.g., scientistic and reductionistic) ontologies that fail to take seriously the ontological postulations

typical of humanistic disciplines (e.g., meanings, values, and the historical past), but this of course by no means entails that all ontologies would be equally valuable or acceptable. Rather, any ontological claim we make must be subordinated to critical scrutiny—scientific, scholarly, and philosophical.

4. James's pragmatist conception of truth should not be characterized merely by drawing attention to the (sometimes unfortunate) claims in *Pragmatism* about the "usefulness" of truth but also, primarily, to his richer employment of the concept in *Pragmatism*, *The Varieties*, and elsewhere: what is at issue is a "true" way of viewing the world—as "sick souls," for instance, taking evil and suffering fundamentally seriously as elements of reality (cf. Pihlström 2020, 2021).

5. These remarks are partly inspired by, though not directly discussions of, Patterson 2018. For pragmatist and transcendental explorations of the problem of evil and suffering in the philosophy of religion, see also Kivistö and Pihlström 2016; Pihlström 2020. In the terminology of my earlier work, we could say that "antitheodicism" (the refusal to approach the problem of evil and suffering in terms of theodicies that would render suffering meaningful or purposive within some grand scheme, theological or secular) is a *condition for the possibility of historical understanding*. No divine or historical teleology can be appealed to in order to justify or excuse the kind of horrendous suffering exemplified by the Holocaust, and introducing such "meaning-making" historical narratives fails to achieve a "true" account (in a pragmatist sense) of suffering. Pragmatism can, I believe, contribute to making sense of this *ethical condition of historical factuality and its representability* by arguing that an antitheodicist account of the irrevocability of past sufferings (as a metaphysical fact about history) and their ethical irreconcilability with any overarching meanings (as also reflected in literature and religion) is a transcendental condition for the possibility of a pragmatically realist account of the humanistic project of seeing our practices of inquiring into the world, and thus our relation to the world more generally, "aright" (to borrow a phrase from the ending of Wittgenstein's *Tractatus*). This deep link between antitheodicism and the humanistic project of inquiry highlights our need to avoid any ideological uses of history—but also the potential excesses of "cancel culture" assuming that we could get rid of irrevocable historical facts merely by destroying monuments or moving history out of our view. On the complex issue of moral judgment in relation to the scholarly practices of historiography, see Gorman 2009. For a highly relevant reading of William James's conception of history (which is hardly a common topic even for pragmatist philosophers of historiography), developing a "non-progressive pragmatist historiography" that integrates a meliorist "turn[ing] toward the past for the sake of improving it in the future" with the "attention to the tragic and traumatic dimensions of history and their role in conditioning the present," see Sheehey 2019, 341–342. I find Sheehey's reading of James mostly congenial to my antitheodicist account of James and pragmatism generally. (Here we already move from the philosophy

of historiography to more speculative and metaphysical philosophy of history, though, and thus beyond the scope of this inquiry.)

6. I would not claim that pragmatic realism is falsified by means of these considerations, though. The fact that it encounters its limits is, however, an indication of the need for thoroughgoing self-critical reflection even by the most ethically sensitive pragmatist philosophers. Our pragmatic realism should never be easy or comfortable.

7. On the problem of comprehension in Holocaust literature studies in its ethical dimensions, see, e.g., Adams 2016. On the tensions between the pursuit of truth in scholarly Holocaust studies (especially historiography) and experientially "truthful" yet not necessarily historically accurate survivor testimony in Holocaust literature, see O'Donoghue 2016. Although this issue cannot be pursued further here, I would be prepared to argue that the pragmatist conception of truth would, again, be well equipped to deal with such tensions in terms of an account of humanistic truth pluralistic enough to cover both historians' scholarly pursuits of truth and the more existential pursuit of truthfulness we find in (nonfictionally intended yet possibly historically inaccurate) survivor testimonies as well as fictional Holocaust literature. There is presumably a fuzzy border line between these subgenres of Holocaust study and writing, and the serious humanistic scholar must appreciate such fuzziness while also maintaining a rigorous philosophical account of the divergences between different ways of pursuing the truth about such an enormously complex historical phenomenon as the Holocaust. For reflections on Holocaust writing, testimony, and truth in the context of Ankersmit's and Hayden White's narrativist philosophy of historiography, see Ankersmit 2001, chapter 6; Butler 2009.

8. These could be connected with a number of virtues—or vices—characteristic of scholarship and learning. For a comprehensive historical study on conceptions of scholarly vices based on early modern sources, see Kivistö 2014.

9. For a pragmatist articulation of vocations of life in terms of an interplay of Peircean habituality and Jamesian will-to-believe existential choices, see Pihlström 2021, chapter 4.

10. This coexistence of contingency and constitutivity is readily comparable to the interplay of the natural and the transcendental explored above, especially in chapter 4.

References

Abela, Paul (1996). "Is Less Always More? An Argument against the Natural Ontological Attitude." *The Philosophical Quarterly* 46, 72–76.
Adams, Jenni (ed.) (2016). *The Bloomsbury Companion to Holocaust Literature*. London and New York: Bloomsbury.
Allison, Henry E. (2004 [1983]). *Kant's Transcendental Idealism: An Interpretation and Defense*. Rev. ed. New Haven, CT: Yale University Press.
Almeder, Robert (1980). *The Philosophy of Charles S. Peirce: An Introduction*. Oxford: Blackwell.
Almeder, Robert (1983). "Scientific Progress and Peircean Utopian Realism." *Erkenntnis* 20, 253–280.
Almeder, Robert (1989). "Peircean Scientific Realism." *History of Philosophy Quarterly* 6, 357–364.
Anderson, Douglas A. and Hausman, Carl R. (2012). *Conversations on Peirce*. New York: Fordham University Press.
Andersen, Hanne (2001). *On Kuhn*. Belmont, CA: Wadsworth.
Andresen, Jensine (ed.) (2001). *Religion in Mind: Cognitive Perspectives on Religious Belief, Ritual and Experience*. Cambridge: Cambridge University Press.
Ankersmit, F. R. (2001). *Historical Representation*. Stanford, CA: Stanford University Press.
Ankersmit, F. R. (2009). "Narrative and Interpretation." In Tucker 2009, 199–209.
Ankersmit, Frank, Domanska, Ewa, and Kellner, Hans (eds.) (2009). *Re-figuring Hayden White*. Stanford, CA: Stanford University Press.
Appelqvist, Hanne (ed.) (2020). *Wittgenstein and the Limits of Language*. London and New York: Routledge.
Armstrong, D. M. (1997). *A World of States of Affairs*. Cambridge: Cambridge University Press.
Armstrong, D. M. (2004). *Truth and Truthmaking*. Cambridge: Cambridge University Press.
Auxier, Randall, Kramer, Eli, and Skowronski, Krzysztof Piotr (eds.) (2020). *Rorty and Beyond*. Lanham, MD: Lexington.

Bagger, Michael (ed.) (2018). *Pragmatism and Naturalism: Scientific and Social Inquiry after Representationalism*. New York: Columbia University Press.
Bernstein, Richard (1995). "American Pragmatism: The Conflict of Narratives." In Herman J. Saatkamp, Jr. (ed.), *Rorty & Pragmatism: The Philosopher Responds to His Critics*. Nashville, TN: Vanderbilt University Press, 54–67.
Bernstein, Richard J. (2010). *The Pragmatist Turn*. Cambridge: Polity Press.
Bhaskar, Roy (1979). *The Possibility of Naturalism: A Philosophical Critique of the Contemporary Human Sciences*. Brighton: The Harvester Press.
Bhaskar, Roy (1991). *Philosophy and the Idea of Freedom*. Oxford and Cambridge, MA: Blackwell.
Bonino, Guido, Jesson, Greg, and Cumpa, Javier (eds.) (2014). *Defending Realism: Ontological and Epistemological Investigations*. Berlin: de Gruyter.
Borges, Jorge Luis (1999). *The Total Library: Non-fiction 1922–1986*. Ed. Eliot Weinberger. Trans. Esther Allen, Suzanne Jill Levine, and Eliot Weinberger. London and New York: Penguin.
Bouveresse, Jacques (2017). *Le mythe modern du progrès*. Marseille: Agone.
Boyer, Pascal (2001). *Religion Explained: The Evolutionary Origins of Religious Thought*. New York: Basic Books.
Brandon, E. P. (1997). "California Unnatural: On Fine's Natural Ontological Attitude," *The Philosophical Quarterly* 47, 232–235.
Bridgman, Percy (1960 [1927]). *The Logic of Modern Physics*. New York: Macmillan.
Brown, James Robert (1994). *Smoke and Mirrors: How Science Reflects Reality*. London and New York: Routledge.
Bruhn, Mark J. and Wehrs, Donald R. (eds.) (2014). *Cognition, Literature, and History*. New York and London: Routledge.
Bruner, Jerome (2004). "James's *Varieties* and the 'New' Constructivism." In Proudfoot 2004a, 73–85.
Burks, Arthur W. (1977). *Chance, Cause, Reason: An Inquiry into the Nature of Scientific Evidence*. Chicago: The University of Chicago Press.
Butler, Judith (2009). "Primo Levi for the Present." In Ankersmit et al. 2009, 282–303.
Campbell, Donald T. (1974). "Evolutionary Epistemology." In Schilpp 1974, 413–463.
Capps, John (1996). "Dewey, Quine, and Pragmatic Naturalized Epistemology." *Transactions of the Charles S. Peirce Society* 32, 634–667.
Capps, John (2000). "Naturalism, Pragmatism, and Design." *The Journal of Speculative Philosophy* 14, 161–178.
Capps, John (2015). "Epistemology, Logic, and Inquiry." In Pihlström 2015a, 81–94.
Carnap, Rudolf (1950). "Empiricism, Semantics and Ontology." *Revue Internationale de Philosophie* 4, 20–40.
Carnap, Rudolf (1963). "Replies and Systematic Expositions." In Schilpp 1963, 859–1013.

Carr, David (1999). *The Paradox of Subjectivity: The Self in the Transcendental Tradition*. Oxford: Oxford University Press.
Cascardi, Anthony J. (2014). *The Cambridge Introduction to Literature and Philosophy*. Cambridge: Cambridge University Press.
Chang, Hasok (2011). "The Philosophical Grammar of Scientific Practice." *International Studies in the Philosophy of Science* 25, 205–221.
Colapietro, Vincent (2016). "The Historical Past and the Dramatic Present: Toward a Pragmatic Clarification of Historical Consciousness." *European Journal of Pragmatism and American Philosophy* 8:2, https://journals.openedition.org/ejpap/623.
Colapietro, Vincent (2021). Review of Viola 2020. *Pragmatism Today* 12:1, 100–106, https://www.pragmatismtoday.eu/summer2021/Review-on-Viola-Tullio-Peirce-on-the-Uses-of-History-Vincent-Colapietro.pdf.
Collingwood, R. G. (1946). *The Idea of History*. Oxford: Oxford University Press.
Conant, James (2000). "Freedom, Cruelty, and Truth: Rorty versus Orwell." In Robert B. Brandom (ed.), *Rorty and His Critics*. Malden, MA and Oxford: Blackwell, 268–342.
Conant, James and Haugeland, John (2000). "Editors' Introduction." In Kuhn 2000, 1–9.
Craig, William Lane and Moreland, J. P. (eds.) (2000). *Naturalism: A Critical Analysis*. London and New York: Routledge.
Creath, Richard (ed.) (1990). *Dear Carnap, Dear Van: The Quine-Carnap Correspondence and Related Work*. Berkeley: University of California Press.
Danto, Arthur C. (1984). "Philosophy as/and/of Literature." *Proceedings and Addresses of the American Philosophical Association* 58, 5–20.
Davidson, Donald (1984). *Inquiries into Truth and Interpretation*. Oxford: Clarendon Press.
Davis, Scott (2018). "Language, Method, and Pragmatism in the Study of Religion." In Bagger 2018, 120–138.
De Caro, Mario and Macarthur, David (eds.) (2004). *Naturalism in Question*. Cambridge, MA and London: Harvard University Press.
De Regt, Herman C. D. G. (1999). "Peirce's Pragmatism, Scientific Realism, and the Problem of Underdetermination." *Transactions of the Charles S. Peirce Society* 35, 374–397.
De Waal, Cornelis (2021). *Introducing Pragmatism*. London: Routledge.
Dennett, Daniel C. (2006). *Breaking the Spell: Religion as a Natural Phenomenon*. London: Penguin.
Dewey, John (1916). *Essays in Experimental Logic*. New York: Dover.
Dewey, John (1936). "What Are Universals?" *The Journal of Philosophy* 33, 253–261.
Dewey, John (1938). *Logic: The Theory of Inquiry*. Boston: Holt, Rinehart, and Winston.
Dewey, John (1957 [1948, 1920]). *Reconstruction in Philosophy*. Rev. ed. Boston: Beacon Press.

Dewey, John (1960 [1929]). *The Quest for Certainty: A Study on the Relation of Knowledge and Action.* New York: G. P. Putnam's Sons.

Dewey, John (1967–87). *Collected Works of John Dewey*, 37 vols. Ed. Jo Ann Boydston. Carbondale: Southern Illinois University Press.

Dewey, John (1989 [1929, 1925]). *Experience and Nature.* 2nd ed. La Salle, IL: Open Court.

Dickstein, Morris (ed.) (1998). *The Revival of Pragmatism: New Essays on Social Thought, Law, and Culture.* Durham, NC and London: Duke University Press.

Diggins, John Patrick (1994). *The Promise of Pragmatism: Modernism and the Crisis of Knowledge and Authority.* Chicago and London: The University of Chicago Press.

Dray, William (1980). *Perspectives on History.* London: Routledge & Kegan Paul.

Dupré, John (2001). *Human Nature and the Limits of Science.* Oxford: Clarendon Press.

Edmundson, Mark (1995). *Literature against Philosophy, Plato to Derrida: A Defence of Poetry.* Cambridge: Cambridge University Press.

Eggington, William and Sandbothe, Mike (eds.) (2004). *The Pragmatic Turn in Philosophy: Contemporary Engagements between Analytic and Continental Thought.* Albany: State University of New York Press.

Evans, David H. (ed.) (2017). *Understanding James, Understanding Modernism.* New York: Bloomsbury.

Faye, Jan (2012). *After Postmodernism: A Naturalistic Reconstruction of the Humanities.* Basingstoke: Palgrave Macmillan.

Felch, Susan M. (ed.) (2016). *The Cambridge Companion to Literature and Religion.* Cambridge: Cambridge University Press.

Fennell, John (2003). "The Three Quines." *International Journal of Philosophical Studies* 11, 261–292.

Feffer, Andrew (1993). *The Chicago Pragmatists and American Progressivism.* Ithaca, NY and London: Cornell University Press.

Feyerabend, Paul (1993 [1975]). *Against Method: An Outline of an Anarchistic Theory of Knowledge.* 3rd ed. London: Verso.

Fine, Arthur (1996 [1986]). *The Shaky Game.* Chicago and London: The University of Chicago Press.

Fine, Arthur (2004). "The Viewpoint of No One in Particular." In Eggington and Sandbothe 2004, 115–129.

Fitz-Hugh, Thomas (1987). *The Philosophy of the Humanities.* Chicago: The University of Chicago Press. (Reissued by Forgotten Books, 2019.)

Fleck, Ludwik (2012 [1935]). *Entstehung und Entwicklung einer wissenschaftlichen Tatsache: Einführung in die Lehre vom Denkstil und Denkkollektiv.* Eds. Lothar Schäfer and Thomas Schnelle. 9th ed. Frankfurt am Main: Suhrkamp.

Foucault, Michel (1970 [1966]). *The Order of Things: An Archaeology of the Human Sciences.* London: Tavistock.

Freeman, Eugene and Skolimowski, Henryk (1974). "The Search for Objectivity in Peirce and Popper." In Schilpp 1974, 464–519.
Frega, Roberto (ed.) (2011). *Pragmatist Epistemologies*. Lanham, MD: Lexington.
French, Steven (1989). "A Peircean Response to the Realist—Empiricist Debate." *Transactions of the Charles S. Peirce Society* 25, 295–307.
Friedman, Michael (1997). "Philosophical Naturalism." *Proceedings and Addresses of the American Philosophical Association* 71:2, 7–21.
Friedman, Michael (1999). *Reconsidering Logical Positivism*. Cambridge: Cambridge University Press.
Friedman, Michael (2000). *A Parting of the Ways*. Chicago, IL: Open Court.
Friedman, Michael (2001). *Dynamics of Reason*. Stanford, CA: CSLI Publications.
Friedman, Michael (2002). "Kant, Kuhn, and the Rationality of Science." *Philosophy of Science* 69, 171–190.
Friedman, Michael (2003). "Kuhn and Logical Empiricism." In Nickles 2003, 19–44.
Friedman, Michael (2007). "Coordination, Constitution, and Convention: The Evolution of the A Priori in Logical Empiricism." In A. W. Richardson and T. Uebel (eds.), *The Cambridge Companion to Logical Empiricism*. Cambridge: Cambridge University Press, 91–116.
Gava, Gabriele and Stern, Robert (eds.) (2016). *Pragmatism, Kant, and Transcendental Philosophy*. London and New York: Routledge.
Gazit, Yael (2019). "Appropriation, Dialogue, and Dispute: Towards a Theory of Philosophical Engagement with the Past." *Journal of the Philosophy of History* 13, 403–422.
Geertz, Clifford (1973). *The Interpretation of Cultures: Selected Essays*. New York: Basic Books.
Geisenhanslüke, Achim (2015). *Die Wahrheit in der Literatur*. Paderborn: Wilhelm Fink.
Gibson, Roger F., Jr. (ed.) (2004). *The Cambridge Companion to Quine*. Cambridge: Cambridge University Press.
Giere, Ronald N. (1996). "From *Wissenschaftliche Philosophie* to Philosophy of Science." In Giere and Richardson 1996, 335–354.
Giere, Ronald N. and Richardson, Alan (eds.) (1996). *Origins of Logical Empiricism*. Minneapolis: University of Minnesota Press.
Gillett, Carl G. and Loewer, Barry (eds.) (2001). *Physicalism and Its Discontents*. Cambridge: Cambridge University Press.
Goldman, Loren (2019). "Revisiting the Social Value of College Breeding." In Clifford S. Stagoll and Michael P. Levine (eds.), *Pragmatism Applied: William James and the Challenges of Contemporary Life*. Albany: State University of New York Press, 31–55.
Goodman, Nelson (1978). *Ways of Worldmaking*. Indianapolis: Hackett.
Gorman, Jonathan (2009). "Ethics and the Writing of Historiography." In Tucker 2009, 253–261.

Gorman, Jonathan (2016). "The Need for Quinean Pragmatism in the Theory of History." *European Journal of Pragmatism and American Philosophy* 8:2, https://journals.openedition.org/ejpap/623.

Grigoriev, Serge and Piercey, Robert (2019). "Introduction." *Journal of the Philosophy of History* 13, 287–301 (special issue: *Pragmatism and the Philosophy of History*).

Gronda, Roberto and Viola, Tullio (eds.) (2016). *Symposium: Pragmatism and the Writing of History. European Journal of Pragmatism and American Philosophy* 8:2, https://journals.openedition.org/ejpap/623.

Gross, Neil (2008). *Richard Rorty: The Making of an American Philosopher*. Chicago and London: The University of Chicago Press.

Grube, Dirk-Martin and Sinclair, Rob (eds.) (2015). *Pragmatism, Metaphysics, and Culture: Reflections on the Philosophy of Joseph Margolis*. Nordic Studies in Pragmatism 2. Helsinki: Nordic Pragmatism Network.

Gunn, Giles (2014). "Is There a Pragmatist Approach to Literature?" *Complutense Journal of English Studies* 22, 41–49.

Gunn, Giles (2017). *The Pragmatist Turn: Religion, the Enlightenment, and the Formation of American Literature*. Charlottesville and London: University of Virginia Press.

Gupta, Chhanda (2002). *Realism versus Realism*. Lanham, MD: Rowman & Littlefield.

Guthrie, Stewart (2001). "Why Gods? A Cognitive Theory." In Andresen 2001, 94–111.

Gutting, Gary (ed.) (2005). *Continental Philosophy of Science*. Malden, MA and Oxford: Blackwell.

Haack, Susan (1998). *Manifesto of a Passionate Moderate: Unfashionable Essays*. Chicago and London: The University of Chicago Press.

Haack, Susan (2004). "Pragmatism, Old and New." *Contemporary Pragmatism* 1, 3–41.

Haaparanta, Leila (1999). "On the Possibility of Naturalistic and of Pure Epistemology." *Synthese* 118, 31–47.

Haaparanta, Leila (2000). "Religious Experience and Contemporary Models of the Mind." In Ghita Holmström-Hintikka (ed.), *Medieval Philosophy and Modern Times*. Dordrecht: Kluwer, 35–44.

Hacking, Ian (1983). *Representing and Intervening: Introductory Topics in the Philosophy of Natural Science*. Cambridge: Cambridge University Press.

Hacking, Ian (2002). *Historical Ontology*. Cambridge, MA and London: Harvard University Press.

Hahn, Lewis Edwin and Shilpp, Paul Arthur (eds.) (1986). *The Philosophy of W.V. Quine*. La Salle, IL: Open Court.

Hall, Richard (2012). "William James on the Humanities." *William James Studies* 9, 120–143.

Hausmann, Frank-Rutger (2011). *Die Geisteswissenschaften im "Dritten Reich."* Frankfurt am Main: Vittorio Klostermann.

Helmer, Christine (2013). "Theology and the Study of Religion: A Relationship." In Orsi 2013, 230–254.

Hempel, Carl G. (1965). *Aspects of Scientific Explanation.* New York: The Free Press.

Hempel, Carl G. (1992). "Eino Kaila and Logical Empiricism." In Ilkka Niiniluoto, Matti Sintonen, and Georg Henrik von Wright (eds.), *Eino Kaila and Logical Empiricism.* Acta Philosophica Fennica 52. The Philosophical Society of Finland, Helsinki, 43–51.

Hesse, Mary (1980). *Revolutions and Reconstructions in the Philosophy of Science.* Brighton: The Harvester Press.

Hickman, Larry (1990). *John Dewey's Pragmatic Technology.* Bloomington: Indiana University Press.

Hickman, Larry (2007). *Pragmatism as Post-Postmodernism: Lessons from Dewey.* New York: Fordham University Press.

Hickman, Larry (2015). "Science and Technology." In Pihlström 2015a, 108–121.

Hildebrand, David L. (2003). *Beyond Realism and Antirealism: Dewey and the Neopragmatists.* Nashville, TN: Vanderbilt University Press.

Hintikka, Jaakko (1976). "Gaps in the Great Chain of Being: An Exercise in the Methodology of the History of Ideas." *Proceedings and Addresses of the American Philosophical Association* 49, 22–38.

Hintikka, Jaakko (1997). *Lingua Universalis vs. Calculus Ratiocinator: A Fundamental Presupposition of Twentieth-Century Philosophy.* Dordrecht: Kluwer.

Hollis, Martin and Lukes, Steven (eds.) (1982). *Rationality and Relativism.* Oxford: Basil Blackwell.

Holm, Poul, Jarrick, Arne, and Scott, Dominic (2015). *Humanities World Report 2015.* Basingstoke: Palgrave Macmillan.

Holton, Gerald (1993). "From the Vienna Circle to Harvard Square: The Americanization of a European World Conception." In Friedrich Stadler (ed.), *Scientific Philosophy: Origins and Developments.* Dordrecht: Kluwer, 47–73.

Honenberger, Philip (ed.) (2016). *Philosophical Anthropology and Naturalism.* Basingstoke: Palgrave Macmillan.

Honnacker, Ana (2018). *Pragmatic Humanism Revisited: An Essay on Making the World a Home.* Basingstoke: Palgrave Macmillan.

Hookway, Christopher (1988). *Quine: Language, Experience and Reality.* Stanford, CA: Stanford University Press.

Horwich, Paul (ed.) (1993). *World Changes: Thomas Kuhn and the Nature of Science.* Cambridge, MA and London: The MIT Press.

Hoyningen-Huene, Paul (1993). *Reconstructing Scientific Revolutions: Thomas S. Kuhn's Philosophy of Science.* Trans. Alexander T. Levine. Chicago and London: The University of Chicago Press.

Humboldt, Wilhelm von (2017). *Schriften zur Bildung.* Stuttgart: Reclam.

Husserl, Edmund (1982 [1936]). *Die Krisis der europäischen Wissenschaften und die transzendentale Phänomenologie: Eine Einleitung in die phänomenologische Philosophie.* Ed. Elisabeth Ströker. Hamburg: Felix Meiner.

Idinopoulos, T. and Wilson, B. C. (eds.) (1998). *What Is Religion? Origins, Definitions, and Explanations.* Leiden: E. J. Brill.

Idinopoulos, T. and Yonan, E. A. (eds.) (1994). *Religion and Reductionism: Essays on Eliade, Segal, and the Challenge of the Social Sciences for the Study of Religion.* Leiden: E. J. Brill.

James, William (1979 [1897]). *The Will to Believe and Other Essays in Popular Philosophy.* In James 1975–88.

James, William (1958 [1902]). *The Varieties of Religious Experience: A Study in Human Nature.* New York: New American Library. (Also in James 1975–88.)

James, William (1975–78). *Pragmatism: A New Name for Some Old Ways of Thinking* (1907) and *The Meaning of Truth: A Sequel to* Pragmatism (1909). Eds. Frederick H. Burkhardt, Fredson Bowers, & Ignas K. Skrupskelis. Cambridge, MA and London: Harvard University Press. (Single-volume paperback ed. 1978.)

James, William (1975–88). *The Works of William James*, 19 vols. Eds. Frederick H. Burkhardt, Fredson Bowers, and Ignas K. Skrupskelis. Cambridge, MA and London: Harvard University Press.

James, William (1987 [1907]). "The Social Value of the College-Bred." In James, *Essays, Comments, Reviews.* In James 1975–88. Also online: https://www.uky.edu/~eushe2/Pajares/jaCollegeBred.html.

Janich, Peter (2000). "Szientismus und Naturalismus: Irrwege der Naturwissenschaft als philosophisches Programm?" In Keil and Schnädelbach 2000, 289–309.

Jardine, Nicholas (2000 [1991]). *The Scenes of Inquiry: On the Reality of Questions in the Sciences.* 2nd ed. Oxford: Clarendon Press.

Jarrick, Arne (2016). "Samla er till större och färre frågor, humanister! En diskussion om det human-vetenskapliga uppdraget." Stockholm: *Årsbok 2016 KVHAA*, 135–146.

Joas, Hans (2017). *Die Macht des Heiligen: Eine Alternative zur Geschichte von der Entzauberung.* Frankfurt am Main: Suhrkamp.

Jung, Matthias (2019). *Science, Humanism, and Religion: The Quest for Orientation.* Basingstoke: Palgrave Macmillan.

Jüngel, Eberhard (2005). "Der Mensch im Schnittpunkt von Wissen, Glauben, Tun und Hoffen: Die theologische Fakultät im Streit mit der durch Immanuel Kant repräsentierten philosophischen Fakultät." In Volker Gerhardt (ed.), *Kant im Streit der Fakultäten.* Berlin: de Gruyter, 1–38.

Kamppinen, Matti (1997). "Religious Models and Problem Solving: A Cognitive Perspective on the Roles of Rationality in Comparative Religion." In J. S. Jensen and L. H. Martin (eds.), *Rationality and the Study of Religion.* Aarhus: Aarhus University Press, 78–98.

Kamppinen, Matti (2001). "Cognitive Study of Religion and Husserlian Phenomenology: Making Better Tools for the Analysis of Cultural Systems." In Andresen 2001, 193–206.
Kant, Immanuel (1998 [1781 = A, 1787 = B]). *Critique of Pure Reason*. Trans. Allen Wood and Paul Guyer. Cambridge: Cambridge University Press.
Keil, Geert (2002). *Quine zur Einführung*. Hamburg: Junius.
Keil, Geert and Schnädelbach, Herbert (eds.) (2000). *Naturalismus: Philosophische Beiträge*. Frankfurt am Main: Suhrkamp. (Contains the editors' introduction, "Naturalismus," 7–45.)
Ketonen, Oiva (1992). "Eino Kaila, Philosopher and Teacher." In Ilkka Niiniluoto, Matti Sintonen, and Georg Henrik von Wright (eds.), *Eino Kaila and Logical Empiricism*. Acta Philosophica Fennica 52. Helsinki: The Philosophical Society of Finland, 66–70.
Kilpinen, Erkki (2002). "A Neglected Classic Vindicated: The Place of George Herbert Mead in the General Tradition of Semiotics." *Semiotica* 142, 1–30.
Kimmerle, Heinz (1978). *Philosophie der Geisteswissenschaften als Kritik ihrer Methoden*. Den Haag: Nijhoff.
Kitcher, Philip (2012). *Preludes to Pragmatism*. Oxford: Oxford University Press.
Kitcher, Philip (2018). "Deweyan Naturalism." In Bagger 2018, 66–87.
Kivistö, Sari (2014). *The Vices of Learning: Morality and Knowledge at Early Modern Universities*. Leiden: Brill.
Kivistö, Sari and Pihlström, Sami (2016). *Kantian Antitheodicy: Philosophical and Literary Varieties*. Basingstoke: Palgrave Macmillan.
Kivistö, Sari and Pihlström, Sami (2017). "The Metaphors of Knowledge and Academic Impact." *Metaphilosophy* 48, 780–797.
Kloppenberg, James T. (2004). "Pragmatism and the Practice of History: From Turner and Du Bois to Today." *Metaphilosophy* 35, 202–225.
Knowles, Jonathan and Rydenfelt, Henrik (eds.) (2011). *Pragmatism, Science and Naturalism*. Frankfurt am Main: Peter Lang.
Kobow, Beatrice (2013). "Was ist 'als-ob'? Die Rolle des fiktiven in der Geschichte." In Christian Schmidt (ed.), *Können wir der Geschichte entkommen? Geschichtsphilosophie am Beginn des 21. Jahrhunderts*. Frankfurt and New York: Campus.
Koistinen, Timo (2019). "Contemplative Philosophy and the Problem of Relativism." In Rydenfelt et al. 2019, 163–172.
Koons, Robert C. (2000). "The Incompatibility of Naturalism and Scientific Realism." In Craig and Moreland 2000, 49–63.
Koopman, Colin (2011). "Genealogical Pragmatism: How History Matters for Foucault and Dewey." *Journal of the Philosophy of History* 5, 533–561.
Koposov, Nikolay (2009). *De l'imagination historique*. Paris: Éditions de l'École des Hautes Études en Sciences Sociales.
Korsgaard, Christine M. (1996a). *Creating the Kingdom of Ends*. Cambridge: Cambridge University Press.

Korsgaard, Christine M. (1996b). *The Sources of Normativity*. Cambridge: Cambridge University Press.

Koskinen, Heikki J. (2004). *From a Metaphilosophical Point of View: A Study of W.V. Quine's Naturalism*. Acta Philosophica Fennica 74. Helsinki: The Philosophical Society of Finland.

Koskinen, Heikki J. and Pihlström, Sami (2006). "Quine and Pragmatism," *Transactions of the Charles S. Peirce Society* 42, 309–346.

Koskinen, Heikki J., Pihlström, Sami, and Vilkko, Risto (eds.) (2006). *Science—a Challenge to Philosophy?* Frankfurt am Main: Peter Lang.

Koskinen, Inkeri (2019). "Relativism in the Philosophy of Anthropology." In Martin Kusch (ed.), *The Routledge Handbook of Philosophy of Relativism*. London and New York: Routledge, 424–434.

Kuhn, Thomas S. (1970 [1962]). *The Structure of Scientific Revolutions*. 2nd ed. Chicago and London: The University of Chicago Press.

Kuhn, Thomas S. (2000). *The Road Since Structure: Philosophical Essays, 1970–1993, with an Autobiographical Interview*. Eds. James Conant and John Haugeland. Chicago and London: The University of Chicago Press.

Kukla, André (1994). "Scientific Realism, Scientific Practice, and the Natural Ontological Attitude." *British Journal for the Philosophy of Science* 45, 955–975.

Kuklick, Bruce (2001). *A History of Philosophy in America: 1720–2000*. Oxford: Oxford University Press.

Kundera, Milan (1986). *L'art du roman*. Paris: Gallimard.

Kusch, Martin (1995). *Psychologism: A Case Study in the Sociology of Philosophical Knowledge*. London and New York: Routledge.

Kusch, Martin (1996). "Sociophilosophy and the Sociology of Philosophical Knowledge." In Ilkka Niiniluoto and Simo Knuuttila (eds.), *Methods of Philosophy and the History of Philosophy*. Acta Philosophica Fennica 61. Helsinki: The Philosophical Society of Finland, 83–97.

Kuukkanen, Jouni-Matti (2015). *Postnarrativist Philosophy of Historiography*. Basingstoke: Palgrave Macmillan.

Kuukkanen, Jouni-Matti (2017). "Moving Deeper into Rational Pragmatism: A Reply to My Reviewers." *Journal of the Philosophy of History* 11, 83–118.

Kuukkanen, Jouni-Matti, D'Oro, Giuseppina, Megill, Allan, Paul, Herman, and Tamm, Marek (eds.) (2019). *Special Issue: Pragmatism and the Philosophy of History. Journal of the Philosophy of History* 13:3.

Laas, Oliver (2016). "Toward Truthlikeness in Historiography." *European Journal of Pragmatism and American Philosophy* 8:2, https://journals.openedition.org/ejpap/623.

Laitinen, Arto (2008). *Strong Evaluation without Moral Sources*. Berlin: de Gruyter.

Lakatos, Imre (1970). "Falsification and the Methodology of Scientific Research Programmes." In Imre Lakatos and Alan Musgrave (eds.), *Criticism and the Growth of Knowledge*. Cambridge: Cambridge University Press, 91–196.

Landgraf, Edgar, Trop, Gabriel, and Weatherby, Leif (eds.) (2019). *Posthumanism in the Age of Humanism: Mind, Matter, and the Life Sciences after Kant*. New York and London: Bloomsbury.
Laudan, Larry (1981). "A Confutation of Convergent Realism." *Philosophy of Science* 48, 19–49.
Laudan, Larry (1984). *Science and Values: The Aims of Science and their Role in Scientific Debate*. Berkeley: University of California Press.
Laudan, Larry (1990). *Science and Relativism: Some Key Controversies in the Philosophy of Science*. Chicago and London: The University of Chicago Press.
Lawson, E. T. (1998). "Defining Religion . . . Going the Theoretical Way." In Idinopoulos and Wilson 1998, 43–49.
Leezenberg, Michiel and de Vries, Gerald (2019). *History and Philosophy of the Humanities: An Introduction*. Amsterdam: Amsterdam University Press.
Leplin, Jarrett (ed.) (1984). *Scientific Realism*. Berkeley: University of California Press.
Leplin, Jarrett (1997). *A Novel Defense of Scientific Realism*. New York and Oxford: Oxford University Press.
Levi, Isaac (1991). *The Fixation of Belief and Its Undoing: Changing Beliefs through Inquiry*. Cambridge: Cambridge University Press.
Lewis, C. I. (1923). "A Pragmatic Conception of the A Priori." *The Journal of Philosophy* 20, 169–177.
Lewis, C. I. (1934). "Experience and Meaning." *The Philosophical Review* 43, 125–146.
Livingston, Paisley (1988). *Literary Knowledge: Humanistic Inquiry and the Philosophy of Science*. Ithaca, NY and London: Cornell University Press.
Lovejoy, Arthur O. (1963 [1913]). *The Thirteen Pragmatisms and Other Essays*. Baltimore: The Johns Hopkins University Press.
Lovejoy, Arthur O. (1964 [1936].) *The Great Chain of Being: The History of an Idea*. Cambridge, MA and London: Harvard University Press.
Luft, Sebastian, Rinofner-Kreidl, Sonja, and Weidtmann, Niels (eds.) (2019). *Phenomenology and Pragmatism*. Special issue of *Phänomenologische Forschungen* 2/2019.
Maddy, Penelope (2000). "Naturalism and the A Priori." In Paul Boghossian and Christopher Peacocke (eds.), *New Essays on the A Priori*. Oxford: Clarendon Press, 92–116.
Malpas, J. (ed.) (2003). *From Kant to Davidson: Philosophy and the Idea of the Transcendental*. London: Routledge.
Mandelbaum, Maurice (1977). *The Anatomy of Historical Knowledge*. Baltimore: The Johns Hopkins University Press.
Margalit, Avishai (2002). *The Ethics of Memory*. Cambridge, MA and London: Harvard University Press.
Margolis, Joseph (1993). *The Flux of History and the Flux of Science*. Berkeley: University of California Press.

Margolis, Joseph (1995). *Historied Thought, Constructed World.* Berkeley: University of California Press.

Margolis, Joseph (2002). *Reinventing Pragmatism: American Philosophy at the End of the Twentieth Century.* Ithaca, NY and London: Cornell University Press.

Margolis, Joseph (2003). *The Unraveling of Scientism: American Philosophy at the End of the Twentieth Century.* Ithaca, NY and London: Cornell University Press.

Margolis, Joseph (2012). *Pragmatism Ascendent: A Yard of Narrative, a Touch of Prophecy.* Stanford, CA: Stanford University Press.

Margolis, Joseph (2019). "Pragmatism and Historicity." *Journal of the Philosophy of History* 13, 302–324.

Marsonet, Michele (1993). "Is Philosophy of Language Really Important for the Foundation of Scientific Realism?" *American Philosophical Quarterly* 30, 283–301.

McDowell, John (1996 [1994]). *Mind and World.* 2nd ed. Cambridge, MA and London: Harvard University Press.

McHenry, Leemon B. (1995). "Quine's Pragmatic Ontology." *Journal of Speculative Philosophy* 9, 147–158.

McKeon, Richard (1990). *Freedom and History and Other Essays.* Ed. Zahava K. McKeon. Chicago and London: The University of Chicago Press.

Mead, George Herbert (2002 [1932]). *The Philosophy of the Present.* Ed. Arthur E. Murphy. Amherst, NY: Prometheus Books.

Medina, José (2002). *The Unity of Wittgenstein's Philosophy: Necessity, Intelligibility, and Normativity.* Albany: State University of New York Press.

Medina, José (2004a). "Anthropologism, Naturalism, and the Pragmatic Study of Language." *Journal of Pragmatics* 36, 549–573.

Medina, José (2004b). "In Defense of Pragmatic Contextualism: Wittgenstein and Dewey on Meaning and Agreement." *The Philosophical Forum* 35, 341–369.

Medina, José (2004c). "Wittgenstein's Social Naturalism: The Idea of *Second Nature* After the *Philosophical Investigations*." In Danièle Moyal-Sharrock (ed.), *The Third Wittgenstein: The Post-Investigations Works.* Aldershot and Burlington, VT: Ashgate, 79–92.

Melnyk, Andrew (2003). *A Physicalist Manifesto: Thoroughly Modern Materialism.* Cambridge: Cambridge University Press.

Mikkonen, Jukka (2013). *The Cognitive Value of Philosophical Fiction.* London: Bloomsbury.

Misak, C. J. (1995). *Verificationism: Its History and Prospects.* London and New York: Routledge.

Misak, Cheryl (2013). *The American Pragmatists.* Oxford: Oxford University Press.

Morgenbesser, Sidney (ed.) (1977). *Dewey and His Critics.* New York: The Journal of Philosophy, Inc.

Morris, Charles (1966 [1937]). "The Concept of Meaning in Pragmatism and Logical Positivism." In Amelie Rorty (ed.), *Pragmatic Philosophy: An Anthology.* Garden City, NY: Doubleday & Company, 374–381.

Morris, Charles (1979 [1937]). *Logical Positivism, Pragmatism and Scientific Empiricism*. New York: AMS Press.
Morris, Charles (1938). "Peirce, Mead, and Pragmatism." *The Philosophical Review* 47, 109–127.
Morris, Charles (1963). "Pragmatism and Logical Empiricism." In Schilpp 1963, 87–98.
Moser, Paul K. and Yandell, David (2000). "Farewell to Philosophical Naturalism." In Craig and Moreland 2000, 3–23.
Mounce, H. O. (1997). *The Two Pragmatisms*. London and New York: Routledge.
Murphey, Murray G. (1994). *Philosophical Foundations of Historical Knowledge*. Albany: State University of New York Press.
Murphey, Murray G. (2003). "A Pragmatic Realism." In Shook 2003a, 285–298.
Murphy, John P. (1990). *Pragmatism: From Peirce to Davidson*. Boulder, CO: Westview Press.
Musgrave, Alan (1989). "NOA's Ark—Fine for Realism." *The Philosophical Quarterly* 39, 383–398.
Mäki, Uskali (2005). "Reglobalising Realism by Going Local, or (How) Should Our Formulations of Scientific Realism Be Informed about the Sciences." *Erkenntnis* 63, 231–251.
Mäki, Uskali (2007). "Putnam's Realisms: A View from the Social Sciences." In Sami Pihlström, Panu Raatikainen, and Matti Sintonen (eds.), *Approaching Truth: Essays in Honour of Ilkka Niiniluoto*. London: College Publications, 295–306.
Nagel, Ernest (1954 [1940]). "Charles S. Peirce, Pioneer of Modern Empiricism." In Nagel, *Sovereign Reason*. Glencoe, IL: The Free Press, 89–100.
Nagel, Ernest (1961). *The Structure of Science*. New York: Harcourt, Brace & World.
Nannini, Sandro and Sandkühler, Hans Jörg (eds.) (2000). *Naturalism in the Cognitive Sciences and the Philosophy of Mind*. Frankfurt am Main: Peter Lang.
Neurath, Otto (1983). *Philosophical Papers 1913–1946*. Ed. and trans. Robert S. Cohen and Marie Neurath. Dordrecht: D. Reidel.
Nevo, Isaac (1992). "Continuing Empiricist Epistemology: Holistic Aspects in James's Pragmatism." *The Monist* 75, 458–476.
Nickles, Thomas (ed.) (2003). *Thomas Kuhn*. Cambridge: Cambridge University Press.
Niiniluoto, Ilkka (1984). *Is Science Progressive?* Dordrecht: D. Reidel.
Niiniluoto, Ilkka (1986). *Truthlikeness*. Dordrecht: D. Reidel.
Niiniluoto, Ilkka (1999). *Critical Scientific Realism*. Oxford: Oxford University Press.
Niiniluoto, Ilkka (2018). *Knowledge-Seeking by Abduction*. Cham: Springer.
Niiniluoto, Ilkka and Pihlström, Sami (eds.) (2020). *Normativity*. Acta Philosophica Fennica 96. Helsinki: The Philosophical Society of Finland.
Niklas, Stefan (2016). "The Anticipated Past in Historical Inquiry: A. O. Lovejoy, C. I. Lewis and E. Wind on Accounting for Knowledge of the Past

within a Pragmatist Theory." *European Journal of Pragmatism and American Philosophy* 8:2, https://journals.openedition.org/ejpap/623.

Norris, Christopher (2000). *Minding the Gap: Epistemology and Philosophy of Science in the Two Traditions*. Amherst: University of Massachusetts Press.

Nubiola, Jaime (2000). "Jorge Luis Borges and WJ." *Streams of William James* 1:3, 7.

Nussbaum, Martha (2010). *Not for Profit: Why Democracy Needs the Humanities*. Princeton, NJ and Oxford: Princeton University Press.

O'Donoghue, Samuel (2016). "The Opacity of Testimony; or, What the Philosophy of Literature Can Tell Us About How to Read Holocaust Narratives." In Selleri and Gaydon 2016, 185–203.

Olafson, Frederick A. (1968). "Philosophy and the Humanities." *The Monist* 52, 28–45.

Olafson, Frederick A. (2001). *Naturalism and the Human Condition: Against Scientism*. London and New York: Routledge.

Olesen, Soren Gosvig (2013). *Transcendental History*. Trans. David D. Possen. Basingstoke: Palgrave Macmillan.

Olsen, Stein Haugom (2016). "The Discipline of Literary Studies." In Selleri and Gaydon 2016, 37–64.

Orsi, Robert (ed.) (2013). *The Cambridge Companion to Religious Studies*. Cambridge: Cambridge University Press.

Orwell, George (1992 [1949]). *Nineteen Eighty-four*. London: Penguin.

Patterson, David (2018). *The Holocaust and the Nonrepresentable: Literary and Photographic Transcendence*. Albany: State University of New York Press.

Peirce, Charles S. (1931–58). *The Collected Papers of Charles Sanders Peirce*, 8 vols. Eds. Charles Hartshorne and Paul Weiss (vols. 1–6), Arthur W. Burks (vols. 7–8). Cambridge, MA: Harvard University Press.

Peirce, Charles S. (1992–98). *The Essential Peirce*, 2 vols. The Peirce Edition Project (Nathan Houser et al.). Bloomington: Indiana University Press.

Phillips, D. Z. (1986). *Belief, Change and Forms of Life*. Basingstoke: Macmillan.

Pihlström, Sami (1996). *Structuring the World: The Issue of Realism and the Nature of Ontological Problems and in Classical and Contemporary Pragmatism*. Acta Philosophica Fennica 59. Helsinki: The Philosophical Society of Finland.

Pihlström, Sami (1998). *Pragmatism and Philosophical Anthropology: Understanding Our Human Life in a Human World*. New York: Peter Lang.

Pihlström, Sami (2003a). *Naturalizing the Transcendental: A Pragmatic View*. Amherst, NY: Humanity Books.

Pihlström, Sami (2003b). "On the Concept of Philosophical Anthropology." *Journal of Philosophical Research* 28, 259–285.

Pihlström, Sami (2004a). "Peirce's Place in the Pragmatist Tradition." In Cheryl Misak (ed.), *The Cambridge Companion to Peirce*. Cambridge: Cambridge University Press, 27–57. (Reprinted in Pihlström 2008, chapter 1.)

Pihlström, Sami (2004b). "Recent Reinterpretations of the Transcendental." *Inquiry* 47, 289–314.
Pihlström, Sami (2005). "A Pragmatic Critique of Three Kinds of Religious Naturalism." *Method and Theory in the Study of Religion* 17, 177–218.
Pihlström, Sami (2008). *"The Trail of the Human Serpent Is over Everything": Jamesian Perspectives on Mind, World, and Religion.* Lanham, MD: University Press of America.
Pihlström, Sami (2009). *Pragmatist Metaphysics: An Essay on the Ethical Grounds of Ontology.* London: Continuum.
Pihlström, Sami (2011a). *Transcendental Guilt: Reflections on Ethical Finitude.* Lanham, MD: Lexington Books.
Pihlström, Sami (2011b). "Contingency, Democracy, and the Human Sciences: Some Challenges for Pragmatic Naturalism." In Knowles and Rydenfelt 2011, 139–152.
Pihlström, Sami (2012a). "A New Look at Wittgenstein and Pragmatism." *European Journal of Pragmatism and American Philosophy* 4:2, https://journals.openedition.org/ejpap/715.
Pihlström, Sami (2012b). "Toward a Pragmatically Naturalized Transcendental Philosophy of Scientific Inquiry and Pragmatic Scientific Realism." *Studia Philosophica Estonica* 5:2, 79–94.
Pihlström, Sami (2013). *Pragmatic Pluralism and the Problem of God.* New York: Fordham University Press.
Pihlström, Sami (2014). "Pragmatic Realism." In Westphal 2014, 251–282.
Pihlström, Sami (ed.) (2015a [2011]). *The Bloomsbury Companion to Pragmatism.* 2nd ed. London and New York: Bloomsbury.
Pihlström, Sami (2015b). "'Languaged' World, 'Worlded' Language: On Margolis's Pragmatic Integration of Realism and Idealism." In Grube and Sinclair 2015, 100–122.
Pihlström, Sami (2016). *Death and Finitude: Toward a Pragmatic Transcendental Anthropology of Human Limits and Mortality.* Lanham, MD: Lexington.
Pihlström, Sami (ed.) (2017a). *Pragmatism and Objectivity: Essays Sparked by the Work of Nicholas Rescher.* London and New York: Routledge.
Pihlström, Sami (2017b). "On the Viennese Background of Harvard Neopragmatism." In Pihlström et al. 2017, 139–166.
Pihlström, Sami (2017c). "Pragmatic Realism, Idealism, and Pluralism: A Rescherian Balance?" In Pihlström 2017a, 7–30.
Pihlström, Sami (2018). "Logical Empiricism between Pragmatism and Neopragmatism." In Maria Baghramian and Sarin Marchetti (eds.), *Pragmatism and the European Traditions: Encounters with Analytic Philosophy and Phenomenology before the Great Divide.* London and New York: Routledge, 251–268.
Pihlström, Sami (2019). "Finnish Versions of Pragmatist Humanism: Eino Kaila and Georg Henrik von Wright as Quasi-Pragmatists." *European Journal*

of Pragmatism and American Philosophy 11:1, https://journals.openedition.org/ejpap/1543.

Pihlström, Sami (2020). *Pragmatic Realism, Religious Truth, and Antitheodicy: On Viewing the World by Acknowledging the Other.* Helsinki: Helsinki University Press.

Pihlström, Sami (2021). *Pragmatist Truth in the Post-Truth Age: Sincerity, Normativity, and Humanism.* Cambridge: Cambridge University Press.

Pihlström, Sami (2022). "On Natural and Transcendental Illusions in Kantian-Pragmatist Philosophical Anthropology." *Journal of Transcendental Philosophy*, https://doi.org/10.1515/jtph-2021-0044.

Pihlström, Sami and Siitonen, Arto (2005). "The Transcendental Method and (Post-)Empiricist Philosophy of Science." *Journal for General Philosophy of Science* 36, 81–106.

Pihlström, Sami, Stadler, Friedrich, and Weidtmann, Niels (eds.) (2017). *Logical Empiricism and Pragmatism.* Vienna Circle Institute Yearbook 19. Cham: Springer.

Plantinga, Alvin (2000). *Warranted Christian Belief.* Oxford: Oxford University Press.

Popper, Karl R. (1972 [1957]). *The Poverty of Historicism.* London: Routledge and Kegan Paul.

Popper, Karl R. (1976 [1963]). *Conjectures and Refutations: The Growth of Scientific Knowledge.* London: Routledge and Kegan Paul.

Popper, Karl R. (1979 [1972]). *Objective Knowledge: An Evolutionary Approach.* Oxford: Clarendon Press.

Popper, Karl R. (1994). *The Myth of the Framework: In Defence of Science and Rationality.* Ed. M. A. Notturno. London and New York: Routledge.

Popper, Karl R. and Eccles, John (1977). *The Self and Its Brain.* Berlin: Springer.

Portella, Elizabeth (2019). "'Caught in Its Movement': Liberalism, Critique, and Dewey's Implicit Philosophy of History." *Journal of the Philosophy of History* 13, 363–383.

Prickett, Stephen (2002). *Narrative, Religion and Science: Fundamentalism versus Irony, 1700—1999.* Cambridge: Cambridge University Press.

Proudfoot, Wayne (1985). *Religious Experience.* Berkeley: University of California Press.

Proudfoot, Wayne (ed.) (2004a). *William James and the Science of Religions: Reexperiencing* The Varieties of Religious Experience. New York: Columbia University Press.

Proudfoot, Wayne (2004b). "Pragmatism and 'an Unseen Order' in *Varieties*." In Proudfoot 2004a, 31–47.

Proudfoot, Wayne (2018). "Pragmatism, Naturalism, and Genealogy in the Study of Religion." In Bagger 2018, 101–119.

Psillos, Stathis (1999). *Scientific Realism: How Science Tracks Truth.* New York and London: Routledge.

Putnam, Hilary (1978). *Meaning and the Moral Sciences*. London: Routledge and Kegan Paul.
Putnam, Hilary (1981). *Reason, Truth and History*. Cambridge: Cambridge University Press.
Putnam, Hilary (1983). *Realism and Reason*. Cambridge: Cambridge University Press.
Putnam, Hilary (1990). *Realism with a Human Face*. Ed. James Conant. Cambridge, MA and London: Harvard University Press.
Putnam, Hilary (1994). *Words and Life*. Ed. James Conant. Cambridge, MA and London: Harvard University Press.
Putnam, Hilary (1995). *Pragmatism: An Open Question*. Oxford and Cambridge, MA: Blackwell.
Putnam, Hilary (2002). *The Collapse of the Fact/Value Dichotomy and Other Essays*. Cambridge, MA and London: Harvard University Press.
Putnam, Hilary (2004). *Ethics without Ontology*. Cambridge, MA and London: Harvard University Press.
Putnam, Hilary (2012). *Philosophy in an Age of Science: Physics, Mathematics, and Skepticism*. Eds. Mario de Caro and David Macarthur. Cambridge, MA and London: Harvard University Press.
Putnam, Hilary (2016). *Naturalism, Realism, and Normativity*. Ed. Mario de Caro. Cambridge, MA and London: Harvard University Press.
Pyysiäinen, Ilkka (2001a). "Cognition, Emotion, and Religious Experience." In Andresen 2001, 70–93.
Pyysiäinen, Ilkka (2001b). *How Religion Works: Towards a New Cognitive Science of Religion*. Leiden: E. J. Brill.
Quine, W. V. (1980 [1953]). *From a Logical Point of View*. Rev. ed. Cambridge, MA and London: Harvard University Press.
Quine, W. V. (1960). *Word and Object*. Cambridge, MA and London: The MIT Press.
Quine, W. V. (1969). *Ontological Relativity and Other Essays*. New York: Columbia University Press.
Quine, W. V. (1981). *Theories and Things*. Cambridge, MA: Harvard University Press.
Quine, W. V. (1986). "Reply to Morton White." In Hahn and Schilpp 1986, 663–665.
Quine, W. V. (1992 [1990]). *Pursuit of Truth*. Rev. ed. Cambridge, MA and London: Harvard University Press.
Quine, W. V. (1995). *From Stimulus to Science*. Cambridge, MA and London: Harvard University Press.
Ramsey, Frank Plumpton (1990 [1927]). "Facts and Propositions." In Ramsey, *Philosophical Papers*. Ed. D. H. Mellor. Cambridge: Cambridge University Press, 34–51.
Reichenbach, Hans (1938). *Experience and Prediction: An Analysis of the Foundations and Structure of Knowledge*. Chicago: The University of Chicago Press.

Reichenbach, Hans (1939). "Dewey's Theory of Science." In Paul Arthur Schilpp (ed.), *The Philosophy of John Dewey*. 3rd ed. La Salle, IL: Open Court, 159–192.

Reisch, George A. (2019). *The Politics of Paradigms: Thomas S. Kuhn, James B. Conant, and the Cold War "Struggle for Men's Minds."* Albany: State University of New York Press.

Rescher, Nicholas (1973). *Conceptual Idealism*. Oxford: Basil Blackwell.

Rescher, Nicholas (1992–94). *A System of Pragmatic Idealism*. 3 vols. Princeton, NJ: Princeton University Press.

Rescher, Nicholas (2000). *Realistic Pragmatism: An Introduction to Pragmatic Philosophy*. Albany: State University of New York Press.

Rescher, Nicholas (2005). "Pragmatism at the Crossroads." *Transactions of the Charles S. Peirce Society* 41, 355–365.

Richardson, Alan W. (2002). "Engineering Philosophy of Science: American Pragmatism and Logical Empiricism in the 1930s." *Philosophy of Science* 69 (3/Supplement), S36-S47.

Richardson, Joan (2014). *Pragmatism and the American Experience*. Cambridge: Cambridge University Press.

Ricoeur, Paul (2004). *Memory, History, Forgetting*. Trans. Kathleen Blamey and David Pellauer. Chicago and London: The University of Chicago Press.

Roberts, David D. (1995). *Nothing but History: Reconstruction and Extremity after Metaphysics*. Berkeley: University of California Press.

Rockmore, Tom (2013). *Art and Truth after Plato*. Chicago and London: The University of Chicago Press.

Rorty, Richard (1979). *Philosophy and the Mirror of Nature*. Princeton, NJ: Princeton University Press.

Rorty, Richard (1982). *Consequences of Pragmatism*. Hassocks: Harvester Press.

Rorty, Richard (1989). *Contingency, Irony and Solidarity*. Cambridge: Cambridge University Press.

Rorty, Richard (1991). *Objectivity, Relativism, and Truth*. Cambridge: Cambridge University Press.

Rorty, Richard (1997). "Religious Faith, Intellectual Responsibility, and Romance." In Ruth Anna Putnam (ed.), *The Cambridge Companion to William James*. Cambridge: Cambridge University Press, 84–102.

Rorty, Richard (1998). *Truth and Progress*. Cambridge: Cambridge University Press.

Rorty, Richard (2004). "A Pragmatist View of Analytic Philosophy." In Eggington and Sandbothe 2004, 131–144.

Rorty, Richard (2007). *Philosophy as Cultural Politics*. Cambridge: Cambridge University Press.

Roth, Paul A. (1987). *Meaning and Method in the Social Sciences: A Case for Methodological Pluralism*. Ithaca, NY: Cornell University Press.

Roth, Paul A. (2020). *The Philosophical Structure of Historical Explanation*. Evanston, IL: Northwestern University Press.

Rouse, Joseph (1996). *Engaging Science: How to Understand Its Practices Philosophically*. Chicago and London: The University of Chicago Press.
Rouse, Joseph (2002). *How Scientific Practices Matter: Reclaiming Philosophical Naturalism*. Chicago and London: The University of Chicago Press.
Rouse, Joseph (2003). "Kuhn's Philosophy of Scientific Practice." In Nickles 2003, 101–121.
Ryan, Frank X., Butler, Brian E., and Good, James A. (eds.) (2018). *The Real Metaphysical Club: The Philosophers, their Debates, and Selected Writings from 1870 to 1885*. Albany: State University of New York Press.
Ryba, Thomas (1994). "Are Religious Theories Susceptible to Reduction?" In Idinopoulos and Yonan 1994, 15–42.
Rydenfelt, Henrik (2019a). "Realism without Representationalism." *Synthese* 198, 2901–2918.
Rydenfelt, Henrik (2019b). "Pragmatist Antinomy." In Rydenfelt et al. 2019, 45–56.
Rydenfelt, Henrik, Koskinen, Heikki J. and Bergman, Mats (eds.) (2019). *Limits of Pragmatism and Challenges of Theodicy: Essays in Honour of Sami Pihlström*. Acta Philosophica Fennica 95. Helsinki: The Philosophical Society of Finland.
Ryder, John (2013). *The Things on Heaven and Earth: An Essay in Pragmatic Naturalism*. New York: Fordham University Press.
Saari, Heikki (1984). *Re-enactment: A Study in R.G. Collingwood's Philosophy of History*. Acta Academiae Aboensis A 63:2. Åbo, Finland: Åbo Akademi.
Saari, Heikki (1991). "Some Aspects of R.G. Collingwood's Doctrine of Absolute Presuppositions." *International Studies in Philosophy* 23, 61–73.
Sandbothe, Mike (2004). "The Pragmatic Twist of the Linguistic Turn." Trans. Lowell Vizenor. In Eggington and Sandbothe 2004, 67–91.
Scheffler, Israel (1982 [1967]). *Science and Subjectivity*. 2nd ed. Indianapolis: Hackett.
Schilbrack, Kevin (2014). *Philosophy and the Study of Religions: A Manifesto*. Chichester: Wiley.
Schiller, F. C. S. (2008). *On Pragmatism and Humanism: Selected Writings 1891–1939*. Eds. John R. Shook and Hugh P. McDonald. Amherst, NY: Humanity Books.
Schilpp, Paul Arthur (ed.) (1963). *The Philosophy of Rudolf Carnap*. La Salle, IL: Open Court.
Schilpp, Paul Arthur (ed.) (1974). *The Philosophy of Karl Popper*, 2 vols. La Salle, IL: Open Court.
Schlette, Magnus, Hollstein, Bettina, Jung, Matthias, and Knöbl, Wolfgang (eds.) (2022). *Idealbildung, Sakralisierung, Religion: Beiträge zu Hans Joas' Die Macht des Heiligen*. Frankfurt am Main: Campus.
Schnädelbach, Herbert (2000). *Philosophie in der modernen Kultur*. Frankfurt am Main: Suhrkamp.

Schulenberg, Ulf (2015). *Pragmatism and Romanticism*. Basingstoke: Palgrave Macmillan.
Segal, Robert A. (1994). "Reductionism in the Study of Religion." In Idinopoulos and Yonan 1994, 4–14.
Segal, Robert A. (1998). "Diagnosing Religion." In Idinopoulos and Wilson 1998, 107–112.
Sellars, Wilfrid (1963). *Science, Perception and Reality*. London: Routledge and Kegan Paul.
Selleri, Andrea and Gaydon, Philip (eds.) (2016). *Literary Studies and the Philosophy of Literature: New Interdisciplinary Directions*. Basingstoke: Palgrave Macmillan.
Sharrock, Wes & Read, Rupert (2002). *Kuhn: Philosopher of Scientific Revolution*. Cambridge: Polity Press.
Sheehey, Bonnie (2019). "To Bear the Past as a Living Wound: William James and the Philosophy of History." *Journal of the Philosophy of History* 13, 325–342.
Sherratt, Yvonne (2013). *Hitler's Philosophers*. New Haven, CT: Yale University Press.
Shook, John R. (1998). *Pragmatism: An Annotated Bibliography 1898–1940*. Amsterdam and Atlanta, GA: Rodopi.
Shook, John R. (2000). *Dewey's Empirical Theory of Knowledge and Reality*. Nashville, TN: Vanderbilt University Press.
Shook, John R. (2002). "Dewey and Quine on the Logic of What There Is." In D. Micah Hester and Robert Talisse (eds.), *Dewey's Logical Theory: New Studies and Interpretations*. Nashville, TN: Vanderbilt University Press (also available online at http://www.pragmatism.org/shook/deweyquine.htm).
Shook, John R. (ed.) (2003a). *Pragmatic Naturalism and Realism*. Amherst, NY: Prometheus Books.
Shook, John R. (2003b). "A Pragmatically Realistic Philosophy of Science." In Shook 2003a, 323–344.
Shook, John R. (2022). *Pragmatism*. Cambridge, MA and London: The MIT Press.
Shusterman, Richard (1992). *Pragmatist Aesthetics*. Cambridge, MA and Oxford: Blackwell.
Siitonen, Arto (1997). "The Pragmatic Turn in the Light of Reichenbach's 'Experience and Prediction.'" In Paul Weingartner, Gerhard Schurz, and Georg Dorn (eds.), *The Role of Pragmatics in Contemporary Philosophy: Papers of the 20th International Wittgenstein Symposium*, 2 vols. Kirchberg am Wechsel: The Austrian Ludwig Wittgenstein Society, 903–909.
Sismondo, Sergio (2004). *An Introduction to Science and Technology Studies*. Malden, MA and Oxford: Blackwell.
Skagestad, Peter (1981). *The Road of Inquiry*. New York: Columbia University Press, New York.
Skowroński, Krzysztof Piotr and Pihlström, Sami (eds.) (2019). *Pragmatist Kant*. Nordic Studies in Pragmatism 4. Helsinki: Nordic Pragmatism Network.

Sleeper, Ralph W. (1986). *The Necessity of Pragmatism: John Dewey's Conception of Philosophy*. New Haven, CT and London: Yale University Press.
Smith, Joel and Sullivan, Peter (eds.) (2011). *Transcendental Philosophy and Naturalism*. Oxford: Oxford University Press.
Smith, Nicholas H. (ed.) (2002). *Reading McDowell*. London and New York: Routledge.
Sokal, Alan and Bricmont, Jean (2003 [1997]). *Intellectual Impostures: Postmodern Philosophers' Abuse of Science*. 2nd ed. London: Profile Books.
Sorell, Tom (1991). *Scientism: Philosophy and the Infatuation with Science*. London and New York: Routledge.
Stadler, Friedrich (1997). *Studien zum Wiener Kreis: Ursprung, Entwicklung und Wirkung des logischen Empirismus in Kontext*. Frankfurt am Main: Suhrkamp.
Stenmark, Mikael (2021). "Worldview Studies." *Religious Studies* 2021, 1–19 (early online).
Stern, Robert (ed.) (1999). *Transcendental Arguments: Problems and Prospects*. Oxford: Clarendon Press.
Stern, Robert (2000). *Transcendental Arguments and Scepticism*. Oxford: Oxford University Press.
Strawson, P. F. (1993 [1959]). *Individuals: An Essay on Descriptive Metaphysics*. London: Routledge, 1993.
Strohmaier, Alexandra (2019). *Poetischer Pragmatismus: Goethe und William James*. Berlin: de Gruyter.
Stroud, Barry (1968). "Transcendental Arguments." *The Journal of Philosophy* 65, 241–256. (Reprinted in Stroud, *Understanding Human Knowledge*. Oxford: Oxford University Press, 2000.)
Suppe, Frederick (1989). *The Semantic Conception of Theories and Scientific Realism*. Urbana: University of Illinois Press.
Tallis, Raymond (1988). *In Defence of Realism*. London: Edward Arnold.
Tamm, Marek (2014). "Truth, Objectivity and Evidence in History Writing." *Journal of the Philosophy of History* 8, 265–290.
Taylor, Charles (1985). *Philosophy and the Human Sciences: Philosophical Papers 2*. Cambridge: Cambridge University Press.
Taylor, Charles (1989). *Sources of the Self: The Making of Modern Identity*. Cambridge, MA and London: Harvard University Press.
Taylor, Charles (1995). *Philosophical Arguments*. Cambridge, MA and London: Harvard University Press.
Thyssen, Johannes (1954). *Geschichte der Geschichtsphilosophie*. Bonn: Bouvier.
Tiles, J. E. (1990 [1988]). *Dewey*. London and New York: Routledge.
Tiles, Mary (2005). "Technology, Science, and Inexact Knowledge: Bachelard's Non-Cartesian Epistemology." In Gary Gutting (ed.), *Continental Philosophy of Science*. Malden, MA and Oxford: Blackwell, 159–175.
Topa, Alessandro (2016). "'I Have To Confess I Cannot Read History So': On the Origins and Development of Peirce's Philosophy of History." *European

Journal of Pragmatism and American Philosophy 8:2, https://journals.openedition.org/ejpap/623.
Toynbee, Arnold J. (1946). *A Study of History*. London: Oxford University Press, 1954.
Tozzi, Verónica (2016). "Dewey, Mead, John Ford, and the Writing of History: Pragmatist Contributions to Narrativism." *European Journal of Pragmatism and American Philosophy* 8:2, https://journals.openedition.org/ejpap/623.
Tucker, Aviezer (ed.) (2009). *A Companion to the Philosophy of History and Historiography*. Hoboken: Wiley-Blackwell.
Tuomela, Raimo (1985). *Science, Action and Reality*. Dordrecht: D. Reidel.
Udehn, Lars (2009). "The Ontology of the Objects of Historiography." In Tucker 2009, 209–219.
Uebel, Thomas E. (ed.) (1991), *Rediscovering the Forgotten Vienna Circle: Austrian Studies on Otto Neurath and the Vienna Circle*. Dordrecht: Kluwer.
Uebel, Thomas E. (1992). *Overcoming Logical Positivism from Within: The Emergence of Neurath's Naturalism in the Vienna Circle's Protocol Sentence Debate*. Atlanta: Rodopi.
Uebel, Thomas E. (1996). "The Enlightenment Ambition of Epistemic Utopianism: Otto Neurath's Theory of Science in Historical Perspective." In Giere and Richardson 1996, 91–112.
Uschanov, T. P. (2006). "On Ladder Withdrawal Symptoms and One Way of Dealing with Them." In Sami Pihlström (ed.), *Wittgenstein and the Method of Philosophy*. Acta Philosophica Fennica, 80, 131–167. Helsinki: The Philosophical Society of Finland.
Vainio, Olli-Pekka (2020). "On Theology and Objectivity: A Northern Point of View to Analytic Theology." *Journal of Analytic Theology* 8, 390–404.
Van Fraassen, Bas (1980). *The Scientific Image*. Oxford: Clarendon Press.
Vihalemm, Rein (2012). "Practical Realism: Against Standard Scientific Realism and Anti-Realism." *Studia Philosophica Estonica* 5:2, 7–22.
Viola, Tullio (2020). *Peirce on the Uses of History*. Berlin: de Gruyter.
Visala, Aku (2011). *Naturalism, Theism and the Cognitive Study of Religion: Religion Explained?* Aldershot: Ashgate (reissued by Routledge, 2016).
Višňovský, Emil (2020a). "Rorty's Humanism: Making It Explicit." *European Journal of Pragmatism and American Philosophy* 12:1, https://journals.openedition.org/ejpap/1878?lang=en.
Višňovský, Emil (2020b). "Science as a Cultural Practice." *Pragmatism Today* 11:2, 96–103.
Von Wright, Georg Henrik (1971). *Explanation and Understanding*. Ithaca, NY and London: Cornell University Press, 2004.
Von Wright, Georg Henrik (1993). *The Tree of Knowledge and Other Essays*. Leiden: Brill.

Weinryb, Elazar (2009). "Historiographic Counterfactuals." In Tucker 2009, 109–119.
Weissman, David (2003). *Lost Souls: The Philosophic Origins of a Cultural Dilemma.* Albany: State University of New York Press.
Westphal, Kenneth R. (ed.) (1998). *Pragmatism, Reason, and Norms.* New York: Fordham University Press.
Westphal, Kenneth R. (2004). *Kant's Transcendental Proof of Realism.* Cambridge: Cambridge University Press.
Westphal, Kenneth R. (2006). "Science and the Philosophers." In Koskinen et al. 2006, 125–152.
Westphal, Kenneth R. (ed.) (2014). *Realism, Science, and Pragmatism.* London and New York: Routledge.
White, Hayden (1973). *Metahistory.* Baltimore: The Johns Hopkins University Press.
White, Hayden (1978). "The Historical Text as a Literary Artifact." In White, *Tropics of Discourse: Essays in Cultural Criticism.* Baltimore: The Johns Hopkins University Press.
White, Morton (1956). *Toward Reunion in Philosophy.* Cambridge, MA: Harvard University Press.
White, Morton (1986). "Normative Ethics, Normative Epistemology, and Quine's Holism." In Hahn and Schilpp 1986, 649–662.
White, Morton (2002). *A Philosophy of Culture: The Scope of Holistic Pragmatism.* Princeton, NJ: Princeton University Press.
White, Morton (2005). *From a Philosophical Point of View: Selected Studies.* Princeton, NJ: Princeton University Press.
Wiebe, Donald (1994). "Beyond the Sceptic and the Devotee: Reductionism in the Scientific Study of Religion." In Idinopoulos and Yonan 1994, 108–126.
Wiggins, James (1998). "What on Earth Is Religion?" In Idinopoulos and Wilson 1998, 133–139.
Williams, Bernard (2006). *Philosophy as a Humanistic Discipline.* Ed. A. W. Moore. Princeton, NJ and Oxford: Princeton University Press.
Winch, Peter (1958). *The Idea of Social Science and Its Relation to Philosophy.* London: Routledge and Kegan Paul.
Winch, Peter (1964). "Understanding a Primitive Society." *American Philosophical Quarterly* 1, 307–324. (Reprinted in Winch 1972.)
Winch, Peter (1972). *Ethics and Action.* London: Routledge and Kegan Paul.
Wisdo, David (1993). *The Life of Irony and the Ethics of Belief.* Albany: State University of New York Press.
Wittgenstein, Ludwig (1953). *Philosophical Investigations.* Trans. G. E. M. Anscombe. Oxford: Basil Blackwell.
Wittgenstein, Ludwig (1993 [1967]). "Remarks on Frazer's *The Golden Bough.*" In Wittgenstein, *Philosophical Occasions 1912–1951.* Eds. A. Klagge and J. Nordmann. Indianapolis: Hackett, 118–155.

Wittgenstein, Ludwig (1969). *On Certainty*. Trans. Denis Paul and G. E. M. Anscombe. Oxford: Basil Blackwell.
Wollheim, Richard (1980 [1968]). *Art and Its Objects*. 2nd ed. Cambridge: Cambridge University Press.

Index

absolute conception of the world, the, 124
Addams, Jane, 31, 53
agnosticism, 98
Allison, Henry E., 148
analytic philosophy, 19, 150
Ankersmit, Frank, 93
anomalies, 65
antirealism: *see* realism vs. antirealism
Apel, Karl-Otto, 150
a priori (pragmatic, relativized), 67, 169, 209n82
Armstrong, David M., 133–134

Beckett, Samuel, 177
Bernstein, Richard, 31
Bhaskar, Roy, 155–156
Bible, the, 135
Bildung, 125, 186n9
Brandon, E. P., 138
Bridgman, Percy, 48
Brown, James Robert, 135
Brown, Matthew, 58

Carnap, Rudolf, 43, 55, 58, 67, 149, 203–204n51
categories, 64
causal powers, 155
Chang, Hasok, 43

China, vii–viii, 217n23
cognitive (cognitivist) study of religion, 159–162
colligatory concepts, 105–106
Collingwood, R. G., 15, 227–228n81
constitution (of reality, of objects), 68, 114
  transcendental, 74, 82, 156, 170
constructive empiricism, 51
constructivism, 41, 114–115, 149, 168 (*see also* idealism; realism vs. antirealism)
contingency, 181–182
correspondence: *see* truth
counterfactuals, 104
COVID-19 pandemic, vii, 12
critical distance, 120, 122, 229n87
critical philosophy, 60 (*see also* transcendental philosophy)
cultural entities, 23

Danto, Arthur, 25
Davidson, Donald, 150
deconstruction, 5
Dennett, Daniel, 157
Dewey, John, 1, 16, 20, 31, 37, 42, 44–53, 57, 59–60, 70–72, 76, 88, 141, 201–202n39, 202n40
digital humanities, 8–9

Index

Dilthey, Wilhelm, 2, 19
Ding(e) an sich (thing in itself, things in themselves), 65
"doubt-belief" model of inquiry, the, 37–38 (*see also* inquiry, theory of)
Dray, William, 15–16
Duhem, Pierre, 47
duty, 179–180

empiricism, 55, 73 (*see also* logical empiricism)
environmental humanities, 9
Erklären vs. Verstehen (explanation vs. understanding), 84, 112, 152, 159–168

facts, factuality: *see* historical facts; realism vs. antirealism
Faye, Jan, 6, 183n1, 185n8
Feyerabend, Paul, 59, 69–70
Fine, Arthur, 77, 130–144, 158 (*see also* natural ontological attitude, the)
Finland, 104, 107–108
first philosophy, 129
Fleck, Ludwik, 99
Foucault, Michel, 6, 35
freedom, 175–176
French, Steven, 51
Freud, Sigmund, 163
Friedman, Michael, 67
fundamentalism, 138, 232n16

Gadamer, Hans-Georg, 150
Gellner, Ernest, 58
Gestaltswitch, 64
God, 11, 95, 97, 111, 161
God's-eye view, 140, 154
Goodman, Nelson, 37
Grenzbegriff, 177

Haack, Susan, 31, 55–56

Haaparanta, Leila, 232n18
Habermas, Jürgen, 150, 156
habits of action (habituality), 37–38, 104
Hacking, Ian, 35, 70
Heidegger, Martin, 150
hermeneutics, 2, 5, 19, 23, 35, 150
Hintikka, Jaakko, 9–10
historical facts, 33, 92, 104, 177
historical ontology, 35, 195n55
historicism, 20, 70, 121, 149
historicity, 35–36
historiography, chapter 3 *passim*
history vs. literature, 22
holistic pragmatism: *see* pragmatism, holistic
Holocaust, the, viii, 29, 177–179, 240n7
Hook, Sidney, 31
Hookway, Christopher, 55
Hoyningen-Huene, Paul, 65, 149
humanism, 24, 112, 122, 198n14
vs. antihumanism, posthumanism, 122
humanities, the, *passim*
as defined, 184n2
see also impact (of the humanities); values (of the humanities); pragmatism
human nature, 139
Humboldtian universities, 7
Hume, David, 147
Husserl, Edmund, 143, 145–146

idealism, 50, 208n74 (*see also* constructivism; realism vs. antirealism)
transcendental, 33, 67–68, 148, 154, 197n9
impact (of the humanities), 7, 125
individual scholarly perspectives, 24
ineffability, 162
inhumanity, 29, 177–178

inquiry, theory of, 23, 37–42 (*see also* "doubt-belief" model of inquiry, the)
  practices of, 68–75, 101, 123
instrumentalism (*see also* realism vs. antirealism; realism, scientific), 3, 42, 44–53, 59, 72, 76–77, 101
  humanistic, 52–53
interdisciplinarity, 8
interests, 115–116
internal realism: *see* realism, internal
interpretive possibilities, 106–108
invariance, 196n5
ironism, 123–124
irony, 107

James, William, 1, 20, 22, 31, 37, 42, 44–53, 59, 63, 72, 80, 82, 88, 91, 103, 109–110, 115–116, 157–158, 163, 190–191n35, 221n50, 239n4–5
Jardine, Nicholas, 70
Joas, Hans, 31
Julius Caesar, 91

Kaila, Eino, 180
Kant, Immanuel, 33, 64–67, 71, 111, 113, 140, 146–148, 150, 169, 186n9
Kaurismäki, Aki, 224n61
Keil, Geert, 139
Ketonen, Oiva, 180
Kierkegaard, Soren, 163
King, Stephen, 107
Kokkonen, Tomi, 183n1
Korsgaard, Christine, 140
Koskinen, Inkeri, 183n1
Kubrick, Stanley, 107
Kuhn, Thomas S., 6, 43, 59–75, 99, 110, 120, 149, 207n66, 207n68, 207–208n71, 208n73
Kundera, Milan, 89
Kusch, Martin, 234n29

Kuukkanen, Jouni-Matti, 92–95, 219n32

Laudan, Larry, 43, 70–72, 76
Leezenberg, Michiel, 6
Leplin, Jarrett, 73
Lewis, C. I., 31, 67
lexicon, 62, 66–67
Linna, Väinö, 107–108, 223n60
literary theory and criticism, chapter 3 *passim*
literature (literary works of art), 4, 17–18
Livingston, Paisley, 16, 21, 102
logical empiricism (logical positivism), 13, 43, 150, 204–205n52
  and pragmatism, 204–205n52
Lovejoy, Arthur O., 9–10

Mach, Ernst, 47
Margolis, Joseph, 17, 31, 34–35, 66, 117, 196n6, 210n85
Marsonet, Michele, 57
Marx, Karl, 163
McHenry, Leemon B. 57
Mead, George Herbert, 31, 53–54, 203n46
meaning(s), 106, 131, 166, 172
  possibility of, 141, 151
Medina, José, 141–142
metaphilosophy, 98–99
metaphors, 88, 174
metaphysical realism: *see* realism, metaphysical
metaphysics, 133–134, 225–224n71
methodological atheism, 167, 238n56
models, 159–160
motivation, 179–181

Nabokov, Vladimir, 18
narrativism vs. postnarrativism (in historiography), 92–95, 187n15, 217n20

naturalism, 16, 20, 27, 56–57, 112, 120, 127–144, 174, 203n49, 230n3–4, 232–233n19–20, 233n23
   hard vs. soft, 76
   of second nature, 141
   pragmatic, 55, 68–75, 212n96
   reductive, 20
   nonreductive, 169
   social, 141
   vs. antinaturalism, 120
   vs. humanism, 112
naturalization, 27, 54, 56, 128–130, 137, 145, 157, 237n45
natural ontological attitude (NOA), the, 129–144, 158, 161, 166, 211–212n92, 229n90 (*see also* Fine, Arthur)
necessity, 147
neopragmatism, 42, 71, 80
Niiniluoto, Ilkka, 39, 73, 102
normal science, 110, 120
normativity, 54, 115, 140
Nussbaum, Martha, 215n13

objects (of humanistic inquiry/research/study), 9–10, 28, 82–83, 198–199n18
   as dependent on inquiry, 50–51
   value-ladenness/value-dependence of, 32–33, 35–36, 85, 113
objectivity, 22, 87, 118, 194n47
O'Brien (a fictional character; *see* Orwell), 90, 118
Olesen, Soren Gosvig, 35, 197n8
ontological commitments, 132, 143
operationalism (operational thinking), 44, 47–48
Orwell, George, 18, 90, 118
Ostwald, Wilhelm, 47
otherness, 175

paradigm(s), 59–68, 120
past, the, 54, 116, 121
Peirce, Charles S., 1, 31, 37–39, 42, 44–45, 48, 51–52, 58, 61, 77, 80, 108–109, 113, 145–146, 200n25, 200n29, 215n16, 218n28, 222n51
phenomenalism, 47
phenomenology, 19, 23, 150, 166
Phillips, D. Z., 160, 163
philosophical knowledge, 28, 128, 132, 134, 144, 146
philosophical methodology, 26, 195n53
philosophy of historiography, 89–98
philosophy of history vs. philosophy of historiography, 4–5, 14–17, 34–35
philosophy of literary theory and criticism, 87–89
philosophy of theology and religious studies, 95–97, 157–168
philosophy vs. literature, 25, 88, 228n84
physicalism, 231n7
Plantinga, Alvin, 231–232n14
pluralism, 10, 59–60, 69, 114, 124, 137, 175, 213n2, 238n3
Poincaré, Henri, 47
politics of the humanities, 100
Popper, Karl R., 15, 43, 48, 102
possibility, 89, 107, 109, 224–225n64
practice(s), 138, 152
pragmatic maxim, the, 37–39, 116
pragmatic realism: *see* realism, pragmatic
pragmatism (in the philosophy of the humanities), *passim*
   holistic, 24, 115–126, 173, 176
   in the philosophy of historiography, 34–35, chapter 3 *passim*
   in the philosophy of literary theory and criticism, chapter 3 *passim*

in the philosophy of science and inquiry, 42–77
in the philosophy of theology and religious studies, chapter 3 *passim*
Kantian, 32–37, 63–64, 86, 113
openness of, 43, 112
transcendental, 33–34, 74–75, 79, 112, 119, 125, 156, 173–174
pragmatist conception of truth: *see* truth, pragmatist conception of
prediction, 49
private language argument, the, 150–151
problem of evil and suffering, the, 239n5
progress, 185n5
Proudfoot, Wayne, 158
problematic situation, 109
Putin, Vladimir, 12
Putnam, Hilary, 20, 31, 36, 43, 56–68, 71, 80, 113–114, 123–124, 142, 207n68

Quine, W.V., 3, 51, 54–58, 61, 67, 72–73, 75, 130–131, 133, 136, 141, 144, 205n53, 205n57, 227n79

Raatikainen, Panu, 236n39
rationality, 83–84, 160
Read, Rupert, 66
ready-made world/objects, 35, 42
"real generals," 25, 28, 103–114, 131
realism (vs. antirealism), 20–21, 26, 39–42, 69, 76–77, 80–82, 91, 112, 130, 136, 153–156, 172, 214n5
convergent, 70
different dimensions of, 39–40, 114
empirical, 33, 67
historical, 115, 218n28

internal, 80, 114
metaphysical, 37, 103, 155, 212n93
modal, 112
pragmatic, 20–22, 36, 41, 59–68, 86, 88, 95, 101–103, 114, 119, 172–176, 178, 192n41
religious and theological, 96
scientific, 39–45, 52, 59–69, 73, 75, 101, 132, 173, 192n41, 199n21, 203n45, 206n59
transcendent, 73, 212n93
transcendental, 155, 212n93
reductionism, 21, 159, 165–167
reenactment, 119
reference, 40, 82, 229n89
Reichenbach, Hans, 67
Reisch, George A., 63
relativism, 3, 20–21, 72, 83–84, 103, 193n43 (*see also* realism vs. antirealism)
religious beliefs, 96, 159–160, 163–164
religious possibilities, 110–111
representationalism, 93
representations, representationality, 82–83, 89, 94, 105
limits of, 177–179
Rescher, Nicholas, 55, 153–156
Ricoeur, Paul, 15–16
Rorty, Richard, 6, 18, 31, 56–58, 69, 77, 80, 91, 123, 131, 156, 175–176, 191n36, 205n54, 216n18
Roth, Paul A., 36, 236n39
Rouse, Joseph, 43, 68–69, 73–74, 211n92
Royce, Josiah, 53
rules, 151
Russia, vii–viii, 12, 217n23

Schleiermacher, Friedrich, 2, 19
Schnädelbach, Herbert, 139

270 | Index

Schulenberg, Ulf, 18
scientific image vs. manifest image, 52
scientific progress, 70
scientific realism: *see* realism, scientific
scientism, 3 (*see also* naturalism, reductive)
Sellars, Wilfrid, 130, 133
Sharrock, Wes, 66
Shook, John R., 57, 73–74, 76
skepticism, 51, 147
Soviet Union, 104
Stenmark, Mikael, 236n43
Strawson, P. F., 146, 148, 150, 153
Stroud, Barry, 146, 148, 150, 153
supernatural, belief in, 159–161

Tamm, Marek, 94–95, 219n32
Taylor, Charles, 19, 192n39
theology, 10–11, 187–188n17, 219n33
    analytic, 97
    as a humanistic discipline, 96–97
theoretical entities, 13, 51, 69, 102
theories, 45–46, 49, 60, 70–71, 81
transcendence, 178–179
transcendental arguments/argumentation, 27–28, 113, 140, 142, 144–157, 165–170, 174
    epistemic vs. semantic, 150
transcendental conditions, 113, 146, 148, 155
transcendental idealism (*see* idealism, transcendental)
transcendental philosophy (*see also* critical philosophy), 32, 125, 143
transcendental subject(ivity), 35
transcendental vs. transcendent, 28–29, 74, 196n3, 235n33
transcendental we, 124
Trump, Donald, 188n22

truth, viii, 40, 80–82, 91–94, 118, 176, 201n34
    as correspondence, 82, 176
    as epistemic, 94
    historical, 90, 94
    pragmatist conception of, 80–82, 91, 176, 213n2
    vs. post-truth, 80
    vs. warranted assertion, 93
truthmakers, 93, 106

universals, 133
Unverhintergehbarkeit, 124

value of the humanities, the, 85, 181–182
values, 22, 86, 100–102, 116–117, 172
value-dependence, value-ladenness, 32, 85, 116, 193n44
van Fraassen, Bas, 51, 73
verisimilitude (truthlikeness), 47
de Vries, Gerard, 6

Weber, Max, 126
Weissman, David, 57
White, Hayden, 16, 90, 92
White, Morton, 17, 31, 34, 71, 115–118, 176, 226n75
Williams, Bernard, 94, 123–124
Winch, Peter, 151–152, 155–156, 158, 163, 233n23
Windelband, Wilhelm, 2
Winston (a fictional character; *see* Orwell), 90–91, 118
Wisdo, David, 163–164
Wittgenstein, Ludwig, 32, 141, 145–146, 150–152, 163, 181
World War II, viii, 12, 104, 108
von Wright, Georg Henrik, 15–16, 189n28

www.ingramcontent.com/pod-product-compliance
Lightning Source LLC
Chambersburg PA
CBHW030530230426
43665CB00010B/836